GREEK LITERARY THEORY AFTER ARISTOTLE

GREEK LITERARY THEORY AFTER ARISTOTLE

a collection of papers in honour of

D.M. Schenkeveld

J.G.J. Abbenes
S.R. Slings
I. Sluiter
(editors)

VU University Press
Amsterdam 1995

VU University Press is an imprint of:
VU Boekhandel/Uitgeverij bv
De Boelelaan 1105
1081 HV Amsterdam
The Netherlands

tel. + 31 20 644 43 55
fax + 31 20 646 27 19

isbn 90-5383-365-x cip

Contents

Preface

In April 1994, friends and colleagues of Dirk Schenkeveld convened in Amsterdam for a symposium celebrating Dirk's 60th birthday. During three beautiful spring days we discussed post-Aristotelian literary theory in an ideal sympotic setting, a wonderful blend of culinary and social delights and intellectual stimuli. Most of the papers presented at the symposium have found their way into the present volume, supplemented by a number of new contributions. It is our pleasure to dedicate this book, one year later, to Dirk Schenkeveld, on the occasion of his retirement as Professor of Greek Language and Literature at the Vrije Universiteit (VU) at Amsterdam.

Dirk Marie Schenkeveld was born at Alkmaar in 1934 and educated at the local Murmellius Gymnasium and at the VU. After a short stint as a high-school teacher of Latin and Greek he was appointed lecturer in Greek at the VU in 1962. In 1971, he succeeded his teacher, the Platonist G.J. de Vries, as a full professor at that institution. This book is primarily intended to honour him as a scholar, so that this is not the place to expatiate on other aspects of his distinguished career. Suffice it to say that his *cursus honorum* includes among many other things the high office of Rector Magnificus of the university, Chair of the Dutch cultural organisation Prins Bernhard Fonds, and Secretary of the oldest Dutch learned society, the Hollandsche Maatschappij der Wetenschappen. A well-loved, erudite and stimulating teacher, Dirk instilled in his students a healthy distrust for authority—somewhat paradoxically, he liked to recall a dictum of his predecessor: 'But, Mr Schenkeveld, surely we people from North-Holland don't just believe what the boss says, do we?' He was a very active supervisor of doctoral dissertations, which benefited from his critical acumen, his emphasis on method and above all his humanity. His graduate students, past and present, showed their gratitude on the occasion of the twenty-fifth anniversary of his tenure at the VU by means of a Festschrift in Dutch[1].

In the course of his scholarly career, Dirk Schenkeveld has made major contributions to his special fields of research, ancient literary criticism, the history of rhetoric and that of the origins and development of ancient grammar. In a striking reversal of the ancient school-curriculum, with its traditional progress from grammar through rhetoric to higher forms of education, he started with studies in ancient poetics and rhetoric: his PhD thesis dealt with Demetrius' *On Style*, and it was followed by numerous articles dealing with, among other things, Philodemus and *οἱ κριτικοί* and Aristarchus' poetics of Homer. Studying ancient views on Homer can provide interesting insights into the history of cultural identity as well as that of literary, rhetorical and linguistic theory, and at one time or another Dirk Schenkeveld has written on all of these. In recent years, his series of 'Studies in the History of Ancient Linguistics' has rightly received wide acclaim.

The theme of this volume is inspired by Dirk's book on Demetrius and his subsequent papers on ancient literary criticism. It covers a wide range of classical authors, including Theophrastus, Philodemus, Cicero, Longinus and Galen. Further topics are philosophical literary theory, the emergence of grammar from poetics, the development of a collection of mythological material in Homeric criticism, fable theory and Byzantine poetics.

It is our hope that this book will stand as a worthy tribute to an inspiring teacher and scholar, and a true *καλὸς κἀγαθός*.

Amsterdam, April 1995

Jelle Abbenes
Simon R. Slings
Ineke Sluiter

---

[1] S.R. Slings - I. Sluiter (eds.), *Ophelos: zes studies voor D.M. Schenkeveld*. Amsterdam 1988.

Publications by D.M. Schenkeveld

1962 De behandeling van stijlgebreken door Aristoteles en Demetrius, *Handelingen van het zevenentwintigste Nederlands Filologencongres*, 113-6.

1964 *Studies in Demetrius On Style*, (PhD thesis Vrije Universiteit) Amsterdam.

1968 Οἱ Κριτικοί in Philodemus, *Mnemosyne* 21, 176-214.

1970 Aristarchus and Ὅμηρος φιλότεχνος. Some Fundamental Ideas of Aristarchus on Homer as a Poet, *Mnemosyne* 23, 162-78.

1971 De zevende Idylle van Theocritus, *Lampas* 4, 169-88.

— Aristoteles en de rechtvaardigheid, *Vredesopbouw* 8, 14-5.

1972 Van Sophocles tot Claus. Toneelstukken over Koning Oedipus (inaugural lecture), Amsterdam.

1975 Theories of Evaluation in the Rhetorical Treatises of Dionysius of Halicarnassus, *MPhL* 1, 93-107.

— Eros in de hellenistische poëzie, *Hermeneus* 47, 114-26.

1976 De waardering van Homerus' poëzie bij de Grieken, *Lampas* 9, 214-42.

— Strabo on Homer, *Mnemosyne* 29, 52-64.

— Aegisthus in Seneca's Agamemnon, in: J.M. Bremer, S.L. Radt, C.J. Ruijgh (eds.), *Miscellanea tragica in honorem Kamerbeek*, Amsterdam, 397-403.

— Xenophon *Hellenica* II 3, 24-9. Een rhetorische analyse, *Lampas* 9, 141-57.

— Macaronilatijn en het eerste Vaticaanse concilie, *Hermeneus* 48, 129-32.

1978 Rhetorica en geschiedschrijving. Thucydides' *Historiae* II 11, *Lampas* 11, 228-36.

— De eerste zinnen (address as Rector Magnificus on the occasion of the *dies natalis* of the Vrije Universiteit), Amsterdam.

— De paradox van het universitaire onderzoek (opening address of the Academic year), Amsterdam.

1979 De universiteit en haar maatschappelijke verantwoordelijkheid (opening address of the Academic year, published in *VU Magazine*, October 1979).

1982 The Structure of Plutarch's De Audiendis Poetis, *Mnemosyne* 35, 60-71.

— Studies in the History of Ancient Linguistics I: ΣΥΝΔΕΣΜΟΙ ΥΠΟΘΕΤΙΚΟΙ and Ο ΕΑΝ ΕΠΙΖΕΥΚΤΙΚΟΣ, *Mnemosyne* 35, 248-68.

1983 Linguistic Theories in the Rhetorical Works of Dionysius of Halicarnassus, *Glotta* 61, 67-94.

1984 Studies in the History of Ancient Linguistics II: Stoic and Peripatetic Kinds of Speech Act and the Distinction of Grammatical Moods, *Mnemosyne* 37, 291-353.

1986 [Review article: R. Janko, Aristotle on Comedy, London 1984], *Gnomon* 58, 212-7.

1988 *Homerus 1752-1988. Visies op het gesprek tussen Hector en Andromache* (Haarlemse Voordrachten XLVIII). Holl. Mij. der Wetenschappen, Haarlem.

— Wat doen we met Homerus? Literaire kritiek in het Hellenisme, *Lampas* 21, 100-10.

— Ancient Views on the Meaning of ΔΑΙΜΩΝ in Iliad Θ 166, *Hermes* 116, 110-5.

— From Particula to Particle - The Genesis of a Class of Words, in: I. Rosier (ed.), *L'Héritage des grammairiens latins de l'antiquité aux lumières*. Actes du colloque de Chantilly, 2-4 septembre 1987. Paris, 81-92.

— Sophocles, de toneeldichter, *Bzzletin* 154, 27-36.

1989 *Iudicia vulgi*: Cicero, De Oratore 3.195ff. and Brutus 183ff., *Rhetorica* 6, 291-305.

— Antiphon, *Or*. V, 8: A case of a dative of purpose?, *Mnemosyne* 42, 474-6.

— Het belang van de kennis van de klassieke talen voor universitaire studies, in: Vrienden van het Gymnasium (red.), *De moeite waard: Beschouwingen over nut en waarde van het Latijn en Grieks*, 37-9.

1990 Studies in the History of Ancient Linguistics III: The Stoic ΤΕΧΝΗ ΠΕΡΙ ΦΩΝΗΣ, *Mnemosyne* 43, 86-108.

— Studies in the History of Ancient Linguistics IV: Developments in the Study of Ancient Linguistics, *Mnemosyne* 43, 289-306.

— (Guest editor of:) Homerus, *Bzzletin*, Den Haag, 175, 1-79.

— Wanneer herkent Penelope Odysseus? Twee eeuwen van interpretatie van een beroemd probleem, *Bzzletin* 175, 20-9.

1991 Figures and Tropes. A Border-Case between Grammar and Rhetoric, in G. Ueding (Hrsg.), *Rhetorik zwischen den Wissenschaften* (Rhetorik-Forschungen 1). Tübingen, 149-57.

— The Philosopher Aquila, *CQ* 41, 490-5.

— Language and Style of the Aristotelian *De Mundo*, *Elenchos* 12, 221-5.

— Theocritus: hij heeft meer geschreven, *Hermeneus* 63, 105-13.

— Versnel en de calvinistische traditie, in M.A. Maurice en S.J. Noorda, *De onzekere zekerheid des geloofs. Beschouwingen in het spanningsveld van geloven en denken*. Zoetermeer, 39-43.

1992 Unity and Variety in Ancient Criticism. Some Observations on a Recent Study, *Mnemosyne* 45, 1-8.

— Prose Usages of ΑΚΟΥΕΙΝ 'To Read', *CQ* 42, 129-41.

— Asteismus, in: G. Ueding (ed.) *Historisches Wörterbuch der Rhetorik I*. Tübingen, 1129-34.

— Aristophanes onder vuur, *Hermeneus* 64, 104-12.

— Alexandrijnse literatuurbeschouwing, *De Gids* 155, 76-80.

1993 The Lacuna at Aristotle's Poetics 1457b33, *American Journal of Philology* 114, 85-9.

— Pap. Hamb. 128: A Hellenistic Ars Poetica, *ZPE* 97, 67-80.

— The Lexicon of the Narrator and his Characters: Some Aspects of Syntax and Choice of Words in Chariton's Chaereas and Callirhoe, in: H. Hofmann (ed.), *Groningen Colloquia on the Novel V*, 17-30.

— Gerrit Jacob de Vries, herdenking, in: *KNAW Levensberichten en herdenkingen 1992*, Amsterdam, 73-80.

1994 Charisius, in: R. Goulet (ed.), *Dictionnaire des philosophes antiques* t. II. Paris, 294-7.

— *Ta asteia* in Aristotle's *Rhetoric*, in: W.W. Fortenbaugh & D.C. Mirhady (eds), *Peripatetic Rhetoric after Aristotle* (RUSCH VI). New Brunswick, 1-14.

— Scholarship and Grammar, in: F. Montanari (ed.), *La philologie grecque à l'époque hellénistique et romaine*, (Entretiens sur l'antiquité classique 40). Vandoeuvres-Genève 1994, 263-301 (-306).

1995 The Linguistic Contents of Dionysius' Παραγγέλματα, in: Vivian Law & Ineke Sluiter (eds.), *Dionysius Thrax and the Technê Grammatikê*. Münster, 41-53.

— De receptie van Homerus bij de hellenistische dichters en filologen, *Kleio* 24, 83-100.

reviews:

1962 W.D. Ross, Aristotelis Ars Rhetorica, *Mnemosyne* 15, 64-5.

1964 C.W. van Boekel, Katharsis, *Mnemosyne* 17, 92-3.

1965 G.A. Kennedy, The Art of Persuasion in Greece, *Mnemosyne* 18, 404-5.

— C.M.J. Sicking, Aristophanes' Ranae, *Mnemosyne* 18, 421-3.

1967 D. Hagedorn, Zur Ideenlehre des Hermogenes, *Mnemosyne* 20, 333.

— G.M.A. Grube, The Greek and Roman Critics, *Mnemosyne* 20, 477-8.

— A.F. Norman, Libanius' Autobiography, *Mnemosyne* 20, 488-9.

1968 M. Fuhrmann, Untersuchungen zur Textgeschichte der pseudo-aristotelischen Alexander-Rhetorik, and M. Fuhrmann, Anaximenis Ars Rhetorica, *Mnemosyne* 21, 91-2.

1969 R. Kassel, Aristotelis de arte poetica liber, *Mnemosyne* 22, 439.

1972 G. Morpurgo-Tagliabue, Linguistica e stilistica di Aristotele, *Mnemosyne* 25, 200-2.

— G. Petzl, Antike Diskussionen über den beiden Nekyiai, *Gnomon* 305-7.

— J.A. Goldstein, The Letters of Demosthenes, *Mnemosyne* 25, 308-9.

1973 K. Pohl, Die Lehre von den drei Wortfügungsarten, *Mnemosyne* 26, 193-4.

— M.H. McCall, Ancient Rhetorical Theories of Simile and Comparison, *Mnemosyne* 26, 296-7.

— E.N. Tigerstedt, Plato's Idea of Poetical Inspiration, *Mnemosyne* 26, 427-9.

1974 R. Kassel, Der Text der aristotelischen Rhetorik, *Mnemosyne* 27, 421-2.

— E. Brooks Jr., P. Rutilii Lupi De figuris sententiarum et elocutionis, *Mnemosyne* 27, 427-9.

1975 A. Scaglione, The Classical Theory of Composition, *Mnemosyne* 28, 215-7.

— F. Cairns, Generic Composition in Greek and Roman Poetry, *Mnemosyne* 28, 425-6.

1976 G.A. Kennedy, The Art of Rhetoric in the Roman World, *Mnemosyne* 29, 89-91.

— M. Dufour & A. Wartelle, Aristote, Rhétorique, t. iii, *Mnemosyne* 29, 195-6.

— W.M.A. Grimaldi, Studies in the Philosophy of Aristotle's Rhetoric, *Mnemosyne* 29, 425-7.

1977 A. Hellwig, Untersuchungen zur Theorie der Rhetorik bei Platon und Aristoteles, *Mnemosyne* 30, 84-5.

1978 J. Soffel, Die Regeln Menanders für die Leichenrede, *Mnemosyne* 31, 99-100.

1980 G. Lindberg, Studies in Hermogenes and Eustathius, *Mnemosyne* 32, 414-5.

1983 J.F. Kindstrand, Isaac Porphyrogenitus, Praefatio in Homerum, and F. Montanari, Studi di filologia omerica antica I, *Mnemosyne* 36, 389-90.

— L. Calboli Montefusco, Consulti Fortunatiani Ars Rhetorica. introd. ed. crit. trad. ital. e comm., *Mnemosyne* 36, 207-9.

1985 J.F. Kindstrand, An Index to Dio Chrysostomus, *Mnemosyne* 38, 217-8.

1986 F.W. Householder, The Syntax of Apollonius Dyscolus, and D. Blank, Ancient Philosophy and Grammar, *Mnemosyne* 38, 424-6.

1987 R. Pretagostini, Ricerche sulla poesia alessandrina, *Mnemosyne* 40, 566-7.

1988 W.H. Mineur, Callimachus' Hymn to Delos, *Mnemosyne* 41, 171-4.

— H. Tarrant, Scepticism or Platonism? The Philosophy of the Fourth Academy, *Ploutarchos* 4, 11-3.

— J.C. Hogan, A Commentary on the Complete Tragedies - Aeschylus, *Mnemosyne* 41, 140.

— L. Montanari, La sezione linguistica del peri hermeneias di Aristotele: I. II testo, *Mnemosyne* 41, 165-6.

— W.J. Slater, Aristophanis Byzantii fragmenta, *Mnemosyne* 41, 178-81.

1989 M. Fusillo, Il tempo delle Argonautiche, *Mnemosyne* 42, 192-203.

— C.W. Wooten, Hermogenes, On Types of Style, transl., *Mnemosyne* 42, 262-5.

1990 Rob. Clavaud, Demosthène, Lettres et Fragments, *Mnemosyne* 48, 212-5.

— Fr. Vian, ed., Les Argonautiques Orphiques, *Mnemosyne* 48, 222-4.

— W. Albert, Das mimetische Gedicht in der Antike, *Mnemosyne* 48, 460-2.

— H. von Thiel, Odysseen, *Mnemosyne* 48, 468-71.

1991 Doreen Innes - M. Winterbottom, Sopatros the Rhetor, *Mnemosyne* 44, 213-6.

— R.A. Kaster, Guardians of language, *Mnemosyne* 44, 271-3.

— D.M. MacDowell, Demosthenes, Against Meidias (Oration 21), *Mnemosyne* 44, 470-2.

— S.-T. Teodorsson, A commentary on Plutarch's Table Talks, Vol. 1, *Mnemosyne* 44, 472-3.

— J. Latacz, Homeros. De eerste dichter van het avondland, *Mededelingen van de Vereniging Vrienden van het Gymnasium* 10,2, p. 7 and *Lampas* 24, 264-5.

1992 B.D. MacQueen, Myth, Rhetoric and Fiction. A Reading of Longus' Daphnis and Chloe, *Mnemosyne* 45, 413-6.

— Th. Cole, The Origins of Rhetoric in Ancient Greece, *Mnemosyne* 45, 387-92.

1994 S. Usher, *Isocrates, Panegyricus and To Nicocles*, *Mnemosyne* 47, 141.

— M. Fusillo - A. Hurst - G. Paduano, Licofrone, Alessandra, *Mnemosyne* 47, 245-6.

— C.M. Mazzucchi, Dionisio Longino, Del Sublime, *Mnemosyne* 47, 249-50.

— P. Cesaretti, Allegoristi di Omero a Bisanzio, *Mnemosyne* 47, 250-1.

— P. Chiron, Démétrios, Du Style, *Mnemosyne* 47, 400-11.

— D.A. Russell, An Anthology of Greek Prose, *Mnemosyne* 47, 432.

— M. Kardaun, Der Mimesisbegriff in der griechischen Antike, *Mnemosyne* 47, 694-6.

— R. Granatelli, Apollodori Pergameni ac Theodori Gadareni testimonia et fragmenta, *Mnemosyne* 47, 697.

— M.-C. Vacher, Suétone, Grammariens et rhéteurs, *Mnemosyne* 47, 697.

1995 A. Rengakos, Der Homertext und die hellenistischen Dichter, *Mnemosyne* 48, 95-7.

Forthcoming:

— Plutarch's Quaestiones Convivales I.1: A Thesis in Disguise, in: P. Swiggers - A. Wouters [on Plutarch]. Leuven.

— Theophrastus. His Rhetorical Works. One Rhetorical Fragment Less, One Logical More, in: *Papers of the 9th Theophrastus Conference* (RUSCH VII).

— Hellenismus, in: G. Ueding (ed.), *Historisches Wörterbuch der Rhetorik*, Tübingen.

— The Study of Language, Rhetoric and Poetics, in: J. Barnes et al. (eds.), *Cambridge History of Hellenistic Philosophy*.

— articles on 'Stoic Philosophers' and 'Philosophical Treatises', in: S.E. Porter et al. (ed.), *A Handbook of Classical Rhetoric in the Hellenistic Period*. Leiden.

Forthcoming review:

— D. Bo, Le principali problematiche del Dialogus de Oratoribus, *Mnemosyne*.

Theophrastus, Source no. 709 FHS&G

William W. Fortenbaugh

Text no. 709 in the new collection of Theophrastean sources[1] comes from the sixth book of Athenaeus' *The Sophists at Dinner*.[2] The speaker in this portion of the work is the philosopher Democritus of Nicomedia (cf. 248d and 262b).[3] He is discussing the evils of flattery, and in connection with this topic (259f-260a) he calls attention to five individuals who had a marked weakness for laughter (259f-260a). After that Democritus jumps from individuals to entire cities. He calls the Tirynthians 'lovers-of-laughter' (our text 709.1) and describes the people of Phaestus as life-long practitioners of wit (261e). Democritus is drawing on a variety of sources, and in the case of the Tirynthians he names Theophrastus. There is no reason to doubt the reference, though we may fault the style of Athenaeus and the jump from individuals to groups of people who are largely unrelated to the theme of flattery.

The Greek text of 709 is not long. I give it here together with an English translation.

> Τιρυνθίους δέ φησι Θεόφραστος ἐν τῷ Περὶ κωμῳδίας φιλόγελως ὄντας, ἀχρείους δὲ πρὸς τὰ σπουδαιότερα τῶν πραγμάτων καταφυγεῖν (3) ἐπὶ τὸ ἐν Δελφοῖς μαντεῖον ἀπαλλαγῆναι βουλομένους τοῦ πάθους καὶ τὸν θεὸν ἀνελεῖν αὐτοῖς, ἣν θύοντες τῷ Ποσειδῶνι ταῦρον ἀγελαστὶ τοῦτον ἐμβάλωσιν εἰς τὴν θάλατταν, παύσασθαι. οἳ δὲ δεδιότες μὴ (6) διαμάρτωσι τοῦ

---

[1] *FHS&G* 2.554-5.

[2] Athenaeus 6.79, 261d-e, 2.81.19-82.4 Kaibel.

[3] Democritus of Nicomedia is introduced in 1.2, 1d, along with his fellow townsman Pontianus. Both are said to be philosophers who excel all in polymathy. Aside from a shared name, there is little reason to connect Democritus with the Presocratic atomist who was born in Abdera and lived six centuries earlier.

λογίου τοὺς παῖδας ἐκώλυσαν παρεῖναι τῇ θυσίᾳ. μαθὼν οὖν εἷς καὶ συγκαταμιχθείς, ἐπείπερ ἐβόων ἀπελαύνοντες αὐτόν, "τί δῆτ';" ἔφη· "δεδοίκατε μὴ τὸ σφάγιον ὑμῶν ἀνατρέψω;" γελασάντων (9) δὲ ἔμαθον ἔργῳ τὸν θεὸν δείξαντα ὡς ἄρα τὸ πολυχρόνιον ἦθος ἀμήχανόν ἐστι θεραπευθῆναι.

'In the work *On Comedy*, Theophrastus says that the people of Tiryns were given to laughter and unfit for more serious affairs. Since they wanted to be released from this condition, they had recourse to the oracle at Delphi and were told by the god that they would be freed, providing that they sacrificed a bull to Poseidon and threw it into the sea without laughter. Fearing that they would not fulfill the oracle, they prevented the children from attending the sacrifice, but one child learned of it and mingled with the people. As they were driving him away with shouts, the child said, "What then? Are you frightened that I shall turn over your victim?" They laughed and so learned by their own action (what) the god showed: (namely) that a long standing habit is incapable of being cured.'

The lesson conveyed by the text—namely, that long standing habits resist change—is immediately understandable, for it is in line with both common sense and Peripatetic doctrine. Theophrastus himself makes the point explicitly in another text preserved in Stobaeus' *Anthology* 2.31.124 = no. 465 FHS&G. The topic is education. The Eresian states the importance of developing good habits and goes on to criticise people who fail to consider the kind of life they wish to lead. He draws an analogy with planning a journey and tells us that once we begin to travel the wrong road, 'turning back is difficult, or rather almost impossible, because time does not provide opportunity to change, and nature is unable to learn what is better, once it is trained in worse ways' (465.16-9). To avoid misunderstanding, I want to underline the caution with which Theophrastus expresses himself. He says that reversal 'is difficult, or rather almost impossible' (χαλεπή, μᾶλλον δὲ σχεδὸν ἀδύνατος 465.16-7). That leaves the door open to an extraordinary event like severe illness, surgery or divine intervention. For Theophrastus, then, the Tirynthians did nothing absurd in consulting the god at Delphi. Their condition could, in theory at least, have been altered by special—in this case divine—intervention. But equally there is nothing unintelligible in their subsequent failure to accomplish a sacrifice without laughing. It is dramatic proof that old habits stubbornly resist change.

I shall return to the subject of curing and treating bad habits later, when I take up the Peripatetic notion of catharsis. At this moment, it may be helpful to relate the form of the story told in 709 to Aristotle's discussion of example (παράδειγμα) in *Rhetoric* 2.20. There, Theophrastus' teacher distinguishes between using actual past events (πράγματα προγεγενημένα) to establish a point and making up examples which serve the speaker's purpose. The former case is illustrated by reference to Darius and Xerxes, who seized Egypt before attacking Greece (1393a30-b3).[4] The latter case is bipartite. There is comparison (παραβολή), which Aristotle elucidates by citing the Socratic use of parallels: a public official ought not to be selected by lot any more than a competitor in an athletic contest or the captain of a ship (1393b3-8). There is also fable (λόγος), which is illustrated twice. First we hear of Stesichorus, who opposed assigning a body guard to Phalaris; he concluded his argument by telling the story of a horse who allowed a man to mount him (1393b8-23). Second, there is mention of Aesop, who defended a demagogue by relating how a fox, when caught in a hole, refused to have fleas removed from his body, for the present fleas had all but sucked their fill of blood (1393b23-1394a2).

If we ask to which category our Theophrastean story belongs, we may be tempted to answer that it must be assigned to the class of actual past events. For the story of the Tirynthians is neither a comparison of the Socratic kind nor a fable in which animals are the principle figures. In addition, we know that Greek cities did consult Delphi in order to find relief from afflictions. The Athenians, for example, did so when oppressed by plague in 596 BCE. The oracle told the Athenians to purify

---

[4] The argument is as follows: Since the Persian kings Darius and Xerxes seized Egypt prior to attacking Greece, the present king should not be allowed to take Egypt, for he will then move against Greece.

the city, which they did and as a result put an end to the plague.[5] Furthermore, the directive of the oracle as reported in 709 contains a qualifier which has parallels in genuine oracles. I am thinking of the way the Tirynthians are told that they will be freed from their condition if they sacrifice to Poseidon *without laughing*. The proviso 'without laughing' may be compared with a similar limitation found in a Delphic response of 431 BCE. When the Spartans asked whether they should renew the war with Athens, the god replied that they will be victorious, fighting *forcefully*.[6] Here the qualifier 'forcefully' is attached to a participle; in 709 the proviso 'without laughing' is part of a conditional clause. In both cases it serves to qualify the god's statement.[7]

If the general motivation for consulting the oracle and the form of the response provide no grounds for doubting the story told in 709, the same cannot be said of the particular motivation: namely, seeking relief from laughter. There is, of course, another story concerning the Delphic oracle in which laughter is a motivating factor. I am thinking of Parmeniscus of Metapontum, who is said to have lost the ability to laugh after visiting the oracle of Trophonius. He went to Delphi and was told that he would regain the ability from 'mother at home'. When his own mother did not cure his condition, he thought himself deceived, until he visited Delos, where a statue of Apollo's mother, Leto, was situated. The unshapeliness of the statue caused him to laugh, and he understood what the Delphic oracle had meant.[8] The story is unlike that of the Tirynthians in that it concerns the loss of laughter by an individual and not intemperate laughter by an entire city. It is, however, similar in that both stories involve insight or understanding which is not only delayed but also subsequent to laughter. More important, the story of Parmeniscus is a

---

[5] Diogenes Laertius 1.110 = no. 13 Parke and Wormell 1956 = no. Q65 Fontenrose 1978. For another example, see no. 584A.332-44 FHS&G.

[6] Thucydides 1.118.3 = no. 137 P&W = no. H5 F.

[7] See the comment of Fontenrose on p. 33.

[8] Athenaeus 14.2, 614a-b = no. 129 P&W = no. Q185 F.

clear fabrication, almost certainly invented to excuse the primitive figure of Leto and to denigrate the oracle of Trophonius.[9] The story of the Tirynthians is equally fictitious. That a whole city would suffer from uncontrolled laughter is incredible, and the wittiness of the story suggests that we are not dealing with an actual past event. No child managed to work his way into a sacrifice and then cause laughter by confusing the Greek words *σφαγεῖον* ('bowl') and *σφάγιον* ('victim'). Even the choice of Tiryns speaks against authenticity. While not as hopeless as the Sybarites,[10] the Tirynthians were unsuccessful in maintaining their position within the Peloponnesus. The comic poet Ephippus makes fun of them in the *Busiris*. He has Heracles say that they are always drunk when they fight, after which Busiris remarks, 'So that's why they always run away.'[11] There is also a report that the Tirynthians consulted the god at Delphi concerning a new homeland, perhaps after a defeat by Argos in 468/7 BCE.[12] The story is almost certainly false, but it is in line with the general reputation of the Tirynthians. They were 'unfit for the more serious affairs' of life (709.2) and therefore not only losers in war but also suitable subjects for a fabricated story about uncontrolled laughter.

Where does this leave us in regard to Aristotle's three kinds of example? If 709 presents a story which is not only witty but also fabricated, perhaps it should be assigned to Aristotle's third class, that of fictitious λόγοι (1393a30). Above I followed standard translations and

---

[9] Parke - Wormell 1956, 1.411-2.

[10] The destruction of Sybaris gave rise to two stories concerning the Delphic oracle: no. 73 P&W = no. Q122 F. and no. 74 P&W = no. Q123 F. The Sybarites' weakness for pleasure was the subject of many anecdotes: see no. 550 and 551 FHS&G.

[11] Athenaeus 10.59, 442d-e = Ephippus fr. 2 *CAF*, 2.251 Kock = fr. 2 *PCG* 5.132 Kassel - Austin.

[12] Ephorus, *FGrH* 70 F 56 = Stephanus of Byzantium, *Ethnika*, s.v. Ἁλιεῖς = no. 315 P&W = no. Q176 F. The date of the defeat is disputed. See Jacoby, *FGrH* vol. 2C1 p. 53-4, who believes that the fall of Tiryns mentioned in this report belongs to an earlier period when Argos dominated the Peloponnesus.

rendered the Greek word λόγος with 'fable.'[13] That seemed sensible given the stories about animals introduced by Aristotle. Nevertheless, the Greek is not so precise and makes room for stories of all kinds including those about men and deities. In addition, the standard collections of Aesop's fables include stories in which humans are the sole actors.[14] More important, there are fables which exhibit striking similarities with 709. I mention two. First, there is the fable of the Weasel and Aphrodite.[15] The animal fell in love with a handsome young man and begged the goddess to turn her into a beatiful woman. Aphrodite obliged; the young man was moved by the woman's appearance, and the two married. Wanting to know whether the woman had undergone a change in character as well as in shape, Aphrodite let loose a mouse. The woman ran after it, and the goddess in disgust changed the woman back into a weasel. The author of the fable then adds a conclusion to the effect that bad men do not modify their character even if they change their appearance. Here, as in 709, a problem is recognised after which there is an appeal to a deity for fundamental change. The deity is or appears to be favorable, but human failure stands in the way. Some things cannot be altered.

[13] E.g., the translation of Rhys Roberts (1924) and that of George Kennedy (1991).

[14] No. 216 Hausrath = no. 200 Perry is of some interest. A mother shows approval when her young son steals, and she continues to show approval as the child grows and engages in ever larger theft. When the son is finally caught and brought into court, the child says he wants to whisper in his mother's ear. When she comes to him, he bites her ear. She reacts indignantly, and he replies that she should have spanked him the first time he stole. The lesson drawn from the story is that what is not blocked at the outset grows ever larger. For our purposes the important point is that we have here a learned habit which need not have developed. In the two fables to which I now turn—the weasel and Aphrodite, and Zeus and the fox—the habits under consideration are different in that they are innate. Which kind of disposition figures in 709 is not immediately clear.

[15] No. 50 H = no. 50 P. I am indebted to Professor William Hansen for calling my attention to this fable and to the one discussed in the next paragraph.

The second fable is that of Zeus and the fox.[16] The god was impressed by the cleverness of the fox and made it king of the animals. Wanting to know whether the fox had experienced a change not only in fortune but also in character, Zeus caused a beetle to pass before the fox. The latter could not control itself, lept up and tried to catch the beetle. The god was disgusted and returned the fox to its former status. The author then adds the observation that worthless men, even if they take on a more brilliant outward appearance, do not alter their nature. Here the similarities to 709 are less striking—no problem sets the story in motion—but they are still real and clear enough. There is a god and a creature which has an unattractive trait. A change for the better is not effected, so that the permanence of a long established character is once again demonstrated.

One difference between these two Aesopic fables and those recorded by Aristotle seems important. It is the difference between a general conclusion and a specific conclusion. In a rhetorical context, the speaker most often tries to persuade his audience to adopt a particular course of action. Hence it is hardly surprising that Aristotle has Stesichorus and Aesop conclude their fables with remarks specifically directed at the people of Himera and Samos (1393b19-23, b32-1394a2). In contrast, the two fables just related conclude with general observations about the permanence of character, and the same is true of 709. That is not to suggest that, given a context, particular conclusions cannot be drawn. In regard to 709, I shall soon have something to say about the matter; but for the moment, I want to underline the general nature of the conclusions and to focus on the idea of worthless character. The fables—those concerning the weasel and the fox—conclude that men who are bad by nature (*οἱ φύσει πονηροί*) do not modify their character; that worthless men (*οἱ φαῦλοι*) do not alter their nature. That suggests a comparison with comedy, for Aristotle defines the genre as an imitation of comparatively worthless people (*μίμησις φαυλοτέρων* *Poetics* 5, 1449a32-3), and the plays of Menander, Theophrastus' pupil (no. 18.12 FHS&G), well illus-

[16] No. 109 H = 107 P.

trate the comic potential of an unattractive and incurable character trait.[17]

Two plays may serve to make the point. First, in *She Who was Shorn* (Περικειρομένη), Menander focuses on an impetuous (*σφόδρος*, 128 OCT) soldier, Polemon, who sets the play in motion with a vehement response to apparent infidelity. Polemon believes that Glycera has betrayed his trust; he cuts off her hair and then bursts into tears (173-4). A large part of the play revolves around Polemon's intense character; and at the end, Menander uses this trait to bring the play to a comical conclusion. Polemon is told to give up his military career, so that he will not act impetuously in the future. His response is first to call upon Apollo and then to ask rhetorically whether he, who has suffered so much, will ever again act impulsively. Finally, depending on how one restores the text, Polemon promises either that he will never again find fault with Glycera, or that he will never, even in a dream, do anything impulsive (1018-20). The response is amusing in its impetuosity and a dramatic indication that, whether or not Polemon gives up military life, he will remain a vehement person.

The second play is the *Grouch* (Δύσκολος). Here Cnemon is presented as a difficult person who prefers to live alone (*μόνος*, 30, 150, 329). In the fourth act, he falls into a well from which he is rescued by Gorgias, his stepson whom he had previously treated with rudeness and even hostility. As a result, Cnemon realises that he was wrong to think himself self-sufficient (713-7) and to suspect the motives of everyone else (718-29). Nevertheless, he cannot free himself from his old habit: he chooses to be alone (869) while others enjoy a banquet next door. That makes possible a lively ending to the play. Cook and slave combine to torment the old man, ultimately picking him up and carrying him off to join the others at their banquet.

---

[17] Caveat: I am not saying that Menander's plays concern only worthless people. Nor do I want to suggest that Theophrastus defined comedy in terms of worthless persons. He appears not to have done so. Nevertheless, worthless types are prominent on the comic stage and therefore merit special consideration in a work *On Comedy* (666 no. 22 FHS&G).

Both plays exploit a truth concerning human character: habits become second nature and cannot be easily changed.[18] That is also the lesson of our Theophrastean text, which not surprisingly makes reference to the Eresian's work *On Comedy* (709.1). That work (no. 666 no. 22 FHS&G) has not survived, so that we cannot be certain how Theophrastus used the example of the Tirynthians to elucidate comedy; but at least four possibilities suggest themselves. First, Theophrastus may have introduced the example not only to illustrate an incurable habit but also to call attention to the fact that humorous traits are often, perhaps most often, foibles which are not in themselves vicious. That is to say, they are not acquired dispositions directed by choice toward some shameful goal. The cases of Polemon and Cnemon can again be instructive. The impetuosity of Polemon is not an ethical failing. It is an innate disposition which gets in the way and causes unintended suffering. In contrast, Cnemon's isolation is an acquired habit, but it too can be distinguished from vice. For it is essentially a stylistic trait which, however regrettable, does not or need not involve a shameful goal and therefore does not in itself invite moral censure.[19]

A second possibility is that Theophrastus used the example of the Tirynthians to elucidate plot. What we have in 709 is, of course, a short anecdote and not the plot of a fully developed comedy. But the anecdote could easily be fleshed out, and in any case it neatly illustrates a truth clearly recognised by Menander: an engrained habit can begin, guide and end a funny story. Furthermore, the anecdote involves no reversal of fortune. The Tirynthians have had a good laugh, but they have not changed their condition. They remain dysfunctional and will eventually be forced to leave their city—at least that was the fate of the historical Tiryn-

---

[18] Cf. Aristotle, *EN* 7.10/*EE* 6.10, 1152a10-33 and *Rhet*. 1.11, 1370a6-7; for commentary, see Fortenbaugh (1984, 192-3).

[19] Here I am concerned only with Cnemon's preference for isolation. His negative judgment concerning the motives of other people is abandoned before the play ends. See the preceding paragraph.

thians.[20] This absence of reversal is a matter of some interest, for in regard to tragedy Theophrastus seems to have followed Aristotle in emphasising change of fortune. The Stagirite calls reversal one of the two most important parts of a tragic plot (*Poetics* 6 1450a33-5), and the Eresian seems to mention it within his definition of tragedy. The definition is preserved by Diomedes and runs as follows: *τραγῳδία ἐστὶν ἡρωικῆς τύχης περίστασις*, 'tragedy is a reversal of heroic fortune' (no.708.6-7 FHS&G).[21] Here Theophrastus does not use the Aristotelian term *περιπέτεια* (*Poetics* 6, 1450a34). Instead he prefers *περίστασις*, which in another context could mean 'circumstance' or 'crisis.' But within the discussion of Diomedes—especially given his subsequent remarks on the tragic shift from joy to grief (708.13-5)—*περίστασις* is almost certainly a variant for *περιπέτεια*.[22] Concerning comedy, we are less well informed. Since Book 2 of the *Poetics* is lost, we cannot be certain whether Aristotle connected comedy with reversal. We can only say that his brief remarks in *Poetics* 1 do not make the connection. In regard to Theophrastus, we have a definition of comedy preserved by Diomedes. It reads: *κωμῳδία ἐστὶν ἰδιωτικῶν πραγμάτων ἀκίνδυνος περιοχή*, 'comedy is a story of private affairs involving no danger' (708.9-10). Here, however, Diomedes does not name Theophrastus. Instead he refers vaguely to Greeks (708.9). Nevertheless, Diomedes does compare the definition of comedy with the Theophrastean definition of tragedy (708.10-6), and that suggests that both definitions are attributable to the

---

[20] See above, note 12.

[21] In vol. 2 p. 553 FHS&G *περίστασις* is translated 'crisis', and 'reversal' is given as an alternative on p. 555 n. 2. Today I would translate 'reversal' and omit the note, reserving discussion for the commentary.

[22] See Usener (1892, 620 n. 81 = reprint (1912-3) 2.294 n. 81), who remarks that *περίστασις* is used in its original sense of 'Umschlag' or 'Umschwung.' Webster (1960, 179 and 1970, 114) translates Theophrastus' definition of tragedy in the following manner: 'a reversal of heroic prosperity.' Aristotle uses *περίστασις* to refer to a shift in wind direction: *Meteor.* 2.6, 364b14 and *Probl.* 26.26, 942b27.

Eresian. Most scholars accept the double attribution,[23] and I do so too. But what especially interests me here is that the definition of comedy seems to include no reference to reversal. It is true that *Lexica* of Hesychius and Photius give 'reversal' as a meaning of the word *περιοχή*,[24] but in our text the more likely meaning is 'story' or 'account.' That agrees with the use of *περιέχειν* in the subsequent definition of mime (709.28). In addition, it is hard to see why Theophrastus would vary his vocabulary if he wanted to make reversal a defining mark of both tragedy and comedy. My guess is that Theophrastus deliberately preferred *περιοχή* to *περίστασις*, because he did not think reversal central to comedy. He recognised that a main character like Cnemon may remain unchanged and unhappy at the end of a play. Indeed, such a character may even get a thumping from a cook and slave. But if the absence of any mention of reversal is understandable,[25] we may be puzzled by the mention of private affairs alone, without any reference to those of the city. In the immediately preceding sentence, Diomedes does mention both 'private and civic fortune' (708.8), so that one looks for some reference to the city in the subsequent definition. Perhaps Diomedes has left something out. Perhaps Theophrastus, if the definition is his, focused on Menander's interest in private life and therefore made no mention of civic fortune. I see no way to decide the matter and prefer to underline the fact that an example is often introduced for the sake of one or two features. That may well be true of the anecdote concerning the Tirynthians. In his work *On Comedy*, Theophrastus may have related the story in order to make a

---

[23] Usener 1892, 620-1 = reprint 2.294-5; Kaibel 1898, 55, 66; McMahon 1917, 45; 1939, 100-4, 126-30; Kroll 1921, 1208, 1214, 1270; Webster 1960, 179; 1970, 114; Stark 1972, 92, 176 n. 29; Janko 1984, 48-52.

[24] Hesychius, *Lex.*, s.v. (3.320.19 Schmidt) and Photius, *Lex.* s.v. (1.82.18 Naber).

[25] The definition is so short that one might ask whether it has been abbreviated by Diomedes or his source. In regard to reversal, I doubt that it has. The omission of any mention of catharsis is more problematic. See below.

point about reversal or character or both, and simply ignored the fact that the story concerns a civic affair.

I come now to the third possibility. Our Theophrastean text concludes with the statement that the people of Tiryns learned (ἔμαθον, 709.9) that long standing habits cannot be cured. Perhaps Theophrastus wanted to call attention to the educational benefits of comedy. While the Tirynthians learned an important lesson through their own actions, the spectators at a comedy can learn the very same lesson from what occurs on the stage. In the *Grouch*, Menander helps the audience grasp the message. Early on he has Gorgias say that Cnemon cannot be reformed either by force or persuasion (250-4); and later Sostratus is made to exclaim 'Oh, intractable character' (ὦ τρόπου ἀμάχου, 869-70). But underlining the message in this way is not necessary. In fact, the playwright may find it amusing to have a stage-figure get things backwards, as Pataecus does in *She Who was Shorn*. He urges Polemon to give up being a soldier in order that he may cease from impetuous behaviour (1016-7); but in fact Polemon is a good soldier, because he is impetuous. As a result, the perceptive spectator laughs at the seriousness of Pataecus as well as the vehemence of Polemon. He enjoys himself while learning or relearning an important truth about human behavior.

The fourth possibility picks up two earlier promises: namely, that I would return to the subject of curing and treating bad habits and that I would consider whether the story of the Tirynthians might not support a particular conclusion. I take up both promises now, for they are related and concern the benefits provided by comic performance. One of these benefits is certainly insight; and given the texts just considered, we can say that a special benefit is clear recognition of the difficulty or near impossibility which confronts men who, after a long period of time, try to change their ways (465.16-7). But that need not be the end of the matter. For men who recognise the impossibility of fundamental change can still take preventive measures to make their condition tolerable.[26] In regard to

[26] Theophrastus is careful not to identify the nature of an individual with necessity (no. 503.2-3 FHS&G), for the person who is powerless in regard to necessity can take steps to counter the effects of nature (cf. no. 504.6-7

emotions like pity and fear, Aristotle points to the cathartic effect of tragic performances (*Poetics* 6, 1449b27-8). Much like persons listening to passionate music, so the spectators at a tragedy are purged and relieved (*Politics* 8.7, 1341b38-40, 1342a14). They experience strong feelings of pity and fright and as a result undergo physiological change. This change is not a permanent cure, but given the pleasures of a good tragedy, most people would welcome such a therapy on a regular basis. The same is, I think, true in regard to laughter. The people of Tiryns may have been hopeless, but there are many people who laugh too much without being totally useless. Moreover, most people are like Parmeniscus of Metapontum; they would not want to lose the capacity for laughter.[27] They would much prefer a short term remedy which brings as much pleasure as it does relief. Perhaps, then, 709 contains an implicit recommendation: embrace comedy for its cathartic effect. Laughter is after all an emotion; and like pity and fright, it may find moderation in repeated release.[28] If that release is found in the theater, then comedy, as well as tragedy, has an important function in the well organised city-state.

Having now run through four possible ways in which Theophrastus could have used the story of the Tirynthians in his work *On Comedy*,[29] I want to call attention to still another feature of the story which is relevant

---

FHS&G). See Fortenbaugh 1984, 232.

[27] In 709.3 we read that the people of Tiryns went to Delphi, *ἀπαλλαγῆναι βουλομένους τοῦ πάθους*. Out of context, the word *πάθος* could refer to the feeling or emotion of laughter, but here it refers to the condition from which the people of Tiryns want to be freed. They want to change a long standing disposition—a *πολυχρόνιον ἦθος* (709.9)—without losing altogether the feeling or emotion of laughter.

[28] Cf. the *Tractatus Coislinianus* in which both tragedy and comedy are said to work a catharsis (lines 7-11 Koster = sec. 2-3 Kaibel = sec. III-IV Janko). Since the definition of comedy in 708.9-10 is quite brief, the omission of any reference to catharsis is probably no indication of Theophrastean doctrine.

[29] Two further possibilities are suggested by Janko: the anecdote 'derives from a discussion of the origins of comedy, or of the comic impulse in man' (1984, 48).

to comedy and generally to theories of humor. I am thinking of the words spoken by the young boy—words already mentioned above in regard to fabrication. When the youth is discovered by the adults, he says, 'What then? Are you frightened that I shall turn over your victim?' (709.8) These words cause the Tirynthians to laugh. Assuming that they were quite nervous in undertaking a sacrifice without laughter and given the fact that they were prone to laugh much of the time, it may be unnecessary to look for a good joke in the boy's words. Nevertheless, such a joke is present. The boy wants to ask whether the adults are frightened that he will turn over a sacrificial bowl. He confuses two cognate Greek words, *σφαγεῖον* ('bowl') and *σφάγιον* ('victim'), and speaks of up-ending the bull. Similarity in sound is behind the boy's confusion and the resulting absurdity evokes laughter from the adults.[30] It cannot be shown that Theophrastus discussed this play on words in the treatise *On Comedy*, but he certainly could have done so, perhaps within a section on the causes of laughter.[31]

Whatever the truth concerning *On Comedy*, it seems certain that Theophrastus had a keen interest in laughter aroused by speech. He wrote a work *On the Ludicrous* (666 no. 23) and commented on a verbal thrust directed by a certain Stratonicus against the actor Simycas (710.7-10). The latter apparently was of large stature but weak in voice. Stratonicus mocked him taking the proverb 'No rotten fish is large' and speaking the words separately. The humourhere depends on the Greek word *οὐδείς* which can mean a 'nobody' and on the reference to fish which have little

---

[30] We may compare Aristotle's *Rhetoric* 3.11. In this chapter, the Stagirite is primarily concerned with urbanities, but he adds 'a footnote' (Schenkeveld 1994, 7) on witty remarks which depend upon a change of letter and are contrary to the expectations of the listener. When they are quickly understood, they are pleasant (3.11, 1412a28-b3).

[31] We may compare the outline of comedy preserved in the *Tractatus Coislinianus*. It contains a division in which laughter arising from speech is marked off from laughter from action, and each half is further divided in accordance with difference in cause (lines 13-30 Koster = sec. 3 Kaibel = sec. V-VI Janko).

or no voice. The joke seems somewhat contrived, but that may be more a matter of reading than hearing. Theophrastus says that Stratonicus delivered the thrust, dividing up the proverb. Pausing would give the listener time to appreciate the meaning of *οὐδείς*; in addition, it would highlight the mention of fish. I suspect that Theophrastus enjoyed making jokes of this kind. He wrote on delivery, and I can imagine him delivering his lectures in a most appealing manner. When discussing tragedy he may well have told the story of Euripides and Archelaus, reserving the phrase 'an account (or tale) of miseries' until the end and speaking it after a pause and with surprising force (708.17-20). Similarly in lecturing on comedy, the Eresian will have related the story of the Tirynthians with considerable relish. He will have mixed an amusing anecdote with a clever one-line joke and added a delivery which brought his students to laughter. Indeed, we hear that Theophrastus, when lecturing, avoided no motion or gesture, and that on one occasion he imitated a gourmet by sticking out his tongue and licking his lips (no. 12.3-4 FHS&G)). Perhaps this flair for effective delivery explains how Theophrastus was able to attract two thousand students (no. 1.16 and 2.7 FHS&G). That figure is round. It may be too high or too low. I assert only that the Eresian understood the comic and regularly practised what he preached.

BIBLIOGRAPHY

FHS&G = *Theophrastus of Eresus: Sources for his Life, Writings, Thought and Influence*, edited by W. Fortenbaugh, P. Huby, R. Sharples & D. Gutas. Leiden 1992.

Fortenbaugh, W., *Quellen zur Ethik Theophrasts*. Amsterdam 1984.

Fontenrose, J., *The Delphic Oracle*. Berkeley 1978.

Kaibel, G., *Die Prolegomena* ΠΕΡΙ ΚΩΜΩΙΔΙΑΣ. Berlin 1898.

Kennedy, G., *Aristotle, On Rhetoric: A Theory of Civic Discourse*. Oxford 1991.

Kroll, W., 'Komödie', Pauly - Wissowa *Realenzyklopädie* 11.1 (1921), 1207-80.

Janko, R., *Aristotle on Comedy*. Berkeley - Los Angeles 1984.

McMahon, A., On the Second Book Of Aristotle's Poetics and the Sources of Theophrastus' Definition of Tragedy, *HSPh* 28 (1917), 1-46.

———, Seven Questions on Aristotelian Definitions of Tragedy and Comedy, *HSPh* 40 (1929), 97-198.

Parke, H., - Wormell, D., *The Delphic Oracle*. Oxford 1956.

Roberts, R., *Aristotle, Rhetoric*. Oxford 1924.

Schenkeveld, D., *Ta asteia* in Aristotle's *Rhetoric*, in: W. W. Fortenbaugh & D. Mirhady (eds.), *Peripatetic Rhetoric after Aristotle* (RUSCH IV). New Brunswick, NJ 1994, 1-14.

Stark, R., *Aristotelesstudien*. München 1972^2.

Usener, H., Ein altes Lehrgebäude der Philologie, *Sitzungsber. d. königlichen Bayrischen Akademie der Wissenschaften* 1892, 4.582-648 = *Kleine Schriften*, Leipzig 1912-13, 2.265-314.

Webster, T.B.L., *Studies in Menander*. Manchester 1960^2.

———, *Studies in Later Greek Comedy*. Manchester 1970^2.

Poetics and Grammar: From Technique to Τέχνη[*]

Pierre Swiggers - Alfons Wouters

> 'La linguistique a des rapports très étroits avec d'autres sciences qui tantôt lui empruntent des données, tantôt lui en fournissent. Les limites qui l'en séparent n'apparaissent pas toujours nettement (...).
> D'autres sciences opèrent sur des objets donnés d'avance et qu'on peut considérer ensuite à différents points de vue; dans notre domaine, rien de semblable (...). Bien loin que l'objet précède le point de vue, on dirait que c'est le point de vue qui crée l'objet, et d'ailleurs rien ne nous dit d'avance que l'une de ces manières de considérer le fait en question soit antérieure ou supérieure aux autres.' (F. de Saussure, *Cours de linguistique générale*, 1916, Introduction; chapters II-III).

1. Introduction

The origin of grammar in Greek antiquity can be—and should be—studied from a twofold point of view: that of the historical constitution of a *discipline*, and that of the gradual delimitation of an *object of study* within a domain of interacting skills and practices. From the first point of view,[1] grammatical science is a discipline which originated in philo-

---

[*] With our thanks to Dr. Ineke Sluiter for her comments on an earlier version of this text.

[1] Elsewhere (Swiggers - Wouters 1994) we have dealt in detail with the influence of philosophical theories on the status, the argumentation and the terminology of ancient grammar. The present study constitutes a complementary analysis, in that it examines the historical delimitation of a grammatical domain.

sophical discussions, and which shows the development from semantic (and referential) preoccupations (such as word-meanings, referential status of names, relationship between language and outer world) to morpho-syntactic questions focusing on the structure of the sentence, and on the establishment of categories of linguistic forms. In this process, Aristotle's *Organon* (and more specifically his *Categories*[2] and his *Peri Hermeneias*) played a crucial role, as did the writings of the Stoic philosophers[3] on types of sentences, types of predicates, and properties of word-classes.

From the second point of view, we have to investigate how a domain was carved out for grammar within a larger field, viz. the study of (literary) speech. Here we have to ask ourselves which specific properties were attached to linguistic structures so that these came to constitute a domain of their own. The purpose of this article, which we take pleasure to dedicate to our friend Professor Dirk Schenkeveld, is to shed some light on the historical formation of the domain of grammar in Antiquity: we will focus our attention on the evolution in the treatment of grammar as a disciplinary object, taking as our point of departure Aristotle's reflections on the study of linguistic expression, and following the development of grammar *in statu nascendi* up to its first systematisation in Dionysius Thrax's *Techne grammatike*, comparing it with Dionysius of Halicarnassus' authoritative treatment of literary composition.[4]

Both studies are an outgrowth of a research project (OT 91/8), funded by the K.U. Leuven, on ancient Greek grammar.

[2] A crucial passage in this respect is *Cat.* 4, 1b25-2a3, in which Aristotle provides a parallel categorisation for conceptual contents and grammatical expressions.

[3] The most important contributions to a scientific conception of grammar were made by the Stoic philosophers Zeno (ca. 332-261 BCE) and Chrysippus (ca. 282-208 BCE). See Diogenes Laertius 7.38-83. Cf. Baratin 1991.

[4] We will not discuss here the fragmentarily preserved works *On Lexis* by Theophrastus (ca. 370-284 BCE) and *On Poems* by Philodemus (ca. 110-40 BCE), although the first may share some ideas with Aristotle's *Poetics* and the second with D.H. For the first, cf. Innes 1985, Kennedy 1989 and Schenkeveld 1993; for the second, cf. Schenkeveld 1968, Innes 1989 and Janko 1991.

2. Aristotle's *Poetics*: the starting-point for the study of 'the use of language'

Scholarly exegesis on the chronology and authenticity of the *Poetics* of Aristotle has focused on the authenticity, and on the various strata in the text; we do not want to take up these discussions which—in the absence of the complete text of Aristotle's *On Poets* and *Homeric Problems* (conserved only in a very fragmentary way)[5]—can only lead to the conclusion that the text as we have it is not a perfectly organised exposition, and that its present (albeit unfinished) state can and should be attributed to Aristotle (as a writer and/or as a teacher).[6] In the present state of our knowledge, the authenticity issue has only restricted relevance.[7] Moreover, the focus on problems of chronology and authenticity has been responsible for the relative neglect of the doctrinal dimension of the *Poetics*, as a reflection on the field of language use.[8] In his *Poetics* Aristotle offers a philosophical reflection on the specificity, species, qualities and uses of literary expression. The specificity of literary/linguistic expression—and ποιητική should be taken as the art, or technique, of literary expression (involving a combination of language, rhythm, and melody; *Po.* 1, 1447a20-2)—is that it *represents life* by means of *articulate speech*. The mimetic dimension explains why literary expression is placed on one line with musical expression, which lacks

---

[5] Cf. for *On Poets*, Rostagni 1926, Janko 1987, 56-65, Halliwell 1989, 149-51 and Janko 1991. For *Homeric Problems*, see Halliwell 1989, 151.

[6] A summary of the attempts to explain and rectify the state of the text is provided by Söffing 1981, 15-22.

[7] See also the position taken by Golden - Hardison 1968, 62; Dupont-Roc - Lallot 1980, 12; Halliwell 1986, 27-9.

[8] Cf. however, López Eire (1980, 19-22: Las funciones del lenguaje en la "Poética" de Aristóteles); Hovdhaugen 1982, 31-9; Halliwell (1986, 344-9: Appendix 4: Aristotle on Language (*lexis*)) and Hennigfeld (1994, 94-103: Sprachanalyse in *Poetik* und *Rhetorik*, esp. 94-7).

λόγος (*Po.* 1, 1447a13-28). In a second stage, Aristotle sets off the art of (literary) speech, although he has no specific name for it:

> *ἡ δὲ [ἐποποιία] μόνον τοῖς λόγοις ψιλοῖς* <*καὶ*> *ἢ τοῖς μέτροις καὶ τούτοις εἴτε μιγνῦσα μετ' ἀλλήλων εἴθ' ἑνί τινι γένει χρωμένη τῶν μέτρων ἀνώνυμοι τυγχάνουσι μέχρι τοῦ νῦν* (*Po.* 1, 1447a28 - 1447b2).[9]
>
> 'But the art which employs words either in bare prose or in metres, either in one kind of metre or combining several, happens up to the present day to have no name' (Hamilton Fyfe 1932, 7).

It is within the field of literary expression that Aristotle seems to have grasped the function of grammar. One of the crucial notions involved in the discussion is that of λέξις, which however receives no specific interpretation in the works dealing with poetics. It is interesting to note that Aristotle, who discusses in his *Poetics* the 'representation' (*μίμησις*) of reality, deals with distinctive properties of poetry (epic, dithyrambic), comedy and tragedy—focusing especially on the mimetical opposition between comedy and tragedy[10]—and relegates the function of language to the discussion of the *μέρη*[11] of tragedy. But, as is clear from his first comments on the role of language, λέξις is a constituent part of (literary) expression:

> *τέταρτον δὲ τῶν † μὲν λόγων † ἡ λέξις· λέγω δέ, ὥσπερ πρότερον εἴρηται, λέξιν εἶναι τὴν διὰ τῆς ὀνομασίας ἑρμηνείαν, ὃ καὶ ἐπὶ τῶν ἐμμέτρων καὶ ἐπὶ τῶν λόγων ἔχει τὴν αὐτὴν δύναμιν* (*Po.* 6, 1450b12-5).
>
> 'The fourth of the literary elements is the language. By this I mean, as we said above, the expression of meaning in words, and this is essentially the same in verse and prose' (Hamilton Fyfe 1932, 29).

This passage is both a correction of and a supplement to the previously given definition of λέξις as the "metrical arrangement of words" (*Po.* 6,

---

[9] We use the Greek text of Kassel's edition (1965). The words between square brackets have been deleted by the editor.

[10] See *Po.* 4, 1447b 24-7.

[11] These *μέρη* are enumerated in *Po.* 6, 1450a7-14.

1449b34-5: *λέγω δὲ λέξιν μὲν αὐτὴν τὴν τῶν μέτρων σύνθεσιν*): in that passage Aristotle provided only a summary characterisation of how λέξις is realised in poetry, whereas in *Po.* 6, 1450b12-5 he considers the function of λέξις as the expression of meaning in discourse. It is this functional appreciation of λέξις which justifies—and thus gives its full sense to—a section whose authenticity has been disputed: the long treatment of λέξις in *Po.* 19-22.[12]

3. *lexis*: the study of speech in Aristotle and Dionysius of Halicarnassus

In Aristotle's *Poetics* the domain of the *lexis* constitutes the common ground for an integrated study of grammar and poetics. This ambivalent position of the *lexis* is partly due to the slow process by which grammar and poetics or rhetoric grew apart (a process which took place after the differentiation, as operated by the Stoics, of dialectics and the study of *lexis*), but it is mainly due to the fact that both grammar and poetics deal with linguistic forms as mimetical elements: for not only is poetical speech *μίμησις* (*Po.* 1, 1447a16;2), it is also a particular manifestation of the mimetical function of ordinary speech, of language in general. This characteristic is noted by both Aristotle, who sees in it a typical feature of man, and by Dionysius of Halicarnassus (D.H.; 2nd half of the 1st cent. BCE), who sees in it the natural driving force of communicative expression:

> *Ἐοίκασι δὲ γεννῆσαι μὲν ὅλως τὴν ποιητικὴν αἰτίαι δύο τινὲς καὶ αὗται φυσικαί. τό τε γὰρ μιμεῖσθαι σύμφυτον τοῖς ἀνθρώποις ἐκ παίδων ἐστὶ καὶ τούτῳ διαφέρουσι τῶν ἄλλων ζῴων ὅτι μιμητικώτατόν ἐστι καὶ τὰς μαθήσεις ποιεῖται διὰ μιμήσεως τὰς πρώτας* (*Po.* 3, 1448b4-8).

---

[12] The section on the λέξις in *Rh.* 3.1-12 will not be analysed here, because it mainly deals with the literary qualities of the λέξις; as to its grammatical contents, the section is inferior to the treatment in *Po.* 19-22, to which references are made. See Ax 1992, 250.

'Speaking generally, poetry seems to owe its origin to two particular causes, both natural. From childhood men have an instinct for representation, and in this respect man differs from the other animals that he is far more imitative and learns his first lessons by representing things' (Hamilton Fyfe 1932, 13).

Μεγάλη δὲ τούτων ἀρχὴ καὶ διδάσκαλος ἡ φύσις, ἡ ποιοῦσα μιμητικοὺς [καὶ θετικοὺς] ἡμᾶς τῶν ὀνομάτων, οἷς δηλοῦται τὰ πράγματα κατά τινας εὐλόγους καὶ κινητικὰς τῆς διανοίας ὁμοιότητας· ὑφ' ἧς ἐδιδάχθημεν ταύρων τε μυκήματα λέγειν καὶ χρεμετισμοὺς ἵππων καὶ φριμαγμοὺς τράγων, πυρός τε βρόμον καὶ πάταγον ἀνέμων καὶ συριγμὸν κάλων καὶ ἄλλα τούτοις ὅμοια παμπληθῆ τὰ μὲν φωνῆς μηνύματα (*varia lectio*: μιμήματα), τὰ δὲ μορφῆς, τὰ δὲ ἔργου, τὰ δὲ πάθους, τὰ δὲ κινήσεως, τὰ δ' ἠρεμίας, τὰ δ' ἄλλου χρήματος ὅτου δή (*Comp.* 16, 62.9-18).[13]
'The great source and teacher in these matters is Nature, who prompts us to imitate, and to coin words which represent things according to certain resemblances which are based on reason and appeal to our intelligence. It is she who has taught us to speak of the bellowing of bulls, the whinnying of horses, the bleating of goats, the roar of fire, the beating of winds, the creaking of ropes, and a host of other similar imitations of sound, shape, action, feeling, movement, stillness, and anything else whatsoever' (Usher 1985, 113-5).

In both authors we find a neat distinction between *thought-contents* and *formal expression,*[14] corresponding to a disciplinary separation between

---

[13] D.H.'s *De compositione verborum* is quoted after the Teubner edition of Usener - Radermacher (1904) by chapter, page(s) and line(s). We also kept at hand the edition (with notes) of Aujac - Lebel (1981).

[14] Aristotle (*Po.* 6) uses the term *dianoia* for the thought-contents, and localises it in 'speeches which contain an argument that something is or is not, or a general expression of opinion' (Διάνοια δέ, ἐν οἷς ἀποδεικνύουσί τι ὡς ἔστιν ἢ ὡς οὐκ ἔστιν ἢ καθόλου τι ἀποφαίνονται); it is distinguished from *lexis*, the formal expression of a content. In *Po.* 19 the study of *dianoia* is assigned to rhetoric, but Aristotle has in view here the pragmatic effects of

dialectics and the study of *lexis*, but the study of linguistic form is still not differentiated into a grammatical-technical one and a stylistic-technical one. At first sight, this may seem awkward, since both Aristotle[15] and Dionysius of Halicarnassus[16] handle a number of grammatical concepts and discuss various purely grammatical matters, which might have justified a disciplinary cut-off point between grammar and poetics. On the other hand, the absence of a disciplinary boundary between both domains seems to find its explanation in the authors' approach. In his *Poetics*, Aristotle is interested in language form as a means of representation, as the 'material' (and also 'efficient') cause of literary expression: in such a global view of language (and its communicative value), there is no place for a distinction between the description of linguistic forms as fitting within a language scheme and the study of these forms as they are used by poets, since in both instances we are dealing with the linguistic means allowing the poet to formulate his literary 'message', and to reshape reality. This is clear from the fact that Aristotle was aware of the continuity between ordinary, commonplace language and literary expression: in the case of literary expression, one must (also) avoid the overuse of rare words, of impossible combinations of words, and of metaphors, and while it should achieve distinction, literary speech must preserve clarity, a

---

they belong within dialectics, which is concerned with propositional types. D.H. is even more explicit in making a twofold distinction between content and form: he opposes *noemata* to *onomata*. *Διττῆς γὰρ οὔσης ἀσκήσεως περὶ πάντας ὡς εἰπεῖν τοὺς λόγους, τῆς περὶ τὰ νοήματα καὶ τῆς περὶ τὰ ὀνόματα, ὧν ἡ μὲν τοῦ πραγματικοῦ τόπου μᾶλλον ἐφάπτεσθαι δόξειεν ἄν, ἡ δὲ τοῦ λεκτικοῦ καὶ πάντων ὅσοι τοῦ λέγειν εὖ στοχάζονται περὶ ἀμφοτέρας τὰς θεωρίας τοῦ λόγου ταύτας σπουδαζόντων ἐξ ἴσου* (*Comp*. 1, 4.6-11). 'In virtually all kinds of discourse two things require study: the ideas and the words. We may regard the first of these as concerned chiefly with subject-matter, and the latter with expression; and all those who aim to become good orators pay close attention to both these aspects of discourse equally' (Usher 1985, 17).

[15] Useful surveys are provided by Weidemann 1991 and by Ax 1992.

[16] Cf. Schenkeveld 1983, who, however, does not discuss *Comp*. ch. 2 (on the history of the word-class system), nor 14-15 (on letters, vowels and consonants).

property which is considered the chief merit of *lexis* in general (*Po.* 22, 1458a34 - 1458b5).[17]

The study of language *forms*, as a means of literary (and ordinary) expression, thus constitutes a domain unified by the choice and the specific use of linguistic elements. This domain does not, at least not in a strict sense, include the study of the logical and psychological aspects of propositional contents or of speech modalities. Both Aristotle and Dionysius of Halicarnassus exclude from their discussion the study of the logical and psychological value of propositions, although linguistic form is also at stake here. According to Aristotle, the issue of the *σχήματα τῆς λέξεως* ('modes of speech') does not have its place in his poetics:

> *τῶν δὲ περὶ τὴν λέξιν ἓν μέν ἐστιν εἶδος θεωρίας τὰ σχήματα τῆς λέξεως, ἃ ἔστιν εἰδέναι τῆς ὑποκριτικῆς καὶ τοῦ τὴν τοιαύτην ἔχοντος ἀρχιτεκτονικήν, οἷον τί ἐντολὴ καὶ τί εὐχὴ καὶ διήγησις καὶ ἀπειλὴ καὶ ἐρώτησις καὶ ἀπόκρισις καὶ εἴ τι ἄλλο τοιοῦτον. παρὰ γὰρ τὴν τούτων γνῶσιν ἢ ἄγνοιαν οὐδὲν εἰς τὴν ποιητικὴν ἐπιτίμημα φέρεται ὅ τι καὶ ἄξιον σπουδῆς. τί γὰρ ἄν τις ὑπολάβοι ἡμαρτῆσθαι ἃ Πρωταγόρας ἐπιτιμᾷ, ὅτι εὔχεσθαι οἰόμενος ἐπιτάττει εἰπὼν "μῆνιν ἄειδε θεά"; τὸ γὰρ κελεῦσαι, φησίν, ποιεῖν τι ἢ μὴ ἐπίταξίς ἐστιν. διὸ παρείσθω ὡς ἄλλης καὶ οὐ τῆς ποιητικῆς ὂν θεώρημα* (*Po.* 19, 1456b8-19).
>
> 'Under the head of Diction one subject of inquiry is the various modes of speech, the knowledge of which is proper to elocution or to the man who knows the master art—I mean for instance, what is a command, a prayer, a statement, a threat, question, answer, and so on. The knowledge or ignorance of such matters brings upon the poet no censure worth serious consideration. For who could suppose that there is any fault in the passage which Protagoras censures, because Homer, intending to utter a prayer, gives a command when he says, "sing, goddess, the wrath"? To order something to be done or not is, he

[17] See Aristotle, *Po.* 22, 1458a18.

points out, a command. So we may leave this topic as one that belongs not to poetry but to another art'[18] (Hamilton Fyfe 1932, 73-75).

Similarly, Dionysius is interested in linguistic form, and not in logical considerations about utterances and propositions. He makes it very clear that he eschews all kinds of dialectical investigations, and that the purpose of his treatise is a different one:

> Ἐγὼ γ' οὖν ὅτ' ἔγνων συντάττεσθαι ταύτην τὴν ὑπόθεσιν, ἐζήτουν εἴ τι τοῖς πρότερον εἴρηται περὶ αὐτῆς καὶ μάλιστα τοῖς ἀπὸ τῆς Στοᾶς φιλοσόφοις, εἰδὼς τοὺς ἄνδρας οὐ μικρὰν φροντίδα τοῦ λεκτικοῦ τόπου ποιουμένους· δεῖ γὰρ αὐτοῖς τἀληθῆ μαρτυρεῖν. οὐδαμῇ δ' οὐδὲν εἰρημένον ὑπ' οὐδενὸς ὁρῶν τῶν γοῦν ὀνόματος ἠξιωμένων οὔτε μεῖζον οὔτ' ἔλαττον εἰς ἣν ἐγὼ προῄρημαι πραγματείαν, ἃς δὲ Χρύσιππος καταλέλοιπε συντάξεις διττὰς ἐπιγραφὴν ἐχούσας "περὶ τῆς συντάξεως τῶν τοῦ λόγου μερῶν" οὐ ῥητορικὴν θεωρίαν ἐχούσας ἀλλὰ διαλεκτικήν, ὡς ἴσασιν οἱ τὰς βύβλους ἀνεγνωκότες, ὑπὲρ ἀξιωμάτων συντάξεως ἀληθῶν τε καὶ ψευδῶν καὶ δυνατῶν τε καὶ ἀδυνάτων ἐνδεχομένων τε καὶ μεταπιπτόντων καὶ ἀμφιβόλων καὶ ἄλλων τινῶν τοιουτοτρόπων, οὐδεμίαν οὔτ' ὠφήλειαν οὔτε χρείαν τοῖς πολιτικοῖς λόγοις συμβαλλομένας εἰς γοῦν ἡδονὴν καὶ κάλλος ἑρμηνείας, ὧν δεῖ στοχάζεσθαι τὴν σύνθεσιν, ταύτης μὲν τῆς πραγματείας ἀπέστην ... (*Comp.* 4, 22.3-23.2).

> 'For my part, when I decided to write a treatise on this subject (viz. of word order), I tried to discover whether my predecessors had said anything about it, especially the philosophers from the Stoa, since I knew that these men paid considerable attention to the subject of language: one must give them their due. But nowhere did I see any contribution, great or small, to the subject of my choice, by any author of repute. As for the two treatises which Chrysippus has left

[18] Aristotle does not specify to what other domain the subject belongs: it cannot be grammar, since (a) this would have been specified by Aristotle, and (b) since the subsequent discussion in *Po.* 20 includes basic grammatical topics. Aristotle may have thought here of dialectics (as a specific field); but it is also possible that no specific disciplinary domain is at stake here: maybe Aristotle is referring to the knowledge of appropriate uses of utterances and speech modes in specific contexts. On the passage, cf. Nuchelmans 1973, 30-1 and Schenkeveld 1984, 292-4.

us, entitled *On the Classification of the Parts of Speech*, they contain, as those who have read the books are aware, not a rhetorical but a logical investigation: they deal with the grouping of propositions, true or false, possible and impossible, admissible and variable, ambiguous, and so forth. These contribute nothing helpful or useful to civil oratory, at least as far as the attractiveness and beauty of style are concerned; and these qualities should be the aim of composition. I therefore abandoned this enquiry' (Usher 1985, 45-7).[19]

4. The general setting of grammar

In Aristotle and Dionysius of Halicarnassus the discussion of grammatical topics is tied up with, or integrated within the analysis of literary or specifically rhetorical issues. Aristotle's *Poetics* has three chapters (20-2) devoted to *lexis*[20]. In chapter 20,[21] Aristotle discusses the (partly hierarchical) build-up of the *lexis*: from letter to syllable, over parts of speech to λόγος (a term which covers phenomena ranging from syntagms to sentences and even a whole text). In chapter 21, Aristotle discusses *formal* aspects of nouns (i.e. composition or its absence, truncation or lengthening of words) and *semantic* ones: it is here that we find a full-fledged theory of metaphorical expression.[22] The chapter ends with a formal-grammatical discussion (avoiding any reference to reality-based categories) of nominal gender:

---

[19] Nevertheless, in ch. 5 D.H. embarks on the question whether there exists a natural order of word-classes and whether it should be followed in the σύνθεσις. Cf. Schenkeveld 1983, 85-9.

[20] Cf. also Ax 1986, 132-6, who indicates (132, n. 53) that in these chapters the basic structure (letters - speech; the parts of speech - the ἀρεταί of speech (in 22)) of the later 'artes grammaticae' can already be recognised.

[21] We are preparing a study on the linguistic contribution of chapter 20 of Aristotle's *Poetics*.

[22] Cf. Swiggers 1984.

> *αὐτῶν δὲ τῶν ὀνομάτων τὰ μὲν ἄρρενα τὰ δὲ θήλεα τὰ δὲ μεταξύ, ἄρρενα μὲν ὅσα τελευτᾷ εἰς τὸ* N *καὶ* P *καὶ* Σ *καὶ ὅσα ἐκ τούτου σύγκειται (ταῦτα δ' ἐστὶν δύο,* Ψ *καὶ* Ξ*), θήλεα δὲ ὅσα ἐκ τῶν φωνηέντων εἴς τε τὰ ἀεὶ μακρά, οἷον εἰς* H *καὶ* Ω*, καὶ τῶν ἐπεκτεινομένων εἰς* A· *ὥστε ἴσα συμβαίνει πλήθει εἰς ὅσα τὰ ἄρρενα καὶ τὰ θήλεα· τὸ γὰρ* Ψ *καὶ τὸ* Ξ *σύνθετά ἐστιν. εἰς δὲ ἄφωνον οὐδὲν ὄνομα τελευτᾷ, οὐδὲ εἰς φωνῆεν βραχύ. εἰς δὲ τὸ* I *τρία μόνον, μέλι κόμμι πέπερι. εἰς δὲ τὸ* Y *πέντε* < * * * >. *τὰ δὲ μεταξὺ εἰς ταῦτα καὶ* N *καὶ* Σ. (*Po.* 21, 1458a8-17).
>
> 'Of the nouns themselves, some are masculine, some feminine, and some neuter. Masculine are all that end in N and P and Σ and in the two compounds of Σ, Ψ and Ξ. Feminine are all that end in those of the vowels that are always long, namely H and Ω, and in A among vowels that can be lengthened. The result is that the number of masculine and feminine terminations is the same, for Ψ and Ξ are the same as Σ. No noun ends in a mute or in a short vowel. Only three end in I, *μέλι, κόμμι, πέπερι*. Five end in Y. The neuters end in these letters and in N and Σ' (Hamilton Fyfe 1932, 83-5).

In Dionysius of Halicarnassus, matters of grammatical interest are harmoniously integrated within a study of linguistic composition, which is structured in function of the various aspects of its central theme: the principles which constitute the merit and the beauty (harmony and pleasure) of literary expression.[23] As indicated by Dionysius of Halicarnassus himself (*Comp.* 6, 27.18-28.2),[24] such an integration involves a threefold

---

[23] Cf. *Comp.* 13, 47.20-2: *ἐξ ἁπάντων δή φημι τούτων ἐπιτηδεύεσθαι δεῖν τὸ καλὸν ἐν ἁρμονίᾳ λέξεως ἐξ ὧνπερ καὶ τὸ ἡδύ.* 'Thus I maintain that beauty in literary arrangement must be pursued by the aid of all those elements that constitute attractiveness' (Usher 1985, 91).

[24] This threefold articulation occurs again in Dionysius' application of this general view to linguistic materials: *πρῶτον μὲν σκοπεῖν, ποῖον ὄνομα ἢ ῥῆμα ἢ τῶν ἄλλων τι μορίων ποίῳ συνταχθὲν ἐπιτηδείως ἔσται κείμενον καὶ πῶς εὖ ἢ* (*varia lectio*: *οὐκ*) *ἄμεινον* (...), *ἔπειτα διακρίνειν, πῶς σχηματισθὲν τοὔνομα ἢ τὸ ῥῆμα ἢ τῶν ἄλλων ὅ τι δή ποτε χαριέστερον ἱδρυθήσεται* (...), *ἐπὶ δὲ τούτοις τὰ ληφθέντα διακρίνειν, εἴ τι δεῖται μετασκευῆς ὄνομα ἢ ῥῆμα, πῶς ἂν ἐναρμονιώτερόν τε καὶ εὐεδρότερον*

study: that of the forms (words) which must be combined in discourse, that of the ways to obtain a harmonious combination by adjusting the word shapes, and that of the procedures of modifying forms in discourse in function of a particular usage.

Dionysius of Halicarnassus distinguishes between two essential properties of stylistic composition:[25] its pleasing character (*ἡδονή*) and its beauty (*τὸ καλόν* or *καλὴ ἁρμονία*).[26]

> *Τάττω δὲ ὑπὸ μὲν τὴν ἡδονὴν τήν τε ὥραν καὶ τὴν χάριν καὶ τὴν εὐστομίαν καὶ τὴν γλυκύτητα καὶ τὸ πιθανὸν καὶ πάντα τὰ τοιαῦτα, ὑπὸ δὲ τὸ καλὸν τήν τε μεγαλοπρέπειαν καὶ τὸ βάρος καὶ τὴν σεμνολογίαν καὶ τὸ ἀξίωμα καὶ τὸν πίνον*[27] *καὶ τὰ τούτοις ὅμοια. ταυτὶ γάρ μοι δοκεῖ κυριώτατα εἶναι καὶ ὥσπερ κεφάλαια τῶν ἄλλων [ἐν ἑκατέρῳ]* (*Comp.* 11, 37.12-9).
>
> 'Under attractiveness I list freshness, charm, euphony, sweetness, persuasiveness and all such qualities; and under beauty impressiveness, solemnity, seriousness, dignity, mellowness and qualities like them. These seem to me the most important, heading the list, so to speak, in either case' (Usher 1985, 71-3).

In his discussion of the *ἡδονή* of literary speech, Dionysius of Halicarnassus specifically deals with the melodic aspects of language, and especially with the pitch accents of words (*Comp.* 11, 40.17-41.12)[28]

γένοιτο (*Comp.* 6, 28.16-29.16). 'They should consider first in what combinations with one another nouns, verbs or other parts of speech will be suitably placed, and how not so well (...). Then they should decide the form in which the noun or verb, or whatever else it may be, will occupy its position more elegantly (...). Next, it must be decided, if any of the selected nouns or verbs requires modification, how it may be fitted in more harmoniously and to better effect' (Usher 1985, 57).

[25] See also *Comp.* 11, 38.9-12.

[26] Cf. Donadi 1986.

[27] Aujac - Lebel (1981, 91; cf. 206) prefer to read *πάθος* ('l'émotion'). Cf. also Donadi (1986, 46 n. 17).

[28] Cf. for a detailed study, Devine - Stephens 1991.

and with the quantity of syllables (11, 42.14-43.3), two issues which belong also within the description of language structure. Other topics dealt with are the variation of sound shapes and word forms (12, 43.18-45.5), the choice of a particular rhythm[29] and sonority, all matters of stylistic elegance. It is within Dionysius of Halicarnassus' discussion of the *καλὴ ἁρμονία* that we find an explicit treatment of grammatical questions, ranging from the level of letters to that of the words. As he notes, the aesthetic qualities of speech depend on the nature, the 'force' or value of the constituent parts:

> *αἰτία δὲ κἀνταῦθα ἥ τε τῶν γραμμάτων φύσις καὶ ἡ τῶν συλλαβῶν δύναμις, ἐξ ὧν πλέκεται τὰ ὀνόματα* (*Comp.* 13, 47.22-48.1).
>
> 'Here as before, the cause resides in the nature of the letters and in the phonetic effect of the syllables, which are the raw material from which the fabric of the words is woven' (Usher 1985, 91).

What follows then is a short technical treatise on *γράμματα*:[30] their number, their nature, their classification, and their combination into syllables. Dionysius of Halicarnassus engages here in a discussion of grammatical issues, or, better, of issues which, while belonging initially to the undivided domain of *λέξις*, became an integrated part of grammatical description: the distinction between vowels (sounding elements: *φωνήεντα*) and consonants (noises: *ψόφοι*), and the subdivision of the

---

[29] Cf. also 11, 42.14-43.3; 12, 46.1-9 and 17, 68.7-70.1 and see D.H.'s analysis (in ch. 18) of the style of various authors: Thucydides, Plato, Demosthenes, Hegesias and Homer. Cf. especially D.H.'s conclusion in 18, 83.19-84.3. See Gentili 1990. On the importance of rhythm, see also Aristotle, *Rh.* 3.8.

[30] For the definition, see *Comp.* 14, 48.3-8: *Ἀρχαὶ μὲν οὖν τῆς ἀνθρωπίνης φωνῆς καὶ ἐνάρθρου μηκέτι δεχόμεναι διαίρεσιν, ἃ καλοῦμεν στοιχεῖα καὶ γράμματα· γράμματα μὲν ὅτι γραμμαῖς τισι σημαίνεται, στοιχεῖα δὲ ὅτι πᾶσα φωνὴ τὴν γένεσιν ἐκ τούτων λαμβάνει πρώτων καὶ τὴν διάλυσιν εἰς ταῦτα ποιεῖται τελευταῖα.* 'Now in the articulate speech of human beings there are prime units admitting no further division, which we call "elements" and "letters": "letters" (*γράμματα*), because they are signified by certain lines (*γραμμαί*), and "elements", because every vocal sound originates in these in the first place, and is ultimately resolved into them' (Usher 1985, 91-3). On the phonetic theories in ch. 14, see Ax 1986, 213-5.

latter into ἄφωνα ('voiceless consonants') and ἡμίφωνα ('semiowels');[31] the length (or length varieties) of each vowel (14, 50.12-52.13); the classification of the ἡμίφωνα, and a description of their articulatory realisation (14, 52.14-54.9); the classification and articulatory description of the ἄφωνα (14, 55.11-57.3); the (relative) length of syllables, according to the length of the vocalic nucleus (15, 57.9-17) and according to the number of units composing the syllable (15, 57.9-59.14). All these issues have of course some relevance for stylistic composition, but taken on their own, they belong elsewhere. Dionysius points this out in a particular instance, viz. when he discusses the number of letters, a problem which is 'after all'—as he feels—of interest to grammarians and philosophers:

> ἀριθμὸς δὲ αὐτῶν ὅστις ἐστίν, οὐ ῥᾴδιον εἰπεῖν ἀκριβῶς, ἐπεὶ πολλὴν παρέσχε καὶ τοῖς πρὸ ἡμῶν ἀπορίαν τὸ πρᾶγμα· οἳ μὲν γὰρ ᾠήθησαν εἶναι τριακαίδεκα τὰ πάντα τῆς φωνῆς στοιχεῖα, κατεσκευάσθαι δὲ τὰ λοιπὰ ἐκ τούτων· οἳ δὲ καὶ τῶν εἰκοσιτεσσάρων οἷς χρώμεθα νῦν πλείω. ἡ μὲν οὖν ὑπὲρ τούτων θεωρία γραμματικῆς τε καὶ μετρικῆς, εἰ δὲ βούλεταί τις, καὶ φιλοσοφίας οἰκειοτέρα (*Comp.* 14, 50.1-8).
>
> 'It is not easy to say precisely what the number of the letters is, for the subject has caused our predecessors much perplexity. Some have thought that there are only thirteen "elements" of sound[32] altogether and that the other elements are formed from these; while others have

---

[31] *Comp.* 14, 49.11-8: οἳ δὲ τριχῇ νείμαντες τὰς πρώτας τε καὶ στοιχειώδεις τῆς φωνῆς δυνάμεις φωνήεντα μὲν ἐκάλεσαν, ὅσα καὶ καθ' ἑαυτὰ φωνεῖται καὶ μεθ' ἑτέρων καὶ ἔστιν αὐτοτελῆ· ἡμίφωνα δ' ὅσα μετὰ μὲν φωνηέντων αὐτὰ ἑαυτῶν κρεῖττον ἐκφέρεται, καθ' ἑαυτὰ δὲ χεῖρον καὶ οὐκ αὐτοτελῶς· ἄφωνα δ' ὅσα οὔτε τὰς τελείας οὔτε τὰς ἡμιτελεῖς φωνὰς ἔχει καθ' ἑαυτά, μεθ' ἑτέρων δ' ἐκφωνεῖται. 'Those who divide the primary and elementary powers of the voice into three give the name "vowels" to all the letters which can be made to produce sound on their own or together with others, and are self-sufficient; "semivowels" to all which are pronounced more effectively in combination with vowels, worse and imperfectly on their own; "voiceless" to all which have no sound on their own, whether perfect or imperfect, but are pronounced in combination with others' (Usher 1985, 93).

[32] Usher's translation ('*elements of speech*') is incorrect.

> thought that there are more even than the twenty-four which we employ today. Now the discussion of these matters belongs more properly to grammar and prosody, or even, if you like, to philosophy' (Usher 1985, 93-5).

This passage is interesting for two reasons:
(A) It supports Saussure's view that a particular field is shaped by a specific point of view ('c'est le point de vue qui crée l'objet'): language phenomena can be studied from the point of view of philosophers, of grammarians, of metricians or rhetoricians, and they assume a particular epistemological status in terms of the approach applied to them;
(B) It offers support for the following hypothesis on the origin of grammar as a discipline: as the study of language structures *in se* and *per se*, grammar developed out of a continuous and global pedagogical activity,[33] in which homogeneous subsets of knowledge (and of usage) were clustered and became the basis of more and more specialised teaching and of increasing theorisation. Between some of these subsets, there were ties as to the material on which they had to draw (this is, e.g., the case of grammar and poetics); between others, the ties were primarily of a methodological nature (e.g., between grammar and philosophy), and they often led to reorientations or radical innovations within one of the interacting fields.

There is, however, much more to this than mere hypothesis. As a matter of fact, if we look at the oldest grammatical treatises, it is clear that these use a global conception of speech, involving no strict distinction between literary and non-literary expression (although the latter is not the primary focus of interest), nor between poetry and prose. We find signs of this fluctuating unity in the rhetorical (and stylistic) treatises. Dionysius of Halicarnassus,[34] for instance, explicitly stresses the continuity between

[33] Interestingly, D.H., *Comp*. 25, 134.21-135.12 makes a reference to the acquisition of a global 'discursive knowledge'.

[34] In one passage (20, 89.5-14) Dionysius discusses the general properties of construing a (narrative) discourse.

good prose and good poetry, although we are dealing with different genres here:

> *ἐγὼ τοὺς λόγους τὸν μὲν ἰδιώτην ἐπιστάμενος ὄντα, τὸν ἀδολέσχην τοῦτον λέγω καὶ φλύαρον, τὸν δὲ πολιτικόν, ἐν ᾧ τὸ πολὺ κατασκευασμένον ἐστὶ καὶ ἔντεχνον, ὅ τι μὲν ἂν τῶν ποιημάτων ὅμοιον εὑρίσκω τῷ φλυάρῳ καὶ ἀδολέσχῃ, γέλωτος ἄξιον τίθεμαι, ὅ τι δ' ἂν τῷ κατεσκευασμένῳ καὶ ἐντέχνῳ, ζήλου καὶ σπουδῆς ἐπιτηδείαν τυγχάνειν οἴομαι. εἰ μὲν οὖν διαφόρου προσηγορίας τῶν λόγων ἑκάτερος ἐτύγχανεν, ἀκόλουθον ἦν ἂν καὶ τῶν ποιημάτων ἃ τούτοις ἔοικεν διαφόροις ὀνόμασι καλεῖν ἑκάτερον· ἐπειδὴ δὲ ὅ τε σπουδαῖος καὶ ὁ τοῦ μηδενὸς ἄξιος ὁμοίως καλεῖται λόγος, οὐκ ἂν ἁμαρτάνοι τις τὰ μὲν ἐοικότα τῷ καλῷ λόγῳ ποιήματα καλὰ ἡγούμενος, τὰ δὲ τῷ μοχθηρῷ πονηρά, οὐδὲν ὑπὸ τῆς τοῦ λόγου ὁμοειδείας ταραττόμενος. κωλύσει γὰρ οὐδὲν ἡ τῆς ὀνομασίας ὁμοιότης κατὰ διαφόρων ταττομένης πραγμάτων τὴν ἑκατέρου φύσιν ὁρᾶν* (*Comp.* 26, 137.16-138.9).[35]
>
> 'Prose style, as I understand it, is of two kinds, that of the ordinary man, by which I mean the current garrulous nonsense, and the language of public oratory, which is in large measure composed with artistry and skill. Whatever poetry I find resembling this garrulous nonsense, I regard as worthy only of ridicule, and I regard as fit for serious imitation only that which resembles the artistic and skilful kind. Now if each sort of prose were called by a different name, it would have been only consistent to call each of the corresponding sorts of poetry also by different names. But since both the excellent and the worthless are called "prose", it may not be wrong to regard as fine that poetry which resembles fine prose, and as bad that which resembles inferior prose, and not to be in any way confused by the identity of terms. The use of similar names for different things will not prevent us from discerning their true nature in either case' (Usher 1985, 233-5).

In another passage Dionysius of Halicarnassus points out that poetic gracefulness is achieved through the specific use, by the aesthetic com-

---

[35] On the links between poetry and prose, see also 6, 29.14-8; 15, 59.8-13; 20, 93.22-94.21.

poser, of words which by themselves are ordinary (*κοινὰ ὀνόματα*; 25, 124.20).

We can note here a few remarkable parallels with grammatical manuals such as the *Techne grammatike* of Dionysius Thrax (ca. 170 - 90 BCE).[36]

(A) The definition of grammar as given by Dionysius Thrax, and the description of its components, testify to a tradition in which grammarians were interested in the wording of literary texts, in the phraseology of literary authors, in the correct recitation and appreciation of works of art:

> *Γραμματική ἐστιν ἐμπειρία τῶν παρὰ ποιηταῖς τε καὶ συγγραφεῦσιν ὡς ἐπὶ τὸ πολὺ λεγομένων. Μέρη δὲ αὐτῆς ἐστιν ἕξ· πρῶτον ἀνάγνωσις*[37] *ἐντριβὴς κατὰ προσῳδίαν, δεύτερον ἐξήγησις κατὰ τοὺς ἐνυπάρχοντας ποιητικοὺς τρόπους, τρίτον γλωσσῶν*[38] *τε καὶ ἱστοριῶν ἀπόδοσις, τέταρτον ἐτυμολογίας εὕρεσις, πέμπτον ἀναλογίας ἐκλογισμός, ἕκτον κρίσις ποιημάτων, ὃ δὴ*

---

[36] We will not enter here into a discussion of the authenticity of this text. See Kemp 1991, 307-15 and the historical survey of the authenticity problem that will be included in the commented English translation of the *Techne* which we are preparing. We would only like to point out that (a) the text fragments adduced here as evidence for our discussion are generally regarded as authentic, i.e. as belonging to the kernel of the manual as it was composed by Aristarchus' disciple; (b) that in the light of the arguments put forward in this article, the general outlook of the *Techne* preserves evident traces of an early composition, at a time when grammar was still strongly tied up with poetry and stylistics, and had not yet become the object of a fully autonomous discussion of phonetic (or graphophonetic), morphological and syntactic phenomena.

[37] The concept of *ἀνάγνωσις* is used here in relation with the reception of a literary text in its prosodic form: *'Ανάγνωσίς ἐστι ποιημάτων ἢ συγγραμμάτων ἀδιάπτωτος προφορά* (*Gramm. Gr.* 1.1, 6.5), 'Reading is the faultless delivery of poems or prose works'.

[38] Cf. for this passage D.H., *Comp.* 25, 124.12-5: *ἐπεὶ καὶ ἡ ἐκλογὴ τῶν ὀνομάτων μέγα τι δύναται, καὶ ἔστι τις ὀνομασία ποιητικὴ γλωττηματικῶν τε καὶ ξένων καὶ τροπικῶν καὶ πεποιημένων, οἷς ἡδύνεται ποίησις*, 'Because the actual choice of words can exert considerable influence, and there is a poetical vocabulary consisting of recondite, unfamiliar and figurative words, and of neologisms, which contribute to the charm of poetry' (Usher 1985, 211).

> *κάλλιστόν ἐστι πάντων τῶν ἐν τῇ τέχνῃ* (*Gramm.Gr.* 1.1, 5.2-6.3).
>
> 'Grammar is the empirical knowledge of the expressions commonly used among poets and prose-writers. Its parts are six [in number]: first, skillful reading in conformity with prosody; second, exegesis of the occurring poetic phrases; third, straightforward account of rare words and realia; fourth, discovery of etymology; fifth, the establishing of analogical patterning; and sixth, judgement on poems, which is the finest part of all those [contained] in the art [of grammar]'.

(B) In the explication of the parts of grammar, we note that the *Techne* attributes an important role to the correct recitation of literary works; for this component the guiding principle is that of *appropriateness* and *adjustment*:

> *Ἀναγνωστέον δὲ καθ' ὑπόκρισιν, κατὰ προσῳδίαν, κατὰ διαστολήν. ἐκ μὲν γὰρ τῆς ὑποκρίσεως τὴν ἀρετὴν, ἐκ δὲ τῆς προσῳδίας τὴν τέχνην, ἐκ δὲ τῆς διαστολῆς τὸν περιεχόμενον νοῦν ὁρῶμεν· ἵνα τὴν μὲν τραγῳδίαν ἡρωϊκῶς ἀναγνῶμεν, τὴν δὲ κωμῳδίαν βιωτικῶς, τὰ δὲ ἐλεγεῖα λιγυρῶς, τὸ δὲ ἔπος εὐτόνως, τὴν δὲ λυρικὴν ποίησιν ἐμμελῶς, τοὺς δὲ οἴκτους ὑφειμένως καὶ γοερῶς. τὰ γὰρ μὴ παρὰ τὴν τούτων γινόμενα παρατήρησιν καὶ τὰς τῶν ποιητῶν ἀρετὰς καταρριπτεῖ καὶ τὰς ἕξεις τῶν ἀναγινωσκόντων καταγελάστους παρίστησιν* (*Gramm.Gr.* 1.1, 6.5-13).
>
> 'The reading should conform to style of delivery, to prosody, and to segmentation—from the style of delivery we grasp the quality, from the prosody the art, from the segmentation the inherent meaning—so as to ensure that we read a tragedy with a heroic flavour, a comedy in a lively way, an elegy with a sharp voice, an epic in a vigorous way, a lyrical poem in a melodic way, and lamentations in a submissive and plaintive way. For when these principles are not observed, it compromises the merits of the poets and renders ridiculous the performance of the readers'.

This appropriateness, respecting the style of the work, its spirit and the overall qualifications of the genre to which it belongs, is an instance of the imperative rule of *τὸ πρέπον*,[39] which is valid for both the receptive side (which is at stake in the *Techne*) and the productive or creative side of literature; the latter aspect is dealt with, e.g., by Dionysius of Halicarnassus, who on several occasions stresses the importance of appropriate and fitting composition:[40]

- *τελευταῖον δὲ ὃ δὴ καὶ πάντων κράτιστον, οἰκείαν ἀποδιδόναι τοῖς ὑποκειμένοις καὶ πρέπουσαν ἁρμονίαν* (*Comp.* 12, 46.15-7).
'Lastly, and what is in fact most important of all, the subject-matter should be arranged in a manner which is natural to it and appropriate' (Usher 1985, 89).

- *ἔτι τις καταλείπεταί μοι λόγος ὁ περὶ τοῦ πρέποντος. καὶ γὰρ τοῖς ἄλλοις χρήμασιν ἅπασι παρεῖναι δεῖ τὸ πρέπον, καὶ εἴ τι ἄλλο ἔργον ἀτυχεῖ τούτου τοῦ μέρους, καὶ εἰ μὴ τοῦ παντός, τοῦ κρατίστου γε ἀτυχεῖ.* (...)
ὁμολογουμένου δὴ παρὰ πᾶσιν ὅτι πρέπον ἐστὶ τὸ τοῖς ὑποκειμένοις ἁρμόττον προσώποις τε καὶ πράγμασιν, ὥσπερ ἐκλογὴ τῶν ὀνομάτων εἴη τις ἂν ἡ μὲν πρέπουσα τοῖς ὑποκειμένοις ἡ δὲ ἀπρεπής, οὕτω δή που καὶ σύνθεσις (*Comp.* 20, 88.1-5 and 11-5).[41]
'One subject still remains for me to discuss: that of appropriateness. All the other adornments must be accompanied by appropriateness. Indeed, if any other function in a speech fails to meet this requirement, it fails to attain the most important end, even if it is not wholly unsuccessful (...).
It is generally agreed that appropriateness is that treatment which is fitting for the actors and the actions concerned. Just as the choice of words may be either appropriate or inappropriate to the subject-matter, so surely may the composition be' (Usher 1985, 155-7).

---

[39] Cf. Pohlenz 1933. The term occurs nowhere in the *Techne*.

[40] See also 17, 68-73 and especially 13, 47.10-20 on the use of an appropriate rhythm.

[41] As noted by D.H., the maxim of appropriateness has an applicability which stretches over the entire field of literary and non-literary expressions. On the concept of *τὸ πρέπον* in D.H., see Nasta 1975, 101-4.

(C) Besides the general setting of grammar as the study of the wording of literary texts, and alongside the underlying principle of observing appropriateness, there is a more 'material' coincidence between stylistic treatises and the first grammatical manuals, viz. the treatment of topics such as accent (*Techne*, § 3), of the *stoicheia* (*Techne*, § 6)[42] and their division into *φωνήεντα* and *σύμφωνα*, the discussion of vowel length,[43] the inventory of word-final elements (*Techne*, § 6 *in fine*) and the detailed treatment of syllable length (*Techne*, §§ 7-10).[44] It is worthwhile to compare a passage already quoted (see *supra*, section 4) from Aristotle's *Poetics*, viz. 21, 1458a8-17, with the strikingly analogous treatment of the same topic in the *Techne*:

> Τελικὰ ἀρσενικῶν ὀνομάτων ἀνεπεκτάτων κατ' εὐθεῖαν καὶ ἑνικὴν πτῶσιν στοιχεῖά ἐστι πέντε· ν̄, ξ̄, ρ̄, σ̄, ψ̄ (...) θηλυκῶν δὲ ὀκτώ· ᾱ, η̄, ω̄, ν̄, ξ̄, ρ̄, σ̄, ψ̄ (...) οὐδετέρων δὲ ἕξ· ᾱ, ῑ, ν̄, ρ̄, σ̄, ῡ (*Gramm.Gr.* 1.1, 15-6).

[42] Compare, e.g., *Gramm.Gr.* 1.1, 9.2-3: *Γράμματα ἐστιν εἰκοσιτέσσαρα ἀπὸ τοῦ ᾱ μέχρι τοῦ ω̄. γράμματα δὲ λέγεται διὰ τὸ γραμμαῖς καὶ ξυσμαῖς τυποῦσθαι* ('There are twenty-four letters, from *α* to *ω*. They are called *grammata* because they are formed by drawn lines, or scratched lines') and D.H., *Comp.* 14, 48.3-8 (quoted *supra*, note 30).

[43] Cf. the strikingly similar passages in the *Techne*, § 6: *Τῶν δὲ φωνηέντων μακρὰ μέν ἐστι δύο, η̄ καὶ ω̄, βραχέα δύο, ε̄ καὶ ο̄, δίχρονα τρία, ᾱ ῑ ῡ. δίχρονα δὲ λέγεται ἐπεὶ ἐκτείνεται καὶ συστέλλεται* (*Gramm.Gr.* 1.1, 10.1-13) ('Of the vowels, two are long, η̄ and ω̄; two are short, ε̄ and ο̄, and three have a twofold quantity. They are called "of twofold quantity", because they can be realised long or short') and in Dionysius' *Comp.* 14, 50.12-6: *ἔστι δὴ ταῦτα τὸν ἀριθμὸν ζ', δύο μὲν βραχέα τό τε ε̄ καὶ τὸ ο̄, δύο δὲ μακρὰ τό τε η̄ καὶ τὸ ω̄. τρία δὲ δίχρονα τό τε ᾱ καὶ τὸ ῑ καὶ τὸ ῡ. καὶ γὰρ ἐκτείνεται ταῦτα καὶ συστέλλεται· καὶ αὐτὰ οἳ μὲν δίχρονα, ὥσπερ ἔφην, οἳ δὲ μεταπτωτικὰ καλοῦσιν.* 'These are seven in number: two are short, ε̄ and ο̄; two long, η̄ and ω̄; and three common, ᾱ, ῑ and ῡ. These latter can be pronounced either long or short, and some call them "common", as I have done, others "variable"' (Usher 1985, 95).

[44] We find a more succinct treatment, with a digression on the *stoicheia* preceding the syllabic nucleus, in D.H., 15, 57.9-59.2. For the definition of the syllable, one can compare *Techne*, § 7 (*G.G.* 1.1, 16.7-17.2) with *Po.* 20, 1456b34-7.

'The elements which figure at the end of unextended masculine nouns in the nominative singular are five [in number]: $\overline{\nu}$, $\overline{\xi}$, $\overline{\rho}$, $\overline{\sigma}$, $\overline{\psi}$ (...). Eight figure at the end of feminine nouns: $\overline{\alpha}$, $\overline{\eta}$, $\overline{\omega}$, $\overline{\nu}$, $\overline{\xi}$, $\overline{\rho}$, $\overline{\sigma}$, $\overline{\psi}$ (...) Six at the end of neuter nouns: $\overline{\alpha}$, $\overline{\iota}$, $\overline{\nu}$, $\overline{\rho}$, $\overline{\sigma}$, $\overline{\upsilon}$.'

5. Looking back

These coincidences in coverage, in subdivisions, and in terminology (although in some instances we can note divergences, testifying to the emergence of a properly grammatical metalanguage)[45] between stylistic or rhetorical treatises and grammatical texts should not surprise us: they are the textual reflection of a didactic and theoretical tradition in which the study of speech was discussed and practised in a global and unified way, and which gave rise to the progressive autonomy of specific subsets, developing ultimately into separate *technai*, albeit with interacting approaches[46] and terminologies, and with partially intersecting domains.

---

[45] A case in point is *ἄρρην* and *θῆλυς* in Aristotle's *Poetics* (21, 1458a9, 10 and 14; cf. *supra*, section 4) compared with the more specifically metalinguistic adjectives *ἀρσενικός* and *θηλυκός* in the *Techne* (cf. English 'male/female' vs. 'masculine/feminine').

[46] An interesting example of an identical approach of language structure in terms of accumulation of building blocks can be found in the opening passage of Apollonius Dyscolus' *De constructione* and in D.H. We quote both texts. *Ἤδη γὰρ καὶ ἡ πρώτη ῥηθεῖσα ἀμερὴς ὕλη τῶν στοιχείων τοῦτο πολὺ πρότερον κατεπηγγείλατο οὐχ ὡς ἔτυχεν ἐπιπλοκὰς ποιησαμένη τῶν στοιχείων, ἀλλ' ἐν τῇ κατὰ τὸ δέον συντάξει, ἐξ ἧς σχεδὸν καὶ τὴν ὀνομασίαν εἴληχεν. ἥ τε ἐπαναβεβηκυῖα συλλαβὴ ταὐτὸν ἀνεδέξατο, εἴγε αἱ ἐκ τούτων συντάξεις ἀναπληρούμεναι κατὰ τὸ δέον ἀποτελοῦσι τὴν λέξιν. καὶ σαφὲς ὅτι ἀκόλουθόν ἐστι τὸ καὶ τὰς λέξεις, μέρος οὔσας τοῦ κατὰ σύνταξιν αὐτοτελοῦς λόγου, τὸ κατάλληλον τῆς συντάξεως ἀναδέξασθαι. τὰ γὰρ ἐξ ἑκάστης λέξεως παρυφιστάμενον νοητὸν τρόπον τινὰ στοιχεῖόν ἐστι τοῦ λόγου, καὶ ὡς τὰ στοιχεῖα τὰς συλλαβὰς ἀποτελεῖ κατὰ τὰς ἐπιπλοκάς, οὕτω καὶ ἡ σύνταξις τῶν νοητῶν τρόπον τινὰ ἀποτελέσει διὰ τῆς ἐπιπλοκῆς τῶν λέξεων. καὶ ἔτι ὃν τρόπον ἐκ τῶν συλλαβῶν ἡ λέξις, οὕτως ἐκ τῆς καταλληλότητος τῶν νοητῶν ὁ αὐτοτελὴς λόγος* (*Gramm.Gr.* 2.2, 2.3-3.2). 'We have seen how the unanalyzable substance unit, the phoneme, long ago was restricted, in that it would not undergo combination at random, but

Keeping this in mind, we should therefore do well not to read and understand texts such as the *Techne grammatike* only from the perspective of the subsequent history of grammar and linguistics: there is also much to learn from reading these texts ‘backwards’, i.e. with an eye at the preceding history of their contents, their subject matters, their philosophical, cultural and pedagogical setting. In short, we should not restrict our analysis to questions such as: What does the author tell us?, What is the ‘technical’ value and importance of his treatment?, What is the relevance of his discussion from our point of view? We should also investigate the conditions and the state of the specific field in question, and address questions such as the following ones:

- How did a particular approach or treatment originate; or, how and why could it have come about at all?
- Is there a particular doctrinal field exclusively reserved for the type of approach or treatment we touch upon in a given text, i.e. are we dealing with already constituted domains of knowledge, or are we confronted with the initial stage of the elaboration of disciplines and disciplinary boundaries?

---

only according to proper rules of structural ordering, from which it in part got its name. The next higher unit, the syllable, adopted the same restriction since structures of syllables, when filled out according to rule, constitute words. And it clearly follows that words, too, being the primes of a regularly constructed complete sentence, must also accept restriction by the structural rules of syntax. For the meaning which subsists in each word is, in a sense, the minimal unit of the sentence, and just as the minimal units of sound compose syllables when properly linked, so, in turn, the structural combining of meanings will produce sentences by combining words. Just as the word is made of syllables, so the complete sentence is made by the grammatical collocation of meanings’ (Householder 1981, 19).—*Τί δὲ τὸ κεφάλαιόν ἐστί μοι τούτου τοῦ λόγου; ὅτι παρὰ μὲν τὰς γραμμάτων συμπλοκὰς ἡ τῶν συλλαβῶν γίνεται δύναμις ποικίλη, παρὰ δὲ τὴν τῶν συλλαβῶν σύνθεσιν ἡ τῶν ὀνομάτων φύσις παντοδαπή, παρὰ δὲ τὰς τῶν ὀνομάτων ἁρμονίας πολύμορφος ὁ λόγος* (*Comp*. 16, 63.4-9). ‘What is the main gist of my argument? It is that the varied effect of the syllables is produced by the interweaving of letters, that the diverse nature of words is produced by the combination of syllables, and that the multiform character of a discourse is produced by the arrangement of the words’ (Usher 1985, 115).

- What does a particular text tell us, explicitly or implicitly, about its own past, and how can we learn more about it, through the comparison with preceding and contemporary achievements?

In fact, these questions are nothing but the dissection of the basic interrogation we ourselves have to face as scholars: where do we stand, and where do we come from?

BIBLIOGRAPHY

Aujac, G. - Lebel, M., *Denys d'Halicarnasse. Opuscules rhétoriques*, Tome III: *La composition stylistique*. Texte établi et traduit (Collection des Universités de France). Paris 1981.

Ax, W., *Laut, Stimme und Sprache. Studien zu drei Grundbegriffen der antiken Sprachtheorie*. Göttingen 1986.

———, Aristoteles, in: M. Dascal et alii (eds.), *Handbücher zur Sprach- und Kommunikationswissenschaft*, Bd. 8, 1. Halbband (*Sprachphilosophie*). Berlin 1992, 244-59.

Baratin, M., Aperçu de la linguistique stoïcienne, in: P. Schmitter (ed.), *Sprachtheorien der abendländischen Antike* (*Geschichte der Sprachtheorie*, vol. 2). Tübingen 1991, 193-216.

Devine, A.M. - Stephens, L.D., Dionysius of Halicarnassus, *De compositione verborum* XI: Reconstructing the phonetics of the Greek Accent, *TAPhA* 121 (1991), 229-86.

Donadi, F., Il "bello" e il "piacere" (osservazioni sul *De compositione verborum* di Dionigi d'Alicarnasso), *SIFC* 3a s. IV (1986), 42-63.

Dupont-Roc, R. - Lallot, J., *Aristote. La Poétique*. Paris 1980.

Gentili, B., Il *De compositione verborum* di Dionigi di Alicarnasso: parola, metro e ritmo nella comunicazione letteraria, *QUCC* 65 (1990), 7-21.

———, Parola, metro e ritmo nel *De compositione verborum* di Dionigi di Alicarnasso, in: R.M. Danese et al. (edd.), *Metrica classica e linguistica. Atti del colloquio Urbino 3-6 ottobre 1988*. Urbino 1990, 9-23.

Gramm.Gr. 1.1 = *Grammatici Graeci,* Pars prima, volumen primum: *Dionysii Thracis Ars Grammatica*. Lipsiae 1883, reprint Hildesheim 1965.

Gramm.Gr. 2.2 = *Grammatici Graeci,* Pars secunda, volumen alterum: *Apollonii Dyscoli De constructione libri quattuor*, rec. G. Uhlig. Lipsiae 1910, reprint Hildesheim 1965.

Golden, L. - Hardison, O.B., *Aristotle's Poetics. A Translation and Commentary for the Students of Literature*. Tallahassee 1968.

Halliwell, S., *Aristotle's Poetics: A Study of Philosophical Criticism*. London 1986.

———, Aristotle's poetics, in: G.A. Kennedy (ed.), *The Cambridge History of Literary Criticism*, vol. 1: *Classical Criticism*. Cambridge - New York - Melbourne 1989, 149-83.

Hamilton Fyfe, W., *Aristotle. The Poetics* (Loeb Classical Library). Cambridge, MA - London 1932.

Hennigfeld, J., *Geschichte der Sprachphilosophie. Antike und Mittelalter*. Berlin - New York 1994.

Householder, F.W., *The Syntax of Apollonius Dyscolus. Translated, and with Commentary*. Amsterdam 1981.

Hovdhaugen, E., *Foundations of Western Linguistics. From the Beginning to the End of the First Millennium A.D.* Oslo 1982.

Innes, D.C., Theophrastus and the Theory of Style, in: W.W. Fortenbaugh et alii (eds.), *Theophrastus of Eresus. On his Life and Work*. New Brunswick, NJ 1985, 251-63.

———, Philodemus, in: G.A. Kennedy (ed.), *The Cambridge History of Literary Criticism*, vol. 1: *Classical Criticism*. Cambridge - New York - Melbourne 1989, 215-9.

Janko, R., *Aristotle, Poetics I with the Tractatus Coislinianus. A Hypothetical Reconstruction of Poetics II. The Fragments of the On Poets*. Indianapolis - Cambridge 1987.

———, Philodemus' *On Poems* and Aristotle's *On Poets*, *CronErc* 21 (1991), 5-64.

Kassel, R., *Aristotelis de arte poetica liber*. Oxford 1965.

Kemp, A., The Emergence of Autonomous Greek Grammar, in: P. Schmitter (ed.), *Sprachtheorien der abendländischen Antike* (*Geschichte der Sprachtheorie*, vol. 2). Tübingen 1991, 302-33.

Kennedy, G.A., Theophrastus, in: G.A. Kennedy (ed.), *The Cambridge History of Literary Criticism*, vol. 1: *Classical Criticism*. Cambridge - New York - Melbourne 1989, 194-6.

López Eire, A., *Orígines de la Poética*. Salamanca 1980.

Nasta, M., L'analyse du langage et la représentation des performances du discours chez Denys d'Halicarnasse, in: *Actes de la XIIe Conférence Internationale d'Études Classiques 'Eirene', Cluj-Napoca, 2-7 octobre 1972*. Bucureşti - Amsterdam 1975, 97-109.

Nuchelmans, G., *Theories of the Proposition. Ancient and medieval Conceptions of the Bearers of Truth and Falsity*. Amsterdam - London 1973.

Pohlenz, M., Τὸ *πρέπον*. Ein Beitrag zur Geschichte des griechischen Geistes, *NGG, Phil.-Hist. Kl.*, 1933, 53-92 = *Kleine Schriften* (ed. H. Dörrie). Hildesheim 1965, 1.100-39.

Rostagni, A., Il dialogo aristotelico Περὶ *ποιητῶν*, *RFIC* 54 (1926), 433-70.

Schenkeveld, D.M., OI KRITIKOI in Philodemus, *Mnemosyne* 21 (1968), 176-214.

———, Linguistic Theories in the Rhetorical Works of Dionysius of Halicarnassus, *Glotta* 61 (1983), 67-94.

———, Stoic and Peripatetic Kinds of Speech Act and the Distinction of Grammatical Moods, *Mnemosyne* 37 (1984), 291-353.

———, Pap. Hamburg. 128: A Hellenistic Ars Poetica, *ZPE* 97 (1993), 67-80.

Söffing, W., *Deskriptive und normative Bestimmungen in der Poetik des Aristoteles*. Amsterdam 1981.

Swiggers, P., Cognitive Aspects of Aristotle's Theory of Metaphor, *Glotta* 62 (1984), 40-5.

Swiggers, P. - Wouters, A., Philosophical Aspects of the *Technê Grammatikê* of Dionysius Thrax, in: P. Swiggers - A. Wouters (eds.), *The Philosophical and Ideological Underpinning of Grammatical and Linguistic Theories* (Departement Linguïstiek, K.U. Leuven, Preprint, no. 149). Leuven 1994, 1-51.

Usener, H. - Radermacher, L., *Dionysii Halicarnassei quae exstant,* vol. VI: *Opuscula II* (Bibliotheca Teubneriana). Lipsiae 1904, repr. Stutgardiae 1965.

Usher, S., *Dionysius of Halicarnassus. The Critical Essays in two volumes*, vol. II (Loeb Classical Library). Cambridge, MA - London 1985.

Weidemann, H., Grundzüge der aristotelischen Sprachtheorie, in: P. Schmitter (ed.), *Sprachtheorien der abendländischen Antike* (*Geschichte der Sprachtheorie*, vol. 2). Tübingen 1991, 170-92.

Cicero and the Division of Virtue

Lucia Calboli Montefusco

1. Introduction

Cicero first deals with the notion of *virtus* near the end of *De inventione* where he gives precepts for the deliberative genre of rhetoric: *virtus*, defined as *animi habitus naturae modo atque rationi consentaneus*, embraces *una vi atque uno nomine* that part of *honestum* which *totum … propter se petitur*, and its *omnes partes* are *prudentia, iustitia, fortitudo* and *temperantia (Inv.* 2.159). Cicero last deals with the same notion when giving his son precepts: *nulla … vitae pars … vacare officio potest in eoque et colendo sita vitae est honestas omnis et neglegendo turpitudo* (*Off.* 1.4). The intervening period is filled by countless passages which attest to his lifelong interest in this matter, and which draw attention to the value of virtue, its διαίρεσις or its parts.

In this regard, however, many problems can be singled out. For example:

1) In the Roman world *virtus* is given a double meaning, being used both in the original sense of the quality par excellence of the *vir* and in the Greek sense of goodness (ἀρετή).[1]

[1] For the distinction between and the overlap of the two meanings of *virtus*, cf. Eisenhut 1973, 14 ff. Particularly with regard to Cicero, cf. the extensive study of (Liebers 1942, 4 ff.), although Eisenhut (1973, 58 n. 151) renders a somewhat unfavourable judgement of it.

2) In the sense of goodness, according to 'philosophical' usage, *virtus* can be an absolute concept (ἡ ἀρετή) or the main head (ἀρετή) which sums up different kinds of human goodness (ἀρεταί, *virtutes*).[2]
3) In this second case *virtus* is divided into its *partes* or *genera*,[3] but unfortunately we find different διαιρέσεις in Cicero's works.
4) The single virtues which are taken into account in the διαιρέσεις do not always appear as parts of a whole, but are sometimes also considered separately.[4]

We could continue illustrating some more aspects of this complicated question, but I think we have matter enough for a quick discussion.

---

[2] As an absolute concept, *virtus* appears, for example, in Cic. *N.D.* 3.87 *propter virtutem enim laudamur et in virtute recte gloriamur* (cf. Weische 1961, 42; Pease 1968, 1206) or *Rep.* 6.25 *suis te oportet inlecebris ipsa virtus trahat ad verum decus*; as a concept which sums up many other *virtutes*, cf. Cic. *de Orat.* 2.343 *virtus autem, quae est per se ipsa laudabilis et sine qua nihil laudari potest, tamen habet pluris partes, quarum alia est <alia> ad laudationem aptior*. Obviously the problem becomes larger when one calls to mind the fact that, under the influence of the Stoics, virtue is frequently taken into account as a whole, because all virtues are *aequales* and *pares* with respect to each other, and whoever has one of them has all of them: Cic. *de Orat.* 1.83; 3.55; 3.136; cf. Leeman-Pinkster 1981, 177; *SVF* 1.200; 3.295; Pohlenz 1948, 127. Aristotle, on the contrary, looks at virtue mostly in the sense of a plurality of ἀρεταί, which he considers in turn as μεσότης between two vices, in the *Ethics* (cf. *EN* 1106b26 f.; b36; 1109a20; *EE* 1220b34 ff.), and in the sense of an ἀρετή constituted of different μέρη, which are themselves ἀρεταί, in the *Rhetoric* (*Rh.* 1366b1 ff.). This distinction, however, is not maintained in *EE* 1220a13 f., where the ἀρετὴ ἠθική appears to be divided into μόρια. Aristotle seems to take into account the absolute notion of virtue (ἡ ἀρετή) only when defining its nature (*EN* 1106b36 ff.; *Rh.* 1366b4 f.) or when opposing to virtue in general a specific virtue (*EN* 1098b30); cf. Eisenhut 1973, 20 f.

[3] On *pars-partes* cf., for example, Cic. *Inv.* 2.159; *de Orat.* 2.343; *Part.* 82; on *genus-genera* Cic. *de Orat.* 2.345; *Brut.* 28; 272; *Part.* 28; 75; 79; 80; *Cael.* 40; cf. Liebers 1942, 118; Eisenhut 1973, 75.

[4] Cf., for example, the four cardinal virtues in Cic. *N.D.* 3.38 f. and the rich commentary of Pease 1968, 1035 ff. On Cicero's use of *virtutes* with the meaning of single virtues, cf. also Eisenhut 1973, 68.

nendus omnis dolor (*Tusc.* 2.31). This contempt of death and pain, Cicero says a few sections later to Brutus, is the distinguishing feature of the *vir*, from which it was called *virtus* and then the name was applied generally to any *recta animi adfectio* (*Tusc.* 2.43):

> *vide ne, cum omnes rectae animi adfectiones virtutes appellentur, non sit hoc proprium nomen omnium, sed ab ea quae una ceteris excellebat omnes nominatae sint. appellata est enim ex viro virtus; viri autem propria maxime est fortitudo, cuius munera duo sunt maxima: mortis dolorisque contemptio. utendum est igitur his, si virtutis compotes vel potius si viri volumus esse, quoniam a viris virtus nomen est mutuata.*

Two elements of this long passage should be stressed: the emphasis on the etymological relationship *vir* - *virtus*[5] and the definition of *virtus* as *adfectio animi*. The first element reveals the original meaning of *virtus*, as the courage of the Roman *civis* in his military or political duties:[6] it is this courage to which Cicero refers when saying, for example, of M. Marcellus *ille vir clarissimus summusque imperator ... cuius virtute captae, misericordia conservatae sunt Syracusae* (*Ver.* 5.84), or of Pompey *dicendum est enim de Cn. Pompei singulari eximiaque virtute* (*Man.* 3),[7] or of himself *mea virtute atque diligentia perditorum hominum coniurationem patefactam esse* (*Catil.* 4.5). Its Greek equivalent is not ἀρετή, but ἀνδρεία, which is defined, for example, in Aristotle's *Rhetoric* as that part of ἀρετή which enables men to face dangers and to respect laws: Arist. *Rh.* 1366b11 ff. Ἀνδρεία δὲ δι' ἣν πρακτικοί εἰσι τῶν καλῶν ἔργων ἐν τοῖς κινδύνοις, καὶ ὡς νόμος κελεύει, καὶ ὑπηρετικοὶ τῷ νόμῳ ('Courage makes men perform noble acts in the

[5] Cf. Varro *L.* 5.73 *virtus ut viritus a virilitate*; Pohlenz 1957, 64; Meister 1967, 4; Grilli 1987, 313 f. Cicero sometimes plays not only on the etymological figure, but also on the alliteration which derives from it: cf. Eisenhut 1973, 12 f.

[6] Cf. Liebers 1942, 11 ff.

[7] Cf. Eisenhut 1973, 63. Many passages of Cicero's speech hint at this warlike *virtus* of Pompey. Regarding this and the other *virtutes imperatoriae* which Pompey combined, cf. Liebers 1942, 104 ff. and Classen 1985, 289 ff.

midst of dangers according to the dictates of the law and in submission to it').[8]

In defining *virtus* as *adfectio animi* Cicero, on the contrary, makes it overlap with the Greek philosophical concept of ἀρετή as goodness. *Virtus*, he says again later in the same work, is an *adfectio animi constans conveniensque* not only *laudabiles efficiens eos in quibus est*, but also *ipsa per se sua sponte separata etiam utilitate laudabilis* and is the origin of *honestae voluntates actiones omnisque recta ratio* (*Tusc.* 4.34).[9] The full meaning of ἀρετή is evident here in all its different aspects: on the one hand *virtus* is itself worthy of praise, on the other hand it is what makes people who have it worthy of praise; moreover at the same time it has both a static and a dynamic dimension (as an *adfectio animi* and as the source of actions). While it does not have any relationship with *utilitas*, it does have a special connection with *honestas*. I cannot attempt to investigate now so many and difficult questions as those which Cicero brings together in his few words. In fact we are facing the main notions of Aristotelian and Stoic ethics, and much literature is available on this subject. I could just remind you of the identity between *virtus* and *honestas / honestum*, which we sometimes see made explicit in Cicero's works (for example in *Fin.* 5.66 *honestum aut ipsa virtus est aut res gesta*

---

[8] For the translations of Aristotle's works I am indebted to the editions in the Loeb Classical Library. Aristotle gives a much more detailed account of ἀνδρεία in the *Ethics* (*EN* 1115a6 ff.; *EE* 1228a29 ff.), where he singles out its different εἴδη. Nevertheless there is no substantial difference: the καλὰ ἔργα of the *Rhetoric* can actually make a pendant to τὸ καλόν, aiming at which, in the *Ethics*, ὁ ἀνδρεῖος ὑπομένει καὶ πράττει τὰ κατὰ τὴν ἀνδρείαν (*EN* 1115b23 f.). On the relationship between ἀνδρεία and military or political life, cf. Cope 1877, 161 f. and Grimaldi 1980, 197 f. About the coincidence *virtus*-ἀνδρεία, cf. Eisenhut 1973, 15. This becomes even more evident when one recalls that in the Latin philosophical canon the proper value of *virtus*, namely its original meaning of distinguishing quality of the *vir*, is expressed by *fortitudo*, the virtue corresponding to ἀνδρεία in the Greek canon: cf. Liebers 1942, 8 f.; Meister 1967, 13.

[9] Cf. Liebers 1942, 121 f.

(for example in *Fin.* 5.66 *honestum aut ipsa virtus est aut res gesta virtute*) and more often simply taken for granted.[10] I could also call attention to the problems involved in the Aristotelian and Stoic definitions of ἀρετή,[11] to the well-known meaning of εὐδαιμονία as ψυχῆς ἐνέρ-

---

[10] The Latin question of the identity *virtus* / *honestas* (*honestum*) is first of all linked to the Greek identity καλόν - ἀρετή. About this Aristotle says in *Rh.* 1366a33 ff. that τὸ καλόν is either what, being desirable in itself, is worthy of praise or what, being good, is pleasant because it is good. 'Αρετή necessarily coincides with it, since ἀρετή is praiseworthy because it is good: Καλὸν μὲν οὖν ἐστιν ὃ ἂν δι' αὑτὸ αἱρετὸν ὂν ἐπαινετὸν ᾖ, ἢ ὃ ἂν ἀγαθὸν ὂν ἡδὺ ᾖ, ὅτι ἀγαθόν. Εἰ δὲ τοῦτό ἐστι τὸ καλόν, ἀνάγκη τὴν ἀρετὴν καλὸν εἶναι. 'Αγαθὸν γὰρ ὂν ἐπαινετόν ἐστιν. Cf. the commentaries to this passage by Cope 1877, 159 and Grimaldi 1980, 193 f. We find here that overlap between an aesthetic and a moral appraisal which appears also in the *Nicomachean Ethics*, where we are explicitly told that τὸ καλόν is what ἀρετή aims at (*EN* 1115b12 f.). The Latin *honestum*, which is defined as what *tale est ut detracta omni utilitate sine ullis praemiis fructibusve per se ipsum possit laudari* (*Fin.* 2.45), is but one of the different words by which the Romans tried to express the meaning of the Greek καλόν when identified with ἀρετή: *Fin.* 3.15 *si una virtus, unum istud, quod honestum appellas, rectum, laudabile, decorum—erit enim notius quale sit pluribus notatum vocabulis idem declarantibus*; cf. *Tusc.* 2.30 and about this whole problem, besides the specific study of Klose (1933, 104 ff.), also Eisenhut 1973, 65 f.; Meister 1967, 13.

[11] The definition of ἀρετή given by Aristotle in the *Rhetoric* (*Rh.* 1366a36 ff. 'Αρετὴ δ' ἐστὶ μὲν δύναμις ὡς δοκεῖ ποριστικὴ ἀγαθῶν καὶ φυλακτική, καὶ δύναμις εὐεργετικὴ πολλῶν καὶ μεγάλων, καὶ πάντων περὶ πάντα) is remarkably different from the definition given in the *Ethics* (*EN* 1106b36-1107a2 Ἔστιν ἄρα ἡ ἀρετὴ ἕξις προαιρετική, ἐν μεσότητι οὖσα τῇ πρὸς ἡμᾶς, ὡρισμένῃ λόγῳ καὶ ᾧ ἂν ὁ φρόνιμος ὁρίσειεν, cf. *EE* 1227b6 ff.). The main difference between them is first of all the use of two words, δύναμις and ἕξις, which have completely different meanings (cf. their definitions in *EN* 1105b23 ff.; *EE* 1220b16 ff.), and secondly the absence in *Rh.* 1366a36 ff. of any προαίρεσις, and, therefore, of the resulting moral aspect. Cope (1867, 96 f.; 1877, 159 f.) points out the difficulty of considering the two definitions as equivalent, because of the different approach Aristotle has to this matter in the *Ethics* and in the *Rhetoric* ('scientific' and 'popular'). In this way he attributes to Aristotle a mistake which Grimaldi (1980, 194 f.), on the contrary, denies to be imputable to him. In Grimaldi's opinion, in fact, *Rhetoric* and *Ethics* mean to underline two different aspects of the same notion of virtue. As to the Stoic definition, τήν τε ἀρετὴν διάθεσιν ὁμολογουμένην (D.L. 7.89 = *SVF* 3.39; 197), the word διάθεσις is opposed to ἕξις, because, although both refer

γειά τις κατ' ἀρετὴν τελείαν ('happiness is a certain activity of soul in conformity with perfect goodness')[12] or to the equally well-known relationship αἱρετόν - ἐπαινετόν. But all this would take us too far and it is better, therefore, for us to concentrate on the matter at hand, namely Cicero's διαίρεσις of virtue.

2. The division of virtue in Cicero's rhetorical works

Well before writing his philosophical works Cicero had dealt with the *partes* or *genera* of virtue three times in the rhetorical treatises. The first passage is towards the end of *de Inventione* and refers to deliberative rhetoric (*Inv.* 2.159 ff.). The second is in the second book of *de Oratore* and refers to epideictic rhetoric (*de Orat.* 2.342 ff.). The third is in the *Partitiones Oratoriae* and refers, as in *de Oratore*, to precepts of epideictic rhetoric (*Part.* 76 ff.). Is there any relationship between them? This looks like a question which could be difficult to answer only on the basis of rhetorical contexts.

When dividing *virtus* in *de Inventione* Cicero deals with the notion of *honestum*. This is, he says, *quod aut totum aut aliqua ex parte propter se petitur* and of which *virtus* consists (*Inv.* 2.159). Together with *utilitas*, in open polemic against Aristotle, it represents the goal of deliberative rhetoric: *Inv.* 2.157 *in deliberativo autem Aristoteli placet utilitatem, nobis et honestatem et utilitatem*. Speaking here of the *partes virtutis* therefore means speaking of the *partes honestatis*.[13] This is not the case

---

to the goods of the soul, ἕξις may indicate intensity changes, whilst διάθεσις has an absolute worth: cf. Pohlenz 1955, 49 and *SVF* 3.104; 105.

[12] *EN* 1102a5 f.; cf. 1098a16 ff.; 1098b30 ff.; 1099b26; 1100b9 ff.; *EE* 1219a39 f. In *Rh.* 1360b14 ff. this activity in accordance with virtue is only one of the many components of εὐδαιμονία: cf. Cope 1877, 73 f.; Grimaldi 1980, 105; Broadie 1991, 24 ff.

[13] In the four *partes honestatis* (*prudentia, iustitia, fortitudo* and *temperantia*), it is easy to recognise the Stoic doctrine of the four cardinal virtues. Nevertheless the very nature of this school handbook lets Cicero deal with such an important matter in a very elementary way; he further divides each one of these main

in *de Oratore*, where Antonius, discussing the function of epideictic speeches, contrasts kinds of goods which are not really praiseworthy, like *genus, forma, vires, opes, divitiae ceteraque quae fortuna det aut extrinsecus aut corpori*, with *virtus*, which is the only praiseworthy good. However, since *virtus* shows itself *in usu ac moderatione* of the listed goods, it breaks down into parts and these parts themselves are *virtutes*, of which *alia est <alia> ad laudationem aptior* (*de Orat*. 2.342 f.). The third and last time Cicero deals with the division of virtue in his rhetorical works is, as I said, within the treatment of the *laudandi vituperandique rationes* in the *Partitiones Oratoriae* (70 ff.). Here we find a particularly interesting statement where Cicero says that there have been many and varied discussions about this point and he is going to sum them up briefly: *Part*. 75 *Sed hic locus virtutum atque vitiorum latissime patens ex multis et variis disputationibus nunc in quandam angustam et brevem concludetur*. Cicero does not present any more detail about these *multae* and *variae disputationes*, but we have good reason to suppose that he is not referring to rhetoricians and to rhetorical precepts.

First of all, right at the end of the *Partitiones*, he claims that all its content comes from Academic philosophy (*Part*. 139 *Expositae tibi omnes sunt oratoriae partitiones, quae quidem e media illa nostra Academia effloruerunt, neque sine ea aut inveniri aut intellegi aut tractari possunt*) and also, he says some years later, from Academic philosophy come those precepts which he learnt in order to become an orator (*Orat*. 12 *fateor me oratorem, si modo sim aut etiam quicumque sim, non ex rhetorum officinis sed ex Academiae spatiis extitisse*). Furthermore in *de Oratore* Cicero had already maintained that the teaching of general questions (θέσεις), a doctrine Antonius and Crassus wish rhetoricians had dealt with (*de Orat*. 2.65; 2.78; 3.109 ff.) and a topic also concerned with *omnis virtutum et vitiorum ... silva* (*de Orat*. 3.118), belongs only to Academic and Peripatetic philosophy. To all this one must add the great influence of the Stoics. In accordance with their doctrine, for example, Cicero defines *virtus* as *animi habitus naturae modo atque rationi consentaneus* (*Inv*.

2.159), and often gives Stoic meanings to single virtues, or, in agreement with Stoic ethics, takes into account the ἀντακολουθία of virtues.[14]

3. The notion of virtue in Aristotle's *Rhetoric* and *Ethics*

Apart from the compelling evidence that within different philosophical schools Cicero could find those *multae* and *variae disputationes* which he refers to in *Part.* 75, the only rhetorical context which includes a treatment of this topic is Aristotle's *Rhetoric*. In dealing with the matter of deliberative rhetoric Aristotle comes to the problem of εὐδαιμονία, the final goal of men.[15] Among its component parts he also mentions ἀρετή (*Rh.* 1360b23), whose definition, however, is deliberately postponed (*Rh.* 1362a14 ff.) to that part of rhetoric which refers to praise (*Rh.* 1366a36 ff.). But, before this, we find Aristotle again briefly concerned with the notion of virtue, which this time comes out in its plural form: *Rh.* 1362b1 ff. καὶ τὰς ἀρετὰς δὲ ἀνάγκη ἀγαθὸν εἶναι ('the virtues also must be a good thing'). Here the focus is on the relationship ἀρεταί - ἀγαθόν, ἀγαθόν being what is desirable in itself or because of which something else is desirable (*Rh.* 1362a20 ff.). In fact virtues are doubly ἀγαθόν: people who have possession of them εὖ διάκεινται and the virtues themselves are ποιητικαὶ τῶν ἀγαθῶν and πρακτικαί (*Rh.* 1362b2 f. 'those who possess them are in a sound condition, and they are also productive of good things and practical'). In other words, virtues are said to have both a static and an active dimension, being at the same time the good disposition of the soul and the source of good deeds. Although no division of ἀρετή is taken into account yet, this plurality is further specified in the kinds of goods Aristotle lists here: among them he

---

[14] Cf. D.L. 7.125 τὰς δὲ ἀρετὰς λέγουσιν ἀντακολουθεῖν ἀλλήλαις (= *SVF* 3.295; cf. 299; 302); Philippson 1930, 362 f.; Pohlenz 1948, 127; 1955, 72. About this link between single virtues in Cicero cf., for example, *de Orat.* 1.83; *Tusc.* 3.17; Leeman-Pinkster 1981, 177.

[15] Cf. *EN* 1097a33 - 1097b6; 1097b22; *EE* 1217a21 ff.; Liebers 1942, 84 ff.; Sherman 1989, 96 f.; Broadie 1991, 3 ff.

mentions δικαιοσύνη, ἀνδρεία, σωφροσύνη, μεγαλοψυχία, μεγαλοπρέπεια καὶ αἱ ἄλλαι αἱ τοιαῦται ἕξεις as virtues of the soul (*Rh.* 1362b12 ff., 'Justice, courage, self-control, magnanimity, magnificence, and all other similar states of mind'). It is only when giving precepts for epideictic rhetoric that Aristotle presents the same ἀρεταί as μέρη ἀρετῆς: *Rh.* 1366b1 ff. Μέρη δὲ ἀρετῆς δικαιοσύνη, ἀνδρεία, σωφροσύνη, μεγαλοπρέπεια, μεγαλοψυχία, ἐλευθεριότης, πραότης, φρόνησις, σοφία ('The components of virtue are justice, courage, self-control, magnificence, magnanimity, liberality, gentleness, practical and speculative wisdom'). The most important of them, he says, are those which are the most useful to people (*Rh.* 1366b3 f.) namely, justice (δικαιοσύνη), courage (ἀνδρεία) and liberality (ἐλευθεριότης). In my opinion this social function of virtue, which is implicit already in its definition (*Rh.* 1366a36 ff. Ἀρετὴ δ' ἐστὶ μὲν δύναμις ὡς δοκεῖ ποριστικὴ ἀγαθῶν καὶ φυλακτική, καὶ δύναμις εὐεργετικὴ πολλῶν καὶ μεγάλων, καὶ πάντων περὶ πάντα, 'Virtue, it would seem, is a faculty of providing and preserving good things, a faculty productive of many and great benefits, in fact, of all things in all cases'), needs to be stressed because upon it Cicero bases his whole division of virtue in *De Oratore*.

When discussing virtue in both the *Nicomachean* and *Eudemian Ethics* Aristotle has a rather different approach to it. First of all, in accordance with the division of the soul into a rational and an irrational part (*EN* 1102a26 ff.; *EE* 1219b26 ff.), he also divides virtue into two forms, distinguishing between intellectual and moral goodness (ἀρεταὶ διανοητικαί - ἀρεταὶ ἠθικαί: *EE* 1220a4; cf. *EN* 1103a3 ff.; 1103a14 f.; 1138b35). The intellectual virtues aim at the truth (*EN* 1139b12 f.), whereas moral virtues have to do with pleasure and pain (*EE* 1220a38 f.; 1222b9 ff.). Both kinds are praiseworthy because, as Aristotle says, 'we praise not only the just but also the intelligent and the wise' (*EE* 1220a5 f.).[16] Nevertheless it is with reference to moral virtue that the social meaning of ἀρετή, a consequence of its active aspect when defined as δύναμις εὐεργετική, succumbs to the statement that ἀρετή is ἕξις

[16] Cf. Buchheit 1960, 134 ff.

προαιρετική, that is a disposition of the soul concerned with choice (*EN* 1106b36).[17] Now, ἕξις being the disposition to good or bad behaviour referring to emotions (*EN* 1105b25 ff.) and προαίρεσις a deliberative appetence of what is in one's power (*EE* 1226b18 f.), the individual aspect is prominent and the emphasis lies here on the meaning of virtue as μεσότης between two extremes, which are both considered vices (*EN* 1107a2 f.), whilst in *Rhetoric* each single virtue is contrasted only with its opposite (*Rh.* 1366b9 ff.). Within both forms of ἀρετή single virtues are then examined at length.

4. Cicero's *de Oratore*

But let me come back to Cicero. Two elements of Aristotle's theory appear to have influenced him: the notion of virtue's utility, which, as I have already mentioned, is best expressed in *de Oratore*, and the distinction between intellectual and moral virtues, which is the starting point for the διαίρεσις in *Partitiones Oratoriae*. As to the first point Antonius, when discussing the value of virtue within epideictic rhetoric, says that praising virtues which *videntur in moribus hominum et quadam comitate et beneficentia positae* gives the audience pleasure (*iucunda auditu*), because all these *non ipsis tam qui eas habent, quam generi hominum fructuosae putantur*; praising virtues which are *in ingenii aliqua facultate aut animi magnitudine ac robore*, on the contrary, pleases the hearers less, because this time these virtues appear to *ornare ac tueri* more *ipsos*

---

[17] The free choice is the condition of moral virtue: *EN* 1106a3 f. αἱ δ' ἀρεταὶ προαιρέσεις τινὲς ἢ οὐκ ἄνευ προαιρέσεως. About the importance of this 'Prohairetic State' cf. the recent analysis of Broadie (1991, 78 ff.). Man becomes virtuous only when, free to choose between evil and good, he deliberately does what is good (*EN* 1112a1 ff.): cf. Eisenhut 1973, 19. In the voluntary aspect of his action (*EN* 1111a22 ff.) appears the indissoluble link between choice and character, that is between φρόνησις and moral virtue; cf. Fortenbaugh 1987, 252; 1993, 453; Sherman 1989, 5; 91; 108. Cicero points out the voluntariness of virtue in *Fin.* 5.36: *alterum autem genus est magnarum verarumque virtutum, quas appellamus voluntarias, ut prudentiam, temperantiam, fortitudinem, iustitiam et reliquas eiusdem generis*; cf. Süss 1966, 63.

... *quos laudamus* than *illos apud quos laudamus* (*de Orat.* 2.343 f.). The meaning of the whole passage becomes clearer if we consider the context carefully. Here Antonius is concerned with the aim the orator has in epideictic rhetoric of stirring *delectatio* in the audience (*Part.* 10; 69), which is obtained through a special kind of style (*Part.* 71 f.) and through the description of special contents (*de Orat.* 2.346 f.).[18] *Gratissima*, he says, *laus habetur* of those actions which appear to be undertaken *a viris fortibus sine emolumento ac praemio* (*de Orat.* 2.346). Therefore the emphasis does not lie here on a systematic division of *virtus*, but on the different *officia ac munera* (*de Orat.* 2.345) of its parts, which are more or less praiseworthy according to the degree of utility of the activities to which they give life. We could even say that moral virtues, like *clementia, iustitia, benignitas, fides, fortitudo in periculis communibus*, represent here the dynamic dimension of virtue, which would agree with Aristotle's definition of ἀρετή as δύναμις only in the epideictic context of the *Rhetoric*. Virtues like *sapientia,*[19] *magnitudo animi, ingenium or eloquentia* itself appear on the contrary much more as individual states, which offer less matter for praise to the orator, since they are less useful to men.[20]

But, if we now turn to details, we see that Cicero is not free from heavy Stoic influences here. Giving to *magnitudo animi* the value of that virtue *qua omnes res humanae tenues ac pro nihilo putantur* (*de Orat.* 2.344) Antonius actually parts from Aristotle's meaning of μεγαλοψυχία, which is defined consistently with its active nature in *Rh.* 1366b17 ἀρετὴ

---

[18] *Delectatio*, in a more general way, played an extremely important role in the doctrine of the *officia oratoris*: cf. Calboli Montefusco 1994, 85 ff.

[19] About the worth of *sapientia* in the Roman world cf., besides Liebers (1942, 80 ff.), the special study of Klima (1971, 3 ff.).

[20] With regard to this passage of *de Oratore* I cannot share the opinion of Peters (1907, 81), namely that we are facing Aristotle's distinction between ἀρεταὶ διανοητικαί and ἀρεταὶ ἠθικαί. *Magnitudo animi* is in fact taken into account by Aristotle (μεγαλοψυχία) as ἀρετὴ ἠθική.

μεγάλων ποιητικὴ εὐεργετημάτων ('virtue productive of great benefits').[21] Much more likely we can recognise in Antonius' *magnitudo animi* that *rerum externarum despicientia* which Cicero in *de Off.* 1.66 considers peculiar to a *fortis animus et magnus* and which finds its equivalent in the Stoic definition of μεγαλοψυχία as ἐπιστήμη ὑπεράνω ποιοῦσα τῶν πεφυκότων ἐν σπουδαίοις τε γίνεσθαι καὶ φαύλοις (Stob. 2.61.15 ff. W. = *SVF* 3.264; cf. 265; 269; 270).[22] Stoic again is the presence of *eloquentia* among the virtues. This was clearly maintained by the Stoic Mnesarchus, according to Antonius' words when referring to his discussions in Athens about the perfect orator and the art of rhetoric (*de Orat.* 1.83 *dicebat ... oratorem ... nisi sapiens esset, esse neminem, atque ipsam eloquentiam ... unam quandam esse virtutem*). Crassus also borrows the same meaning from Stoic doctrine (*de Orat.* 3.55 *est enim eloquentia una quaedam de summis virtutibus*), when he requires of the orator the full knowledge of things. It is just in order to give him that *virtutum omnium cognitio* without which no praise is possible that Antonius here has dealt with this matter longer than he himself wanted to (*de Orat.* 2.348).

5. Cicero's *Partitiones Oratoriae*

Much deeper, however, is Cicero's discussion of this topic in *Partitiones Oratoriae*. Within the well-known tripartite division of *bona* which are at the origin of any praise, he says that *multa et varia facta in propria virtutum genera sunt digerenda* (*Part.* 75). Only when it is *gesta* according to virtue does each *res* appear *honesta ... summeque laudabilis* (*Part.* 79). This is again consistent with the epideictic context which Cicero is dealing with: while looking for the *voluptas* of his audience the orator

---

[21] When dealing with μεγαλοψυχία in his *Nicomachean Ethics*, Aristotle mentions important details: here he says that μεγαλόψυχος is only that man who is perfect because he excels in what is great in each virtue; in this sense μεγαλοψυχία appears indeed to be κόσμος τις ... τῶν ἀρετῶν (*EN* 1123b25-1124a3).

[22] Cf. Knoche 1935, 49 n. 220; Liebers 1942, 77 ff.; Pohlenz 1967, 40 ff.

needs to emphasise the relationship virtue - action,[23] also stressed some sections later in the conclusion of this part (*Part.* 82 *tum quae quisque senserit dixerit gesserit ad ea quae proposita sunt virtutum genera accommodabuntur*; cf. *de Orat.* 2.345). To this first statement Cicero appends a quite remarkable *digerere in genera*. Its starting point is, as I said, the Aristotelian distinction between intellectual and moral virtues: *Part.* 76 *Est igitur vis virtutis duplex: aut enim scientia cernitur virtus aut actione.* To *scientia* belongs what is called *prudentia* or *calliditas* or *sapientia*, to *actio* what is called *temperantia*, which *moderandis cupiditatibus regendisque animi motibus laudatur*. Both of them are further divided according to their reference to the individual or to society. *Prudentia in suis rebus* is therefore *domestica*, *prudentia in publicis rebus* is *civilis*. More problematic is the division of *temperantia* (*Part.* 77 f.). For under this main head Cicero considers all moral virtues, but in a complicated relationship to each other. *Temperantia in suis rebus* can actually appear either in fortunate or in unfortunate situations (*in rebus commodis—in rebus incommodis*). In the first case it shows itself either *ea quae absunt non expetendo* or *ab eis quae in potestate sunt abstinendo*. In the second case it is called *fortitudo*, when it *venientibus malis obstat*, or *patientia*, when it *quod iam adest tolerat et perfert*. At this point Cicero introduces the notion of *magnitudo animi*, which seems to overlap his dichotomous way of dividing: *quae autem haec uno genere complectitur, magnitudo animi dicitur; cuius est liberalitas in usu pecuniae simulque altitudo animi in capiendis incommodis et maxime iniuriis et omne quod est eius generis.* We will come back later to the meaning of this sentence. Moving now to *temperantia* with reference to social relationships (*in communione*), Cicero says that this part is called *iustitia*, which in turn has different names: *erga deos religio, erga parentes pietas, creditis in rebus fides, in moderatione animi advertendi lenitas, amicitia in benevolentia.* Still not happy, he adds two more virtues as *quasi ministrae comitesque sapientiae*,

---

[23] In this regard the distinction Aristotle makes between ἔπαινος and ἐγκώμιον is interesting: the former is the praise due to virtue, the latter the praise due to virtuous works (*EN* 1101b31 ff.; *EE* 1219b8 ff.): cf. Buchheit 1960, 134; 162; Hellwig 1973, 138.

namely dialectic and rhetoric (*Part.* 78), and finally considers *verecundia* as *custos ... virtutum omnium dedecus fugiens laudemque maxime consequens* (*Part.* 79).

6. Philosophical influences on Cicero's division of virtue

Looking back on this whole διαίρεσις we must note that Cicero was very honest indeed when he described his short discussion on this topic as a synthesis of several others (*Part.* 75). If we were to choose which one most influenced him, we should acknowledge that quite a few Stoic elements are woven into a Peripatetic-Academic fabric. Thus I cannot believe Knoche's claim in his study on *magnitudo animi*; in referring to his division of virtue, Cicero—he maintains—'weist ... unverkennbar darauf hin, dass er hier eine nicht akademische Lehrmeinung einfügt' (1935, 51). Neither can I share Pohlenz's opinion,[24] which was accepted by Knoche (1935, 53), that here Cicero is clearly influenced by Panaetius. In my opinion these assertions are not sufficiently supported by the comparison between the first distinction *scientia* - *actio* and Diogenes Laertius' testimony about Panaetius: Παναίτιος μὲν οὖν δύο φησὶν ἀρετάς, θεωρητικὴν καὶ πρακτικήν (D.L. 7.92). Trying to confirm it by comparing *Partitiones* and *de Officiis*, as Knoche does (1935, 52),[25] can even be misleading. First of all nobody could deny that Panaetius' distinction also has Peripatetic roots.[26] There is no doubt about that. Cicero himself was well aware that the Stoics were accustomed to "stealing" their notions, as appears from his quite rude statement in *Fin.* 5.74 (*Stoici restant ... totam ad se nostram philosophiam transtulerunt; atque ut reliqui fures earum rerum quas ceperunt, signa commutant, sic illi ut sententiis nostris pro suis uterentur, nomina tamquam rerum notas mutaverunt*). Aristotle's distinction between ἀρεταὶ διανοητικαί and ἀρεταὶ

[24] Pohlenz 1933, 75 n. 3.

[25] Cf. in this regard already Peters 1907, 81.

[26] Cf. Peters 1907, 73 n. 1.

ἠθικαί (*EN* 1103a4 f.) is therefore certainly also at the bottom of Panaetius' doctrine. We could moreover remember that the whole teaching of the θέσεις, divided into a *genus cognitionis* and a *genus actionis* (*de Orat*. 3.111 ff.; *Part*. 62 ff.; *Top*. 81 ff.), exhibits a very similar distinction and that this distinction is, since *de Oratore*, explicitly attributed to Peripatetic and Academic philosophy.[27] Turning now to the Stoic context of *de Officiis* (cf. *Off*. 1.6 *Sequimur igitur hoc quidem tempore et hac in quaestione potissimum Stoicos*), where Cicero probably follows Panaetius' writing on τὸ καθῆκον, we see that Cicero, dealing with the notion of *honestum*, divides it into four parts here (*Off*. 1.15 ff.). But he does not simply list them as he did in *Inv*. 2.159; rather he opposes to the first of these parts, which *in perspicientia veri sollertiaque versatur*, the last three, which, on the contrary, aim *ad eas res parandas tuendasque, quibus actio vitae continetur*. To the first part belong *sapientia* and *prudentia*, theoretical and practical wisdom, because *omnis ... cogitatio motusque animi aut in consiliis capiendis de rebus honestis et pertinentibus ad bene beateque vivendum aut in studiis scientiae cognitionisque versabitur* (*Off*. 1.19). To the other group belong *iustitia, magnitudo animi* and *temperantia*. Therefore, the four cardinal virtues (wisdom, courage, justice and temperance), which, recalling Plato's belief,[28] constituted one of the foundations of Stoic doctrine, are here distributed in a ratio of one to three, according to their different natures.

Beyond the first analogy in the structure, i.e. the main division into *scientia* and *actio*, however, the διαίρεσις of *Partitiones* departs from the treatment of virtue which Cicero presents in *de Officiis*. Peculiar to

---

[27] Cf. Calboli Montefusco 1986, 45 ff.

[28] Cf. Plato *R*. 427e οἶμαι ἡμῖν τὴν πόλιν, εἴπερ ὀρθῶς γε ᾤκισται, τελέως ἀγαθὴν εἶναι ... Δῆλον δὲ ὅτι σοφή τ' ἐστὶ καὶ ἀνδρεία καὶ σώφρων καὶ δικαία. Plato often deals with virtue: cf. Mutschmann 1906, xiv; 16; Peters 1907, 79; Eisenhut 1973, 20. In *Off*. 1.63 Cicero quotes Plato with regard to the opposition *scientia/calliditas; fortitudo/audacia* (*Mx*. 246e; *La*. 197b); cf. Pohlenz 1967, 43 n. 3. Wehrli (1950, 79) underlines the fact that the Stoics have taken from Plato even the concept of the one virtue which partially reveals itself in the different virtues.

Partitiones is actually not only the fact that *temperantia* sums up all moral virtues,[29] but also the distinction drawn between the individual and the social aspects of both wisdom and temperance. In this regard we must be careful not to confuse this distinction with the Stoic one between *cognitio* and *actio*, which gives a social value only to the latter (*Off.* 1.153 *cognitio ... manca quodam modo atque incohata sit, si nulla actio rerum consequatur. Ea autem actio in hominum commodis tuendis maxime cernitur; pertinet igitur ad societatem generis humani; ergo haec cognitioni anteponenda est*). When, in *Partitiones*, *prudentia* is given the double meaning of *prudentia in suis rebus domestica, in publicis civilis* (*Part.* 76), this is again an indisputable inheritance from Aristotle. Looking at his *Nicomachean Ethics* we find the same idea expressed in a surprisingly similar way: *φρόνιμος*, says Aristotle, is he who is able to investigate what is good for himself and, more generally, for mankind; *φρόνησις* therefore is the virtue possessed by *οἰκονομικοί* and by *πολιτικοί*: *EN* 1140b9 ff. *Περικλέα καὶ τοὺς τοιούτους φρονίμους οἰόμεθα εἶναι, ὅτι τὰ αὑτοῖς ἀγαθὰ καὶ τοῖς ἀνθρώποις δύνανται θεωρεῖν· εἶναι δὲ τοιούτους ἡγούμεθα τοὺς οἰκονομικοὺς καὶ τοὺς πολιτικούς* ('men like Pericles are deemed prudent, because they possess a faculty of discerning what things are good for themselves and for mankind; and that is our conception of an expert in domestic economy or political science'). Then, when *temperantia* is divided *in suas res* and *in communes res* and is called *magnitudo animi* with reference to its individual aspect, and *iustitia* with reference to its social aspect, we have a quite remarkable difference as to the meaning of *temperantia* as it is considered in *de Officiis*. Considering it as a main head under which other virtues are taken into account has in fact nothing to do, in my opinion, with the prominence given to temperance relative to the other parts of *honestum*, as Merchant and Sternkopf maintain in their studies on *Partitiones*.[30] In the three passages taken into account to support their opinion, namely *Off.* 1.93,

---

[29] Sternkopf (1914, 71) is inclined to recognise in this peculiarity of *Partitiones* a possible Academic origin.

[30] Merchant 1890, 56; Sternkopf 1914, 70 f.

Fin. 2.47 and *Tusc.* 3.16, the notion of temperance appears indeed to be a wider principle which involves all the other virtues, including *prudentia*; and this principle has the well-known meaning of πρέπον, as is best shown in *Off.* 1.93 *Sequitur ut de una reliqua parte honestatis dicendum sit, in qua verecundia et quasi quidam ornatus vitae, temperantia et modestia omnisque sedatio perturbationum animi et rerum modus cernitur. Hoc loco continetur id, quod dici Latine decorum potest, Graece enim πρέπον dicitur.*[31] It is not difficult to recognise here the function which in *Partitiones* is attributed to *verecundia* as *custos ... virtutum omnium dedecus fugiens laudemque maxime consequens* (*Part.* 79).[32]

But let me come back again to *temperantia in suas res* (*Part.* 77). The first difficulty here is the introduction of *magnitudo animi* as a comprehensive notion. The question is, of course, whether this means that *magnitudo animi* includes all four parts into which Cicero had already divided *temperantia in suas res*, as is my opinion, or only the last two (*fortitudo* and *patientia*), as is Knoche's view. There are three reasons why I cannot share Knoche's preliminary statement that here we are facing 'die Abhandlung der vier stoischen Kardinaltugenden: *sapientia, temperantia, magnitudo animi, iustitia*. Deren dritte, die *magnitudo animi*, wird als die Zusammenfassung zweier speziellerer *virtutes* bezeichnet (§ 77), der *fortitudo* ... und der *patientia*' (1935, 51). First of all, by looking at things in this way, *temperantia* would be given the value of *species* and not the value of *genus*, which seems to be at odds with the dialectic method of division which Cicero uses here. Secondly we must not forget that ever since Aristotle and the later Peripatetic tradition, the notion of μεγαλοψυχία had been inclusive of bad and good fortune, which would perfectly agree with Cicero's division *in rebus commodis* and *in rebus incommodis*. Μεγαλοψυχία is defined in the small

[31] Rhetoric borrowed the same notion from philosophy and the orator was requested to respect it at all times, as best appears in the famous passage of Cic. *Orat.* 70; cf. *de Orat.* 3.210 ff. On this topic cf. Philippson 1930, 386 ff.; Pohlenz 1933, 72 ff.; 1967, 60 ff.; Desmouliez 1976, 266 ff.

[32] Cf. Büchner 1957, 313 f.; Lossmann 1967, 330 ff.

treatise on virtues and vices attributed to Aristotle as that *ἀρετὴ ψυχῆς καθ' ἣν δύνανται φέρειν εὐτυχίαν καὶ ἀτυχίαν, τιμὴν καὶ ἀτιμίαν* ('goodness of spirit that enables men to bear good fortune and bad, honour and dishonour') ([Arist.] *de Virt. et Vit.* 1250a14 f.), and in the *Nicomachean Ethics* *μεγαλόψυχος* is said to be that man who will behave *μετρίως* with respect to any kind of good and bad fortune (Arist. *EN* 1124a13 ff.). Turning then to *de Officiis* we see that Cicero too, still dealing with *magnitudo animi*, says that *ut res adversas, sic secundas inmoderate ferre levitatis est* (*Off.* 1.90). Finally, in my opinion, it should be stressed that Cicero, in joining together *liberalitas in usu pecuniae*[33] and *altitudo animi in capiendis incommodis et maxime iniuriis et omne quod est eius generis* (*Part.* 77) as special characteristics of *magnitudo animi*, means to sum up the ingredients of its wide content. Indeed he says in *de Officiis* that two things are distinctive of a *fortis animus et magnus*: one is that *rerum externarum despicientia*, which we have seen mentioned also in *de Oratore*, the other is doing *res ... magnas ... et maxime utiles, sed ut vehementer arduas plenasque laborum et periculorum* (*Off.* 1.67). The latter is what he means by *altitudo animi*; the former also includes *liberalitas*: *Off.* 1.68 *nihil enim est tam angusti animi tamque parvi quam amare divitias, nihil honestius magnificentiusque quam pecuniam contemnere, si non habeas, si habeas, ad beneficentiam liberalitatemque conferre.*

Turning now to justice, which is *temperantia in res communes*,[34]

---

[33] Cf. Sternkopf 1914, 72; Heuer 1941, 63 ff.

[34] As social virtue *iustitia* is particularly emphasised within the philosophical canon: Cic. *Off.* 1.20 *latissime patet ea ratio, qua societas hominum inter ipsos et vitae quasi communitas continetur*. Only justice in fact guarantees the human social order, since it is only by observing it that each one is happy to possess what belongs to him (cf., for example, Cic. *Fin.* 5.65 *quae animi affectio suum cuique tribuens atque hanc ... societatem coniunctionis humanae munifice et aeque tuens iustitia dicitur* and already Arist. *Rh.* 1366b9 f. Ἔστι δὲ δικαιοσύνη μὲν ἀρετὴ δι' ἣν τὰ αὑτῶν ἕκαστοι ἔχουσι) and one does not injure other people unless in self-defence: Cic. *Off.* 1.20 *iustitia primum munus est, ut ne cui quis noceat, nisi lacessitus iniuria, deinde ut communibus pro communibus utatur, privatis ut suis*. On this basic function of justice cf. also Peters 1907, 82

we must remember that Cicero particularly loved this topic. Several times he comes to single out its different aspects, once again in *Part.* 129 ff. within the treatment of questions of *qualitas* which are concerned with *ius*;[35] twice in *de Inventione*, in 2.65 ff., when referring to *partes iuris* as *loci argumentorum* for questions of *qualitas negotialis*, and in 2.160 ff. in his διαίρεσις of *honestum*; once in *Fin.* 5.65 where, he says, to justice *sunt adiunctae pietas bonitas liberalitas benignitas comitas quaequae sunt generis eiusdem* and, finally, twice in *Topica*, when exemplifying the difference between *partitio* and *divisio* (28) and, some sections later, in his overview of theoretical theses (90).[36] Behind all these passages lie philosophical meanings. The Academy since Plato, the Peripatos since Aristotle and then the Stoics had all distinguished between different forms of justice.[37] It was always, however, a matter of social relationships. Being just means doing what is best not only for oneself but also for other people. In this sense, says Aristotle, justice is the only ἀρετὴ τελεία (*EN* 1129b31 ff.).

At this point Cicero adds rhetoric and dialectic as *virtutes* which are linked to *sapientia*. This is again a philosophical inheritance. Crassus, for example, in *de Orat.* 3.65 thanks the Stoics because *soli ex omnibus eloquentiam virtutem ac sapientiam esse dixerunt*. In *Acad.* 1.5 Cicero himself, arguing against the Epicureans who *nullam ... artem esse nec dicendi nec disserendi putant*, says that, on the contrary, the other philosophical schools consider both to be virtues. In accordance with this

---

f.; Ibscher 1934, 19 ff.; Pohlenz 1948, 132; 1967, 25 ff.; Bretone 1992, 338 n. 69.

[35] Cf. Calboli Montefusco 1986, 93 ff.

[36] Some of these passages have been studied with particular interest not only by philologists, but also by romanists, because they constitute the starting point for a reconstruction of the Roman juridical system: cf. Riposati 1947, 217 ff.; Nörr 1972, 10 ff.; Stein 1978, 21 ff.; Bretone 1992, 333 ff.

[37] Cf. e.g. Plato *Grg.* 507b; *Euthphr.* 12e; Arist. *EN* 1130b5 ff.; *Rh.* 1374a25 ff.; [Arist.] *de Virt. et Vit.* 1250b20 ff.; *SVF* 3.264; Mutschmann 1906, 5 ff.; Sternkopf 1914, 72 ff.; Riposati 1947, 221 ff.

claim his *perfectus orator* joins to the *facultas ornatissimae orationis* (*de Orat*. 1.76) the understanding of dialectic and philosophy (cf., for example, *de Orat*. 1.17; 1.19; 1.34; 3.80). In this sense ethics represents Cicero's greatest concern: not only as a philosopher, but also as an orator he feels compelled to deal with the notion of virtue, *honestum*, and of its single parts. He does it all his life long, from *de Inventione* to *de Officiis*, both in rhetorical and in philosophical contexts: only when coupled with *sapientia* can rhetoric be useful to people,[38] Cicero first says in the introduction to *de Inventione* (1.1 ff.); to live according to *temperantia, prudentia, fortitudo, iustitia* is his final advice to his son at the end of his life (*Off*. 3.177 ff.).

BIBLIOGRAPHY

Barwick, K., *Das rednerische Bildungsideal Ciceros*, Abhandlungen der Sächsischen Akademie der Wissenschaften zu Leipzig, Philol.-hist. Klasse, Band 54, Heft 3. Berlin 1963.

Bretone, M., *Storia del diritto romano*. Roma - Bari 1992.

Broadie, S., *Ethics with Aristotle*. New York - Oxford 1991.

Buchheit, V., *Untersuchungen zur Theorie des Genos Epideiktikon von Gorgias bis Aristoteles*. München 1960.

Büchner, K., *Humanitas Romana. Studien über Werke und Wesen der Römer*. Heidelberg 1957.

Calboli Montefusco, L., *La dottrina degli "status" nella retorica greca e romana*. Hildesheim 1986.

———, Aristotle and Cicero on the "officia oratoris", in: W.W. Fortenbaugh - D.C. Mirhady (eds.), *Peripatetic Rhetoric after Aristotle*. RUSCH VI, New Brunswick - London 1994, 66-94.

Classen, C.J., *Recht, Rhetorik, Politik. Untersuchungen zu Ciceros rhetorischer Strategie*. Darmstadt 1985.

[38] On this *sapientia* required of the orator cf., among others, Barwick 1963, 69 ff.; Klima 1971, 102 ff..; Classen 1986, 46 ff. Several times Cicero points out the ethical function of the orator: cf. Schulte 1935, 13.

———, Ciceros "orator perfectus": ein "vir bonus dicendi peritus"?, in: S. Prete (ed.), *Commemoratio. Studi di filologia in ricordo di Riccardo Ribuoli*. Istituto internazionale di Studi Piceni. Sassoferrato 1986, 43-55.

Cope, E.M., *An Introduction to Aristotle's Rhetoric, with Analysis, Notes and Appendices.*, London and Cambridge 1867.

———, *The Rhetoric of Aristotle, with a Commentary by* E.M. Cope, revised by J.E. Sandys, Volumes I, II and III. Cambridge 1877, reprint Salem, N.H. 1988.

Desmouliez, A., *Cicéron et son goût. Essai sur une définition d'une esthétique romaine à la fin de la République*. Bruxelles 1976.

Eisenhut, W., *Virtus Romana. Ihre Stellung im römischen Wertsystem.* München 1973.

Fortenbaugh, W.W., Un modo di affrontare la distinzione fra virtù etica e saggezza in Aristotele, *Museum Patavinum* 5 (1987), 243-58.

———, Theophrastus on Law, Virtue, and the Particular Situation, in: R. Rosen - J. Farrell (eds.), *Nomodeiktes. Greek Studies in Honor of Martin Ostwald*. Ann Arbor 1993, 447-55.

Grilli, A., *Marco Tullio Cicerone, Tusculane, Libro II, testo, introduzione, versione e commento*. Brescia 1987.

Grimaldi, W., *Aristotle, Rhetoric I, A Commentary*. New York 1980.

Hellwig, A., *Untersuchungen zur Theorie der Rhetorik bei Platon und Aristoteles*. Göttingen 1973.

Heuer, K.H., *Comitas - facilitas - liberalitas. Studien zur gesellschaftlichen Kultur der ciceronischen Zeit*. Münster 1941.

Ibscher, G., *Der Begriff des Sittlichen in der Pflichtenlehre des Panaitius. Ein Beitrag zur Erkenntnis der mittleren Stoa*. München 1934.

Klima, U., *Untersuchungen zu dem Begriff sapientia von der republikanischen Zeit bis Tacitus*. Bonn 1971.

Klose, F., *Die Bedeutung von honos und honestus* (Diss. Breslau). Breslau 1933.

Knoche, U., *Magnitudo animi. Untersuchungen zur Entstehung und Entwicklung eines römischen Wertgedankens*, Philologus, Supplementband 27, Heft 3. Leipzig 1935.

Leeman, A. - Pinkster, H., *M. Tullius Cicero, De oratore libri III, Kommentar, 1. Bd.: Buch I, 1-165*. Heidelberg 1981.

Liebers, G., *Virtus bei Cicero*. Dresden 1942.

Lossmann, F., Verecundia, in: H. Oppermann (ed.), *Römische Wertbegriffe*. Darmstadt 1967.

Meister, K., Die Tugenden der Römer, in: H. Oppermann (ed.), *Römische Wertbegriffe*. Darmstadt 1967, 1-22.

Merchant, F.I., *De Ciceronis Partitionibus oratoriis commentatio*. Berlin 1890.

Mutschmann, H., *Divisiones quae vulgo dicuntur Aristoteleae, praefatus edidit testimoniisque instruxit Hermannus Mutschmann*. Lipsiae 1906.

Nörr, D., *Divisio und Partitio. Bemerkungen zur römischen Rechtsquellenlehre und zur antiken Wissenschaftstheorie*. Berlin 1972.

Pease, A.S., *M. Tulli Ciceronis, De natura deorum libri III*. Darmstadt 1968.

Peters, C., *De rationibus inter artem rhetoricam quarti et primi saeculi intercedentibus*. Kiel 1907.

Philippson, R., Das Sittlichschöne bei Panaitius, *Philologus* N.F. 39 (1930), 357-413.

Pohlenz, M., *Die Stoa. Geschichte einer geistigen Bewegung*. Göttingen 1948.

———, *Die Stoa. Geschichte einer geistigen Bewegung*, 2. Band: *Erläuterungen*. Göttingen 1955.

———, *Ciceronis Tusculanarum disputationum libri V, Mit Benutzung von Otto Heines Ausgabe*. Erstes Heft: Libri I et II. Stuttgart 1957.

———, *Antikes Führertum. Cicero De officiis und das Lebensideal des Panaitius*. Amsterdam 1967.

———, Tὸ πρέπον, Ein Beitrag zur Geschichte des griechischen Geistes, *NGG, Phil.-Hist. Kl.* 1933, 53-92 = *Kleine Schriften* (ed. H. Dörrie). Hildesheim 1965, 1.100-39.

Riposati, B., *Studi sui "Topica" di Cicerone*. Milano 1947.

Schulte, H.K., *Orator. Untersuchungen über das ciceronianische Bildungsideal*. Frankfurt am Main 1935.

Sherman, N., *The Fabric of Character: Aristotle's Theory of Virtue*. Oxford 1989.

Stein, P., The Sources of Law in Cicero, *Ciceroniana* N. S. 3 (1978), 19-31.

Sternkopf, P., *De M. Tulli Ciceronis Partitionibus Oratoriis*. Münster 1914.

Süss, W., *Cicero. Eine Einführung in seine philosophischen Schriften (mit Ausschluß der staatphilosophischen Werke)*. Akademie der Wissenschaften und der Literatur, Abhandlungen der Geistes- und Sozialwissenschaftlichen Klasse, Jahrgang 1965, Nr. 5. Wiesbaden 1966.

Wehrli, F., *Straton von Lampsakos*. Die Schule des Aristoteles. Basel 1959.

Weische, A., *Cicero und die neue Akademie. Untersuchungen zur Entstehung und geschichte des antiken Skeptizismus*. Münster 1961.

Greeks, Romans, and the Rise of Atticism

Jakob Wisse

1. Introduction

The man honoured with the symposium of April 1994 and with this collection is, of course, a Hellenist. Nevertheless, he has not just now and again invoked evidence from Latin authors; he has actually published on Latin material. I am thinking of his interesting contribution to the 'Cicero on Tatnic' conference, published in 1988. I, following his example, will try to show that studying Greek and Latin material in close conjunction is, in the case of the rise of Atticism, not only natural, but actually indispensable.[1]

It may be in order to begin by stating, in very broad terms, what I understand by Atticism, so as to preclude misunderstandings. What I shall call Atticism is the movement—both Roman and Greek, and particularly in rhetoric as well as prose literature in general—that harks back to the old models of the classical Athenian period, especially but not exclusively Lysias. I have concluded that the beginnings of the movement seem to belong in the first century BCE.

What I will not try to do is to discuss the causes and antecedents of the rise of Atticism.[2] I shall chiefly confine myself to some more down-to-earth problems: when was Atticism initiated, by whom, and what were the ways in which such a movement and such ideas were transmitted. In trying to answer these questions and to devise a picture that is perhaps more plausible than those presented so far, my main aim is to draw some

---

[1] I want to thank Nancy Laan for several forms of help with this piece, and Doreen Innes for the stimulating discussions on this and similar topics during the symposium. All errors and infelicities are, of course, mine alone.

[2] Cf. below n. 22.

threads together. The questions themselves are far from new, and the material used as well as many of the analyses will also be familiar. The issue of Atticism, after all, has been amply discussed in the past, especially in the last quarter of the 19th century: the names that come to mind are those of Rohde, Kaibel, Wilhelm Schmid, and especially of Norden (in his *Antike Kunstprosa*), Radermacher and Wilamowitz.[3] Unfortunately, however, the secondary literature as a whole resembles a jungle more than anything else, in more than one sense. To start with, as has been pointed out some years ago by Goudriaan (1989, esp. 635-6), academic manners were not always as they should have been. For example Wilamowitz, in his famous article from 1900, 'Asianismus und Atticismus', does not deign to mention the name of Wilhelm Schmid, but he does characterise Schmid's suggestion that the movement started on Rhodes as 'eine kaum fassbare Verkehrtheit' (1900, 49).[4] From this jungle fight it was, of course, Wilamowitz himself who emerged as the winner—not because his article is faultless or even particularly lucid, but chiefly, it seems, because of his overriding authority. As a result, that stage of the debate virtually ended in 1900. Of more recent scholars, Dihle has been rather influential, but he did, at least to my mind, obscure the issue rather than illuminate it, not only by his fanciful handling of the ancient evidence, but also by misrepresenting earlier scholarship.[5] This is another way in which the secondary literature resembles a jungle: not only is a

---

[3] See bibliography for the titles, and the very useful survey of the debates of the period by Goudriaan 1989, 595-677.

[4] Goudriaan 1989, 635. Schmid's suggestion was made in his Antrittsrede (1898, 11: Goudriaan 1989, 634), which I have not seen.

[5] E.g., when trying to establish a firm connection between Stoicism and the *genus subtile* (1957, 185), he presents Cotta, the Academic spokesman in *de Natura Deorum*, as a Stoic, as well as Torquatus (either the Epicurean spokesman in *de Finibus*, or his father who once ridiculed the Stoics: *Fin.* 1.39); also, he reports (1957, 170 n. 2) that Wilamowitz (1900) discussed 'das Aufkommen des Attizismus in Griechenland', though Wilamowitz himself put the beginnings of the movement in Rome (below, § 5).

real consensus still very difficult to reach, but also the various opinions are often hard to disentangle.

This is, I hope, already sufficient excuse for my again taking up the issue. What I will do is, as the saying goes, to proceed from the known to the unknown. I will take as my point of departure the two relatively secure phases of the Atticist movement in the first century BCE, viz. the Roman phase of ca. 50 BCE, and the Greek phase associated with Dionysius of Halicarnassus of ca. 25 BCE. From there, after an intermezzo where the problems are defined with some more precision, I will move on to the question of the relationship between these two phases, and to the problem of the first beginnings of the movement.

2. The two secure phases

2.1 Roman Atticism

We know about Roman Atticism, of course, through Cicero's works, especially the two rhetorical works published in 46 BCE, *Brutus* and *Orator*. What emerges quite clearly from these is a general and relatively undisputed picture of the main characteristics of the movement. The Atticists favoured the use of a pure Latin as they saw it, and more especially a style that was simple and elegant. Their models were the classical Athenian orators Lysias and Hyperides; particularly Lysias they saw as the Attic orator *par excellence*. All the oratory of the period from ca. 300 BCE until their own time they rejected as being 'Asianist', by which they chiefly meant overdone and bombastic. And in this criticism they included Cicero's emotional style, which they likewise regarded as swollen and bombastic. Cicero answers their challenge in *Brutus* and *Orator* by pointing out, among other things, that in persuading an audience, his oratory was far more effective than theirs. He also emphasises that Demosthenes, who often used an emotional style, was no less truly 'Attic' than the simple and subdued Lysias. In other words, Cicero claims that he himself, in following Demosthenes, has as many rights to the title of Atticist as his opponents.

What also emerges clearly from *Brutus*, and is confirmed elsewhere, is that the leader of the movement was C. Licinius Calvus, who, in this same work, is spoken of as dead.[6] And as Bowersock writes (1979, 59), here the trouble begins: when did the movement start? It is commonly assumed that Cicero's *de Oratore*, published at the end of 55 BCE, does not address the issue of Atticism, whereas the works of 46 BCE do. The usual inference is that Roman Atticism emerged between 55 and 46. Calvus, then, must have died ca. 47.

But, as Bowersock rightly emphasises (1979, 61), this cannot be right. Calvus is never heard of after 54. That is, our numerous records of the eventful years of power politics and civil war between 54 and 46 do not mention this ambitious, gifted young man, who left 21 books of speeches that Tacitus could still read (*Dial.* 21.1), and who was very active in the years 56-54. As Münzer saw (1926, 433), this means that he must have died in 54 or 53. Since he was the leader of the Atticists, the movement must, then, have begun well before 54.[7]

This seems to create a new problem, for we might be tempted to think, with Bowersock (1979, 61-5) and others,[8] that Roman Atticism virtually died with Calvus in 54/53; after all, neither in *Brutus* nor in *Orator* does Cicero mention other, living adherents of the movement. This would make oddities of these two works: written in 46, they would address an issue that was definitely old hat. Bowersock's solution (1979, 62) is to suggest that Cicero was an 'ageing person', who 'could still feel strongly on tired topics'. But even apart from the circularity of such

---

[6] *Brut.* 283; 284; cf. *Fam.* 15.21.4 (probably from the end of 46: see Shackleton Bailey's commentary).

[7] On Calvus' activities in 56-54 see esp. Münzer 1926, 430-3. Note also that he is not attested to have held any office. All this fits in very well with a birth-date for Calvus in 82, which was convincingly defended by Sumner (1973, 149), less well with the date of 88 that was favoured by Münzer (1926, 429-30).

[8] Similarly, in particular, Douglas (1955, 242; 1966, xii-xiv; 1973, 125-6—but contrast 1973, 127), who, however, puts Calvus' death in 47 or not much earlier (1966, xiii and ad 283).

analyses, this will not do. It requires us to imagine that Cicero has written these two works only to refute a man who was at least seven years dead—a behaviour for which 'feeling strongly on tired topics' is surely an understatement. We must suppose that Calvus had followers who were active in 46. Cicero, of course, does not mention them in *Brutus*; but that is because he explicitly refrains from discussing living orators (*Brut.* 231), with only some exceptions *honoris causa*, such as those of Marcellus and Caesar, who are treated by the other interlocutors (248-62). Actually, he does speak of Atticists and imitators of Lysias in the present tense.[9] Moreover, a well-known passage in a letter to Atticus from 44 BCE (*Att.* 15.1a.2) makes it clear that Brutus was at least inclined to follow Calvus: Cicero there discusses a speech by Brutus and describes it as 'Attic' in the sense of the Atticists, i.e. elegant and unemotional.

What, then, of the virtual absence of Atticism from the earlier *de Oratore*? Contrary to what is usually assumed, the work may show some traces of the budding controversy,[10] but Atticism is still indeed at most a marginal concern. A natural explanation is that the movement was not yet strong enough to provoke Cicero to write a (lengthy) defence.

So, unless we are prepared to take Cicero for a complete fool, we may safely infer the following: the beginnings of Roman Atticism must be put between 60 and 55, with Calvus in a leading role; in 55, when writing *de Oratore*, Cicero did not yet consider the movement worth refuting at length; but after Calvus' death in 54/53, it gained more adherents and this forced Cicero to defend himself in 46. These statements, of course, do not exhaust the matter by far, but for my purpose they may serve as a starting point.

2.2 Dionysius and other Greeks

I can be fairly brief about the second relatively secure phase, which is marked especially by Dionysius of Halicarnassus and the man he once

---

[9] E.g., 64; 67; 285-91 *passim.*

[10] Esp. in 3.25-37: see the introduction to this passage in Leeman - Pinkster - Wisse (forthc.).

calls his 'dear friend',[11] Caecilius of Caleacte. Dionysius arrived in Rome in 30 or 29 BCE,[12] and probably not too long afterwards wrote what is for us an extremely valuable document: the *Preface* to *On the Ancient Orators*. Our own time, he writes, at last sees the victory of the Attic Muse over the mindless, bombastic style from Asia that has dominated from the time of the death of Alexander the Great. This resurgence and victory of the Attic style, he says, is due to the good taste of the Romans, the masters of the world (a point to which I will come back). What we see here is a Greek Atticism with the same basic characteristics as the Roman version of 30 years earlier.

However, there is one difference: Calvus had obviously designated Lysias and Hyperides as the only true models, but Dionysius values almost all the 'classic' Attic orators, not only Lysias and Hyperides, but also Demosthenes, and even the verbose Isocrates. On the other hand, his 'friend' Caecilius seems, like Calvus, to have favoured Lysias above all other models.

3. Intermezzo

So far, so good—more or less. Before tackling any further questions, it seems a good idea to try to characterise the Atticist movement a little more accurately and to formulate more clearly the chief problems that I want to address.

3.1 The nature of Atticism

When I call Atticism a 'movement', that is only because I know no better term. It was in fact a movement, if we understand the term loosely. For what Cicero describes, and what Dionysius describes, is not a movement in the sense of a closed school of thought, with official members, and an official policy and programme. It is, however, a movement in the sense of a fashion or a trend, based on a set of only more or less coherent ideas

---

[11] *Pomp.* 3.20, 240.14: τῷ φιλτάτῳ Καικιλίῳ.

[12] *Ant. Rom.* 1.3.4 with 1.7.2.

that is shared by a number of people. The variation in the choice of models well illustrates the absence of a coherent programme: the extremists, Calvus on the Roman side and perhaps Caecilius on the Greek, accept really only Lysias; Dionysius adds Demosthenes, Isocrates, Isaeus and others. What counts, then, is not whether someone subscribed to a definite programme, but whether he was an Atticist in his own eyes or in those of his contemporaries.[13] For instance, Cicero's letter mentioned above (*Att.* 15.1a.2) is enough reason to connect Brutus with the movement.

What the Roman and Greek variants conspicuously have in common is the rejection of the oratory and prose literature from the whole period that we call Hellenistic, i.e., the period beginning with the death of Alexander in 323: the style of this period is regarded as bombastic and labeled 'Asianism', as allegedly originating from Asia Minor. Accordingly, both variants had for their chief butt someone from this area and from this period, viz. Hegesias of Magnesia,[14] who lived ca. 300 BCE or somewhat later.

Thus in the Atticist view, literary history is divided into three periods: first, a 'classical' period, located in the glorious past of classical Athens; then, a falling off, a long period of decline and degeneration; and finally, their own time, which is at last striving to restore and revive the glory of the past. It seems a good idea, as Thomas Gelzer has advocated, to use the term 'classicism' for such a tripartite view of history.[15] Of course, it may be disputed whether or not this use of the term is really ideal, but for now at least, I will use it in this sense. A precise term for this concept is attractive because it alerts us to the fact that the same

---

[13] This implies that the history of the movement does not coincide in any straightforward manner with the history of oratorical styles: see below. Cf. also the sensible, though over-polemical remarks of Douglas (1973, 125-7).

[14] Cf. Cic. *Brut.* 286-7; *Orat.* 226; 230; D.H. *Comp.* 4.11, 9.9-15; 18.21-9, 79.9-84.3; Strabo 14.1.41.

[15] Gelzer 1979, esp. 9-12; actually, he adds the presence of a specific theory about the qualities that mark the 'classical' period.

tripartite view of history had asserted itself in a number of other disciplines already. I cannot reiterate the evidence here, but the same idea seems to have taken root in the visual arts as early as 150 BCE: at least some sculptors around that time saw themselves as reviving the high standards of the past after a period of decline that had started ca. 300 BCE.[16] The same pattern established itself in philosophy around 90 BCE at the latest: e.g., in the view of Antiochus of Ascalon, Plato and his immediate followers in the early Academy had devised the true philosophy, which had been betrayed in the period after that (see *Fin.* 5.9-14). In other words, classicism was rife in our period, and Atticism must surely be connected with this general trend.

Atticism, then, is by nature a form of classicism, i.e., it has this particular tripartite view of history. What deserves emphasis is that this view need by no means be true. To an important extent, it is a form of image building, for by this view the proponents of the movement proclaim themselves to be the restorers of the classical standards. Wilamowitz (1900, 1-8) already pointed out (and this was perhaps his most important contribution) that 'Asianism' was not, at least not originally, the name of a real movement or even of a real stylistic period: it was a term of abuse coined by the Atticists to disparage the period they rejected. This view of history may be untrue in another sense also: the proponents of a renewed 'Attic' style may try to attain this ideal and may try to write like their classical models, but this does not mean they will actually do so. To begin with, they are not necessarily imitating every aspect of their models. More importantly, they may be very bad judges of their own efforts. The style of Dionysius himself, it has been observed, was far less innovative and truly Attic than he would probably have liked to think. But this does not alter his view of himself or his ideals, and he remains an Atticist.[17]

---

[16] Plin. *Nat.* 34.49-52, cf. Preisshofen 1979, 269-71 .

[17] An extreme illustration of a discrepancy between stylistic ideal and stylistic practice is the much earlier case of Hegesias, who was later considered the typical Asianist, and whose fragments do show a style that is rather hard to

The discrepancy between theory and practice need cause no surprise, if only because to a native speaker of Greek, the inclusion of even a limited number of 'Atticisms' must already have given his style and language a recognisable Attic flavour. It does, however, imply that much caution is necessary in the analysis of the style of Dionysius and other Atticists. Only a very careful synthesis in the field of the stylistic practices of the relevant authors (and this is not yet, as far as I know, available)[18] would be meaningful here and could tell us something about the Atticist movement as such.

Much more could be said, especially about the relationship between language and style. That, however, would take us too far afield. It is time to go back to the rise of the movement.

3.2 The problem

What we have is two securely dated movements which are very much alike, the earlier one Roman, the slightly later one Greek. It is, to my mind, clearly unacceptable to separate them, as Dihle, for example, seems to do,[19] and to pretend they have little to do with each other. Most scholars have indeed posited some sort of connection. There are, however, quite a number of possibilities regarding the precise nature of this connection. First, as in the view of Norden (1898) and again of some moderns, the movement may be originally Greek, and early, i.e., stemming from the early second century BCE. The two movements we have looked at would then, probably, be independent descendants of this earlier one. A second possibility was favoured by Wilamowitz (1900, 31-51). It resembles the first, but puts the origin around 60 BCE with Greeks who

---

swallow: surprisingly, Hegesias considered himself a follower of Lysias! (*Brut.* 286: H. imitated Charisius who imitated Lysias; *Orat.* 226: H. imitated Lysias.)

[18] Lasserre 1979 is rather unsatisfactory.

[19] Dihle (1977, 176), mainly as a result of his excessive emphasis on the grammatical aspect. Thus also Douglas, explicitly (1973, 125 n. 89) or implicitly (1966, xii-xiv: only the Latin variant discussed), though he had earlier, with much hesitation, given the Greek side some attention (1955, 242-3).

worked in Rome. Both these variants are in line with the old and still dominant belief that the Romans, in the first place, took all their ideas from the Greeks, and in the second place, cannot possibly have influenced Greek thought. As to the latter point, many scholars, of course, have looked down on Dionysius of Halicarnassus (cf. Goudriaan 1989, 666-75), but it seems they usually looked down on the Romans even more: even in his case, the suggestion that he might have been influenced by Roman ideas has, until rather recently, hardly been seriously entertained. Bowersock, though with hesitation, broke at least this taboo, and advocated a third possibility (1979, esp. 67; cf. also Innes 1989, 245-6). Though he did cling to a Greek origin of the movement, around 65, he supposed that the Atticism of Calvus and his friends must have led to the Atticism of Dionysius. As I will presently set forth, my view, which may be regarded as a development of Kennedy's (1972, 241-2; 351-3), goes one step further: I think the movement was originally Roman, and was passed on to Greeks working in Rome.

In what follows, I shall begin by arguing that the first alternative, the early dating, is virtually impossible. Then I shall try to show that a Roman origin is the most natural hypothesis in view of what our sources tell us. And finally, I will address the question that was already a central issue in Bowersock's article: if Atticism was originally Roman, how did it reach Dionysius, Caecilius and their fellow Greeks?

4. The origins

Norden, in his *Antike Kunstprosa*, put the origins of Atticism ca. 200 BCE. The reason, it seems, was not so much a wish to avoid crediting the Romans with the movement, but his tendency to interpret every criticism of bombastic style as Atticism. He saw the whole history of style as a battle between Asianism and Atticism.[20] So when the early second

[20] See Norden 1898, esp. 149-51.

century geographer and historian Agatharchides (as quoted by Photius)[21] criticised Hegesias for his puerile and bombastic style, this was for Norden a sign of Atticism. However, this procedure would make even Aristotle into an Atticist, and it is fairly clear (as Radermacher already remarked (1899, 355)) that in Agatharchides' criticism the characteristic features of the Atticist movement were still lacking: he did not appeal to classical models, he did not call Hegesias an Asianist, and there is no sign of the classicistic three-period view of history.[22]

The early dating has recently been revived by Preisshofen in his contribution to the *Entretiens* on Classicism at Rome, published in 1979. And as the proceedings of this colloquium show, this dating was acceptable to most of the other participants. His reason is the turn to classicism in the visual arts around 150 BCE (mentioned above § 3), with the typical three-period scheme applied to art history. This scheme, he thinks, cannot have originated in theories of sculpture or painting, but must have derived from rhetoric. Therefore, rhetorical classicism, i.e. Atticism, must be earlier than 150 BCE That this should have been so readily accepted is a little surprising: it is unclear why rhetoric should be the first candidate for having devised the scheme. And what we know of second-century rhetoricians does not encourage the view: they were busy with other things, such as quarreling among themselves over *status* theory, and with the philosophers over education.

Some additional evidence is also available to date the movement in the first century. Cicero, in *Orator* 89, speaks of *istis novis Atticis*, 'these modern Attics'; in *Brutus* 284, he writes that Calvus *ipse errabat et alios etiam errare cogebat*, Calvus 'was in error himself and caused others to err with him'. Taken by itself, this might only concern the recent, Roman version of Atticism. However, Dionysius in his *Preface* also consistently speaks of Atticism as a fairly recent phenomenon, e.g. in 3.3, 6.8-9,

---

[21] Agatharch., *GGM* 1.119.33-122.24 = Phot. *Bibl.* 250 (446a16-447b5), containing Hegesias *FGrH* 142 T3; F 6-14.

[22] Radermacher is in general very good on the antecedents of Atticism (1899, 351-60), as on a number of other issues: his article deserves more attention.

where he talks of the change for the better: τηλικαύτης μεταβολῆς ἐν τούτῳ τῷ βραχεῖ χρόνῳ γεγενημένης ('such a great change having come about in this brief period of time').[23] The two passages from Cicero and the passage from Dionysius strongly confirm each other. They point to a date of ca. 60 BCE for the beginning of Atticism as a whole.

5. The originators

Who originated the movement? As I have already said, for most scholars it has been natural to posit a Greek origin. Wilamowitz is a good example. Having mentioned Dionysius' statement that Rome had a decisive influence, he writes (1900, 45), speaking about the 60's and 50's BCE: 'Schon damals galt, was er [Dionysius, JW] von Rom sagt, dass es als Centrum der Welt den Ton angab; aber Römer können ihn unmöglich angegeben haben'. The Greeks in Rome, Wilamowitz concluded, rethought their classics, and inaugurated classicism. Dihle (1977, 170-4) even thought he could pinpoint the Greek grammarian Philoxenus of Alexandria as the instigator of the Roman variant.[24]

But why, we must ask, should it have been Greeks? Let us see what Dionysius says in the beginning of the third chapter of his *Preface* (3.1, 5.21-6.1 U.-R.):

> αἰτία δ' οἶμαι καὶ ἀρχὴ τῆς τοσαύτης μεταβολῆς ἐγένετο ἡ πάντων κρατοῦσα Ῥώμη πρὸς ἑαυτὴν ἀναγκάζουσα τὰς ὅλας πόλεις ἀποβλέπειν καὶ ταύτης τε αὐτῆς οἱ δυναστεύοντες κατ' ἀρετὴν καὶ ἀπὸ τοῦ κρατίστου τὰ κοινὰ διοικοῦντες, εὐπαίδευτοι πάνυ καὶ γενναῖοι τὰς κρίσεις γενόμενοι, ὑφ' ὧν κοσμούμενον τό

[23] Cf. 1.1, 3.5 τῷ καθ' ἡμᾶς χρόνῳ; 1.2, 3.10 ἐν ... τοῖς πρὸ ἡμῶν χρόνοις; 2.2, 4.23 ὁ καθ' ἡμᾶς χρόνος; 2.3, 5.6) τὸν παρόντα χρόνον; 2.3, 5.10 ταχεῖαν τὴν μεταβολήν (cf. 2.4, 5.11-4); 2.5, 5.18 νεωστί. Dionysius' wording is not very precise and can easily be brought in line with Cicero's testimony (*contra* Dihle 1977, 164).

[24] Though not of the Greek variant (cf. above with n. 19).

τε φρόνιμον <ἑκάσ>της[25] πόλεως μέρος ἔτι μᾶλλον ἐπιδέδωκεν καὶ τὸ ἀνόητον ἠνάγκασται νοῦν ἔχειν.

'I think the cause and the origin (ἀρχή) of this great change to be almighty Rome which forces all the cities to look to her for guidance, and those who rule her virtuously and administer the world in all good faith: they are well educated and noble in their judgements, and because they have honoured the sensible element of <each> city this has gained even more strength, and the foolish element has been forced to be sensible.'

In itself, this is not decisive. I don't think we should insist on ἀρχή, 'origin'; Dionysius does not clearly speak about the origin of the movement, only about the reason for its success. Moreover, he might just be flattering his patrons. But let us again look at *Brutus* 284: Calvus 'was in error himself and caused others to err with him'. If we take this at all seriously, as I think we must, Calvus himself was the originator of the movement. This may be clinched by the following observation: in *de Oratore*, Cicero repeatedly ridicules Greek rhetoricians and their like as impractical and pretentious people. If Atticism had been originated by Greeks, it is therefore hard to imagine that he would have missed the opportunity to ridicule it in *Brutus* and *Orator* as one of those fanciful and impractical Greek notions; after all, the impractical nature of Atticism is one of his persistent arguments against it (e.g. *Brut.* 289-90). But he does nothing of the sort: neither *Brutus* nor *Orator* contains even a hint at such a Greek origin. The coterie of Calvus, then, produced not only the neoteric poets, but also Atticism, with Calvus himself in the leading role. And in 46, as we have seen, Brutus and others were still continuing the movement.

---

[25] In the context, the τῆς πόλεως of the MSS seems impossible to interpret. Hurst (1982, 859) seems to take it as referring to Rome, which doesn't make much sense; the reference of 'de la cité' in Aujac's Budé ed. is unclear to me; and Usher, in his Loeb edition, translates 'of the population'! A distributive phrase is called for, referring (as does the earlier πόλεις) to the Greek cities.

6. The transmission

This seems to leave us with a problem: how did an originally Roman movement manage to influence Greek rhetoricians? It is again Bowersock who has addressed this issue, for although he thinks a Greek must have been initially responsible for Roman Atticism (1979, 63), he does take Dionysius seriously (1979, 66), and reckons with decisive Roman influence on the Greek movement. Bowersock's own solution, however, is slightly odd. He writes that 'the relation between the two Atticist movements can be most naturally explained by reference to Q. Aelius Tubero, the patron of Dionysius' (1979, 68): it is Tubero who 'reviewed with [Dionysius] the whole controversy over Atticism and Asianism' (1979, 69). Here we see the prosopographical method, with its reliance on individual relationships, at its weakest. Is Dionysius supposed to have reacted with so much enthusiasm that he took it upon himself to spread the word to all the Greek cities? Such a restricted, personal transmission is already implausible in itself.

Moreover, in his *Preface* Dionysius writes about a broad Greek movement, which has already been going on for some (short) time; and in the passage just quoted in § 5, he mentions the influence of Romans (in the plural). What seems to have happened is that the movement spread through intensive contacts between Roman and Greek intellectuals, probably at first in Rome, though soon also elsewhere.[26] That is to say, in more fashionable terms, there must have been an intellectual network in Rome consisting of both Greeks and Romans.

Now the concept of a 'network' is a very useful one, but we must beware of possible misunderstandings. Quite recently, I heard a Renaissance scholar use it in the sense of 'circle': he spoke of some humanist 'and his network'; and if we don't look out, the 'Scipionic circle', which

---

[26] Innes (1989, 246) likewise suggests 'mutual cross-fertilisation between Greeks and Romans' regarding Atticism, but with much hesitation, and in a context where she stresses a general 'Greek lack of interest in Roman literature' (1989, 245). Like most others, she seems to assume that the movement probably started among Greeks, though again with much (justified) caution.

has at last been ruled out of court, will enter again under the name of the 'Scipionic network'. This is not what I am referring to when I use the term 'network'. What I mean to say is that there must have been many contacts, of various sorts and varying intensity, between numerous Greek and Roman intellectuals.

Now it may well be asked whether there is any other evidence, apart from Atticism itself, for such a network, and for the hypothesis that Greeks seriously took notice of the Romans and their ideas. There is indeed such evidence. Already in the 60's and 50's BCE at least some of the numerous Greeks who worked in Rome as grammarians, rhetoricians, etc., occupied themselves with the Latin language and Latin literature. Elizabeth Rawson has assembled the evidence. We may think, for example,[27] of Cornelius Epicadus, a freedman of Sulla's, who wrote, among other things, on the technical subject of Roman cognomina. There was Alexander Polyhistor, who must have used Latin sources for his history of Rome; Ateius Philologus, who also dealt with Greek and Latin, worked until perhaps 30 BCE. This already takes us much further in time—and there must be much more material, into the Augustan age.

Let me illustrate this by means of the case of a remarkable though far from likeable man: L. Cestius Pius. Despite his Roman name, he was a Greek, who had made a name for himself as a rhetorician or declaimer in his native Smyrna or in Asia in general. Already in that stage of his career, he vehemently disliked and attacked Cicero, as appears from the following anecdote that Seneca the Elder tells us (*Suas*. 7.12-3). Cicero's son, governor of Asia somewhere in the 20's, once invited Cestius to a dinner party. Cicero Junior was in his cups and kept forgetting who Cestius was, so finally a slave said: *hic est Cestius, qui patrem tuum negabat litteras scisse* ('this is Cestius, the one who said that your father couldn't read and write'). Young Cicero was not pleased: he had Cestius flogged immediately—which, Seneca says, was only right. Now Cestius,

---

[27] Also, a number of Greek grammarians took Latin to be derived from the Greek Aeolic dialect, and even wrote works 'On the Latin language': Hypsicrates of Amisus, Philoxenus, Tyrannio (the Elder or the Younger: cf. Rawson 1985, 69).

we may venture to say, took his revenge: he came to Rome to become one of the most famous and sharp-tongued declaimers of Augustan times; he is mentioned very frequently by Seneca the Elder, where he appears, even for a declaimer, as an extremely conceited and aggressive man. But what is most remarkable about him is that, though a Greek (cf. Sen. *Con.* 9.3.13), he only declaimed in Latin. Moreover, a famous pupil of his, Argentarius, also a Greek, did the same (*ib.*). And from the way Seneca reports this, it is clear that though such a restriction was unusual, a Greek declaiming in Latin was in itself not at all considered exceptional.

This is, I think, already strong evidence for the existence of a truly Graeco-Roman cultural 'network' throughout the relevant period, but it must be only a fraction of what can be found. Although I have not yet looked systematically at the material, I think that Seneca the Elder is bound to yield more.[28] What I hope to be able to do in the near future is to attempt to reconstruct at least part of this network, just as the late Elizabeth Rawson has done for the end of the Republican period. In my opinion there is a real challenge here, for a number of developments, such as that of Augustan literature as a whole, might need to be rethought from this perspective.[29]

7. Conclusion

However that may turn out, I hope to have shown that, despite the confusing number of opinions on the beginnings of Atticism, it may not, in the end, be too hard to choose between them and to devise an overall picture. Of course, I have left aside several issues and glossed over some problems that may turn out to be nasty ones, especially that of the relation between language and style; not to mention the question of the subsequent

---

[28] See already the list of the declaimers mentioned by Seneca in Bornecque 1902, 143-201.

[29] I have not been able to take into account White's study (1993), which seems to offer a very interesting analysis of Augustan poetry in the context of a chiefly Roman network.

history of the movement in Latin and in Greek and the light this might throw on its beginnings. Also, the material is scanty, and every new piece of evidence may shatter all our carefully constructed schemes. Nevertheless, considering the actual evidence we have, I hope my picture, as it is, is a plausible one: it was in the coterie of Calvus that Atticism took shape ca. 60 BCE; it spread through a Graeco-Roman network, to emerge, for us, as a Greek phenomenon in Dionysius of Halicarnassus. And as to this Graeco-Roman network, it will no doubt be possible to unearth some representatives who are less repulsive than Cestius Pius.

BIBLIOGRAPHY

Bornecque, H., *Les déclamations et les déclamateurs d'après Sénèque le Père*. Lille 1902.

Bowersock, G.W., Historical Problems in Late Republican and Augustan Classicism, in: *Le classicisme à Rome* (1979), 57-75.

Le classicisme à Rome aux 1ers siècles avant et après J.-C., ed. H. Flashar. (Entretiens sur l'antiquité classique 25). Vandoeuvres-Genève 1979.

Dihle, A., Analogie und Attizismus, *Hermes* 85 (1957), 170-205.

———, Der Beginn des Attizismus, *A&A* 23 (1977), 162-77.

Douglas, A.E., M. Calidius and the Atticists, *CQ* 5 (1955), 241-7.

———, *M. Tulli Ciceronis Brutus*. Oxford 1966.

———, The Intellectual Background of Cicero's *Rhetorica*: A Study in Method, *ANRW* I.3 (1973), 95-138.

Gelzer, Th., Klassizismus, Attizismus und Asianismus, in: *Le classicisme à Rome* (1979), 1-41.

Goudriaan, K., *Over classicisme. Dionysius van Halicarnassus en zijn program van welsprekendheid, cultuur en politiek*. Unpublished diss. Vrije Universiteit Amsterdam, 1989.

Hurst, A., Un critique grec dans la Rome d'Auguste: Denys d'Halicarnasse, *ANRW* II.30.1 (1982), 839-65.

Innes, D.C., Augustan Critics, in: G.A. Kennedy (ed.), *The Cambridge History of Literary Criticism. Vol. I: Classical Criticism*. Cambridge 1989, 245-73 (ch. 8).

Kaibel, G., Dionysios von Halikarnass und die Sophistik, *Hermes* 20 (1885), 497-513.

Kennedy, G., *The Art of Rhetoric in the Roman World*. Princeton 1972.

Lasserre, F., Prose grecque classicisante, in: *Le classicisme à Rome* (1979), 135-63.

Leeman, A.D. - H. Pinkster - J. Wisse, *M. Tullius Cicero. De oratore libri III: Kommentar. 4. Band: Buch II,291-367; Buch III,1-95*. Heidelberg (forthcoming).

Münzer, F., Licinius 113, Pauly - Wissowa, *Realenzyklopädie* 13.1 (1926), 428-35.

Norden, E., *Die antike Kunstprosa vom VI. Jh. v. Chr. bis in die Zeit der Renaissance*. Leipzig 1898.

Preisshofen, F., Kunsttheorie und Kunstbetrachtung, in: *Le classicisme à Rome* (1979), 263-77.

Radermacher, L., Studien zur Geschichte der antiken Rhetorik IV: Ueber die Anfänge des Atticismus, *RhM* 54 (1899), 351-74.

Rawson, E., *Intellectual Life in the Late Roman Republic*. Baltimore 1985.

Rohde, E., *Der griechische Roman und seine Vorläufer*. Leipzig 1876.

———, Die asianische Rhetorik und die zweite Sophistik, *RhM* 41 (1886), 170-90.

Schenkeveld, D.M., *Iudicia vulgi:* Cicero, *De oratore* 3.195 ff. and *Brutus* 183 ff., *Rhetorica* 6 (1988), 291-305.

Schmid, W., *Der Atticismus in seinen Hauptvertretern* (5 vols.). Stuttgart 1887-1897.

———, *Ueber den kulturgeschichtlichen Zusammenhang und die Bedeutung der griechischen Renaissance in der Römerzeit* (Antrittsrede Tübingen). Leipzig 1898.

Sumner, G.V., *The Orators in Cicero's Brutus: Prosopography and Chronology* (Phoenix Suppl. XI). Toronto 1973.

White, P., *Promised Verse. Poets in the Society of Augustan Rome*. Cambridge, MA - London 1993.

Wilamowitz-Moellendorff, U. von, Asianismus und Atticismus, *Hermes* 35 (1900), 1-52.

Οἱ κριτικοί: A Reassessment

James I. Porter*

1. The problem: finding common ground

Any discussion of the '*kritikoi*'—the euphonist literary critics known to us from Philodemus—must perforce begin with their name, and then with their names. The difficulty is that we only have the names of a handful of critics (Heracleodorus, a certain 'Milesian', Andromenides, Crates of Mallos) and the name, or rather the label, they appear to share ('*kritikoi*'); but nowhere in the extant fragments of Philodemus' *On Poems* are the two kinds of name conjoined.[1] No named critic is ever called a '*kritikos*' by Philodemus, not even Crates. Look elsewhere and you look in vain: none of Philodemus' euphonist opponents are mentioned by any ancient source, with the exception of Andromenides and Crates, while

* It is a great pleasure to present this essay in honour of Dirk Schenkeveld, who is one of the pioneers on the subject of *οἱ κριτικοί* in Philodemus. The essay represents work in progress, and it was prompted in part by recent work that is also in progress. It therefore remains partly conjectural. Special thanks are due to David Blank, Richard Janko, André Laks, to participants of the Philodemus conference held at UCLA in May of 1994, to the editors of this volume, and to the generosity of the International Institute and the office of the Rackham Dean at the University of Michigan, for a travel grant which permitted me to participate in the symposium on post-Aristotelian Criticism in Amsterdam in April of 1994.

[1] The name of an erstwhile 'Pausimachos' turns out to have been a phantom, in the light of Constantina Romeo's recent autopsy.

these latter are nowhere else associated with euphonist criticism.[2] The problem I have just outlined is surely one of the more puzzling enigmas in the history of literary criticism. How could an entire school of thought vanish almost without a trace, as unexpectedly as it appeared?

One answer has been powerfully, and persuasively, put forward by David Blank (1994): the school never existed to begin with, at least not as a self-conscious group that called themselves '*kritikoi*'. 'Rather,' Blank writes, 'the name is Philodemus' own device for referring to particular theorists who he believed had certain views in common' (1994, 55; cf. 60 n. 28). This must surely be right, as far as Philodemus' use of the name is concerned. But the argument that '[p]robably all these theorists held different views, from which Philodemus abstracts ... one point in common' (roughly, a concession to the sense of hearing in the evaluation of poetry, *ib.*, 61) leaves the door open to an even stronger implication, one not clearly endorsed or rejected by Blank. For implicitly there is the worry that Philodemus has fashioned his collection of critics by looking to their lowest common denominator. And if he has, then the '*kritikoi*' could turn out to share very little in common at all—or else, too much.[3] I believe that this worry, which is a valid and interesting one, can be turned around by putting it in a different form. If the theorists in question do not form a school, how identifiable are they as a group? And given that

---

[2] On the early history of the term '*kritikos*', cf. Clem. *Strom.* 1.16.79; Sch. D.Thr. 3.24, 448.6; Pfeiffer 1968, 157-8; and generally Schenkeveld 1968, 177-9. The term is never a sure index of critical affiliations, e.g., D.L. 7.200 (SVF 2.16, Chrysippus' work Πρὸς τοὺς κριτικούς); Plu. 1095c = Epic. fr. 5 Us. (cf. 1096a); ps.-Plato *Ax.* 366e (see Russell 1989, 21). In none of these cases do we know that the critics in question espoused a theory of euphony, or that they didn't. Other occurrences of the term clearly rule out the reductive implications assigned to euphony by the Philodemean '*kritikoi*', e.g. Schol. in D.H. *Aesch. Or.* 3.90 = vol. 5, p. 254 U.-R.; Schol. in Dem. 307b1.

[3] This is at least suggested by one of the formulations by Demetrius of Laconia of a position that appears to be identical to, or consistent with, their theory: 'reason along with hearing' (cf. Blank 1994, 61). So stated, Aristoxenus, Diogenes of Babylonia, and Andromenides all qualify for the title of '*kritikos*', which now threatens to be voided of distinctive significance.

Philodemus, at least, seems to have been successful at identifying them as a group, how likely is it that they could have failed to make the same identification themselves?

This last question can only be answered speculatively. But it is not a matter of speculation that the range of euphony theories found in Philodemus is remarkably narrow. They all represent some version of the thesis that the presence or absence of euphony alone, which is judged by the ear, determines whether a poem is good or bad (cf. Blank 1994, 60). And since this is the case, the euphonism espoused by these critics must have been not only a feature of their criticism, but distinctive of it as well. In a word, the '*kritikoi*' known to us only through Philodemus were reductively and prominently euphonist. This can hardly be accidental, and it is surely significant. The relevant question to ask, then, is not why the '*kritikoi*' vanish outside of Philodemus, but how Philodemus comes to report them at all. One clue is to be found in a passage that on Richard Janko's new ordering of the papyri would fall at least 75 columns, or a little less than half-way, into a book of *On Poems* (whether it is Book 1 or 2 is still controversial).[4] Here, someone in the first person, probably Philodemus,[5] promises to 'demolish those of their <arguments> which will be thought to establish their common ground, *which is inconsistent with my view too*' (ἐγὼ δ[ὲ τού]των ἀναιρήσομαι τὰ ν̣[ο]μισθησόμενα τὸ κοινὸν κατασκευάζειν, ὃ κἀμοὶ μάχεται, *P.Herc.* 460 fr. 24.5-9 = Tr. B fr. 19 = col. 75* Janko). We can reject the idea that Philodemus has imposed a group identity on his opponents *tout court*, for the simple

[4] Cited after Janko's edition in progress (forthcoming), whose translations I have followed throughout. Janko's systematic re-ordering of the columns, which is still tentative (hence the asterisks), is convincing, but it remains to be proved (he assigns the fragment to *On Poems* 1). On Dorandi's competing reconstruction of the treatise (Dorandi 1992 and 1993; cf. Hausrath 1889), the fragment falls in the middle of *On Poems* 2. A note on underscored Greek characters which appear below: these represent a change made by an editor in the reading of either the papyri or the *disegni*, according to the convention being adopted by the Philodemus Translation Project.

[5] So Schächter 1928, 444; Hausrath 1889, 234; Blank 1994; and now Janko, who formerly supposed the speaker to be Crates (*ad loc.*).

reason that some of that identity has already been constituted in advance for him. The telltale phrase ὃ κἀμοὶ μάχεται suggests this by itself. Philodemus, I wish to argue, has been preempted by Crates of Mallos.[6] This will not affect the general thesis that Philodemus in some sense consolidates the euphonists, but it will give him a new rationale for doing so, and it will help us to pinpoint in just what sense he does consolidate them.

Here it will prove useful to follow Philodemus in making a distinction he was capable of making, namely between Crates on the one hand and the '*kritikoi*' taken as an ensemble on the other. As emerges from *On Poems* 5, Crates and the '*kritikoi*' he opposes himself to (cf. ὃ πρὸς τοὺς κριτικοὺς λέγει, col. 27.7-8 Mangoni) are not in perfect agreement over the issues involved in euphonic criticism, and Philodemus will have known this in the same way that he came to know about these other critics at all: through the polemics of Crates. This thesis has most recently been advanced by Richard Janko, to whose forthcoming edition the present essay is greatly indebted. Crates enjoys an exceptional prominence in Philodemus' treatise, and Philodemus' dependency on him for information about the '*kritikoi*' is to be suspected.[7] I believe that this insight can be refined, and the acuity of Blank's thesis has provided a good stimulus to do so. But for now, I wish to focus on the problem of the identity of views that can be seen to obtain among Philodemus' euphonist opponents

---

[6] The situation is in fact parallel to another in Demetrius of Laconia's *On Poems*, which is well described by Blank: 'Demetrius, like Philodemus, criticizes both groups of theorists and individuals against the background of those groups; perhaps the individual is his source, while the group consists of those cited in his source' (1994, 61).

[7] In columns prior to col. 75* we can detect Crates' polemics with other euphonists; these continue into the sequel. This was first noticed by Jensen (1923, 159) and developed by Schächter (1928, 444). See further Rispoli 1986, 118-34 and 119 n. 16. Philodemus' dependence on Crates is an easy inference to make based on *On Poems* 5 alone (see below; and, e.g., Asmis 1991, 146). Janko's brilliant systematisation of the surviving papyri from *On Poems* makes a compelling case for extending this insight into *P.Herc.* 994 (Bk 2 or 3) and into other parts of Book 1*.

against a polemical background that is *not* of Philodemus' making. Only a radically incomplete sketch will be possible. I leave aside the question of the name these critics shared ('*kritikoi*'), or rather, how Crates' opponents acquired this label: the question is secondary to the issue of what it is that joins and separates Crates and the '*kritikoi*', which is to say, what it is that will have *prompted* Philodemus to treat them in the way that he does (in what way remains to be seen). In what immediately follows, my comments will be organised around three general areas in which Crates and the '*kritikoi*' can be seen to have both converged and diverged in their views on literature. This discussion will eventually lead to an alternative picture of the way it came about that Philodemus sought to establish their 'common ground'.

1.1 τὸ ἴδιον

The concept of 'the particular' is possibly the most distinctive article of faith held in common by Crates and the '*kritikoi*', and the cornerstone of their other teachings. Since this is the least controversial element of their euphonism, I will restrict myself to what I take to be its more controversial implications. The doctrine is plainly spelled out in a passage from *P.Herc.* 1676 col. 6, which gives us one of the better attested mentions of '*kritikoi*' in *On Poems*:[8] 'it stands as <engraved> in [stone] for all the *kritikoi* that euphony, which appears on the surface <of a composition [*synthesis*]>, is *idion* ["particular"; or "peculiar to it"], while the meanings and the expressions must be concluded to be external and common (*koinon*)'.[9] The thrust of this position is not just that the specific nature of poems lies in their sound, but that their value *as poems* lies in this single dimension. Poems are valued on the basis of verbal arrangement

---

[8] Of the six instances in which the term '*kritikos*' appears to have survived in *On Poems*, only three are secure enough to warrant discussion (these will be discussed below).

[9] *καὶ τὸ τὴν μὲν | [ἐπιφαι]ν̣ομένην [ε]ὐφωνί | αν ἴδιον [εἶν]αι, τὰ δὲ νοή{ι} | ματα καὶ [τ]ὰς λέξεις ἐκτὸς | εἶναι καὶ κοινὰ συνάγεσ | θαι δεῖ[ν, πα]ρὰ πᾶσι μὲν ὡς | ἐν̣ [στή λ]ηι μέ[ν]ε̣ι τοῖς κρι | τικοῖ[ς* (*P.Herc.* 1676 col. 6 = Tr. C col. 17; cf. Romeo 1992, 166-7).

(*synthesis*), which in turn is valued both for the pleasant sound it gives rise to and *per se*—these amount to the same thing—, but without regard for meaning, which is to say all that is encompassed by plots and characters and even places (everything, in other words, that falls under *hypothesis*). As another fragment puts it, 'Good poets are first in their class and alone endure through no other reason than the sounds' that their poetry gives rise to (col. 75*). To hold this is already to hold quite a lot. And it is to exclude quite a lot as well.

One casualty of this critical reduction is the relation of appropriateness (*to prepon*) that conventionally binds together meaning and expression.[10] That is the plain lesson of a neighboring column,[11] but it also flows from their view of what is *idion*. There need be no *necessary* correlation between expression and what is expressed, because neither is central to the poet's primary objective: *psychagogia* through euphony. Moral concerns fall by the wayside (once poems are looked at *as* poems, καθὸ ποιήματα), as do concerns for clarity. Meaning needn't even be recognisable, 'so long as <the poet> doesn't fail at what is his *idion*' (euphony).[12] The tool of *metathesis*, or rearranging verses, was an attempt to prove this very point: change the shape of a verse and its *idion* will be lost, even though the meaning and the words haven't changed.[13] Here, the '*kritikoi*' surprisingly distance themselves from Eratosthenes (Strab. 1.2.3). Euphonic pleasure (*psychagogia*), tied to properties other than the formal ones isolated by Eratosthenes, is immediate and somatic; it is an intimate pleasure of the body, and inaccessible to the mind, which cannot take in the sensuous particularities of poems. Meanwhile, the mind enjoys pleasures of its own, namely those which the artistry of poems

---

[10] Schenkeveld 1968, 186.

[11] *P.Herc.* 1676 col. 4.9-17 = Tr. C col. 15; cf. Andromenides, *ap. P.Herc.* 1081a fr. 40 = Tr. D fr. 4 = 145*.

[12] 1047a fr. 21 + 1081a fr. 8 = Tr. C col. 2.

[13] Cf. *P.Herc.* 1676 cols. 6-7 = Tr. C cols. 17-18; 1073a fr. 19.1-3 = Tr. B fr. 35 = 65*.

gives rise to (what might be called the 'critical' pleasures), for art and technique are the less immediate but no less important cause of sounds that please the ear. Accounting for the immediate and 'remoter' pleasures of poetry on one and the same theory leads to interesting dilemmas and potential misunderstandings. Not surprisingly, there are traces of a debate between Crates and the '*kritikoi*' on some of this.[14] These differences notwithstanding, on one point there was unanimous agreement: the particulars of poetry afford unrivalled pleasure, and even ecstasy of a sort. Poetry, so conceived, is in many ways sublime.[15] It may just turn out that the real source of ecstasy lies not in the application of the theory, but in its postulation. But that is another story.

1.2 Synthesis and sound

Sounds may be naturally beautiful or ugly, but sounds do not occur in isolation, and in fact they do not occur naturally at all whenever they do occur. Rather, they appear in combination (in *synthesis*), and anyway, what a poet is after is not sound but euphony. Thus, *xi* or *sigma* can be

---

[14] Thus, Crates' occasional complaint that his opponents failed to spell out the 'causes' of poetic excellence misleadingly suggests that they denied the existence of such causes. His appeal to the element which 'actualises' excellence (*P.Herc.* 460 fr. 27b = Tr. B fr. 21 + 1073a fr. 17 = B fr. 20 col. 2 = 66*) isn't foreign to at least one of his opponents: *πρὸς μέντοι τ[ὸ] | γράφεσθαι τὸ πόημα ἴσον | ἔν τε τῆι ὕλῃι καὶ τῶι ἐνερ | γοῦντι αὐτήν κτλ* (*ib.*, 6-9). But some of the dispute is over the question whether composition or euphony is the 'cause', not whether the artist lies causally behind the one factor or the other (see below).

[15] One might profitably compare the use of *καιρίως* in *On the Sublime* 1.4, a somewhat depreciated *hyphos* ('whole texture') standing to the poem as *poiesis* the way *hypsos* ('sublimity') stands to the poem as *poiema*, which is to say, as euphony, pleasure, exaltation, domination—all notions set to critical work by Crates and the '*kritikoi*'. There are other parallels, for instance sound that is 'noble', 'binding' metaphors (e.g., glue) as applied to verbal compositions, and Corybantic ecstasies (which can be linked back with [Long.] 1.4 by way of D.H. *Dem.* 22, a passage much indebted to the '*kritikoi*'). Needless to say, *synthesis* is reckoned one of the five 'sources' of sublimity at [Long.] 8.1.

either pleasant or unpleasant in combination with other letters,[16] even if, when taken in isolation (as ἁπλῆ φωνή), they will be one or the other;[17] sounds can be mixed well or badly; sounds in sequence create 'modifications' (πτώσεις)[18] as do repetitions;[19] prosodic features, like accents and aspirations, can affect the sounds negatively or positively.[20] The examples are all from Crates, who seems to be taking a hard line against other euphonist theories.[21] What he would have us believe, though his statements do not always support him, is that it is the individual sounds themselves, and not their *synthesis* (arrangement), that contain all the 'reasons' or 'causes' one needs to account for aural pleasure or pain (ὁ ἦχ[ος] | αἴτιός ἐστ[ι]ν).[22] His current adversary, apparently one of the '*kritikoi*' and an advocate of *synthesis*, seems to have been indifferent to the intrinsic sound qualities of letters, on the same principle as is enunciated elsewhere in *On Poems*, namely that 'what is pleasant to the hearing and what is [enunciated] with difficulty are identical' (*P.Herc.* 994 frr. 22.22-23.1 = Tr. A cols. e-f), by which must be meant that these things *can* be identical, depending on how the sounds are arranged.[23] This adversary and other critics like him held that *synthesis*

[16] *P.Herc.* 460 fr. 22 = Tr. B fr. 7 col. 1 = 78*.

[17] *P.Herc.* 460 fr. 19 + fr. 14a.12 = Tr. B fr. 5 col. 1 = 81*; cf. 994 fr. 20.25 = Tr. A col. c.

[18] *ib.* 81*; cf. *P.Herc.* 1073a fr. 9b = Tr. B 23 col. 1 = 99*.

[19] 81*.

[20] *P.Herc.* 460 fr. 6 = Tr. B fr. 9 col. 2 = 108*.

[21] Cf. Rispoli 1986, 133; Janko, *ad loc.*

[22] *P.Herc.* 460 fr. 14.24-5 = Tr. B fr. 6 col. 1 = 92*; cf. 78*.

[23] At *P.Herc.* 1676 cols. 8-12 = Tr. C cols. 19-23 a '*kritikos*' is under discussion, one who seems to hold that *synthesis*, not the sounds *per se*, can alter the relative ease or difficulty of pronouncing sounds (cf. esp. col. 8); a similar view reappears later in the same book (*P.Herc.* 994 fr. 10 = Tr. A fr. 10).

is the cause of pleasure; they reasoned, for example, that if a repetition of sounds causes pleasure, the cause is in the repetition, not in the sound that is repeated. Crates appears to be denying this,[24] and the same lack of agreement is reported in Book 5. The conflict is too easily stereotyped as a difference over the value of euphony (the absolute value of euphonic sounds) as against *synthesis* (their relative and relational value). But this is *prima facie* unlikely: euphony is not a sound but a product of sounds. Why should Crates have resisted this obvious conclusion? Chance euphony is not a sign of poetic excellence in Crates' eyes (*On Poems* 5 cols. 27-8); sounds must be artistically *arranged* to be aesthetically compelling; and this concession to arrangement is made in several of his teachings as enumerated above. Let me briefly launch a different hypothesis about how this divergence between Crates and the opposition played itself out.

All his claims about the native qualities of letters as sounded notwithstanding, Crates in fact proceeds on the opposite assumption. He compares two Homeric phrases, ἐρευγομένης ἁλὸς ἔξω (*Il.* 17.265) and ὀρυκτὴν τείχεος ἐκτός (*Il.* 9.67 = 20.49). Both 'cause great delight due to their sound; but if we exchange them [i.e., the two prepositions], we change them for the worse'. And so, he concludes, 'there is no other cause apart from the *sounds*'.[25] Let us note three anomalies: first, Crates is focusing not on the native sounds of letters but on their *accents* (if you like, their 'accidents'); second, he is admiring not sounds in isolation but as elements in a *sequence* (here, one in which substituting ἔξω for ἐκτός would disrupt the dappled effect of alternating pitches); third, the sounds of the letters taken by *themselves* display no obviously pleasant characteristics (none that are in question, at least).[26] So, what is to be made of

---

[24] As in *P.Herc.* 460 fr. 5 = Tr. B fr. 4 col. 1 = 111*, where cacophony, unpronounceability and displeasure are causally linked together by Crates.

[25] *P.Herc.* 1073a fr. 9a = Tr. B fr. 23 col. 1 + 1073a fr. 15b = fr. 10 col. 1 = 85*; for discussion of the details of this passage, see Janko, *ad loc.*

[26] As Janko well points out, *ad loc.*

Crates' theory of euphony based on sound, as opposed to combination? Crates himself gives the answer: 'Just as in an instrument, and even more so in a bow, there will be no harmony *in the whole* (ἐν τοῖς ὅλοις)' unless there is 'relaxation and tension'.

Clearly, Crates' theory of *stoicheia* is a theory about the dynamic *relations* that obtain among the letters and the sound-effects produced thereby 'in the whole' far more than it is about the natures of individual sounds in some absolute and unchanging sense. And even if Crates' focus in the present passage is not meter *per se* but the natural accents of words, as Rispoli has remarked (1986, 127), whatever these accents are 'by nature' is crucially overridden by their artistic arrangement, and this is the source of aesthetic pleasure. Would the '*kritikoi*' disagree? Not in principle, surely; they can hardly have meant anything else.[27] But their means of illustration might have differed from Crates'. We do not know, for instance, that they applied euphonic criteria to word-accents (although in this Crates was preceded by the musicologists and by Hieronymus of Rhodes).[28] The refusal of Crates' opponent to correlate sound quality with ease of pronunciation—which doesn't please Crates—is just another way of reaching after a standard of euphony, and it is a pungent lesson in the overriding goal they both shared: accounting for pleasing *collocations* of sound.[29] On the fundamental issues—euphony, the prerequisites of artistry and technique, and even the fact of arrangement—there can have been no disagreement. At stake, at times, may be at most a difference of taste. (The euphonic criterion is far from being stable, or immune to subjective disagreements.) But the bulk of the evidence suggests that

---

[27] Cf. Ardizzoni 1953, 84-90; Pace 1992, 91-2, n. 4.

[28] Aristox. *Harm.* 10.24, 18.15 Meib.; Hieron. *ap.* Philod. *Rhet.* 4 cols. 16a.13-18a.8; D.H. *Isoc.* 13 = fr. 52 Wehrli; see Janko *ad loc.* for discussion.

[29] Much as he might have wished to, Crates can't seek refuge in the claim that there are two different and exclusive activities, the 'collocation' of sounds (e.g. *synaphe*) and the *synthesis* of sounds or of linguistic components taken as sound (cf. Rispoli 1986, 133): these are one and the same thing. On *synthesis* as 'letter-arrangement', cf. Schenkeveld 1968, 198.

Crates' quarrels with the '*kritikoi*' were not over matters of taste (for instance, whether a given verse from Homer is euphonic or not), but over the way to account for and evaluate sound. The supreme value of sound with respect to meaning is, however, axiomatic on both accounts.

1.3 Sense and sensation

Any discussion of meaning must start with a bewildering passage from Book 5 (it was alluded to earlier), in which Crates is reported as saying that 'it is not convincing to praise the sense [i.e., meaning], on the grounds that this sort of thing <sc., the sense> is outside art (*a-technos*)'. If that is what he stated, Philodemus writes, '<then> what he says against the *kritikoi* he would himself be rejecting, when <in fact> they agree <with him> that the sense is outside art, <nor is it> known by the mind but by the trained sense of hearing—which explains why he praises the sense too.'[30] There are textual difficulties with the passage, which comes late in the exposition and is compressed; but some of the contortion must be due less to Philodemus' visible desire to convict Crates of self-contradiction than to Crates' confusing polemics. Here, a parallel text shows that we must mentally supply a missing adverb: 'it is unconvincing to praise the sense *εὐθύς*, *without further ado*', 'whenever the sense <of hearing> (*ἡ αἴσθησις*) receives pleasure'.[31] Both parties

---

[30] *εἴπερ ἔτ' εἶπε τὸ "μ̣ὴ | πιθανὸν εἶναι τὴν δι | άνοιαν ἐπαινεῖν, ἀτέ | χνου γε δὴ τοῦ τοιούτου | ὄντος", ὃ πρὸς τοὺς κριτι | κοὺς λέγει παραιτο[ῖτ] ἄν, | ὁμολογούντων ἄτεχνον | εἶναι, <οὐδ' εἶναι> λόγωι τ[ε]τριμμέ | νηι δ' ἀκοῆι̣ γνωστόν, <δι> | όπερ καὶ τὴν διάνοιαν | ἐπαινεῖ{ν̣}* (*On Poems* 5 col. 27.3-13). Janko's emendation, in angle brackets, is preferable to Gomoll's | *<οὐκ> εἶναι λόγωι*. An alternative punctuation and translation are possible for the relative clause: 'if Crates added this claim ..., which he makes against the *kritikoi*, he would be refuted' (so Janko); and for the last tag (reading *ὅπερ*): 'which is to praise the sense too'.

[31] *P.Herc*. 228 fr. 1a.7-21 Mangoni: *πάντα | δ' ἐμπείρως [θε]ωρούμε- | [ν]α κρίνεται, ἐπεὶ "οὔτε | θέματα πιθανὸν εἶνα[ι], | μαρτυρούσης γοῦν εἰς | τοῦτο τῆς ἀκοῆ[ς, ο]ὔθ̣' ὅ | [τ]αν ἡ αἴσθησι[ς] ἥδηται, | [ε]ὐθὺς καὶ τὴ[ν διά]νοιαν | [πιθ]ανὸν ἐ[παι]νεῖν, ἀτέ | χνου [γ]ε τοῦ σ̣[...]γ ὄντος"*.

crucially view meaning as an *aesthetic* property of poetry, or so it seems, but Crates' view appears to have been subtly different from that of the critics he opposes. What does that difference amount to?

We can begin with *atechnos* ('outside art'). This term is partially illuminated by Sextus' *Against the Grammarians*, where Crates' or Cratetean views about what falls outside the provenance of the critic's, and presumably the poet's, art are exposed: it is τὸ ἱστορικόν, roughly, content (*hypothesis*), which consists of material that lacks method and is therefore not amenable to it (ἐκ τῆς ἀμεθόδου ὕλης, *M.* 1.254; 265-7). This is all familiar territory, in light of the preceding pages (content, one could say, is not an *idion* of poems), and it is confirmed by another papyrus scrap.[32] Crates' claim is extreme (and may mark a radicalisation beyond Andromenides, as the same scrap indicates). Given Crates' cavalier attitude towards Homer's meaning—his tendency to extrapolate from the surface meaning of the text (traditional *hypothesis*) and to look for more satisfying hidden meanings (*hyponoiai*)—his claim is perhaps more readily understandable. But in what way is meaning 'known' by the sense of hearing?

Here we must jump ahead to *On Poems* 5 cols. 28-9, where Philodemus writes: 'Either it is reasonable that words receive their sense *via* the ear; or it is true that a poem's meanings have to be judged, and that whenever we praise the composition we should not detach (ἀποσπᾶ[ν]) it from the underlying <sense>.'[33] The first half of the claim is obscure, and may be nothing more than a *reductio* of Crates' position. The second half has a history that can be traced. 'Αποσπᾶν is a pointed reversal of Crates' teaching, exposed in earlier books, that while sound can provide a

---

[32] 'But <Crates> says that arguments and ... [meanings] are outside the art <of poetry>' (ὁ δὲ ἔ̓ξω || τῆς τέχνη[ς εἶναι τούς τε] | λόγους καὶ [... τὰ διανο] | ήματα; *P.Herc.* 1074a fr. 3c cols. 1-2 = Tr. D frr. 13 + 42 = cols. 117-8*).

[33] ἦ πρὸς λ[ό] | γον ἐστὶ τὸ διὰ τῆς ἀκο | ῆς τὰς λέξεις παραδέ- || χεσθαι τὴν διάνοιαν ἢ ἀ | ληθὲς δ[εῖν τὰ νο]ούμενα ἐν ποήμ̣[ασι]ν̣ κρίνε- σ | θαι̣, καὶ μηδ' ὅταν τὴν | σύνθεσιν ἐπαινῶμεν, ἀ | ποσπᾶ[ν] αὐτὴν τῶν ὑπο | τεταγμένων.

certain natural gratification (*χάριν*), at the same time a reader can be distracted (*περισπᾶσθαι*) by other factors, for instance by the attention claimed by meaning.[34] Sound and sense, it would seem, are fatally related: attend to the one and you naturally lose sight of the other. The dilemma is apparent: for 'it would be terrible if the sound were deprived of its *idion* whenever the sense becomes apparent'.[35] But that is the dilemma of the euphonist, not of you and me. Or is it? In a parallel passage, the same statement appears in slightly different form: 'In the case of people speaking pure Greek (*hellenismos*), the sound creates what is peculiar (*to idion*) to the language [or: "to the sense"]—wouldn't it be terrible for <sound> to be deprived of <its peculiarity> on account of pure Greek?', that is to say, on account of a sound's corresponding to pure Greek, the language that, after all, exhibits the very peculiarities Crates would have us attend to.[36] Here we can begin to make out how Crates' euphonism is not just a theory about poetry but a theory of language. Euphonism receives its justification by virtue of being rooted in the nature of expression; and we are all, now, euphonists of a sort. A brief hypothesis about how the various parts of his theory work together can be sketched in quickly.

---

[34] It is the reader who is distracted, even though the texts sometimes speak of the 'sound' being distracted from or towards the sense: *P.Herc*. 994 col. 6 = Tr. A col. 6 ~ *P.Herc*. 460 fr.15.13-15 = Tr. B fr. 23 col. 2 = 89* ~ *P.Herc*. 1073 fr. 6.19-21 = Tr. B fr. 23 col. 3 = 90*: *ὅσα μ[ὴ] περισ[πᾶ | τ]αι μὲν εἰς τὰ νοούμ[ε]να*; cf. *P.Herc*. 994 col. 17.15-6 = Tr. A col. 17.

[35] *δεινὸν δ', ὡς ἐλέγε | [τ]ο* (sc. *P.Herc*. 460 fr. 15), *εἰ παρὰ τὸ τὴν διά | [ν]οιαν βλέπεσθαι ἀπο | [στ]ερηθήσε`τ´αι ὁ ἦχος [το]ῦ ἰδίου* (*P.Herc*. 460 fr. 9.6-10 = Tr. B fr. 26 = 100*).

[36] *P.Herc*. 460 fr. 15.7-13 = Tr. B fr. 23 col. 2 = 89*: *καὶ ἐπὶ | τῶν ἐλληνιζόντων ὁ | μὲν ἦχος ἀποτελεῖ τὸ | ἴδιον κατὰ τὴν δ[ι]ά[λεκτον]* (Gomperz : *δ[ι]ά[νοιαν* Hausrath) | (*ἦ δεινὸν ἂν εἴη [τὸ] διὰ | τὸν ἐλληνισμὸν ἀπο | στερεῖσθαι*). In context, *[τὸ] διὰ* (Gomperz) seems preferable to *[τὰ ἴ]δια* (Usener); in any event, the alternative ('... wouldn't it be terrible for pure Greek to be deprived of its peculiarities?') leaves the point unaffected.

Crates' position is that what is distinctive about the sound of an utterance (*to idion*) gives a distinctive character to the language in which the utterance is expressed, if not to the sense itself.[37] In fact it is the sound that leads the mind *to* the sense;[38] but the sense *qua* sense can in turn distract the reader from that same set of characteristics (*ta idia*) which drew the mind to them, and which only the ear can judge. On Crates' view, aesthetic characteristics just are the distinctive characteristics of a given language (with Hellenism defining Greek in its purest and most 'natural' condition);[39] and these are bound up with the sense, though just how still needs to be specified. Philodemus' comment that Crates perversely conflates together sound and sense, the mind and the hearing, confirms this for us, though it does not capture the fact, which Philodemus could recognise when he liked, that sound and sense for Crates are in competition and not just in collaboration.[40] Crates' theory is full of meaningful equivocations (rather than 'conflations'). His otherwise strange claim from Book 5 that it is not the meaning that is the object of literary criticism, but neither is that object to be conceived as without meaning either (col. 28.26-9), points ahead to his theory of allegoresis, but more immediately it refers back to the problems outlined above. It states in concentrated form what it takes two tries to say in other contexts: that what enchants those who apprehend poetry is 'not the sound

[37] See *P.Herc.* 460 fr. 15.7-10 in the foregoing note and the discussion by Rispoli (1986, 119).

[38] When sounds are clustered according to rules for word division, 'signification (ἡ ἀποσημασία) occurs naturally (κατὰ φύσιν)', otherwise not (*P.Herc.* 460 fr. 7 = Tr. B fr. 8 = 105*). 'Naturally' here means according to the nature of the Greek language. 'Signification' denotes signification in general, not given meanings (these are not felt by Crates to be fixed by sound or by nature; see below).

[39] Cf. *P.Herc.* 994 col. 6 = Tr. A col. 6. On 'natural' see preceding note.

[40] *P.Herc.* 994 col. 5.21-2 = Tr. A col. 5: τὸ φύρειν ὁμοῦ διάνοιαν ἀκοῆι (and compare the sequel). The verb is possibly filched from Crates and turned against him; cf. *P.Herc.* 460 fr. 17.16 = Tr. B fr. 11 col. 2 = 83*.

itself without the sense' but the two 'combined';[41] but it is the sound, not the sense, which enjoys 'leadership' (*ἡγεμονία*) in poetry.[42] Sound and sense will necessarily be combined in such a way as to preserve the *idion* of language as defined by Crates; and sound will be pre-eminent, both as a guide to sense and as sovereign aesthetically. If this is right, then Crates has found a brilliant way to make his euphonist case (the argument is unparalleled by any ancient author): meaning isn't utterly sacrificed to the imperatives of euphony; rather, euphony is the irrational criterion of the rational character of language—which can be experienced and apparently enjoyed in its aesthetic character.

It is a precarious position, but Crates seems to have thrived on such precariousness. What is more, Crates may have actually used his theory of sound to liberate the signifier, which is 'natural', from its signified, which is conventional. The *idion* of a given expression involves a *reference* to meaning, but not the apprehension of meaning as such. Another way of putting this is that an expression necessarily has meaning, but not necessarily any one, particular meaning. Thus, the apparent or surface meaning needn't be fixed but only a habitual *phantasia*;[43] strictly, the sense needn't even be evident for the linguistic function to obtain (this is

[41] *P.Herc.* 460 fr. 9.12-8 = Tr. B fr. 26 col. 1 = 100*: *ọὐ τὸν ἦχον αὐτὸν | [ἄνευ* (*[ἄνευ* Porter : *[χώρις* Hausrath : *[τῶν* Gomperz) *ὑ]ποτεταγμένων, ... ὅταν δέ | [τις τά]δε μεί[ξας ἐ]πικρ[α | τ]ῇ ἡμῶν εἰς [τ]ὴν ἐπι[| π]ρ̣έπειαν ἀνακ[ει]νῶν.*

[42] *P.Herc.* 994 col. 21 = Tr. A col. 21.

[43] Cf. *P.Herc.* 1073a fr. 16a.3-4 = Tr. B fr. 33 = 68*. The term occurs elsewhere in connection with Andromenides; Crates apparently used *emphasis* in a similar sense (e.g., at *P.Herc.* 460 fr. 5.12 = Tr. B fr. 4 col. 1 = 111*). I take this point to be virtually confirmed by *P.Herc.* 460 fr. 28 col. 2 = Tr. E fr. 22 col. 1 = 62*, where Crates' position is that it is not impossible that beauty is to be found in all the features of poems in question (these seem to be related to *hypothesis*, because in question are features that are not *idia*); but if so, it is not 'by necessity' that *τὸ καλόν* is found where it is, but (presumably) by convention.

true, if provocative);[44] and the door is now wide open to *hyponoia*—not quite as allegory, but as a justifiably 'other', and *unconventional*, way of reading poems. Here at last we have a link between euphonist criticism and *sphairopoiia*: this is how Crates gets from the line to the circle.[45]

The contrast with the '*kritikoi*' can be speculated about very briefly, because we have so little to go on. If the statement that they 'praise the sense without any further ado (εὐθύς)' is in fact directed against them, it can only be so if they praise (which is to say, pass a favorable aesthetic judgment on) the sense *qua* the way it sounds, for they cannot have praised the sense *qua* sense. Heracleodorus, opposed by Crates and in all probability a '*kritikos*', claimed that meanings in general do not move us; they are not psychagogic; and even lack of clarity in meaning (ἀσάφεια) cannot stand in the way of a poem's poetic value or effects. Crates would have agreed with all of this up to a point. But perhaps what was objectionable to him was the way the '*kritikoi*' too readily cashed out the sense as sound (treating sound as the immediate phonic equivalent of sense), especially if this prevented them from developing a satisfying theory of

---

[44] δ]ιάνοια οὐ βλέ[πεται καὶ] | κ̣αταλείπετα[ι τὸ ἀνα | κ]ινοῦν κατὰ τ[ὸν ἦ | χο]ν (*P.Herc*. 460 fr. 9.3-6 = 100*). For the immediate sequel, see n. 35 above. This is far stronger than Crates' claim that euphony determines word-choice at the expense of sense, as in *P.Herc*. 994 cols. 10-1 = Tr. A cols. 10-1.

[45] See Porter 1992, 112-4, where I broached this problem without yet having discovered a satisfying solution to it. With the link made, there are further questions. What is the status of the meanings discovered in Homer? Demonstration that Homer represents the spherical nature of the universe ought to be the demonstration *par excellence* of a '*koinon*'. Is a *koinon* devoid of aesthetic value? Perhaps as a *koinon* it is, but Crates appears to be doing much more than isolating common conceptions in Homer with his *sphairikos logos*. Nor is it clear why the poetic qualities of an *idion* should exhaust the whole of aesthetic value (either in poetry or beyond it). I hope to return to this intriguing set of problems at a later date.

ambiguity, homonymy, or of alternative meanings (such as *hyponoiai*), concerns that were dear to Crates.[46]

Elsewhere, Crates introduced an analogous subtlety that he may have likewise found missing in his opponents' account. Irrational euphony and pleasure are for Crates the immediate criterion of good poetry, but not its ultimate criterion. In the last analysis, the evaluation must be of the method and art of a composition ('the *logos* of its *techne*'); otherwise, chance euphony would have an equal claim to excellence, and aesthetic appreciation would be in vain (*On Poems* 5 col. 28). But even so, it is the ear that 'judges'. It is just possible that his euphonist predecessors collapsed these two 'moments', grossly in Crates' eyes. If so, then Crates once again equivocates meaningfully where his opponents rushed headlong into an apparently unfettered sensualism. On the other hand, given their emphasis on the art of composition as a source of euphony, we may have reason to suspect yet one more polemical reading by Crates of his opponents. At any rate, the sense of language for Crates is not transparent to the ear as sound; it is more like a distraction of the mind, tied more or less weakly, but in any case not indissolubly, to sound, which has attractions of its own. On his more nuanced and more painstakingly grammatical view of language,[47] sense and sound subtly interact in a myriad of ways, but always in a productive and precarious tension that he could only resolve (not reduce) by resorting to an enlarged and enriched concept of the *idion*, borrowed from his predecessors, the '*kritikoi*'.

---

[46] In his discussion of sound and sense, Crates cites the example of *νηὸς ἰσχάδα* from Sophocles to illustrate how considerations of sound prevail, despite the (here, obscene) ambiguity of the phrase ('fig-iron', 'anchor'), col. 89* ~ *P.Herc.* 994 col. 5 = Tr. A col. 5. For an account, see Janko 1991. Either Crates defended the surface sense of the word as conventional or habitual, or he defended the sound as prevailing by itself and by distracting us from its meanings.

[47] This is what I take to be the meaning of *logikos* in connection with Crates, whose criticism turns on *logika theoremata*, or literary principles, which are logical, methodical, and based on the empirical observation of poetic phenomena (*On Poems* 5 col. 28; cf. D.H. *Dem.* 47-9 and 52; *Comp.* 5, 27.12-5).

2. Alignments

The question of who the '*kritikoi*' were is necessarily bound up with the question why it is that we know of their existence only through Philodemus. The simple answer is the mere existence of Crates of Mallos, the most prominent literary critic besides Aristarchus in the last two centuries BCE. It was Crates who initially consolidated them, at least doxographically; and as he was more interested to emphasise his superiority to their views, it is this difference that comes out in *On Poems*, not any dissonances within their 'ranks'. Thus, it is correct, methodologically, for Philodemus to attempt to pierce through Crates' arguments in order to determine just what those arguments come down to. And I see no reason to distrust Philodemus' instincts in this matter. How diverse a group they were is uncertain. What seems certain is that in places Philodemus is overriding Crates' polemics against other euphonists, by picking out a feature of both their programs that genuinely deserves to be used in identifying them as critics of a special and singular stamp (as in col. 75* above). Realigning their views in this way is of course not a disinterested undertaking: undoing Crates' polemics is itself polemical.[48]

This explanation is consistent with Book 5, where Crates is shown to concur with the '*kritikoi*' when he believes himself to be dissenting from their views—another polemics overridden not just by Philodemus, but by the obvious facts of agreement (ὁμολογούντων, col. 27.9-13). A few columns earlier, Crates is said to have been mistaken about (or 'diverged from') Heracleodorus and his fellow-travellers, and Andromenides too (though he believes himself to be in full agreement with the latter). Here is the text, which now comes equipped with two variant restorations: ἀποτ[υγ]χάνει τοιγαροῦν [τ]ῆς Ἡρακλεοδώρου καὶ τῶν ὁμοίων δόξης—[οὐ γ]ὰρ τὴν σύνθεσιν, ἀλλὰ τὴν ἐπιφαινομένην [α]ὐ[τῆι] φωνὴ[ν] ἐπ[αι]ν[οῦ | σι (ἐπ[αι]ν[οῦ | σι—Delattre et Monet : ἐπ[αι-]ν[εῖ | —ῶς Kentennich) κ]αὶ τῆς Ἀνδρομενίδ[ου | π]ά̣ντη<ι> γε

[48] That col. 75* has a programmatic ring to it is undeniable—so much so, in fact, that Hausrath (1889) deduced, wrongly, that this column (= fr. 1 H.) derived from the beginning of the book roll that contained it.

νομίζων ὁ | [μο]λογεῖν αὐτὸν καὶ διὰ || [πα]ντὸς τοῖς εἰρημέ-νοις.[49] With the new conjecture by Daniel Delattre and Annick Monet, which is a welcome confirmation of the reading offered above, we must take ἀποτ[υγ]χάνει to mean 'is mistaken about', not 'hat nicht dieselbe Ansicht wie' (Jensen). Crates is mistaken about his opponents—who we can be almost certain are '*kritikoi*'—'for it isn't composition but the euphony supervening on it that they praise'. This is the more natural reading of ἀποτυγχάνει.[50] But it isn't true that the '*kritikoi*' do not praise composition even if Crates falsely claims that this is all they do praise. And how is Crates 'mistaken' about Andromenides? These distortions can be written off to Philodemus' polemic, while the alternative reading is in many ways less appealing: why at his point should Philodemus present Crates' case as Crates presented it—and as Philodemus nowhere else does?[51] So, if the text has been rightly construed, once again the obvious facts of agreement cancel out the main thrust of Crates' claims to difference.

The differences that do emerge elsewhere among all the protagonists (and there may only have been a handful—probably no more than those named at the start of this paper) are not compelling; Philodemus clearly wasn't impressed, and nor should we be.[52] As we saw, Crates sought to

---

[49] I am grateful to André Laks and David Blank for their helpful comments on this passage, along lines similar to those suggested by the conjecture that was arrived at independently by Daniel Delattre and Annick Monet. All these suggestions were communicated to me (for the most part orally) at the time of the UCLA Philodemus conference in May of 1994.

[50] As Jensen also knew; cf. Jensen 1923, 154 (ll. 4-5).

[51] See esp. *P.Herc.* 1676 col. 6, cited at n. 9 above, if Crates is to be understood in the reference to 'all the *kritikoi*': in that context *synthesis* and euphony are of equal value, euphony being a function of *synthesis*.

[52] Compare *On Poems* 5 col. 23 where Philodemus breaks down anonymous opponents (φασί [τ]ινες) into two groupings (they are obviously '*kritikoi*'). 'Some' hold that the aesthetic quality of a poem lies in its *synthesis*, even 'if the sense should be unknown'; 'others' advance *synthesis* as the criterion of poetic

distinguish himself from his euphonist predecessors by granting a privileged status to sound rather than to composition, claiming that the '*kritikoi*' held the opposite. In practice, it is a distinction that he simply cannot maintain. Philodemus rightly resists this gambit, and he points out that Crates' opponents, too, were committed to the pre-eminence of euphony—once explicitly (in Book 5, as above), but everywhere else merely by attributing to them the doctrine that 'euphony supervenes on composition' without further comment. That Philodemus hasn't simply *awarded* them this doctrine is guaranteed by a number of considerations, including his fidelity as a witness, but especially by the details of their literary criticism and by the logic by which composition and euphony *must* go hand in hand. A '*kritikos*' could pass effortlessly back and forth between the two contested concepts, as does the unnamed opponent at *P.Herc.* 1676 col. 7 (= Tr. C col. 18), who believes that 'the composition in and of itself (*καθ' αὑτήν*) produces *psychagogia*' (ll. 12-7), a belief he takes to be equivalent to a claim about euphony (ll. 7-12). It is a complex claim that Philodemus, moreover, is at pains to refute in both its parts.[53] The distinction does not seem to have been an issue until Crates came along and made it one, somewhat factitiously. And by the time we reach Dionysius of Halicarnassus, who probably underwent the influence of both Crates and his opponents (though he fails to acknowledge this), it is no longer an issue again. All the evidence suggests that Crates probably exaggerated his distinctness from the '*kritikoi*' he attacked, as Philodemus senses. Philodemus was right, then,

---

excellence, 'even if the sense should be wholly absent or distorted'. Clearly, it is a difference that doesn't make much of a difference.

[53] That the claim was about euphony follows from Philodemus' rejection of it. Whether the phraseology ('euphony that appears on the surface of the composition') stems from the opponent or is Philodemus' own gloss is harder to make out here, but not, for instance, at col. *P.Herc.* 466 fr. 7.1-3 = Tr. E fr. 10 = 34*, where its occurrence is internal to a reported exposition, although the exact source (probably either Crates or Andromenides) remains uncertain.

to establish the common ground they shared.[54] And if by '*hoi kritikoi*' he sometimes understands Crates' literary critical opponents and sometimes understands Crates too, the usage may be confusing, but it is not false.

Of course, this only pushes the problem of the identity of the '*kritikoi*' back a stage, which at a certain level of detail, given the state of the evidence, is bound to be irretrievable. But a few discriminations are in order. First, strictly speaking, *no* differences in opinion ought to have separated 'Heracleodorus and those like him', who appear to have been united by a common view (τ]ῆς Ἡρακλεοδώρου καὶ τῶν ὁμοίων δόξης). Philodemus cannot have invented *this* '*koinon*'. And so it only remains to ask whether any other critics among those whose teachings were exposed in Crates' treatise were also opposed by him for embracing the cause of *synthesis* instead of euphony. 'Aristo' has been put up as one candidate.[55] The name is worth dwelling on for a moment.

Philodemus faults 'Aristo' for smuggling the extraneous criterion of euphony ('the non-existent euphonies of the "*kritikoi*"') into his theory of poetry, and specifically into his criteria of excellence for *synthesis*. It is hard to believe that by his statement (κ]αὶ συν[ε] | πενηνέχθαι ταῖς ἀγε[νῆ] | τοις εὐφωνίαις τῶν κ[ρι]τικῶν, *On Poems* 5 col. 21.14-7) Philodemus means to say that 'Aristo' just *is* one of the '*kritikoi*'. And if he did not mean to say this, then holding a euphonic doctrine clearly isn't enough to warrant inclusion in the group as constituted, say, by Philodemus. Possibly, this is a telltale sign that Crates did not discuss 'Aristo' in his exposition of those critics whom Philodemus understands by '*kriti-*

[54] It is tempting to see in '*koinon*' (col. 75*) another swipe at their teachings on 'what is thought to be *koinon*'. The interpretation offered above represents a revision of my earlier view (Porter 1989), although the following still appears to stand: '[T]here may have been genuine points of disagreement between Crates and the "*kritikoi*" ... But by the same token, it was precisely because [they] shared a certain amount of ground in common that Crates may have found reason for disputing some of the finer points of the *synthesis*-doctrine they shared' (175).

[55] See Blank 1994, 60 with n. 28, and 61.

koi',[56] and so (one might conclude) the term is reserved for those opponents specifically addressed by Crates—and for Crates in so far as his position is indistinguishable from theirs. But the '*kritikoi*' appear to be unlike 'Aristo' in other respects. His view of meaning is nuanced in a way that theirs is not, in part because he does not hold meaning to be reducible to a *koinon*.[57] It is obvious that 'Aristo' merely found it useful to resort to a euphonist argument as part of a larger theoretical (and indeed, dialectical) construction. Euphonism is not his starting-point but an accessory, to be adduced only once all other grounds for praising a poem (chiefly moral grounds) have been shown wanting. In fact, to judge from the exposition, 'Aristo' did not evolve the theory in a technical way. My guess is that he borrowed the main lines of the theory ready-made, possibly from the same critics exposed by Crates, though again this is uncertain. At all events, if Crates opposed himself to '*kritikoi*', we may safely speculate it was to the group constituted by Heracleodorus and his ilk, not to Andromenides (π]ἀ̣ντη<ι> γε νομίζων ὁ | [μο]λ̲ογεῖν αὐτὸν καὶ διὰ || [πα]ντὸς τοῖς εἰρημένοις),[58] and not to 'Aristo'.[59]

It might be objected that the '*kritikoi*' could have practised euphonist criticism as a means to other ends as well, which only goes to show that euphonism is a lowest common denominator that serves not only to unite critics but (in the end) to divide them. This is a difficult claim to assess.

---

[56] A certain Philomelus, possibly an Epicurean, appears to be Philodemus' immediate source for 'Aristo's' teachings (*On Poems* 5 col. 12.10).

[57] See Porter 1994, 80-1 with n. 90 for this point and *passim* for the following points.

[58] Andromenides has even been speculated to have been Crates' teacher (Asmis 1992, 145). Heraclides of Pontus is another case that needs to be examined.

[59] Greenberg (1955, 166) argues vigorously, but unconvincingly, that Heracleodorus is not to be deemed one of the '*kritikoi*'. He is misled in part by a false understanding of *atechnos* in *On Poems* 5 col. 27 (cf. Mette 1952, 184.6), which refers not to *synthesis*, which is precisely '*entechnos*', but to meaning, which is not. It would be most economical to assume that the 'Milesian' from the end of Tr. A is Heracleodorus, not some supernumerary.

Euphonism needn't be subordinated to 'other ends'; it only needs to be compatible with them, especially if the starting assumption is that poets remain 'first' in their class in virtue of the sounds they produce alone, or that the *idion* of poetry (euphony) constitutes its excellence (*agathon* or *arete)*.[60] Crates, evidently, could practice his *sphairikos logos* without compromising his euphonism. If other '*kritikoi*' went on to do equally strange things to poets' words, themes, and images, they would nonetheless be identical in their common point of departure, which *is* unique among ancient literary critics. Much still remains be said about their name, but the evidence we have gives no indication whatsoever as to the originator of the *special* sense of '*kritikos*'.[61] Philodemus' use of the term seems to presuppose, not posit, the special sense.[62] More than this, we cannot say.[63]

---

[60] Cf. *P.Herc*. 1676 col. 7 = Tr. C col. 18; *ib*., col. 12 = Tr. C col. 23.

[61] For the meaning of '*kritike*' Blank (1994, 57-9) points to the passage from *On Music* 4 col. 136* Delattre (= col. 22 Neubecker), about which a different story is equally possible. There is no need to entangle the '*kritikoi*' with Diogenes of Babylon's *ethos*-theory of music: the '*kritikoi*' firmly reject all moral evaluations of poetry. But a connotation very much active in the term *kritike* (and '*kritikos*') is sensory discernment, as passages from [Philod.] *On Sensation* show, where, moreover, a further allusion to '*kritikoi*' is surely in evidence (cf. cols. 31b-33b Monet = frr. 23-5 Scott; Porter 1989, 174 n. 139). Plainly, the 'special' sense of '*kritikos*' has to do with the reduction of poetic discrimination to sensory discrimination. Crates' own use of the term may be ironic and aimed against Plato (with S.E. *M*. 1.79, cf. Pl. *Plt*. 260); it is in any case un-Stoic and has no obvious affinities with Diogenes of Babylon's theory.

[62] This is true of every occurrence of the term in Philodemus, not least in *On Music* 4 (*τοῖς ὀνομαζομένοις κριτικοῖς*). Nowhere do we get the impression that Philodemus is coining the usage. That he has is only an assumption. It is at least as possible that Crates, in collecting his adversaries together, dubbed them '*kritikoi*', only to revoke their claim to the title and to assert it for himself.

[63] On the somewhat parallel problem of *οἱ καλούμενοι μουσικοί*, see now Wallace (forthcoming).

3. Philosophy and literary criticism: some prospects

Philodemus so often reminds us of how little we know about antiquity. Were it not for him we would have *no* way of knowing that Crates of Mallos practised euphonic criticism—there simply is not a shred of evidence in any of his other testimonia to show or even suggest that he did. Philodemus' testimony on the history of poetics is all the more precious for this reason. Even so, no available account of the '*kritikoi*' is capable of explaining why Philodemus, and not some other ancient, should be a source of information on critics like these at all—let alone why he spilled so much ink on them. Book 1, we learn, treated 'the euphony of sequential letters and the like';[64] book 2 covered, inter alia, 'Crates' theory of letters'.[65] One book is lost (either 1 or 3), and only ten columns of book 4 have survived. But the end of book 5 (almost all that remains of the book) contains, I think, a clue. The historical sequence traced there seems to be evolutionary, though it has never been identified as such. In a word, what it traces is the ascendancy of *synthesis* as a commanding perspective in ancient literary criticism after Aristotle: on this view, compositional qualities are praised as paramount—in virtue of themselves, their euphonies, and the various pleasures they entail.

If the final survey in book 5 is any indication, given its placement and its sudden reprise of earlier motifs, we are entitled to the guess that this new emphasis in literary criticism was Philodemus' primary concern throughout the *whole* of *On Poems*. (Indeed, if Dorandi's assignment of books is right, then the first *three* books were extensively if not exclusively devoted to euphony.) What was the attraction? Possibly, Philodemus is reflecting Crates' powerful influence. But there is a deeper reason as well. The empiricism and the sensualism that Crates and the '*kritikoi*' adopted presented a genuine philosophical threat to the Epicurean outlook and therefore required refutation—not only because it challenged some of the basic premises of Epicurean epistemology, but also

---

[64] *P.Herc.* 994 col. 31.4-10 = Tr. A col. 31.

[65] *On Poems* 5 col. 29.7-17.

ERRATA

p. 65, 2nd paragraph, last sentence: "And the beginnings of the movement, as I will try to show, seem to belong in the first century BCE.".

p. 71, 3rd paragraph, second sentence, insert before "Thomas Gelzer: "for instance".

p. 71 note 14, read D.H. *Comp.* "4.11, 19.9-15 ...".

p. 72, first paragraph, forelast sentence, read: (see e.g. *Fin.* 5.9-14).

p. 75, last paragraph, first sentence, read (instead of "Some additional evidence is also available"): "Some additional evidence gives us positive reasons".

p. 77, first paragraph, first sentence, read (instead of "all the cities"): "the cities in their entirety".

p. 79, second paragraph, forelast sentence, delete "also".

p. 80, second paragraph, second sentence, insert before: "Seneca the Elder": "for instance".

because it appeared to return to an Epicurean a distorted image of himself (compare, for example, the Cyrenaics' challenge to the Epicureans for according primacy to the senses instead of the mind in aesthetic perception).[66] The striking reappearance of empiricist views very like those held by the '*kritikoi*' in Philodemus' philosophical work *On the Senses* reinforces this possibility.[67] But let me emphasise that Philodemus' view of literary criticism is parochial and therefore a distortion of the historical reality. The trend towards *synthesis* was probably less pronounced than he makes it out to be. Were there time, one would need to paint a different picture, on a larger canvass and with a bigger brush. That picture would be more static than Philodemus'. It would go back to the earliest systematic studies of music and poetry,[68] two areas which never ceased to be thought together, and forward to the author of *On the Sublime*, who would remember Crates and the '*kritikoi*' not for their restricted views of literature, but for the ways in which they opened up new dimensions in criticism and new avenues to sublimity. For they too, in the last analysis and in their own way, were working in the tradition of the sublime.

---

[66] Plu. *Quaest. conv.* 647a-b: 'This, my good Epicureans,' I said, 'is considerable evidence for the Cyrenaics, who argue against you that the pleasures got from sights and sounds don't lie in vision or in the sense of hearing but in the mind'. See further Porter (1995), esp. 629-30.

[67] Cf. above n. 61.

[68] The language of Crates' poetics as a whole seems borrowed from harmonic theory, though with important modifications which still need to be explored. With *On Poems* 5 col. 27.18-21, *τὸ φάσκειν* "*δι[α]γινώσκεσ | θαι τὴν ὑπάρχουσαν ἐν | τοῖς ποιή[μ]ασ[ι]μ φυσικὴν | διαφορὰν τῆι ἀ̣κ̣οῆι*", cf. Theophr. (arguing against mathematically based music theory) *ap.* Porph. *Comm. in Ptol. Harm.* 62.21-30 Düring: *ἡ γὰρ αὐτῶν φύσει διαφορὰ αὐτάρκης ἔσται εἰς τὴν τῶν μελῶν γένεσιν, καὶ εἴδησις ἔσται τῶν διαφορῶν. οὐκέτι γὰρ ἔσονται διαφοραὶ παρὰ τὰ πλήθη ἀλλὰ παρὰ τὴν ἰδιότητα τῶν φωνῶν, ὥσπερ ἐν τοῖς χρώμασιν.*

BIBLIOGRAPHY

Ardizzoni, A., ΠΟΙΗΜΑ: *Ricerche sulla teoria del linguaggio poetico nell'antiquità*. Bari 1953.

Asmis, E., Crates on Poetic Criticsm, *Phoenix* 46 (1991), 138-69.

Blank, D., Diogenes of Babylon and the *κριτικοί* in Philodemus: A Preliminary Suggestion, *CErc* 24 (1994), 55-62.

Dorandi, T., Per una ricomposizione dello scritto di Filodemo, Sulla Poetica, *ZPE* 91 (1992), 29-46.

———, Precisazioni su papiri della *Poetica* di Filodemo, *ZPE* 97 (1993), 81-86.

Greenberg, N.A., *The Poetic Theory of Philodemus* (diss. Harvard University, 1955). New York - London 1990.

Hausrath, A., Philodemi *περὶ ποιημάτων* libri secundi quae videntur fragmenta, *NJPhP*, Suppl. 17 (1889), 213-76.

Janko, R., (ed.), *Philodemus, On Poems 1* (forthcoming).

———, Philodemus Resartus: Progress in Reconstructing the Philosophical Papyri from Herculaneum, *Proceedings of the Boston Colloquium in Ancient Philosophy* 7 (1991), 271-308.

Jensen, C., *Philodemos über die Gedichte, Fünftes Buch*. Berlin 1923.

Mangoni, C., *Filodemo. Il Quinto Libro Della Poetica*. Napoli 1993.

Mette, H.J., *Parateresis: Untersuchungen zur Sprachtheorie des Krates von Pergamon*. Halle 1952.

Nardelli, M.L., *Due Trattati Filodemei Sulla Poetica*, in F. Sbordone (ed.), *Ricerche sui papiri ercolanesi*, vol. 4, Napoli 1983 = 'Tr. D, E'.

Neubecker, A.J., *Philodemus, Über die Musik IV. Buch*. Napoli 1986.

Pace, N., *Problematiche di Poetica in Filodemo di Gadara* (diss. Università degli Studi di Milano). Milano 1992.

Pfeiffer, R., *The History of Classical Scholarship from the Beginnings to the End of the Hellenistic Age*. Oxford 1968.

Porter, J.I., Philodemus on Material Difference, *CErc*. 19 (1989), 149-78.

———, Hermeneutic Lines and Circles: Aristarchus and Crates on the Exegesis of Homer, in: R. Lamberton - J. Keaney (eds.), *Homer's Ancient Readers: The Greek Epic's Earliest Exegetes*. Princeton 1992, 67-111.

———, Stoic Morals and Poetics in Philodemus, *CErc* 24 (1994), 63-88.

———, In Search of an Epicurean Aesthetics, in: G. Giannantoni (ed)., Epicureismo greco e romano, *Elenchos* (special issue, 1995), 613-30.

Rispoli, G. M., Eufonia ed ermeneutica: origine ed evoluzione di un metodo filologico e critico-letterario, *Koinonia* 10-12 (1986), 118-34.

Romeo, C., Per una nuova edizione del *P.Herc.* 1676, *CErc.* 22 (1992), 163-7.

Russell, D.A., Arts and Sciences in Ancient Education, *Greece and Rome* 36 (1989), 210-24.

Sbordone, F., [*Φιλοδήμου περὶ ποιημάτων*] *tractatus tres* in F. Sbordone (ed.), *Ricerche sui Papiri Ercolanesi*, vol. 2 (Napoli 1976) = 'Tr. A, B, C'.

———, *Sui Papiri della Poetica di Filodemo*. Napoli 1983.

Schächter, R., De Homero in Philodemi *περὶ ποιημάτων* l. II laudatio, *Eos* 31 (1928), 439-46.

Schenkeveld, D.M., Oἱ *κριτικοί* in Philodemus, *Mnemosyne* (1968), 176-214.

Wallace, R.W., Music Theorists in Fourth-Century Athens, in: Memorial vol. for G. Comotti (forthcoming).

Longinus: Structure and Unity

Doreen C. Innes

Longinus, as I shall follow convention in terming the author of *On the Sublime*, uses the formal structure of a textbook. He begins with preliminaries, where he introduces main themes, and analyses related neighbouring faults. He lists five sources, promises to analyse the characteristics of '*each* type', *καθ' ἑκάστην ἰδέαν τούτων* (8.1), and continues to remind us of this schema. Thus figures 'follow next in their due place' (16.1 *ἐφεξῆς τέτακται*), and word-arrangement is 'the fifth of the headings contributing to the sublime which I set out at the beginning' (39.1 *ἡ πέμπτη μοῖρα τῶν συντελουσῶν εἰς τὸ ὕψος, ὧν γε ἐν ἀρχῇ προὐθέμεθα*). The final chapter is a surprise in its unusual form, a reported dialogue between an unnamed philosopher and Longinus, but, as we shall see, its contents form a satisfying climax.

Textbook structures elsewhere offer a sequence of preliminaries, analysis under formal headings and final appendices,[1] but Horace's *Ars Poetica* is a particularly interesting parallel. Horace similarly starts with key themes (*ars*, unity and propriety) and neighbouring faults (1-37). He then analyses poetry under the three headings set out in 38-41 (arrangement, diction and content), and adds a formally distinct section on the poet's aims and virtues (295 ff.). Yet Horace in practice subverts this formal superstructure; he deliberately blurs transitions (where indeed *is* the transition to content?[2]). Instead he highlights a set of interlocking key

[1] Appendices are partly the equivalent of modern footnotes, but see below on 43 as an example of more organic use in Longinus.

[2] The favoured candidates are 119 and 153. But note the term *res* already in 73 ff. on the link of metre and content (and indeed already 49). This fits Horace's emphasis on the interlocking relationship of words and content (38-41, cf. 311).

themes; and he ends, like Longinus, with a grand finale, which reiterates key themes and provides an insight into reasons for failure—the picture of the undisciplined mad poet, who claims freedom but lacks *ars*.

Longinus also subverts *his* carefully constructed superstructure. To take the most obvious problem, why is there no independent analysis of the second of the five sources, emotion?—precisely the source which is the most original and whose exclusion by Caecilius evokes immediate polemic and justification (8.2-4). The long lacuna in 9.4 must make us cautious, but the transition at the end of 15 is crucial, since 15.12 formally concludes the first source on sublimity of thought, and 16.1 formally introduces figures as the next logically following topic. Yet 15.12 makes no mention of emotion. The most stimulating attempt to solve this notorious problem is by Donald Russell (1981). Yet I doubt the five-source schema of 8.1 can have only a temporary purpose, part of a careful preparation for a defence of Plato. Some formal explanation will have been given in the long lacuna beginning in 9.4, and my own favoured explanation is that the second source, 'vehement and inspired emotion' (8.1 *τὸ σφοδρὸν καὶ ἐνθουσιαστικὸν πάθος*) is primarily and typically found in conjunction with the first source. Great thought, we are told, is often found without emotion, and Longinus immediately offers an example and suitable contexts, but, significantly, he gives no example of suitable emotion without greatness of thought. He also (8.2) excludes low, ignoble emotions, such as pity, grief and fear, and what he particularly recommends is the opposite, 'noble emotion', *τὸ γενναῖον πάθος*, a type which will combine emotion and nobility of thought, and it is this which more than anything will inspire our speech (8.4). Emotion as a source of sublimity on its own without nobility of thought will be a very curious beast—though it will presumably cover the ecstasy of madness. I explore this question elsewhere (Innes 1995). But whatever the details of his explanation, I accept that Longinus preserved the validity of his five-source superstructure throughout the work[3] and presented emotion as a source which is important but only rarely, if ever, autonomous.

It is also often claimed that 15.12 is an incomplete summary of 9-15: it includes imitation and imagination, the topics of 13.2-15, but it omits sublimity from density of detail in 10 (and can therefore also omit emotion, a very dubious argument). But I agree with Mazzucchi (1990) that 10-13.1 are not on sources of sublimity but on methods of intensifying thoughts—by *con*cise selection and by *ex*pansion (αὔξησις), methods which Longinus aptly distinguishes by his use of vocabulary, amassing words beginning συν- and ἐπι- respectively. Mazzucchi rightly compares the distinction of thoughts and approaches, ἔννοιαι and μέθοδοι, in Hermogenes (e.g. 218-9 Rabe).

One final detail on formal structure: 43, on petty diction, is formally an appendix out of due order (diction was discussed in 30-8). It can be defended simply as an appendix, and it runs on smoothly enough from the preceding topic on faults of arrangement. But I suggest a more integral function. It concerns failure of the sublime and acts as a gliding transition to the final chapter on reasons for a lack of sublimity. After the paean of praise of sublimity in the digression in 33-6 (also of the power of word-arrangement in 39), the discussion of the fifth source has already moved towards an emphasis on negative aspects, (1) an absence of the first source, sublimity of thought (good arrangement can compensate for that lack, 40.2-3), and (2) 'what makes arrangement petty' (41-2; note that 41 begins μικροποιόν, 'what makes *petty*'). Then 43 provides a further example of such pettiness, this time 'pettiness in diction' (μικρότης τῶν ὀνομάτων). This all sets the scene for the final chapter on what is effectively pettiness of nature, that absence of sublimity of thought which causes the current dearth of sublime writers. If we also look back over the whole structure, 41-3, placed near the end, are on opposite faults of technique, and thus balance the account of neighbouring faults of thought (and emotion) which comes near the beginning, in 3-5.

---

[3] He has, for example, already written two books on arrangement, but for his present project 'necessarily' (ἐξ ἀνάγκης) he includes some brief discussion (39.1).

The apparent anomalies of structure are therefore part of a careful scheme, and as Longinus himself says (20.3 of a flurry of anaphora and asyndeta), 'thus his order is disordered, and his disorder conversely contains order', *οὕτως αὐτῷ καὶ ἡ τάξις ἄτακτον καὶ ἔμπαλιν ἡ ἀταξία ποιὰν περιλαμβάνει τάξιν*. Longinus did not wish us to forget or disregard the textbook structure, but he did wish us also to see its limitations, and I follow Donald Russell closely in his emphasis on gliding transitions and the way in which one section is linked to the next by common themes. My own aim is to examine ways in which that structure of five apparently divisible categories is subverted in ways which emphasise a view of sublimity as an organic whole. The omission of emotion as a separate category of analysis is in itself a signal of that approach.

Take the most important formal transition, from the innate to the technical sources, the same passage which we have already examined for its omission of emotion (15.12). Longinus uses a typical textbook transition of the type 'so much for "x", now for "y"', but in 16.2 ff. he blurs that formal distinction by launching directly into an analysis of the Marathon oath of Demosthenes (18.208), in which he continues the emphasis on the primacy of the two innate sources. The example is also about Chaeronea, as is the last example in the previous chapter (15.10), thus resuming the noble idea of fighting for freedom. Then too, like Homer (9.7), Demosthenes presents men like gods (16.2 'deifying ... like gods', *ἀποθεώσας ... ὡς θεούς*, 16.3 'immortalising', *ἀπαθανατίσας*). The Marathon oath also picks up the theme of *mimesis*, the creative emulation of a predecessor. It illustrates the irrelevance of merely verbal *mimesis* (16.3 Eupolis is not Demosthenes' source), and so reminds us of the true *mimesis* of spirit which he championed in 13.2-14, and which, in another gliding transition, he then illustrated under the next topic, imagination, where Euripides emulates an idea of Aeschylus and improves it,[4]

---

[4] Russell (1981, 79-80) terms the Euripides example 'a partial success'; but compare the similar reaction of nature to the epiphany of Poseidon, a passage explicitly admired in 9.8. For Aeschylus' less successful personification of a building, compare Longinus' disapproval in 4.6 of Plato's personification of walls

by turning an over-grotesque personification of a building feeling ecstasy into the sublime notion of a whole mountain sharing ecstasy at the epiphany of Dionysus (15.6). Key themes of greatness of thought and *mimesis* thus continue past the formal transition to analysis of technique—and, as we shall see, they continue through to the end, into 44.

Also significant is the choice of Demosthenes as the first example within the technical sources, since it heralds his prominence generally within the technical sources; contrast the leading role played earlier by Homer, who provides the first examples of the first source (8.2 and 9.2). Yet it is also Demosthenes who is the first author named in the whole work (2.3; cf. 1.2, the first quotation, a passage probably assumed by Longinus to be by Demosthenes). He is also already highlighted within the first source: his dense intensity of style is distinguished from those of Plato and Cicero (12.3-5), and it is Homer, Plato and Demosthenes who are the prime models for *mimesis* (14.1; cf. 36.2). But it is Demosthenes[5] more than the other two who combines the two innate sources and who best illustrates the ideal partnership or ἀλληλουχία of nature and technique (36.4; cf. 2.2-3, 22.1)—and it is this partnership which dominates Longinus' analysis of the technical sources—and which, likened to that between light and shade (17.2), significantly concludes the analysis of Demosthenes' Marathon oath, the first example to appear under the technical sources.

At the end of the treatment of figures there is another formal conclusion, but it is no mere textbook transition. It succinctly summarises the relationship of emotion to sublimity in a memorable antithesis: 'emotion is as much a part of sublimity as ethos is of pleasure' (29.2 πάθος δὲ ὕψους μετέχει τοσοῦτον ὅποσον ἦθος ἡδονῆς). The significant placement emphasises the importance of emotion, πάθος. Emotion, as we were told in 8.2-4, is important but not always necessary, and within each of

---

left 'to sleep and not rise up' (Pl. *Lg*.778d).

[5] Demosthenes also fits Longinus' primary interest in oratory: he aims to produce a work of use to 'those active in public affairs', πολιτικοὶ ἄνδρες (1.2, cf. 17.1); note also his use of 'the orator', ὁ ῥήτωρ, in 9.3, 11.2.

the other four sources Longinus sets next to each other examples with and without emotion (e.g. love and storms in 10.1-6, or the varied series in 23, 32 and 40). Emotion has, however, been particularly prominent within the treatment of figures (e.g. 19-21 on asyndeton; note also 38.3 where Longinus recommends emotion 'as I said before also in the use of figures'). Longinus therefore aptly ends his analysis of figures by recalling the importance of emotion.[6] This key theme is what matters, not what can be casually dismissed as 'so much unnecessary technical detail' (29.2 *ἐκ παρενθήκης τοσαῦτα πεφιλολογῆσθαι*).[7]

Digressions similarly emphasise main themes, as they may elsewhere, as in Sallust's *Catiline* and *Jugurtha* (e.g. *Cat*. 36.4 ff. and *Jug*. 37 ff.), Cicero's *Brutus* (esp.181 ff. and 284 ff.) and Horace's *Ars Poetica* (e.g. 60 ff.). These are no purple patches, they serve as focal points, asserting or reiterating main themes. So Russell (1981, 73): 'the most carefully composed and memorable parts of the book ... [they] are discursive additions to the scheme, and not integral to it, though they clearly are integral to the author's general purpose.'

Lacunae preclude certainty, but the extant text offers a striking pattern. All the digressions are in the form of comparisons, all focus on the nature or *φύσις* of the author, and they move from comparison of two works by a single author (Homer's *Iliad* and *Odyssey* in 9.11-5), to comparisons of similar and contrasting authors (Demosthenes and Plato, Demosthenes and Cicero in 12.3-5); and from individual admired models of the past to the more general and crucial digression on the nature of genius and flawless mediocrity in 33-6.

---

[6] It may also be significant that emotion is absent from the immediately preceding analysis of the figure of periphrasis (28-9.1). This is a figure particularly open to misuse, even in Plato: Longinus may implicitly suggest that it is safer to use figures with emotion.

[7] He similarly disdains unnecessary multiplication of examples, 22.4; contrast Caecilius (1.1, 4.2).

Patterns of imagery provide yet another form of unity.[8] Take, for example, the image of competition for victory and the first prize (key terms are those referring to first place, victory and competition, e.g. *πρωτεύειν* / *τὰ πρωτεῖα*, *τὰ νικητήρια* and *ἀγών*).[9] Thus at the beginning and end of the work the sublime is what wins first place for authors (1.3, 44.2); in our mimesis of past masters we contend like athletes for first place (13.4); and within a network of competitive imagery within the genius/mediocrity digression, Hyperides is a good all-rounder, who is often second but never gets the top prize (34.1), and it is Demosthenes who is always victorious over orators of every age (34.4); we are all, finally (35.2 ff.), born as competitors or spectators, marvelling at nature as if at a great festival and stirred to go beyond normal horizons to gain the eventual prize of victory (*τὰ νικητήρια*) from eternity itself (36.2).

A particularly prominent source of imagery is provided by the mighty forces of nature such as light, sun, thunderbolts, fire, rivers and sea. These too come to a climax in the genius/mediocrity digression (33-6). Longinus here richly exploits and pulls together imagery which he has previously used of particular authors, most notably in the digressions: so Homer is the Ocean, and the stream from which Plato draws (9.13, 13.3); Plato is himself a broad sea, and he flows smoothly (12.3, 13.1), whereas Demosthenes is like a rushing torrent of emotion (32.1). Water imagery links all three of Longinus' main models for our imitation, and in 35.4 this imagery comes to a climax, as Ocean and great rivers represent all great writers of genius, and are set above small, useful streams which do not evoke instinctive awe and admiration.[10]

---

[8] I shall not here give parallels for what are traditional areas of imagery, such as Homer as Ocean, Demosthenes as thunderbolt. I am also selective, omitting in particular imagery from vocabulary of inspiration, e.g. 8.4, 13.2, 16.2. For a useful list of the most colourful images, see Matelli 1987, 183-90, for parallels see the commentaries of Russell 1964 and Mazzucchi 1992.

[9] See 1.3; 13.4; 14.2; 33.1; 33.4; 34.1; 34.4; 35.2; 36.2; 44.2.

[10] Longinus inverts Callimachean praise of small springs; but for possible polemic also against the plain-style Atticism praised by Caecilius, note that imagery of such streams is also applied to prose authors: so Plato's plain style is

A still more pervasive nexus of imagery is that of light, fire, sun and thunderbolts. Demosthenes is a thunderbolt, as is the impact of sublimity itself (12.4, 1.4), whereas Cicero is a spreading fire, which also blazes but has greater mass (12.4). Where there is powerful imagination 'the factual aspect is concealed since it is *encircled by* light' (15.11 *τὸ πραγματικὸν ἐγκρύπτεται περιλαμπόμενον*); and, in an extended series of images in 17.2, if it is 'encircled by the light' of grandeur, artifice 'sinks out of sight' (*περιλαμφθεῖσα ... δέδυκε*), and the brilliant light of Demosthenes' passion hides the artifice of his figures, just as (in a double simile from nature and art) 'dim lights disappear in the surrounding light of the sun' (*τὰ ἀμυδρὰ φέγγη ἐναφανίζεται τῷ ἡλίῳ περιαυγούμενα*), or, in a painting, light throws the rest into shade. The sun is an apt symbol for the supremacy of nature or *φύσις*, but it also links Demosthenes back to Homer whose *Iliad* is like the bright noonday sun, the *Odyssey* like the setting sun, still grand but less intense (9.13). The link is all the stronger if Longinus asks us to remember that the sun's supremacy over other stars had been applied to Homer in an epigram of Leonidas (*AP*. 9.24 = 30 Gow-Page).[11]

Light and fire imagery then, like water imagery, comes to a climax in 33-5, and in a triple crescendo it also marks the end of three successive stages of the digression: (1) flawed genius is superior to flawless mediocrity, and the quick succession of examples ends with Pindar and Sophocles: both show flawed genius, 'they blaze vehemently but are often inexplicably extinguished' (33.5 *ἐπιφλέγουσι τῇ φορᾷ, σβέννυνται δ' ἀλόγως πολλάκις*); (2) so too, in an extensive comparison of two specific authors, Hyperides is inferior to Demosthenes, and the climax of the praise of Demosthenes is that we are blinded as 'he thunders and dazzles us' with his brilliance (34.4 *καταβροντᾷ καὶ καταφέγγει*); and then (3) in the culminating image of the whole digression, we marvel not

---

pure like the clearest springs (D.H. *Pomp.* 2) and Lysias is *puro tamen fonti quam magno flumini propior* (Quint. *Inst.* 10.1.78).

[11] The comparison itself is common, e.g. Quint. *Inst.* 8.5.29, Lucr. 3.1044 (of Epicurus), and see Nisbet-Hubbard (1970) on Hor. *Carm.* 1.12.48.

at small fires but at the fires of heaven—or at Etna's volcano, where the earth's convulsions throw up rivers of fire,[12] a final image which no doubt deliberately combines both fire and water (35.4).

The rich use of imagery within the digression in 33-5 is in itself striking, and is particularly apt, since it is a digression within an analysis of imagery, the use of metaphor and simile.[13] It also exploits and brings to a climax strands of imagery which are almost absent from the final chapter.[14] This will be deliberate: they come to their own separate climax in 33-5,[15] and there is a different focus with a correspondingly different range of imagery in 44.

Why, asks the philosopher in this final chapter, do sublime authors no longer exist? Why do we have authors able only to persuade and please?[16] Is it the lack of political freedom (44.1)? In reply, Longinus reaffirms that the author's own nature is the prime source of sublimity

---

[12] Rivers are in themselves a banal image to describe the flow of lava (e.g. [Arist.] *Mu.* 4, 395b); but Longinus shows his own literary claims to join the list of sublime authors with a deliberate echo of Pindar (*P.* 1.21 ff.; cf. 33.5) and the suggestion of violent disruption on the vast scale he admires in Homer in 9.6, *ἀναρρηγνυμένης μὲν ἐκ βάθρων γῆς*, 'when the earth is broken apart from its depths'.

[13] Longinus is, as often, his own example: see Innes 1994, 36-53, esp. 48 ff.

[14] Minor isolated use: 44.3 *ἔπαθλα*, *συνεκλάμπει*, and *νάματος*; 44.6 *καταβυθίζουσι*; 44.10 *ἐπικλύσειαν*.

[15] Hypothetically, the lacuna in 37.1 (a continuation of the analysis of metaphor) might include further examples of such imagery: if so, it would remain true that imagery from natural phenomena has some restrictions on its use, since it is virtually absent from what precedes the first and follows the last lacuna, 1-9.4 and 38-44. The lacuna in 9.4 also prevents us from knowing if the imagery found in both 9.1-3 and 44 was further supported in the lacuna (an attractive notion), but it remains significant within our extant text that the same imagery links two passages at structurally important points on the crucial importance of greatness of thought.

[16] Sublimity evokes a strong emotional impact, stronger than persuasion or pleasure, and it rejects the merely smooth or elegant: on this key theme cf. 1.4; 3.4; 10.4; 10.6; 15.9; 21.1; 29.2; 33.5; 39.1.

(44.6 ff.). To create sublime literature even in an age of moral decline, we must not let our inborn potential greatness of thought wither away, but aim at posterity. Longinus thus fulfils his opening promise to show how we may 'develop our nature' to produce sublimity (1.1 *τὰς ἑαυτῶν φύσεις προάγειν*), that we should nurture a mind (cf. e.g. 9.1) which despises desires such as wealth (cf. 7.1), and looks upwards[17] to seek what is immortal (44.8; cf. e.g. 36.3 and especially 36.1, where sublimity raises us up towards the greatness of god's mind). In short, it aims beyond the ephemeral to the whole of eternity, *πρὸς τὸν αἰῶνα* (44.9; cf. 1.3; 4.7; 9.3; 14.3; 34.4; 36.2).

These themes also conclude two patterns of imagery, (1) freedom, slavery and imprisonment, and (2) pregnancy, births and growths. Both appear also in 9.1-3, before the huge lacuna in 9.4, and it may seem significant that they appear precisely at the beginning of the discussion of the first source, greatness of thought—the very absence of which is seen as the key to the loss of sublimity at the very end of the work, in 44.

Imagery of freedom runs throughout the final chapter: first (44.1-5), the philosopher laments the loss of political freedom as a prison which stunts the sublime; he looks to *external* causation and the imagery is of imprisonment and maiming of the *body*; then Longinus in reply (44.6 ff.) looks to the freedom of the *mind* or spirit, and uses imagery of *internal* freedom. This recalls 9.3 where slavery of the mind is incompatible with sublimity, since 'those who think the petty thoughts *of slaves*' (*μικρὰ καὶ δουλοπρεπῆ φρονοῦντας*) cannot produce anything worthy of eternity. This enslaved mind is in contrast to the sublime mind which is 'as if *pregnant* with noble excitement' (9.1 *ὥσπερ ἐγκύμονας ... γενναίου παραστήματος*), and we can compare such a truly creative mind with the mind which is absorbed in ephemera, and will, 'as it were, miscarry and certainly *bring nothing to term* with regard for *the view of posterity*' (14.3 *ὥσπερ ἀμβλοῦσθαι, πρὸς τὸν τῆς ὑστεροφημίας ὅλως μὴ τελεσφορούμενα χρόνον*). These aborted stillbirths contrast with the true pregnancy of inspiration (13.2), where the creative stimulus of a predecessor

[17] Cf. Pl. *R.* 586a ff., quoted in 13.1.

is like the inspiration which fills the Delphic Sibyl and makes her '*pregnant*' (ἐγκύμων) with the divine power. The vivid image is a natural development from the pervasive vocabulary of creativity, especially γεννᾶν, γόνιμος, ἐντίκτω (all three of which appear in 44[18]); so for example (7.2) the audience feels 'as if it has itself created what it has heard' (ὡς αὐτὴ γεννήσασα ὅπερ ἤκουσεν). False creation is analogously described as like the false hollow swellings of the body (3.4 and 7.1), and in music it effects '*bastard* copies and likenesses of persuasion, not *legitimate* activities, as I said, proper to human nature' (39.3 εἴδωλα καὶ μιμήματα νόθα ἐστὶ πειθοῦς, οὐχὶ τῆς ἀνθρωπείας φύσεως, ὡς ἔφην, ἐνεργήματα γνήσια).

All this imagery is richly expanded in 44, where Longinus explains the loss of sublimity in terms of the stunting of the mind, as false emotions are allowed entry and then in turn, in exotic genealogical fantasy, create succeeding generations of further false offspring, such as desire for wealth and pleasure: as a result our innate potential withers away. These images include some deliberate vocabulary echoes of previous passages: thus the false offspring produce their own still worse children, who are 'not their *bastard* offspring but entirely *legitimate*', (44.7 οὐ νόθα ἑαυτῶν γεννήματα ἀλλὰ καὶ πάνυ γνήσια; cf. 39.3 quoted above); men no longer look up, no longer have concern for *the view of posterity* (ὑστεροφημία), and it is now destruction which *is brought to term* (44.8 τελεσιουργεῖσθαι; cf. 14.3 quoted above).

One final image in 44 is that of judgement in the law-court, 44.9: such imagery has appeared earlier: in 14.2 we must imagine the scrutiny of our work by great authors of the past as if at a lawcourt or theatre where they are *judges* (κριταῖς) and witnesses of sublimity; and in 33.4 sublime authors get 'the *vote* of first place' (τὴν τοῦ πρωτείου ψῆφον) for their greatness of thought; I suggest that this image recalls the role of the true *literary* critic, especially Longinus himself, as just such a judge or κριτής. Literary judgement too must be free and truthful (cf. 1.2; 7.4;

[18] Cf. γεννᾶν 2.1; 5; 6; 15.1; 15.12; 18.2; 38.4; 44.7; 44.11; γόνιμος 8.1; 31.1; 44.3; ἐντίκτω 16.3; 44.7.

34.1). References to his own judgement frame the genius digression (33.1 and 36.4), and Caecilius, by contrast, is the critic biassed by the two emotions of prejudiced hostility and favouritism (32.8).[19] The free judgement of the true critic is thus part of the wider notion of that inner freedom of mind which Longinus champions in 44. We are, he continues (44.9), as if 'taken prisoner' (*ἠνδραποδισμένοι*), so can we expect to find still 'any free judge of greatness' (*ἐλεύθερόν τινα κριτὴν τῶν μεγάλων*)? Are we to be ruled or free, 'let out as if from a prison', *ὥσπερ ἐξ εἱρκτῆς ἄφετοι* (44.10)?

The final chapter also points up the pervasive intertextuality, as theory, imagery and quotation all support each other in reinforcing key ideas. Escape from prison was an example in 15.9 (D. 24.208), and it is the concluding image cited from Plato's elaborate imagery of the body in *Timaeus* 65c-85e, when the soul is 'released free' from the body (32.5 *μεθεῖσθαι τε αὐτὴν ἐλευθέραν*; note that 'free' is the final and emphatic word in the sentence). Quotations which implicitly or explicitly assert the value of freedom are also more generally pervasive, such as those illustrating the fight of Greece against Persia or Athens against Macedon (15.10; 16.2 ff.; 22.1-2; 32.2).[20]

I have briefly indicated the use of such patterns of examples elsewhere (Innes 1994, 44-5; 49); thus Homer is a sun (9.13), so compare the previous examples of the light of creation ('let there be light and there was light'), followed by the light Ajax demands to let him fight (9.9-10);[21] I suggest here some more instances, restricting myself to Longi-

---

[19] The two emotions are described as *ἀκρίτοις*: may this difficult and disputed word mean 'lacking true judgement' or 'not appropriate to a true critic'?

[20] On these examples as part of the heroic spirit, see Segal 1987, 207-17, esp. 215-6. For Longinus it is freedom of mind or soul which characterises an Ajax or a Demosthenes.

[21] The examples also contribute gliding transitions between traditional categories of sublime thought (cf. Hermog. *Id.* 243 f. Rabe): gods, the divine and the heroic. Longinus avoids the formal use of textbook subdivisions but offers examples from each: cosmic disruption by gods, cosmic creation of light, and heroic demand for god to create light.

nus' favoured area of the mighty forces of nature: Cicero and Demosthenes are like fires (12.3-4), and Homer's madness (9.11) is compared to a destructive fire raging in the mountains; note too that the fire is raging in the mountains, and mountains are among the great natural phenomena of the earth, like Etna's fiery volcano in 35.4, the Aloadae piling mountain upon mountain to build a path to heaven (8.2), and the response to a god's epiphany that 'the whole mountain shared the ecstasy' (15.6 *πᾶν δὲ συνεβάκχευ' ὄρος*; cf. 9.8 when at Poseidon's epiphany 'the high mountains and woodland trembled', *τρέμε δ' οὔρεα μακρὰ καὶ ὕλη* ...).

Another example from nature is the image of stormwinds to suggest Demosthenes' forcefulness (20.3 *ὡς αἱ καταιγίδες*): compare forceful winds and storms in several quotations, especially 10.4-7, where some are successful, as in Homer's storm (10.5), in contrast to the failures of the *Arimaspeia* and Aratus (10.4 and 6), which are then immediately followed by the successful shipwreck in Archilochus (10.7). Outside this tight nexus of four successive examples illustrating failure and success, add 9.14 on the successful storms of the *Odyssey*, and the failure in detail of Herodotus' storm (43.1; but the thought, significantly, was a good one). Winds appear specifically in the storms cited from Homer (like Homer, it is forceful) and Herodotus (it gets tired!), and, to add another example of failure, the description of Boreas, the north wind, is said to be confused and lacking forcefulness (3.1): the thought is good but taken to an extreme of bombast.

I could add examples of heaven and far horizons (8.2; 9.4-5; 9.6; 9.8; 9.9; 15.4), all examples of the first source, nobility of thought, and all mirroring sublimity's own transcendence of the ordinary horizons of the cosmos (e.g. 35.2 ff.); but let me conclude: Longinus is his own best example, whether we consider the microcosm of minor points of technique such as 18.1 (the topic of rhetorical questions is introduced by rhetorical questions) or the macrocosm of overall unity. Longinus may seem concerned only with examples of sublimity from short passages or poems, but he himself illustrates, on a larger scale, the unity he praised in 10.1: to select 'what is most appropriate', *τὰ καιριώτατα*, and to combine them densely 'to be able to form a single body', *καθάπερ ἕν τι* σῶμα ποιεῖν δύνασθαι.[22] *On the Sublime* has true unity from interlocking key themes, examples and imagery, and the apparently separate limbs of the five sources (8.1) themselves merge together, a symbol of that single cohesive organic unity.

BIBLIOGRAPHY

Innes, D.C., Period and Colon: Theory and Example in Demetrius and Longinus, in: W.W. Fortenbaugh - D.C. Mirhady (eds.) *Peripatetic Rhetoric after Aristotle*. RUSCH VI. New Brunswick - London 1994, 36-53.

———, Longinus, Sublimity and the Low Emotions, in: Doreen Innes - Harry Hine - Christopher Pelling (eds.), *Ethics and Rhetoric*. Oxford 1995 [forthcoming].

Matelli, E., Struttura e stile del περὶ ὕψους, *Aevum* 61 (1987), 131-247.

Mazzucchi, C.M., Come finiva il περὶ ὕψους?, *Aevum Antiquum* 3 (1990), 143-162.

———, *Dionisio Longino Del Sublime*. Milan 1992.

Nisbet, R.G.M., - Hubbard, Margaret, *A Commentary on Horace, Odes I*. Oxford 1970.

Russell, D.A., *'Longinus', On the Sublime*. Oxford 1964.

———, Longinus Revisited, *Mnemosyne* 34 (1981), 143-55.

Segal, C., Writer as Hero: the Heroic Ethos in Longinus, On the Sublime, in: J. Servais et al. (eds.), *Stemmata. Mélanges de philologie, d'histoire et d'archéologie grecques offerts à Jules Labarbe*. Liège - Louvain-la-Neuve 1987, 207-17.

[22] Here again we see linking use of imagery and quotations. The Sappho quotation which follows itself illustrates unity of body and soul (10.2-3; compare the body/tabernacle examples from Xenophon and Plato in 32.5 ff.); and for imagery drawn from the body compare 11.2; 21.2; 30.1; 40.1; 43.5.

Some Aesthetic Views of Dio Chrysostom and Their Sources

Zsigmond Ritoók

Dio Chrysostom is not considered an important classic of aesthetics[1] and perhaps not without reason, though recently an important paper attempted to prove that Dio did have a more or less consistent theory of aesthetics, founded on a philosophy of culture, and another one, that he made some good observations at least with regard to the aesthetics of poetic production.[2] Still, however eclectic his aesthetic views may be, as it is generally admitted they are, they may be of interest because of their eclectic nature: from what sources does an educated man of this age derive his views on art and literature, an educated man whose profession is the art of words! A systematic review of all his statements on literary and art criticism, and a comparison with their possible sources, may even show how well Dio understood them: did he only more or less superficially echo them or apply them as they suited him, or was his understanding deeper and did he even improve upon what he read in other critics? This, nevertheless, goes beyond my present aim, which is only to make a contribution to such an investigation.

What Dio has to say on literature can be traced back to various authorities. Some of his statements go back, in the final analysis, to the

---

[1] The only work which treats Dio as a literary critic comprehensively is M. Valgimigli's book. The latest authorative summary of his whole critical activity is that by Russel 1989. The author of the latest monograph on Dio, Desideri, denies that Dio was a literary critic; according to Desideri he was a politician and even his literary criticism is determined by his political views, cf. 1978, 474; 484.

[2] T. Szepessy in the postface to his Hungarian translation (with a rich commentary) of *Or.* 21 in the periodical *Antik Tanulmányok* 29 (1982), 127-33; cf. also Seeck 1990.

sophists, especially to Gorgias,[3] but is is rather doubtful if he knew these from first hand or only from handbooks, or indeed, in some cases, from Plato's refutation of them, since in his whole speech on Socrates he speaks of the sophists, including Gorgias, in the spirit of Plato ('they made much money', 'they delivered many speeches, which, however, do not make the slightest sense': 54.1). And even if this could be explained from the aim of the speech (glorification of Socrates as against the sophists), the statement in the same speech that 'the speeches of those admired sophists are lost and nothing but their names has remained' (54.4) suggests that Dio can hardly have read the texts of the sophists themselves.

By contrast, he was the more familiar with the works of the Socratic school: Plato, Xenophon, Antisthenes; several of his statements concerning aesthetics are traceable to them. According to Dio, Antisthenes established, prior to Zeno, that some things in Homer are said *κατὰ δόξαν*, others *κατὰ ἀλήθειαν* (53.5).[4] Beauty is a sort of light, he says (21.14; 12.52): this must be Socratic (cf. X. *Smp.* 1.9; Pl. *Phdr.* 250b). A king must not listen to slackened harmonies and must not pay attention to indecent and riotous art, Dio says (2.55), in this echoing Plato again (*R.* 395d-396d; 398d-399e; etc.).

Nevertheless, his statements are not always in harmony with each other. He says, again in agreement with Plato (and, of course, with others as well) that Homer does not tell the truth with regard to the gods (11.17-8, cf. Pl. *R.* 377d-379e, etc.). Still, he asserts that Homer is not only an excellent chastiser (*σωφρονιστής* 2.54), but also that he has taught beneficial and useful things regarding virtue and vice (53.11) and even that Homer undertook to educate people like Socrates (55.11), while Plato refused to accept Homer as an educator (*R.* 559c-600e; 605c-607a, etc.),

---

[3] *καιρός*: 71.6, cf. VS 90, 19-20 and Gorgias VS 82 B 13; oratory and poetry as *γοητεία*: 2.19; 12.71; cf. 82 B 11.10; poetry as *φάρμακον*: 11.42, cf. VS 82 B 11.14; *ἀπάτη*: 32.5, cf. VS 82 B 23.

[4] For a thorough examination of this passage see Hillgruber 1989, 15-24, with a history of the problem.

let alone one like Socrates.[5] This, however, can be accounted for by the different aims of the speeches: in *Or.* 11 Dio wants to prove that the whole *Iliad* is a fictional story, which is why he makes use of all possible arguments that suit this purpose, while in *Or.* 53 and 55 he wants to extol Homer in all respects, and consequently he makes use of other, not less old and acknowledged arguments (cf. Ar. *Ra.* 1034-6; X. *Smp.* 4.6, etc.). There are, however, other, more interesting disagreements where Dio seems to follow different authorities. The aim of the present paper is to discuss some of these cases.

Plato maintains that poets, not knowing what truth is, cannot express it either, unless they are possessed by a god (*Ion* 598d-e; *R.* 598d-601b, etc.). Thus, if not led by a god, they are led by the expectations and pleasure of the masses (*R.* 602b; *Lg.* 656c-657e; 668a-b, etc.). The orators, on the other hand, do not even care for the truth, their ambition is merely to say the probable (*εἰκός*, *Phdr.* 267a, cf. 260e). The word *εἰκός* appears in Dio too, but not concerning rhetoric, but in connection with poetry or at least fictional prose.

Dio discusses the word several times when speaking of tragedy or of myths treated in tragedies. In the speech in which he compares the several plays on Philoctetes of the three great tragedians, he calls attention to the issue how strange it would have been if—as in the drama of Aeschylus—the Lemnians would not even have seen Philoctetes and helped him. 'It is probable that he met some aid, even if only scantily' (52.8: *εἰκὸς μὲν τυγχάνειν αὐτόν, σπανίως δέ*). In the speech which treats the Nessus and Deianeira myth (elaborated by Sophocles and at least mentioned by Archilochus, fr. 285-88 West), Dio talks with an anonymous interlocutor and points to some elements of the story which are not credible (*πιθανόν*). The interlocutor is afraid that in this way the myth will be destroyed. 'By no means—Dio answers—if we consider how it happened and how it is probable to have happened' (60.3: *ὡς ἐγένετο καὶ εἰκός ἦν γενέσθαι*). And a little later, the text runs as follows:

---

[5] For Dio as an educator, see Kindstrand 1973, 125-7; Desideri 1978, 481-2; on Homer's wisdom: Kindstrand 1973, 124-7; on the divine origin of education: Kindstrand 1973, 115-9.

'Deianeira after having heard it [the words of Nessus, as interpreted by Dio] paid no cursory attention to the words, but considered how rightly the Centaur had spoken, as it was probable (*ὥσπερ εἰκός ἦν*), since she wished to have her husband under her control' (60.5).

This, however, is not simply a question of usage: it reveals also Dio's view of poetry (fictional prose) in general. In his fourth speech on kingship he presents a dialogue between Alexander the Great and Diogenes. In the introduction he says: 'I should like to tell the probable course of their conversation' (4.3: *ὡς δὲ εἰκός ἐκείνοις γενέσθαι τὴν συνουσίαν ἐκείνην εἴποιμ' ἄν*). That is to say: the dialogue may be fictitious, but it must suit the requirements of probability. The same teaching lies, negatively formulated, in a remark of *Or.* 11. Dio's intention is to prove that Homer did not tell the truth regarding the Trojan war or at least badly distorted it. According to the epic tradition, Helen became the wife of Deiphobus after Paris' death and the Trojans did not return her to Menelaus, although they could have saved their city by doing so. 'Nothing of this is probable or possible' (11.70: *τούτων οὐδὲν εἰκὸς οὐδὲ δυνατόν*; cf. also 11.72; 11.137). Even more important is perhaps the question with which he finishes his expose of the story of Chryses: 'Do you wish to hear how things really happened or how it would have been good for things to have happened?' (61.18: *Σὺ δὲ πότερον ἀκούειν θέλοις ἂν ὡς γέγονεν ὄντως ἢ καλῶς εἶχε γενέσθαι*. I have accepted Emperius' emendation instead of the version of the manuscripts': *γέγονε πάντως*).

The two other adjectives which Dio used together with *εἰκός* in the texts quoted above, namely 'possible' (*δυνατόν*) and 'credible' (*πιθανόν*) seem also to be of a certain importance. They are used more than once. Homer describes the royal palace of Alcinous and Menelaus respectively 'surpassing what is real (*ἀληθές*) and almost what is possible (*δυνατόν*, 79.1)'. Aeschylus 'did not bother to make Odysseus credible' (*πιθανός*), while Euripides 'showed the greatest intelligence and credibility' (*πιθανότης*: 52.14; cf. 52.9; 11; 11.107; etc.).

Poetic representations should be, then, probable, possible, credible. This triad of requirements is not Platonic, but Aristotelian. It was Aristotle who applied *εἰκός*, this technical term of rhetoric, as a term and as a criterion in judging poetry (cf. *Po.* 1451a28; 38; b9; etc.; for *δυνατόν*: 1451a39; 1460a27 etc.; *πιθανόν*: 1451b16 etc.). Even one of Dio's telling examples is Aristotelian. When discussing the incredible things and lies that Homer tells, Dio mentions Hector running around the city and Achilleus following him (and nor overtaking him, no matter how quick-footed he was, cf. 9.17), while the Achaeans gaze at them as if attending a spectacle and nobody helps Achilleus (11.107-8). Aristotle mentions the same case as proof that epic admits strange things, which would be ridiculous in the theatre (*Po.* 1460a13-7).[6] This coincidence is the more remarkable because Homer does in fact explain the situation: Achilleus forbade the Greeks to pursue or kill Hector (*Il.* 22.206-7).

The closing sentence of an argument in the Trojan speech is certainly Aristotelian. In order to prove that the Trojans were not defeated, Dio recounts the achievements of the Trojans after the alleged sack of Troy as accomplished facts and concludes by saying: 'A thing which happened was possible to happen' (11.139: *τὸ γενόμενον δυνατὸν γενέσθαι*). The same is told, of course in a different (and more suitable) context, by Aristotle: 'things which happened are obviously possible ones' (*Po.* 1451b17-8: *τὰ γενόμενα φανερὸν ὅτι δυνατά*).

Finally, the closing question of *Or.* 61 ('Do you wish to hear how things really happened or how it would have been good for things to have happened?') brings to mind Aristotle's words about the difference between the historian and the poet: the former tells things which happened, the latter things which could happen, as it is possible that they happened (*Po.* 1451a36-b19);[7] and, as Dio's remark in 4.3, quoted above, proves, he tried to compoe his fictitious dialogues according to this principle.

Perhaps Aristotle, or Aristotle too, may be suspected to lurk behind 55.12, where Dio claims that Plato had good reasons for giving names to his interlocutors: 'to comprehend men from their words and words from

---

[6] Cf. also Valgimigli 1913, 44.

[7] As Desideri 1978, 489 sums up the tenor of this passage: a false story that makes sense is better than a verified one without sense, a formulation which recalls that of Aristotle, *Po.* 1461b11-2, though Desideri does not refer to it.

the men is not easy for others than philosophers and educated people'. He then proceeds by maintaining that Plato when representing a boaster presents at the same time boasting and, further, refers to many figures in the epics whom Homer presents as representatives of certain characteristics or qualities who are characterised as such by their words and deeds (55, 14-21).[8] Besides, Dio, emphasises here as well that Homer does not speak at random; and in another speech he points out that in several cases a person's clothes, house and way of life are described in accordance with his character (2.39-43).[9]

Aristotle points out in the *Poetics* that according to their character (ἦθος) and way of thinking (διάνοια) people possess a certain quality (1449b37-8) and adds a little later that ἦθος is 'that according to which we say that the acting persons are of a certain quality' and that by διάνοια he means parts (of the tragic dialogue) in which 'they prove something or deliver a view by speaking' (1450a5-8). Some pages later he states again that characters of a tragedy 'will have ἦθος if their speech or action reveal a decision' (1454a17-8). Words and deeds are connected and they make clear a person's qualities and way of thinking. A similar passage can be found in the *Rhetoric*, where Aristotle expounds that regarding elocution the author has to take into consideration the kind of person in question as well as his habits, 'according to which he has a certain quality' and 'if he selects words appropriate to the habit, he will create the character' (1408a25-31). This seems to be similar to Dio's view.[10]

Dio, then, seems to have understood Aristotle, though not his full philosophical depth. The work of art, he says, (1) need not cling to the particulars of reality, but it must be probable and credible. He applies (2) the requirement of probability to both poetry and fictional prose, i.e. he

---

[8] Kindstrand 1973, 134-5.

[9] I do not see why Valgimigli thinks—with reference to *Rh.* 1368b32 ff. and *Po.* 1452a1 ff.—that this is directed against Aristotle.

[10] Desideri 1978 traces this opinion back to the Stoics, with reference to Str. 1.2.3; Strabo, however, only says that the wise is the only poet.

treats fictional literature as a whole according to the same principle. This outlook was initiated by Aristotle (who in turn borrowed some ideas from Gorgias), who complains (*Po.* 1447b9-13) that in Greek there is no common name for poetry and Socratic dialogues. Aristotle's view was developed by Theophrastus (fr. 64; 65 Wimmer) and by the Stoics (Str. 1.2.6). Dio further emphasised (3) the importance of the harmony of elocution and character—undoubtedly a commonplace notion even before Aristotle, but for Aristotle elocution is indicative of character, and so it is for Dio (both are even indicative of the other). He adds that the presentation of the surrounding must also be in harmony with, or even indicative of the character. Finally—this too may perhaps be mentioned—as an author also he himself composed his dialogues according to these principles, as he constantly kept in mind what was probable both in physical and in psychological respect.[11]

Dio, further, has something to say about the relation between the poet and his audience. Homer, the poet of kings, had no success among peasants (2.12); it is impossible that Homer, though being a beggar, did not sing to the taste and at the pleasure of those with whom he curried favour (11.15); Homer overstated the feats of the Greeks when performing his poems to the ignorant crowd and so he was not refuted even by those who knew things well (11.92). The poet's activity and impact depends, then, on the kind of audience. But this is not all Dio has to say. 'We think we will find the thoughts of the people expressed especially in the poets... For it is clear that if the poem were not in keeping with the sentiments of the people, if it would not exhibit the same views as their own, they would not like and praise the poets as wise and brave men who tell the truth.' The poet is the spokesman (*προφήτης*) of the people[12] and says the same things (*συνήγορος*) as they (7.98-101).

This is a view which we know from Plato, and Aristotle follows suit, though in a totally different context. Plato utters it with contempt (e.g. *R.* 602b), in Aristotle it follows from the principle, accepted by Dio as well,

[11] Cf. Desideri 1978, 487-9.

[12] According to *Or.* 36.42 the poet is the *προφήτης* of the Muses.

that the poet has to compose according to probability (εἰκός), the probable being, in Aristotle's definition, 'that which people know to happen mostly or not to happen, or to exist or not to exist' (*APr.* 70a4-5; cf. *Rh.* 1357a34-b1). People thus recognise somehow their own world in the poet's work. Again, Dio lacks the philosophical depth of the two masters; he simply takes the view as a thing agreed upon and known, obviously from his own oratorical experience. Nevertheless, he sees clearly that there is an interaction between the poet and his audience: they depend in a certain sense upon each other.[13]

An audience, however, is not homogeneous and even the inferior should be allowed some sort of relaxation; this is, of course, inferior itself, but the artist must have the right to amuse the masses too, even if by some perverted sort of art—as Aristotle points out in the *Politics* (1342a18-28). This idea, too, may be found in Dio: he acknowledges that shoddy and worthless spectacles are also necessary and to be permitted 'because of the frailty of the masses' and sometimes even the better may need this kind of entertainment (32.45).

Dio mentions Aristotle several times, though never in the contexts of the aforementioned passages. How did Dio know about Aristotle's views? From commentaries of the age, which incorporated several of his statements?[14] From his Ἀπορήματα Ὁμηρικά?[15] Dio refers to Aristotle's works only once: 'Aristotle himself, with whom, it is said, literary scholarship (κριτική τε καὶ γραμματική) began, treats the poet [Homer] in many dialogues, admiring and extolling him for the most part' (53.1). Dio could have received his knowledge, accordingly, from the dialogues of Aristotle, which were read by most educated people. The Aristotelian views which we know from the *Poetics* he probably knew from the

[13] Desideri (1978, 473, cf. also 476) speaks of the interaction of poet and popular belief.

[14] Kroll 1915, 609-10.

[15] Valgimigli 1913, 42 ff., rejected by Kroll 1915.

dialogue Περὶ ποιητῶν, in which Aristotle expounded ideas similar to those found in the *Poetics*.

The idea that Dio was influenced by Aristotle is, of course, not a new one. As early as 1902, W.A. Montgomery collected many passages from the Homer scholia, especially from Porphyry, which recall some passages of Dio's *Or.* 11. Dio and these scholia, then, must have a common source, and Montgomery maintained this was Aristotle. I do not wish to examine all these parallels (in my opinion not all of them are convincing). Rather, I have tried to make it probable that Dio took his knowledge or at least some important elements of it from Aristotle himself, probably mainly from his dialogues, but I don't want to exclude the possibility that he knew of other works too.[16] Furthermore, it is my claim that Aristotle's influence on Dio is not confined to *Or.* 11, that it goes beyond some details, and that Dio learned from Aristotle more than what he says about Homer. Aristotle's views, blended with the opinions of others, especially with those of Plato, determine Dio's whole view of poetry and even his own way of composition.

BIBLIOGRAPHY

Desideri, P., *Dione di Prusa. Un intellettuale greco nell'Imperio Romano*. Messina - Firenze 1978.

Hillgruber, M., Dion Chrysostomos 36 (53) 4-5 und die Homerauslegung Zenons, *MH* 46 (1989), 15-24.

Hintenlang, A., *Untersuchungen zu den Homer-Aporien des Aristoteles*, diss. Heidelberg 1961.

Kindstrand, J.F., *Homer in der zweiten Sophistik*. Uppsala 1973.

Kroll, W., Randbemerkungen, *RhM* 70 (1915), 609-10.

Montgomery, W.A., Oration XI of Dio Chrysostomos. A Study in Sources, in: *Studies in Honour of Basil L. Gildersleeve*. Baltimore 1902, 405-12.

---

[16] In the first place, the ἀπορήματα are relevant here. As Hintenlang 1961 has proved, Porphyry used this work of Aristotle's, and numerous comments recall the *Poetics* too.

Russell, D.A., Dio of Prusa, in: G.A. Kennedy (ed.), *The Cambridge History of Literary Criticism* I. Cambridge 1989, 299-302.

Seeck, G.A., Dion Chrysostomos als Homerkritiker (Or. 11), *RhM* 133 (1990), 97-107.

Valgimigli, M., *La critica letteraria di Dione Crisostomo*. Bologna 1913.

The Mythographus Homericus

Franco Montanari*

1. Introduction

The so-called *Mythographus Homericus* (henceforth MH) is one of the many interesting issues in the field of ancient Homeric scholarship and mythography. In the light of the progress of research and the new evidence obtained above all from papyri, I would argue that it is of interest to reconsider this text globally and to review the main questions it raises. I will thus mainly be concerned with its origin and its historical-cultural position.

Before providing a definition of what is meant by the term MH, a few words are required on the so-called D-scholia to Homer, an important corpus of Homeric scholia which includes a considerable amount of glossographical and paraphrastic material as well as a good deal of *zetemata*, mythographical *historiae* and some other material.[1] The D-scholia are the most widespread scholia corpus in Byzantine manuscripts: they were first edited by Janus Lascaris (Rome 1517, the *Iliad*), and by Franciscus Asulanus (Venice 1528, the *Odyssey*) and remained almost the only scholia widely used and known until Villoison published the Venetian scholia in 1788, though subsequently falling into neglect. After the *editiones principes* of Lascaris and Asulanus, the D-scholia were reprinted several times in different forms, but no modern critical edition has so far been produced. The great edition of the Scholia vetera to the *Iliad* by H. Erbse includes the scholia derived from VMK (*Viermännerkommentar*, a

---

* English translation by Rachel Barritt.

[1] Moreover, the *D-scholia* are usually provided in the codices by the *hypotheseis* (book summaries).

compilation of materials taken from Didymus, Aristonicus, Nikanor, Herodianus) together with the so-called *Scholia exegetica*: the element still needed to complete the set of the *Scholia vetera* to the *Iliad* is precisely the corpus of D-scholia. For about a century now, interest in this class of scholia has been growing.[2] I myself have been working on an edition of the D-scholia to the *Iliad* for several years and here I use texts from Iliadic D-scholia drawn from my provisional collation. The D-scholia to the *Iliad* are much richer and quantitatively more extensive than those to the *Odyssey* (I thus believe that the corpus of D-scholia to the *Odyssey* can be included in a new edition of the complete *Odyssey* scholia).[3]

The glossographical material of the D-scholia, providing a 'translation' of Homeric lemmata represented by single words or short expressions into an easier and more understandable form of Greek, carries on the ancient *Scholia minora* or glossaries, which are widespread in many papyri from the first century BCE to the seventh century CE. The same glossographical material is also found in the so-called *Lexeis Homerikai* (very close to the D-scholia), in Apollonius Sophista and in many streams of Greek lexicography. Indeed, this is in itself a highly interesting feature of the D-scholia, but it is not the subject I intend to focus on at this time.

The mythographical material is represented by a fairly large group of short stories of varying length (*historiae*), providing mythographical accounts whenever the Homeric text offers a suitable opportunity. Such *historiae* usually have the following structure: they are introduced by the Homeric lemma providing the link with the text of the *Iliad* or the *Odyssey*, which is followed by the main body of the comment with a mythological account; finally, at least in most cases, one finds a subscription attributing the content of the *historia* to some authority: ἡ ἱστορία

[2] *Status quaestionis* in Montanari 1969; cf. Schmidt 1976; Snipes 1988; Montanari 1994.

[3] It is reported that an edition of the Scholia to the *Odyssey* is being prepared by A.R. Dyck.

παρὰ τῷ δεῖνα or (*ὡς*) *ἱστορεῖ ὁ δεῖνα, οὕτως ὁ δεῖνα*;[4] at times, however, the subscription is missing. These mythographical *historiae* are precisely what is meant by 'MH' in the corpus of the Homeric D-scholia transmitted by the codices. Its ancient predecessor is represented by similar mythographical *historiae* on papyrus fragments, for which the name MH is also used. Thus when we talk about the MH, we are dealing with that whole set of mythographical *historiae* on Homer found in papyrus fragments as well as in the D-scholia.

The corpus of *Iliad* D-scholia contains some two hundred mythographical *historiae*, while a significantly smaller number are to be found in the D-scholia to the *Odyssey*. As for the papyri, they provide a markedly richer testimony today than was available twenty or even only ten years ago and are composed of about ten pieces, eight for the *Iliad* and two (of which one is doubtful) for the *Odyssey*. The list at the end of this article stands to my knowledge as the complete repertory of MH fragments available to date. However it should be kept in mind that there exists a multitude of papyri containing remains of mythographical narrations, among which it is quite likely that some fragment of the MH may be hidden. If fate has resulted in loss of the Homeric lemma and of the subscription in the fragment and if the preserved *historia* turns out to be noticeably different from that present in the D-scholia or indeed if it is not present at all in the D-scholia, then identification of the papyrus text will be extremely difficult and always open to doubt. Fortunately, however, the undisputed pieces do offer sufficient material for satisfactory evaluation.

Let us begin with a few general observations on the papyrus fragments of the MH. First, we will consider their chronological distribution. The oldest piece dates back to the period between the end of the first century and the beginning of the second century CE (*Il.* 002, cf. also 004), but most of the pieces belong to the second century CE. From the third century CE we have one papyrus of the *Iliad* (008) and the only

[4] But one can also have *ὡς γὰρ ἱστορεῖ ὁ δεῖνα* and then the *historia* (e.g. Hellanicus in *D-sch.* on *Iliad* 3.144).

certain piece of evidence of the *Odyssey* (001); the latest find, a parchment codex referring to the *Iliad* (007), dates from the fifth century. As for the book formats, the largest group consists of the papyrus rolls datable roughly to the second century CE (*Il.* 001, 002, 003, 005, 006);[5] there are also two papyrus codices of the third century CE (*Il.* 008; *Od.* 001) and a parchment codex from the fifth century CE (*Il.* 007). Taken together, these pieces provide a range of findings stretching from about the first to the fifth century CE and presenting the various book formats that were widespread in the imperial age.

Of particular interest, from this point of view, is the ostrakon *Iliad* 004 (*PSI* 1000), dating from the 1st-2nd century CE, in which a small remnant of the *historia* to *Iliad* 13.217-8 has been identified.[6] In all likelihood this was no more than a limited copying exercise from a text that must obviously have borne the title of the book, the Homeric lemma and the corresponding *historia* (or possibly a group of *historiae*).

N 216-8 *εἰσάμενος φθογγὴν ᾿Ανδραίμονος υἷι Θόαντι*
ὅς πάσῃ Πλευρῶνι καὶ αἰπεινῇ Καλυδῶνι
Αἰτωλοῖσιν ἄνασσε

Ostrakon PSI 1000.

1]... *τῆς* N
ὃς πάσῃ] Π̣λευρῶνι καὶ αἰπεινῇ Καλυδῶνι
3 *Αἰτωλὸς ὁ ᾿Ε]ν̣δυμίωνος παῖς κατήντησ-* N 217
εν εἰς ᾽Απιν ?]

1 *τῆς* N (poss. (*᾿Ιλιαδὸς*) *ἱστο]ρ̣ί̣α̣ι*) Salvadori 2-4 suppl. Salvadori: *εἰς ᾿Επειόν, ὃς ἦν ᾿Ε]ν̣δυμίωνος παῖς, κατήντησ<εν>* ¦ *ἡ βασιλεία* ed. pr.

Sch. D N 217. **Πλευρῶνι καὶ Καλυδῶνι**: *ἀντὶ τοῦ Πλευρῶνος καὶ Καλυδῶνος, εἰσὶ δὲ πόλεις Αἰτωλίας*. **CHV La**

[5] I will disregard *Od.* 002, a papyrus roll of the third century CE, of uncertain identification.

[6] The text had previously been given a doubtful attribution to an unknown tragedy: cf. *TrGF* II F 709 (= adesp. 323 d Nauck - Snell).

P.Ryl. 536: *Scholia minora* N 198-562

Recto → col. 1.12-13 Π]λευρὼν καὶ [Καλυδών πόλεις Αἰτωλίας [N 217

Sch. D N 218. **Αἰτωλοῖσιν ἄνασσε**: Αἰτωλὸς παῖς μὲν ἦν Ἐνδυμίωνος, ὃς ἀκούσιον φόνον δράσας ἔφυγεν εἰς τὴν ἀπ' αὐτοῦ προσαγορευθεῖσαν Αἰτωλίαν κἀκεῖ τεκνοῦται Πλευρῶνα, ἀφ' οὗ ἡ ἐν Αἰτωλίᾳ πόλις Πλευρὼν ἐκλήθη. τούτου δὲ γίνονται δύο παῖδες Κούρης τε καὶ Καλυδών, ἀφ' ὧν ἄλλαι δύο πόλεις ἐν Αἰτωλίᾳ προσαγορεύθησαν. **ACHRV La**

Sch. ex. N 217-8. **ὃς πάσῃ Πλευρῶνι <καὶ αἰπεινῇ Καλυδῶνι / Αἰτωλοῖσιν ἄνασσε>**: Αἰτωλὸς ὁ Ἐνδυμίωνος, Ἠλεῖος τὸ γένος, Ἆπιν ἀκουσίως τὸν Φορωνέως ἀνελὼν φεύγει εἰς τὴν ἀπ' αὐτοῦ Αἰτωλίαν προσαγορευθεῖσαν, ἴσχει δὲ παῖδα Πλευρῶνα, οὗ ἐγένοντο Κούρης καὶ Καλυδών, ἀφ' ὧν αἱ πόλεις. οὕτω Δηΐμαχος (FGrHist 65 F 1). **T**

The tiny remnant of the ostrakon is sufficient to indicate that it is not the remains of a glossary, as can be seen by comparing it with the *D-Sch.* to 13.217 and with *P.Ryl.* 536: on the contrary it was a genuine *historia*, as confirmed by comparing it with *D-Sch.* to 13.218 and with *Sch.ex.* to 13.217-8, which preserve two different versions that can fairly certainly be traced back to the same original source (unfortunately, no evidence on papyrus is available for this particular *historia*). The presence of the verb *κατήντησεν* suggests that the story of the fight between Endymion's son Aetolus and Apis, followed by the involuntary killing, was more extensive in the ostrakon source than the more concise form in the scholia. In any case, this utilisation is eloquent testimony to the popularity of the MH already in the second century.

The second observation is that the material in our possession allows us to state that the MH provided a systematic mythographical commentary to the entire *Iliad* and the entire *Odyssey*. *PSI* 1173 (*Od.* 001), dating from the third century CE, is the only certain papyrus for the *Odyssey*, but it is also one of the most interesting fragments and the most extensive one: from this papyrus codex parts of eight leaves are extant, in which *historiae* to books 3, 11, 13 and 14[7] can be recognised. This was therefore an exemplar that undoubtedly covered the entire poem (in forty or so pages?). For the *Iliad* the documentation is richer: 003 (*P.Oxy*. 3830 + *P.Lit.Lond.* 142), a papyrus roll of the second century CE, has preserved parts of books 7, 8, 9; 005 (*P.Oxy*. 3003), also a papyrus roll of the second century CE, offers remains of books 13, 14, 15; 006 (*P.Oxy*. 4096), another papyrus roll of the second century CE, covers books 18-24;[8] the other pieces of evidence present *historiae* to books 1, 13, 19, 20, and among these there are the remains of a papyrus codex of the third century CE (008) and the remains of a parchment codex of the fifth century CE (007). For the *Iliad* we have no extant exemplar similar to papyrus codex PSI 1173 of the *Odyssey*, which covers no fewer than twelve books (from 3 to 14), but *Iliad* 006 (*P.Oxy*. 4096) is even more extensive as far as the quantity of text preserved is concerned and offers fragments of a papyrus roll with remains from books 18-24, covering a total of seven books and extending to the end of the poem. The overall set of findings ranges from book 1 to book 24 and provides unequivocal evidence that this type of erudite exegesis existed for the whole of the *Iliad* as well.

The evidence available to date also indicates that the MH was in circulation quite separately from any other kind of exegetic material. This is a point worth noting, since the imperial age is dotted with examples of rich miscellaneous commentaries of highly diversified content: discussions on text constitution intermingled with exegetic material, grammatical disquisitions, matters of antiquarian interest and so on. In the framework of Homeric scholarship, there is certainly no lack of *hypomnemata* offering a rich array of contents, yet it would appear that the MH circulated quite independently, unaccompanied by other material, appearing in

---

[7] One of the eight fragments is unidentified and could belong to yet another book.

[8] The edition in the *P.Oxy.* series will be prepared by P. Schubert, to whom I would like to express my heartfelt thanks for the information concerning the papyrus.

copies containing only the isolated *historiae*. The findings that have come to light so far have provided ample confirmation that this was indeed the general rule. A similar case is that of the glossographical material called *Scholia minora*, mentioned at the beginning of this paper: this material is present in a large number of glossaries (taking both the *Iliad* and the *Odyssey* together, the total is close to one hundred), in which Homeric lemmata represented by single words or short expressions are accompanied by a 'translation' into an easier and more understandable form of Greek. Indeed the numerous fragments of glossaries (*Scholia minora*) and a considerable number of papyri of the MH demonstrate that during the imperial age these two streams of Homeric scholarship each enjoyed considerable autonomy and were widespread at several different levels, even in schools. Literal translation into a currently used language and mythographic explanation (in different forms and with different intentions) are the two most ancient forms of Homeric exegesis, traceable back to at least the fifth century BCE: at the same time they also supplied the most substantial amounts of materials that eventually contributed to forming the corpus of Homeric D-scholia.

2. Structure and origin of the MH

How was the MH built up? How did it originate? Some time ago the MH was regarded merely as a sort of mythographical handbook, differing little from many other similar works in circulation, which could have been a school compilation and was certainly not considered a high level work. Such a view was derived from the opinions expressed by E. Schwartz, E. Maass, E. Bethe and J. Panzer towards the end of the last century. Schwartz went as far as to deny that the subscriptions of the *historiae* in the Homeric D-scholia could be awarded any reliability at all and he rejected the indications of sources contained therein. When discussing the indirect use of sources in Ps.-Apollodorus *Bibliotheca*, he refused to accept the view that, on account of the subscriptions, the *historiae* in the D-scholia should be regarded as genuine excerpts from the authors cited. Rather, he argued, they had derived from the use of compendia similar to

Ps.-Apollodorus *Bibliotheca* and the subscriptions were no more than quotations placed at the end, which could refer to a single variant or to a part of the story, and only in a few fortunate exceptions, when the compiler had taken the entire story from an author and had cited the latter, did they encompass the entire *excerptum* without substantial error.[9] Such a view was also shared by E. Bethe, who identified the origin in a 'compendium fabularis historiae',[10] and by E. Maass, who then claimed that the *historiae* were not the fruit of Homeric exegesis, but derived instead from a 'mythologisches Handbuch', probably dating from the second century CE and similar both to Ps.-Apollodorus and to Ps.-Hyginus.[11]

Following a similar line of thought, J. Panzer contended that the origin of this material was to be found in a separate handbook of mythology: its textual tradition as mythographical D-scholia, he maintained, was of a later date and wholly secondary: 'Hoc igitur ex iis quae supra disputavimus pro certo opinor habemus, aliunde *ἱστορίας* reliquiis scholiis D adscriptas esse ... ad explicanda Homeri verba *ἱστορίας* primitus non fuisse destinatas contendo ... Compendio debentur mythologico Apollodori bibliothecae simillimo'.[12] Thus the true origins of the MH were kept at one remove from the framework of Homeric scholarship[13] and high erudition, on the assumption that its historical-cultural status was that of a fairly late and rather low-level mythographical compendium, based on indirect knowledge gleaned from manuals, and only subsequently used to enrich collections of Homeric scholia with

---

[9] Schwartz 1881; synthesis in Schwartz 1894, 2878.

[10] Bethe 1887, 80-90.

[11] Maass 1884, 537 n. and 563-4.

[12] Panzer 1892, 61-3; cf. also Wilamowitz 1925, 76-7.

[13] I should add that a different opinion was in fact expressed: Schwarz 1878 believed that the *historiae* derived from a mythological commentary on Homer, but his opinion and arguments were decidedly refuted by Panzer 1892, 61-2.

mythographical notes: none of these could be viewed as particularly erudite, despite the presence of subscriptions containing many great names of the noblest Greek literature, for the subscriptions were not held to be valid.

The first observation that needs to be made at this point is that the view outlined so far was based exclusively on an examination of the *historiae* in the Homeric D-scholia and could not benefit from any evidence from papyri. The first MH papyrus was edited in 1903 (*Il.* 002), but taken in itself, it was still far from providing a clarification of the true nature of the problem. The richest one, *PSI* 1173 (*Od.* 001), was not published until 1932. Naturally, comparisons with the Homeric scholia were made within the general framework of speculation on ancient precedents of Byzantine scholiastic *corpora*, but little progress was achieved on this particular problem and the specific question of what had now become known as the MH was not taken up again. It is my belief that we now need to adopt a different approach, grounded on more careful and painstaking analysis of the materials at hand: it needs to be emphasised that the papyri have supplied crucial evidence on this matter, evidence which was not available earlier and failed to be awarded due consideration subsequently.

Without taking into consideration the MH fragments on papyrus, P. Lünstedt 1961 likewise devoted a dissertation to the subscriptions of the *historiae* in the D-scholia: to his mind, examination of the verifiable subscriptions, i.e. those referring to extant authors, tended to lead to a substantially positive assessment concerning their validity. The essence of the results achieved by Lünstedt deserves to be emphasised at this point. First and foremost, it was shown that the subscriptions are not without grounds, and that there exists a genuine link with the author cited in each subscription: elements are shown to come frequently not only from the author's text but also from the scholia to this text and can therefore be traced back to ancient commentaries. One should not make the mistake, he reasoned, of thinking that the general intention of the subscriptions is always that of indicating a veritable 'source' for the *historia* as a whole, for it may be also a suggestion of a parallel text or a learned comparison (indeed, the very concept of trying to evaluate them strictly as 'sources' has constituted a false presupposition of research on these subscriptions). He therefore claims that the basic reliability of the subscriptions resides in the fact that the reference to the author cited does actually exist in some way, inasmuch as the authors they quote deal with at least a part of the relevant *historia*. On the other hand, the conclusion that they should not be taken as an indication of global 'sources' of the scholion is corroborated by the presence of elements derived from other sources as well, i.e. ancient comments on the cited author himself or parallel texts by other authors. This is a rather crucial difference in approach, although somewhat cautious.[14] The fact that the subscription does not indicate the 'source' of the whole of the material of the *historia* is in itself no longer seen by Lünstedt as the crucial factor: what is decisive is that the author cited (and at times also the ancient exegesis to the author) should have a genuine direct link with the content of the scholion.

Along the same lines, M. van der Valk[15] claims that the material of the mythographical D-scholia does not appear to be worse or more recent than that found in parallel versions contained above all in the exegetical scholia to Homer. In fact, he goes as far as to cast out Schwartz's hypothesis according to which the MH was built up exclusively with the use of handbooks and therefore contains only low-level and late material. Overall, then, although the author cited is often pertinent only to a part of the content of the *historia*, Van der Valk concludes in favour of the basic reliability of the subscriptions of the scholia, despite revealing skepticism in more than a few cases.[16]

---

[14] Lünstedt (1961, 36) concluded that the last word had not yet been said as regards the negative judgement passed by Schwartz and urged further investigation of those subscriptions that were not directly verifiable, i.e. those pertaining to lost authors.

[15] Van der Valk 1963-4, I 7 (*The mythographical D scholia*), 303-413.

[16] For subscriptions citing the *Kyklos* cf. also Janko 1986, 51-5, esp. 52-3.

The last couple of decades have seen the publication of several studies by G. Arrighetti,[17] who has been able to make use of the evidence furnished by the papyri and thus to set up an explicit linkage between the papyrus fragments of the MH and the *historiae* in the Homeric D-scholia. The term 'commentary'[18] is now confidently used for the MH, the origins of which are seen as lying in the exegetic activity carried out in the highest circles of Hellenistic-Roman scholarship. I myself put forward the same opinion several years ago, as I began to investigate the D-scholia,[19] and my conviction is constantly being strengthened by acquisition of new data and new arguments.

The papyrus fragments show that, even in the most ancient forms that have come down to us, what we now call MH is properly a commentary on the Homeric poems, following the text step by step and linked to it by the quotation of lemmata: each *historia* takes as its starting point some feature mentioned in the poetic text, which may even be just a single word or an expression that is felt to call for an explanation or an extended comment. It was a mythographical commentary, by which I mean a commentary dealing with a specific subject-matter, and to continue calling it a 'handbook' of Homeric mythology would be misleading: it was a commentary which had a fairly widespread circulation from the first century CE onwards and continued in circulation throughout the imperial age. In all identified MH fragments the order follows that of the Homeric text and the lemmata are always present; moreover in *P.Oxy.* 3830 (*Il.* 003), in *P.Schubart* 21 (*Il.* 007) and in *P.Berol.* 13282 (*Il.* 008) the lemmata are in *ekthesis*, a characteristic of the commentary. In some cases one also finds a form of title in passing from one book to another: *PSI* 1173 (*Od.* 001) fr. 5 *recto* preserves the end of book 11 and the

[17] Arrighetti 1968; 1977[1]; 1977[2], 52-4; 1987, 204-10.

[18] Turner 1968, 119 (= 138), had defined *PSI* 1173 (*Od.* 001) as a *hypomnema*: in contrast, for *PSI* 1173 and for *P.Schubart* 21 (*Il.* 007), Turner 1977, nr. 207 and nr. 206 respectively, uses the term scholia.

[19] Montanari 1979, 14-5; cf. Janko 1986, 51-5, with interesting observations on the *D-sch.* on *Il.* 23.346 (subscription to Kyklikoi) and the story of Cycnus.

beginning of book 12, which is indicated by 'Οδ(υσσείας) μ. Forms of title are also found at two points in *P.Oxy.* 4096 (*Il.* 006); a title is also present in the ostrakon *Il.* 004, see above.

By chance, one piece suggests an extremely interesting line of inquiry. Mention has already been made several times of codex PSI 1173 (*Od.* 001), with *historiae* to several books of the *Odyssey*, a large part of which deal with the heroines Odysseus encounters in 11.235-332: in frgs. 2-4 there remain parts of six *historiae* to 11.321-2 and 326, followed directly by a piece (in fr. 4 *verso*) of the *historia* on Eurypylus at 11.519-20. A papyrus of *Odyssey* book 11, *P.Mil.Vogl.* 259, a small fragment dating from 1st-2nd century CE, provides evidence of the initial parts of 11.292-310 and definitely has a *diple* before 11.298 and perhaps the trace of another *diple* before 11.305.[20]

Odyssey 11	*historiae* in *PSI* 1173	*historiae* in *D-sch.*	*P.Mil.Vogl.* 259
287 Pero		XXX Pherecydes	
290 Iphicles		XXX missing	
298 Leda		XXX neoteroi	---------- diple
305 Iphimedea			diple ? ----------
321 Phaedra	---------- XXX fr.2 Asclepiades	XXX Asclepiades	

[20] *Ed. pr.* by D. Del Corno, *P. Mil. Vogliano*, VI, Milano 1977, nr. 259, 1-3; corrections to the *ed. pr.* (in which the transcription of one line was omitted) in Moretti 1993, 96. Through the kind assistance of G.Bastianini I was able to see the original of the fragment preserved at the Istituto di Papirologia of the University of Milan.

Procris	XXX fr.2 missing	XXX Pherecydes	
321-2 Ariadne	XXX fr.3 missing	XXX Pherecydes	
326 Maera	XXX fr.3 Pherecydes	XXX Pherecydes	
Clymene	XXX fr.3-4 Hesiod	XXX Hesiod	
Eriphyle	XXX fr.4 Asclepiades	XXX Asclepiades	
519-20 Eurypylus	XXX fr.4 v missing ----------	XXX Acusilaus	

The situation is summarised in the chart, in which the broken lines indicate the fractures in the fragments, leading one to regret that so little is preserved of *PSI* 1173 and *P.Mil.Vogl.* 259.

The use of the *diple* by Alexandrian philologists to indicate discussion of exegetic questions, including questions of antiquarian interest, is well known: thus even if for 11.298 (*καὶ Λήδην εἶδον, τὴν* Τυνδαρέου *παράκοιτιν*) the scholia and codices highlight a grammatical problem concerning the form of the genitive Τυνδαρέου or Τυνδάρεω, I regard it as likely that the presence of this *diple* or of these two *diplai* in the tiny Milan fragment is to be related to the presence of a mythographical comment on the character cited in the line.[21] This fascinating suggestion

[21] In *PSI* 1173 the *historiae* are separated from one another by a long horizontal line, which one hesitates to define as a *paragraphos*: it may be purely by coincidence that the same is seen in *P.Mil.Vogl.* 259, where before 11.298 and before 11.305 there remains a piece of interlinear separation line which, even allowing for the small part of column preserved, would appear to be rather too

admittedly appears to rest on somewhat shaky foundations: however, it will be seen below that, when considered together with certain other elements, the idea begins to acquire a little more plausibility.[22]

3. The papyri

Thus what we know of the MH has come down to us through two different forms of transmission: the group of papyrus fragments dating from Roman times traceable to the first through firth centuries CE and the *historiae* contained in the corpus of the Homeric D-scholia preserved in a few codices of the Byzantine age. If we consider the papyrus fragments and compare them with the text of the D-scholia, we observe first and foremost that no papyrus fragment shows exactly and totally the same text as the D-scholia manuscripts, no papyrus fragment is totally and absolutely different from the D-scholia manuscripts: thus it is not unknown for the text of a given *historia* on a shattered and fragmentary papyrus in one case to be reconstructable on the basis of the D-scholion, whereas in another case one may well find that comparison with the corresponding D-scholion does not allow the lacunae of the papyrus to be integrated. Sometimes the papyrus texts are richer and more extensive, whereas at other times it is the papyri that present an abridged and impoverished version. But in general, despite the often considerable differences, there is a basic similarity among all the sources of evidence, showing beyond a shadow of doubt that the papyri preserve what must be regarded as the ancient precursor of the *historiae* of the Homeric D-scholia, i.e. that the *historiae* in D can be traced back to a mythographical commentary on Homer of the imperial age, which is known thanks to papyrus fragments and is called MH. It is therefore fully legitimate to regard the papyrus fragments and the Homeric D-scholia as phases of the transmission of the MH, as we have been doing so far, in a line of transmission within which

---

long for a normal *paragraphos*.

[22] Of course, inquiry into *diple* preservation for lines provided with *historia* in the scholia is what is needed at this point.

the characteristics—similarities as well as differences—can all be provided with a plausible explanation.

The possibility of comparing two extant papyri both presenting the same *historia* is for the moment extremely limited. This is indeed regrettable, as it would be highly instructive to be able to benefit from at least a few such comparisons. We have only one case in which a *historia* to the same Homeric line appears in two papyri, namely the *historia* at 20.403-4 found both in *P.Oxy.* 4096 (*Il.* 006) and in *P.Berol.* 13282 (*Il.* 008): the two versions are similar and parallel but not identical, and a few differences can be spotted. For the *historia* at 20.147, *P.Schubart* 21 (*Il.* 007) and *P.Berol.* 13282 (*Il.* 008) have a notably more extensive version compared to the corresponding D-scholion, but the former preserves the beginning of the *historia* and the latter the final part: consequently, we cannot tell whether the two editions had identical texts.[23] However, I believe it is doubtful that exactly the same text will ever be found in two papyri, that is, that we will ever find two papyrus copies of exactly the same version of MH. For as so often happens in this kind of text, each individual copy represented a different version and copyists or redactors felt relatively free to modify or adapt the text as they produced a new exemplar. Furthermore I would also argue that it is highly probable that the first compilation of the D-scholia was not composed by copying one single exemplar of MH, but rather the redactor D may well himself have produced a new version based on more than one single copy at his disposal (as indeed he did when using his sources for the glossographic material). Now, because a new version always involves a certain amount of changes, this can explain why one finds the above described situation of similarities and differences with the papyrus versions. Even the fact that at times the author cited in the subscription may strictly speaking be associated with only a part of the *historia* is not always to be taken as representing the original situation, for it could be due to the process of transmission and manipulation of the exegetic material starting from

[23] Cf. Montanari 1985, 235-6.

learned products of the Hellenistic and Roman age up to the Byzantine scholia.

As far as the crucial element represented by the subscriptions is concerned, the whole range of possibilities can be observed.

N 302	om. *P.Oxy*. 3003	Pherecydes *D-Sch.*
A 38 Τενέδοιο	Myrsilus & Euripides (?) P.Hamb. 199	om. *D-sch.*
Θ 479	Euphorion *P.Oxy*. 3830	om. *D-sch.*
A 263	om. *P.Oxy*. 418	om. *D-sch.*
H 44	Anticleides *P.Oxy*. 3830	Anticleides *D-sch.*
Y 53	Demetrius of Scepsis *P.Schubart* 21	Demetrius of Scepsis *D-sch.* (ad Y 3)
γ 4	Hellanicus *PSI* 1173	Hellanicus *D-sch.*
λ 321 Phaedra	Asclepiades *PSI* 1173	Asclepiades *D-sch.*
λ 326	Pherecydes *PSI* 1173	Pherecydes *D-sch.*
λ 326	Hesiod *PSI* 1173	Hesiod *D-sch.*
λ 326	Asclepiades *PSI* 1173	Asclepiades *D-sch.*

λ 582	Asclepiades *PSI* 1173	Asclepiades *D-sch.*
ν 259	Lycophron *PSI* 1173	Lycophron *D-sch.*
N 301	subscr.??? *P.Oxy.* 3003	Apollodorus *D-sch.*
Y 307	subscr.??? *P.Berol.* 13282	Acusilaus *D-sch.*

First of all one notices a large number of agreements between the papyri and the scholia manuscripts. But on the other hand there are also differences: for instance *P.Oxy.* 3003 (*Il.* 005) omits the subscription at the end of the *historia* at 13.302, while the D-scholion preserves the subsciption to Pherecydes. On the other hand, *P.Hamb.* 199 (*Il.* 001) shows the subscription (a double one, to Myrsilus and possibly Euripides)[24] at 1.38 Τενέδοιο, while the corresponding D-scholion has lost it. The same happens in *P.Oxy.* 3830 (*Il.* 003), which preserves the subscription to Euphorion at 8.479, lost in the corresponding D-scholion.[25] For 1.263 the subscription is lost both in *P.Oxy.* 418 (*Il.* 002) and in the manuscripts; but in contrast: *P.Oxy.* 3830 (*Il.* 003) and the D-scholion preserve the same subscription to Anticleides for 7.44; *P.Schubart* 21 (*Il.* 007) and the D-scholion preserve the same subscription to Demetrius of Scepsis for the *historia* at 20.53 (which in the D-scholion is found at 20.3); in *PSI* 1173 (*Od.* 001) seven subscriptions are preserved and all of them agree perfectly with the corresponding D-scholion (3.4 Hellanicus;

[24] *Ed. pr.* 25-6: ἱστοροῦσιν] / Μύρτιλος καὶ Ἐ[υριπίδης; Luppe (*ZPE* 56 (1984), 31-2): οὕτως] / Μύρτιλος καὶ Ἐ[υριπίδης. For the second name Euripides is preferred because he wrote a tragedy on Tennes; I wonder however whether the association with Myrsilus of Methymna might not lead one to prefer—since the topic focused on is Tenedos—another author of *Lesbiaka*, so possibly: Μύρτιλος καὶ Ἐ[λλάνικος? (cf. *P.Oxy.* 3711? see comm. to fr. 1, I 10-7; II 15-7).

[25] For the subscription to Eratosthenes in the *historia* to 9.447 of the same papyrus, cf. *infra*.

11.321 [Phaedra] Asclepiades; 11.326 Pherecydes, Hesiod, Asclepiades; 11.582 Asclepiades; 13.259 Lycophron); in *P.Oxy.* 3003 (*Il.* 005) there was a subscription at 13.301 but the name is lost *in lacuna*, and the D-scholion attributes the *historia* to Apollodorus; in *P.Berol.* 13282 (*Il.* 008) there was a subscription at 20.307 but the name is lost *in lacuna*, and the D-scholion attributes the *historia* to Acusilaus. Thus when analysing the subscriptions, it can be seen that the range of possiblities includes agreement between papyri and manuscripts of D both in presence and in omission, as well as differences involving greater richness either in the papyri or in the manuscripts of D (subscription preserved in the papyrus and lost in D, subscription preserved in D and lost in the papyrus).

It is remarkable, however, that when the subscription has survived both in the papyri and in the manuscripts, there is always agreement between them. That is, at least so far, there has in effect never been a discrepancy in the attribution of the same *historia*, in that the same *historia* has never been ascribed to different authorities in different pieces of evidence. This is of course a most important connection as well as a clear sign of the reliability of the tradition by which the subscriptions have survived within the corpus of the D-scholia, where such subscriptions cannot be considered a later addition. Generally the subscriptions belonged to the original form of the MH and have been well preserved in the D-scholia.

There is one exception to this general rule that is well worth taking into consideration. In *P.Oxy.* 3830 (*Il.* 003), for the *historia* at 9.447 (the Phoenix story), the first editor[26] suggested that it might be possible to reconstruct in the papyrus a subscription to Eratosthenes from the traces of fr. 3 II 21: thus she argues that ἡ̣ δ' ἱστορία] | παρ' Ἐρ̣[ατοσθέ]ν̣ει (ll. 20-1) is to be preferred to a possible παρ' Εὐ̣[ριπί-δηι].ει, which would leave us with a highly problematic].ει at the end, but she prudently refrains from integrating the text. The reconstruction of the name Eratosthenes is put forward rather more confidently by Has-

[26] M.A. Harder in *P.Oxy.* LVI.

lam,[27] who however also compares it with the different subscription of the same *historia* in the corresponding D-scholion: ἡ ἱστορία παρὰ τῷ ποιητῇ, παρὰ γὰρ τοῖς τραγικοῖς διαλλάσσει.[28] This is undoubtedly an anomalous case. Haslam's explanation is as follows: 'In the light of the papyrus subscription it is clear that the (formally atypical) subscription in A [*scil.* in ACH, that is in *D-sch.*] is not a preservation lost in the other parts of the tradition, but an addition consequent on the loss of the Eratosthenes subscription'.[29] Therefore the copy or copies of the MH available to the redactor of the Iliadic D-scholia lying at the origin of our tradition had lost the subscription for the Phoenix-*historia* at 9.447: then somewhere along some branch of the tradition[30] an unknown hand filled the gap with a subscription created *ad hoc*.

No connoisseur of scholiastic literature will be startled to find that the editor of the Byzantine corpus or the copyist/user of a manuscript did not hesitate to boldly insert or add material or blend together materials of varying origin or epitomise materials with differing degrees of precision. Even if the form of the subscription does not strike me as being particularly atypical,[31] I regard this as a plausible explanation. However, one

---

[27] Haslam 1990, 34-6: cf. W. Luppe, *Gnomon* 64 (1992), 292.

[28] For the subscription Haslam knows only the text of A, but it is also found in C and H, and therefore in branch *u* of the tradition, while it does not appear in branch *v*: therefore either it was present in the archetype and *v* omitted it, or else it was not present in the archetype and was added only in *u*. For the manuscripts and the tradition of D-scholia to the *Iliad* cf. Montanari 1979; 1984; 1994.

[29] Haslam 1990, 34 n. 1.

[30] Cf. n. 28.

[31] For the reference to Homer himself, cf. the subscriptions (all to the *Iliad*) above all to 13.66, but also to 3.443, quoted infra. Double subscriptions are by no means rare: *P.Hamb.* 199 (*Il.* 001) has been cited for the subscription to Myrsilos and Euripides (?) at 1.38 Τενέδοιο; cf. infra the subscriptions at 2.145, 3.242, 13.66. For a generic reference such as οἱ τραγικοί cf. κατὰ τοὺς τραγικούς to 1.7, but one can also make a comparison with οἱ κυκλικοί (e.g. 3.242 quoted *infra*, and 18.486; 19.332; 20.346; 20.660), οἱ ῥητορικοί to 1.50

may still wonder whether, given the very small part extant, restoration of the name of Eratosthenes in the papyrus should be considered as definite, or whether Euripides could still be an outside possibility, or even something else.[32] In any case, this kind of exception certainly does not invalidate the general observation of absence of discrepancies between the papyri and the D-scholia in attribution of the same *historia* and the assertion that the subscriptions belonged to the original form of the MH and have been well preserved in the D-scholia.[33]

4. Sources and subscription

A peculiar and interesting case is represented by the *historia* at *Iliad* 1.264, which is worth taking into consideration. This *historia* is preserved in *P.Oxy*. 418 (*Il*. 002) as well as in the D-scholia and the form is quite similar:

> *Sch. D* A 264. **Καινέα τ'**: καὶ τὸν Καινέα. ὁ δὲ Καινεὺς 'Ελάτου μὲν ἦν παῖς, Λαπίθων βασιλεύς. πρότερον ἦν παρθένος εὐπρεπής, μιγέντος δὲ αὐτῇ Ποσειδῶνος, αἰτησαμένη μεταβα-

---

or possibly even πολλοὶ ἐμνήσθησαν to 6.130 (quoted *infra*). Comparisons between Homer and tragedy are also not without parallels: e.g. to 1.7 concerning Agamemnon's family. Cf. Lünstedt 1961, 1-6.

[32] Cf. *Sch. ex.* (*vel* Porph.) *Iliad* 9.453 *c* = Sosiphanes 92 F 6 *TrGF*, Euripides p. 621 *TGF*²: the link between *sch.* 9.453 *c* and the *historia* to 9.447 is found in *TGF*², *l.c.*, and is also mentioned by Lünstedt, *l.c.* Thus one might think of something like παρ' Εὐριπίδηι καὶ Σωσιφάνει, which would perhaps give a name to the τραγικοί cited in the *D-sch.*: however, this would appear to be too long for the lacuna in the payrus fr. 3 II 21 unless there were some abbreviations, for which in this same papyrus cf. fr. 1-2 I 1, 13; therefore perhaps e.g. παρ' Εὐρ(ιπίδηι) κ(αὶ) Σωσιφάνει.

[33] Thus Haslam 1990, 34 n. 1: 'Discrepancy in attribution between the D-scholia and a papyrus witness, apart from mere presence or absence of the subscription, would be unique. It becomes increasingly clear that the subscriptions were part and parcel of the original work, and trustworthy, but were subject to omission and to mistaken reparation.'

λεῖν εἰς ἄνδρα ἡ νεᾶνις[34] *ἄτρωτος γίνεται γενναιότατος τῶν καθ' αὐτὸν ὑπάρξας. καὶ δήποτε πήξας ἀκόντιον ἐν τῷ μεσαιτάτῳ τῆς ἀγορᾶς, θεὸν τοῦτο προσέταξεν ἀριθμεῖν· δι' ἣν αἰτίαν ἀγανακτήσας ὁ* Ζεὺς, *τιμωρίαν τῆς ἀσεβείας παρ' αὐτοῦ εἰσεπράξατο. μαχόμενον γὰρ αὐτὸν τοῖς* Κενταύροις *καὶ ἄτρωτον ὄντα, ὑποχείριον ἐποίησε· βαλόντες οἱ προειρημένοι δρυσί τε καὶ ἐλάταις ἤρεισαν εἰς τὴν γῆν. μέμνηται δὲ αὐτοῦ καὶ* 'Απολλώνιος *ἐν τοῖς* 'Αργοναυτικοῖς *λέγων οὕτως·* "Καινέα *γὰρ δὴ πρόσθεν ἔτι κλείουσιν ἀοιδοὶ* | Κενταύροισιν *ὀλέσθαι, ὅτε σφέας οἶος ἀπ' ἄλλων* | *ἤλας' ἀριστήων· οἱ δ' ἔμπαλιν ὁρμηθέντες* | *οὔτε μιν ἀγκλῖναι προτέρω σθένον οὔτε δαΐξαι,* | *ἀλλ' ἄρρηκτος ἄκαμπτος ἐδύσατο νειόθι γαίης* | *θεινόμενος στιβαρῇσι καταΐγδην ἐλάτῃσιν*" (A.R. 1.59-64). **ACHV**

P.Oxy. 418.9-22[35]

A 264 **[Καινέα τ' 'Εξαδιό]ν** ***τε καὶ ἀντίθεον*** **Πολυφήμον**

[ὁ Καινεὺς 'Ελάτου] *μὲν παῖς,* Λαπίθων *δὲ* βασιλε[ύς,
[*πρότερον παρθέ*]*νος εὐπρεπὴς ἐγένετο·* δ[
[*μιγέν*]*τος αὐτῇ* Ποσειδῶνος, *αἰτησα*[*μέ-*
[*νη μεταβαλεῖν νε*]*ανίας ἄτρωτος γίνεται·* γ[*εν-*
[*ναιότατος δὲ τ*]*ῶν καθ' ἑαυτὸν ὑπάρξας, τον*[
[*τῆς ἡγε*]*μονίας οὐκ ἐβάστασεν. ἐξευ*[*τε-*
[*λίσας δὲ καὶ το*]*ὺς θεοὺς παρ' οὐ*[*δεν ἐποιή-*
[*σατο καί ποτε πή*]*ξας ἀκόντιον ἐν* [*μέσῃ τῇ*
[ ] *ἀγορᾷ, τοῦτο θεὸν π*[*ροσέτα-*
[*ξε νομίζειν·* Ζεὺ]ς *δὲ ἀγανακτήσα*[ς Κενταύ-
[*ροις πολεμοῦν*]*τα, καίπερ ἄτρωτο*[*ν ὄντα ὑπο-*

[34] Probably *νεανίας legendum*: cf. *P.Oxy.* 418.13 and n. 36.

[35] The papyrus itself is lost and no photograph exists. I give the text of the *ed. pr.* by Grenfell & Hunt, adding punctuation, breathings, accents, *iota mutum*. Besides: 12 *ποσιδωνος* pap.—13]*ανειας*, corr.]*ανιας* pap.; *γεινεται* pap.—20 *ατροτο*[, corr. *ατρωτο*[pap.—22 *ηρισαν* pap.

[χείριον ἐποίησε]ν· ἐλάταις γὰρ κα[ὶ δρυσίν
[οἱ Κένταυροι] αὐτὸν ἤρεισαν εἰς [γῆν.[36]

The papyrus text seems to contain something more in ll. 11-2 and ll. 14-6, but at the end of the story (ll. 17-22) it is a little shorter than the D-scholion (ll. 4-7).[37] But while the papyrus text stops when the story is finished,[38] in the scholion we find the quotation of Apollonius Rhodius, 1.59-64, that is to say the explicit reference to the authority, not a simple reference of the kind we can read for instance at *Iliad* 3.237: ὡς Ἀπολλώνιός φησιν ἐν δευτέρῳ Ἀργοναυτικῶν. This explicit quotation could just as easily have been replaced by one of the normal forms of subscription, something like ἡ ἱστορία παρὰ Ἀπολλωνίῳ or (ὡς) ἱστορεῖ Ἀπολλώνιος or οὕτως Ἀπολλώνιος, but in actual fact it was not, and this shows that here the text of the scholia preserves a more learned and richer version of the MH than this particular papyrus: I think this version was a more ancient one, since it is well known that the citations of the authorities are the first to be lost in transmission of erudite material (as is frequently observed in lexicographical works). It is therefore far more probable that the quotation was originally present and was then omitted in certain copies, rather than being absent originally and added at a later date. What we have, in fact, is a typical case of the process of impove-

---

[36] 11-2 δ[ιὰ | δὲ τὸ κάλλος Blass *apud ed. pr.*—14-5 τὸν [μέ | γαν ὄγκον Blass *apud ed. pr.*—17-8 ἐν [μεσαι | τάτῃ τῇ] ἀγορᾷ *brevius*: ἐν [τῷ με | σαιτάτῳ τῆς ἀγορᾶ<ς>?—18-9 poss. τοῦτο θεὸν π̣[ροσέταξεν ἀριθμεῖν· Ζεὺ]ς δὲ κτλ.

[37] Cf. *ed. pr.*: 'This [scil. the *D-sch.*] is almost identical with the papyrus, but is more compressed in some parts and more expanded in others. As before, the papyrus exhibits the better text, (1) by avoiding the repetition of ἦν in the first sentence, (2) by having νεανίας in place of ἡ νεᾶνις which is detrimental to both sense and construction, and in the light of the papyrus should be corrected to νεανίας.'

[38] At least as far as we can see in the edition, since the papyrus itself is lost: but it seems to me quite unlikely that the papyrus edition could have committed such a blunder as to fail to indicate whether there was some more text between ll. 22 and 23.

rishment of exegetic material, from a more erudite version to one that was reduced and simplified. Such an example should be carefully kept in mind. The *historia* of the MH gives more mythological material than that which can be strictly extracted from Apollonius' lines: this could be due to the cultural level of the comment at the origin and some material may possibly have been borrowed from commentaries or scholia to the passage. For instance in the collection of Apollonius' scholia we have a mythographical comment giving the detail—not present in Apollonius' lines—of Caeneus' transformation from a woman into an invulnerable man, an element that the *historia* does furnish. It is well to recall Lünstedt's remarks concerning *historiae* containing material which derives jointly from the text of the author cited in the subscription and from ancient comments to the given author.

But investigation into this case can go beyond the confines of what is strictly speaking the evidence of the MH. There is an extremely interesting parallel in *P.Oxy.* 1611, a substantial fragment of a *hypomnema* to an unknown work,[39] of which there remain erudite comments deprived of the lemmata of the work to which the commentary refers, but still introduced by the typical ὅτι (*scil.* τὸ σημεῖον ὅτι): thus this was probably already an *excerptum* from the original *hypomnema*. A section of this text, ll. 38-96, has a close bearing on the questions under discussion here, though naturally we do not know what sparked the comment. The comment opens with the quotation of a passage from Theophrastus, *On Kingship* 2, on the subject of Caeneus' spear.[40] It then goes on to say that Theophrastus' statement must be elucidated with the help of the story related by Acusilaus of Argos and at this point Acusilaus' text itself is given,[41] and it shows a number of elements similar or parallel to the

[39] Attention to this text and its relevance for the purposes of the present discussion is due to Arrighetti 1968: later in Arrighetti 1977[1]; 1977[2]; 1987, 204-10.

[40] Theophrastus fr. 600 FHS&G.

[41] *FGrHist* 2 F 22.

Caeneus' *historia* of the D-scholia and of *P.Oxy.* 418, to which it is in fact much closer than that which one finds, say, in the Apollonius Rhodius scholia. Afterwards, the passage taken from Acusilaus is used by the author of the *hypomnema* to explain the proverbial expression *τῷ δόρατι ἄρχειν τὸν* Καινέα, to which he referred in the passage from Theophrastus, and it is further used as the launch pad for discussion of a passage from the *Alcmeon in Corinth* by Euripides.[42] It can thus be seen that the excerptum offered by *P.Oxy.* 1611 is extremely erudite and far removed from the simplicity of the *historiae* of the MH: but in any case it does give an idea of the possible origin of this material. In the exegesis of *Iliad* 1.264 the passage from Acusilaus could well have been utilised together with Apollonius Rhodius (and maybe other material as well?) in an erudite commentary rich in references and doctrine such as that constituted by *P.Oxy.* 1611, and the whole could therefore represent a typical source used by the MH. Certainly, one could perfectly well have found, as indeed occurred elsewhere, that the MH had preserved the *historia* with a subscription like *ἡ ἱστορία παρὰ* 'Ακουσιλάῳ (as for instance is observed in *Iliad* 20.307 and *Odyssey* 11.519-20) or (as mentioned above) like *ἡ ἱστορία παρὰ* 'Απολλωνίῳ or else *ἡ ἱστορία παρὰ* 'Ακουσιλάῳ *καὶ* 'Απολλωνίῳ. But instead, in this case, in one exemplar of the MH (*P.Oxy.* 418) we find the *historia* shorn of any subscription, and in another (the D-scholia) we have the *historia* with an explicit citation, this time not lost as so often happens but preserved in literal form, similarly to what one finds in *excerpta* from commentaries such as *P.Oxy.* 1611.

Another rather interesting case is offered by the *historia* on *Iliad* 1.399-400, still preserved in *P.Oxy.* 418 and in the D-scholia.

A 399-400 *ὁππότε μιν ξυνδῆσαι* 'Ολύμπιοι *ἤθελον ἄλλοι*
"Ηρη *τ' ἠδὲ* Ποσειδάων *καὶ* Παλλὰς 'Αθήνη

[42] Fr. 73a *TGF*[2] Suppl.

Ariston. A 400 *a.* **Παλλὰς Ἀθήνη**: ὅτι Ζηνόδοτος γράφει "Φοῖβος Ἀπόλλων". ἀφαιρεῖται δὲ τὸ πιθανόν· ἐπίτηδες γὰρ τοὺς τοῖς Ἕλλησι βοηθοῦντας <***>. **A**

Sch. ex. A 400 *b.* **Ἥρη τ' ἠδὲ Ποσειδάων καὶ Παλλὰς Ἀθήνη**: πιθανῶς τοὺς Ἀχαϊκοὺς θεοὺς ἠχθρευκέναι Διΐ φησιν, ἵνα ἀκούοιτο Θέτις. τινὲς δὲ γράφουσι "καὶ Φοῖβος Ἀπόλλων"· τοῦτον γὰρ εἰκὸς ἠχθρευκέναι μὴ φέροντα τὸν ζῆλον τῆς ἐκείνου τυραννίδος· ὅθεν Ἥραν μὲν δεῖ, τοὺς δὲ Λαομέδοντι ὑποτάσσει. οἱ δὲ Ἥραν μὲν διὰ τὸ πολλαῖς μίγνυσθαι, Ποσειδῶνα δὲ διὰ τὸ πλεονεκτεῖσθαι εἰς τὴν διανομήν, Ἀθηνᾶν δὲ διὰ τὸ ἀναγκασθῆναι ζευχθῆναι Ἡφαίστῳ. **bT**

Cf. *sch. ex.* 399-406 et *sch. ex.* 400 *c.*

Sch. D A 399-400. **ὀππότε μιν ξυνδῆσαι <Ὀλύμπιοι ἤθελον ἄλλοι | Ἥρη τ' ἠδὲ Ποσειδάων καὶ Παλλὰς Ἀθήνη>**: γράφεται "καὶ Φοῖβος Ἀπόλλων". Ὀλύμπιοι δὲ ἄλλοι οἱ Τιτᾶνες· καὶ γὰρ ἐν ἄλλοις "μάλα γάρ κε μάχης ἐπύθοντο καὶ ἄλλοι οἵ περ ἐνέρτεροί εἰσι θεοὶ Κρόνον ἀμφὶς ἐόντες" (O 224-5). **CHRV**

Ζεὺς παραλαβὼν τὴν ἐν οὐρανῷ διοίκησιν περισσῶς τῇ παρρησίᾳ ἐχρῆτο, πολλὰ αὐθάδη διαπρασσόμενος. Ποσειδῶν δὲ καὶ Ἥρα καὶ Ἀπόλλων καὶ Ἀθηνᾶ ἐβούλοντο αὐτὸν δήσαντες ὑποτάξαι. Θέτις δὲ ἀκούσασα παρὰ τοῦ πατρὸς Νηρέως (ἦν γὰρ μάντις) τὴν Διὸς ἐπιβουλήν, ἔσπευσε πρὸς αὐτόν, ἐπαγομένη Αἰγαίωνα φόβητρον τῶν ἐπιβουλευόντων θεῶν· ἦν δὲ θαλάσσιος δαίμων οὗτος, καὶ τὸν πατέρα Ποσειδῶνα κατεβράβευεν. ἀκούσας δὲ ὁ Ζεὺς Θέτιδος, τὴν μὲν Ἥραν ἐν τοῖς καθ' αὑτοῦ δεσμοῖς ἐκρέμασε, Ποσειδῶνι δὲ καὶ Ἀπόλλωνι τὴν παρὰ Λαομέδοντι θητείαν ἐψηφίσατο, τῇ δὲ Θέτιδι τὴν Ἀχιλλέως τιμὴν εἰς τὰ μετὰ ταῦτα ἐταμιεύσατο. ἱστορεῖ Δίδυμος (Schmidt p. 179 fr. 1). **ACHRV**

P.Oxy. 418.9-22[43]

A 399 **ὁππ[ότε μιν] ξ[υν]δῆσαι Ὀλύμπιοι ἤ[θε]λ[ον ἄλλοι**

γράφ[ου]σί τινες "καὶ Φοῖβος Ἀπόλλων"· φ[ασὶ γὰρ
ὅτι Διὸς ἐπικρατέστερον χρωμένου [τῇ τῶν
θεῶν βασιλείᾳ, Ποσειδῶν τε καὶ Ἥρα κα[ὶ Ἀπόλ-
λων ἐπεβούλευσαν αὐτῷ. Θέτις δὲ γνοῦσα [παρὰ
Νηρέως τοῦ πατρὸς, ὃς μάντις ἦν, δηλοῖ τῷ [Διὶ
τὴν ἐπιβουλὴν καὶ σύμμαχον παραδίδωσι τ[ὸν
Αἰγαίωνα ἑκατόγχειρον Ποσειδῶνος παῖδα [
Ζεὺς δὲ Ἥραν μὲν ἔδησεν, Ποσειδῶνι δὲ κ[αὶ
[Ἀπόλλω]ν̣ι προστάσσει θητεῦσαι Λαομέδον[τι[44]

For line 400 we have (as is shown in Aristonicus' scholion and in the *Scholia exegetica*) an ancient *varia lectio* of Zenodotus, which replaces Athena by Apollon as the third god involved in the plot against Zeus. The scholia show that Aristarchus rejected Zenodotus' text, saying that Homer had purposely chosen three pro-Greek gods to plot against Zeus because Zeus had listened to Thetis' prayers against the Greeks (explaining Homer by Homer). The *sch. ex.* reports Zenodotus' reading, ascribing it to *τινές*, but on account of the presence of Apollo among the gods hostile to Zeus the *sch. ex.* preserves an element that is lost in Aristonicus' scholion, namely, that Apollo is portrayed as having rebelled because he could no longer bear Zeus' tyranny: such an explanation would appear to allude to some sort of plot against the king of the gods, who is then said to have punished them by putting Hera in fetters and sending Apollo and Poseidon off to be servants of Laomedon.

The mythographical account of *P.Oxy.* 418 is from the very beginning closely related (*φασὶ γάρ*) to the variant (without Zenodotus' name, but with *τινές*, l. 24, as happens in the *sch. ex.*), and consequently later on it names Poseidon, Hera and Apollo as the three gods in the plot (ll.

---

[43] Cf. n. 35.

[44] 26 *ποσιδων* pap.—30 *αιγεωνα*, *εκατονχειρον*, *ποσιδωνος* pap.—31 *ποσιδωνι* pap.

26-7). Similarly in the D-scholia[45] the quotation of the variant is connected with the *historia*, after which four gods, with a degree of unsophisticated syncretism, are named as enemies of Zeus, namely Poseidon, Hera, Apollo and Athena (l. 6). Yet curiously, in its last part the scholion says that the well known punishments were inflicted upon Hera, Poseidon and Apollo (ll. 9-11), and this is in accordance with Zenodotus' text. This discrepancy suggests a rather rough and ready summarised version made by someone who may perhaps have shied away from a longer version and from more detailed discussion of how interpretation of the passage could depend on which text was accepted. The subscription to Didymus is preserved in D (l. 12): but unfortunately the papyrus is damaged here and we cannot state whether there was one or not. In any case, the presence of the variant is also an important feature indicating a learned origin, certainly preserved in the MH on papyrus in a linkage which I think is very likely to be the original one. The text of *Iliad* 1.399-400 takes on a different meaning depending on whether the name is Athena or Apollo: in the former case, the ill-will of three deities towards Zeus deals with issues strictly internal to the *Iliad*, while in the latter case there is an allusion to an ancient story of a struggle among the gods, following which the walls of Troy were built at the time of Laomedon and then the first destruction of Troy was carried out by Heracles. It therefore seems to me perfectly reasonable to deduce from this picture that Didymus told the story in the commentary to 1.399-400, thereby discussing the textual variant: as a result, the *historia* became closely linked to Didymus in later arrangements of the material, and in the transmission of the MH the subscription ἱστορεῖ Δίδυμος is found.

It should not be forgotten that Aristonicus' scholion makes it clear beyond a shadow of doubt that the rejection of Zenodotus' reading was due to Aristarchus. The scholion begins with ὅτι, *scil.* τὸ σημεῖον ὅτι,

---

[45] Despite the fact that in some manuscripts the first part of the scholia to the passage is separated from the *historia*: it can be observed that A omits the first part of the *D-sch.* (present in CHRV) probably because information concerning the variant, in A itself or more properly in its model, was already given in Aristonicus' scholion (which unfortunately is mutilated).

or rather ἡ διπλῆ περιεστιγμένη ὅτι, as was the norm for scholia illustrating an Aristarchean argument against Zeonodotus' text.[46] It is thus Aristarchus who preferred the text naming the three enemy deities as Hera, Poseidon and Athena because this is *pithanon*, inasmuch as it is linked to the promise made to Thetis by Zeus at the beginning of the *Iliad*: any idea of a reference here to an ancient plot by Hera, Poseidon and Apollo, harking back to the old story of Laomedon and all its consequences, seems unacceptable to Aristarchus. This is an application of the criterion of 'explaining Homer by Homer' and the same criterion guides the Aristarchean interpretation of the Διὸς βουλή at *Iliad* 1.5, as reported by the scholia to this line and indeed by a particularly rich D-scholion. This *D-sch.* states that it is thought by some that the Διὸς βουλή refers to Zeus' intention of relieving the earth of the excessive quantity of men and their wickedness, by causing many to perish in the two great wars of Thebes and Troy; on the other hand, according to Aristarchus and Aristophanes the Διὸς βουλή at 1.5 should be taken merely as Zeus' intention to keep the promise to Thetis of honouring Achilles by bringing about the defeat of the Acheans. Here too we find one interpretation referring to the mythical macrocontext and a contrary one that remains internal to the *Iliad*. This problem is discussed in the scholia, which point out that Aristarchus and Aristophanes opted for the second approach: particularly extensive among these scholia is the above mentioned *D-Sch.* to 1.5, endowed with a learned quotation from the Cyclic poem *Cypria*.[47] That this scholion belongs to the MH is in my view highly probable, even though we do not have the typical ἡ ἱστορία παρὰ τῷ δεῖνα or *similia*.

---

[46] A small detail can be added: the monster Briareos or Aegaeon, whom Thetis summons to the aid of Zeus, in the Homeric text, 1. 402, is called ἑκατόγχειρον, an epithet that is absent in the *D-sch.* but preserved in the papyrus, l. 30: no scholia are extant for this word, but Apollonius Sophista 65.15 says: ὁ Ἀρίσταρχος κατὰ τὸ μυθικὸν ἑκατὸν χεῖρας ἔχοντα κτλ.

[47] Fr. 1 Bernabé.

The presence of a grammarian such as Didymus in the subscriptions to the *historiae*, alongside poets, historians and mythographers, constitutes a feature we would do well to reflect on.[48] The name of Didymus also appears for the *historia* to *Iliad* 22.126-7 οὐ μέν πως νῦν ἐστὶν ἀπὸ δρυὸς οὐδ' ἀπὸ πέτρης | τῷ ὀαριζέμεναι. The *D-sch.* contains an explanation of the proverbial expression in this line (and such a situation is by no means surprising for the ancient exegesis of poets,[49] with a reference to the nomadic life of mankind in ancient times, when women would give birth in rocky caves and hollow oak trees: the scholion then closes with the subscription ἡ ἱστορία παρὰ Διδύμῳ.[50] It is clear that here the 'anthropological' explanation of the origins of the proverb is in no way strictly connected with the Homeric contextual use, where Hector uses it with paradoxical force as if to say: this is certainly not the right moment to meet Achilles the way a boy and a girl have a tender meeting behind an oak-tree or a rock. However in the *D-sch.* a much more general explanation is given,[51] which could have belonged to an extensive learned excursus in a commentary on the Homeric line: indeed, the material of such an excursus may well have been available to Didymus, who was the author of the Περὶ παροιμιῶν. This is therefore a highly plausible subscription, despite the fact that its relation with the Homeric text is generic rather than specific. Furthermore, a case such as this shows that the *historiae* of the MH could also involve notable variety of content, even though the strictly mythographical material was by far the most prominent.

---

[48] Schmidt 1854, 182 and again 213-4, claimed it was possible to go as far as to hypothesise that the scholia with the subscription ἡ ἱστορία παρὰ τῷ δεῖνα could be traced back to Didymus (this is also mentioned by Lünstedt 1961, ii).

[49] Cf. above the proverb concerning Caeneus' spear in *P.Oxy.* 1611.

[50] Schmidt 1854, 182 fr. 15.

[51] Which, if anything, calls to mind Hesiod *Theogony* 35 (and this could perhaps have been cited as a parallel).

It is also worth noting that even the mythographical content was not always of the same standard type: a divergence from the simple short story to which the *historiae* generally restrict themselves is found for example in the *D-Sch.* to *Iliad* 2.103, a *historia* dedicated to the epithet ἀργεϊφόντης, which begins with an etymological exegesis, continues with a lengthy aetiological explanation starting from Zeus' love for Io, and closes with a subscription to Apollodorus: ἡ δὲ ἱστορία πλατύτερον κεῖται παρὰ 'Απολλοδώρῳ ἐν τῇ α' (ἐν δευτέρῳ A).[52] The brief scholion immediately preceding it on the same Homeric line contains an etymological explanation of the epithet διάκτορος, which in this line is, as always, used together with ἀργεϊφόντης: I contend that what we have at this particular point in the scholia is the separate presence of two pieces deriving from a unified treatment composed of etymological interpretations and mythological aetiologies on the epithets of Hermes διάκτορος ἀργεϊφόντης. This content cannot fail to remind us of the Περὶ θεῶν of Apollodorus of Athens.

In order to offer a few more examples of subscriptions taken from the D-scholia that I consider to be particularly noteworthy, I would also like to recall the following items. Space prevents me from commenting on them one by one, but I believe that even the short text of these subscriptions stands as a testimony of traces of true scholarly investigation.

B 145 ... ἱστορεῖ Φιλοστέφανος καὶ Καλλίμαχος ἐν Αἰτίοις.
Γ 242 ... ἡ ἱστορία παρὰ τοῖς Κυκλικοῖς, καὶ ἀπὸ μέρους παρ' 'Αλκμᾶνι τῷ λυρικῷ.
Γ 443 ... ὡς δηλοῖ ὁ ποιητὴς διὰ τῶν ἑαυτοῦ λόγων.
Z 130 ... τῆς ἱστορίας πολλοὶ ἐμνήσθησαν, προηγουμένως δὲ ὁ τὴν Εὐρωπίαν πεποιηκὼς Εὔμηλος.
N 66 ... ἡ ἱστορία παρὰ Καλλιμάχῳ ἐν Αἰτίοις καὶ παρ' αὐτῷ τῷ ποιητῇ ἐν τῇ δ' τῆς 'Οδυσσείας (488 ff.) παχυμερῶς.

---

[52] On this *historia* cf. Lünstedt 1961, 26-8, who correctly interprets πλατύτερον with the meaning of 'more extensive and detailed' (*ausführlicher*), i.e. as a specific observation concerning the comparison.

5. Conclusion

This list could indeed be extended, but I believe that the evidence provided so far will certainly be sufficient to allow constructive conclusions.

I believe the MH derives from reliable sources belonging to the field of Homeric scholarship and of learned mythography. Some compiler built up the MH by borrowing from sources with mixed material, like *hypomnemata* or other learned products, and shaping it into a veritable specialised commentary which, from a certain point of time onwards, circulated separately. This is a by no means unusual case in which reduced, epitomised and simplified or specialised forms gained favour at the expense of the products of the great scholarly tradition, inasmuch as many of the fragments of *hypomnemata* or *syngrammata* that have come down to us on papyri dating from the early centuries of the imperial age are already in epitomised form. The MH may have assumed its present form, as shown in the papyri, just after the Augustan age: Didymus is quoted, the most ancient papyrus still preserved dates back to the 1st-2nd century CE and the ostrakon discussed above is of the same date. It was then presumably copied in this form all through the Roman age, finally ending up in the first compilation of our D-scholia.[53] Naturally, along the way it underwent important and substantial modifications and, as was to be expected, its quality declined, at least from a scholarly point of view, while yet retaining traces of its high-level origins. Quite frequently, breaks in the continuity and complexity of exegetical analysis must have occurred, with the result that some elements are now found in different scholia, so that it is not always possible to reconstruct the integrity of the line of argument and the links between different parts and types of materials. I am of course aware that having overall learned origins does not provide an exception-free rule and does not necessarily imply absolute reliability of all the final results. I consider the subscriptions in general to be reliable in the sense we have seen in this discussion, but it is clear that

---

[53] Put together in the Protobyzantine period or at the very beginning of the Byzantine Renaissance: the most ancient manuscript dates from the second half of the ninth century: cf. bibliography at n. 28.

case-by-case examination must be carried out with possibly different outcomes. However, my overall assessment is that we can be reasonably sure that the material contained in the MH must not be viewed as deriving from a fairly late and low-level mythographical compendium, based merely on indirect manualistic knowledge. On the contrary, it appears to me that there is strong evidence that somebody made a selection from high-quality learned commentaries of the Alexandrian age, thereby producing this mythographical commentary to Homer, which was transmitted in later centuries in a number of versions. Most of the material, in my view, probably comes from the Alexandrian tradition, but there is no reason to take this as a strict constraint on interpretation of each single element. As is only natural in this sort of product, materials from different sources may have been added or conflated at varying points in time. For instance, it is impossible to say at which stage elements of allegorical interpretation were included in the main body of mythological erudition, but this is hardly surprising in the eclectic and miscellaneous products of the Roman age. As a matter of fact, within the corpus of the D-scholia, allegorism does not figure prominently, but its presence should be noted in a few important passages.[54] In the evidence available from the papyri, on the other hand, to date no passages of allegorical exegesis have been discovered.

I would like to conclude by pointing out that the hypothesis of the origin and transmission of the MH sketched here can be set within a typology that is far from unusual in the history of (Homeric) scholarship. An interesting parallel I would mention, *mutatis mutandis*, is the Homeric lexicon of Apollonius Sophista, on which an interesting state-of-the-art survey was given recently by M. Haslam. Apollonius has come down to us in epitomised form from only one complete manuscript, the codex *Coislinianus gr.* 345 of the tenth century and from a handful of papyrus fragments from the Roman age (1st-6th centuries). These papyri vary

---

[54] I would like to remind for instance of *D-sch.* on *Il.* 5.385, where one finds allegorical interpretations adduced in opposition to Aristarchus; equally important is *D-sch.* on *Il.* 20.67, where an articulated allegorical explanation of the battle of the Gods is given.

considerably in form and version, and clearly each copy is the outcome of an individually made selection: none of them is identical with the *Coislinianus* text, but similarities and differences are intermingled. The text has undergone sundry modifications over time and in the different exemplars: 'How different can two texts be, and still be regarded as texts of the same work? ... In that sense they are different works. But each of them may still have a right to be called Apollonius' lexicon. That lexicon was a discrete textual entity, originating as such at a particular time and place, and its subsequent textual instability did not compromise its ontological integrity. This is what distinguishes the lexicon from what modern scholars collectively label *scholia minora*. As a popular reference work, it could change without losing its identity, and could exist simultaneously in multifarious forms ... Adaptability and success went hand in hand'.[55] So also for Appolonius we have a series of fragmentary papyri covering different parts of the lexicon and the instability of the text can be seen from a comparison with what is found in the *Coislinianus*: here too, at times it is the tenth century codex that presents the richer text and a form closer to the original, whereas at other times it is the exemplar on papyrus. More complex glosses were simplified and among the first elements to be lost were literal citations of authors; text impoverishment created imprecision affecting names and arguments of scholars who supported this or that interpretation. The materials for setting up an alphabetic Homeric lexicon were available in the whole gamut of Homeric scholarship (*hypomnemata* and *syngrammata* as well as the rich and ancient production of glossaries), from whence they could successfully be extracted and organised: 'The full range of the lexicon's material was available in ready-packaged form, requiring only reassembly'.[56] All in all, there are many elements in the history of the origin and tradition of Appolonius Sophista that bear a high similarity to what we have reconstructed for the MH. Perhaps the greatest differences lie firstly in the fact that an authorial name is known for the lexicon of Appolonius Sophista, whereas the

[55] Haslam 1994, 108-9; 114.

[56] Haslam 1994, 44.

MH was probably composed by an obscure grammarian working with the aid of good erudite sources; and secondly by the fact that the lexicon of Appolonius has been preserved as an independent entity in a Byzantine codex, even though in a strongly epitomised form, while the MH has been preserved within the Byzantine corpus of the D-scholia, forming one of its main sources.

Ilias

001. A 38, 39.
P.Hamb. 199 r—Vol. pap., IIp.
Ed. pr. B. Kramer, *P.Hamb. III*, 1984, 25-34; cf. W. Luppe, *ZPE* 56 (1984), 31-2.

002. A 263, 264, 399.
P.Oxy. 418 (Pack[2] 1164)—Vol. pap., I-IIp.
Ed. pr. B.P. Grenfell - A.S. Hunt, *P.Oxy. III*, 1903, 63-5.

003. H 8 (?), 44, 86; Θ 479; I 447.
P.Lit.Lond. 142 + *P.Oxy.* 3830 (Pack[2] 1188)—Vol. pap., IIp.
Ed. pr.: *P.Lit.Lond.* 142 (Brit. Mus. inv. 1605): H.J.M. Milne, *P.Lit. Lond.*, 1927, 121; cf. R. Pfeiffer, *Philologus* 92 (1937), 16-8 = *Ausgew. Schr.*, München 1960, 39-41; H. Erbse, *Sch. Iliad.* II, 1971, 392-3, *Sch. Iliad.* VII, 1988, 266, 300—*P.Oxy.* 3830 (+ *P.Lit. Lond.* 142): M. A. Harder, *P.Oxy. LVI*, 1989, 37-44; cf. M. Haslam, *BASP* 27 (1990), 31-6; W. Luppe, *Gnomon* 64 (1992), 291-3, *APF* 39 (1993), 9-11.

Θ 479: v. 003.

I 447: v. 003.

004. N 217.
PSI 1000 (Pack[2] 2463)—Ostrakon, I-IIp.

Ed. pr. P. Viereck e G. Vitelli, *PSI* VIII, 1927, 209; v. L. Salvadori, *CCC* 9 (1988), 259-62.

005. N 301 (?), 302, 459; Ξ 319; O 229.
P.Oxy. 3003—Vol. pap., IIp.
Ed. pr. P. J. Parsons, *P.Oxy. XLII*, 1974, 15-9.

Ξ 319: v. 005.

O 229: v. 005.

006. Σ [, T], Y, Φ, X, Ψ, Ω.
P.Oxy. 4096—Vol. pap., IIp.
Ed. pr. P. Schubart, *P.Oxy. LXI*, 1995

007. T 326/32; Y 53, 147.
P.Schubart 21 = *P.Berol.* 13930 (Pack[2] 1203)—Cod. perg., Vp.
Ed. pr. W. Schubart, *Gr. Lit. Pap.*, Berlin 1950, 45-7; cf. B. Snell, *apud ed. pr.*; R. Merkelbach, *APF* 16 (1956), 117-8; Turner 1977, nr. 206; Montanari 1985, II, 235-6; W. Luppe, *APF* 31 (1985), 5-11.

Y: v. 006.

Y 53, 147: v. 007.

008. Y 147, 307, 404.
P.Berol. 13282—Cod. pap., IIIp.
Ed. pr. W. Müller, *Forsch. u. Berichte* 10 (1968), 118-9; cf. Montanari 1985.

Φ, X, Ψ, Ω: v. 006.

Odyssea

001. γ 4, 91; λ 321-2, 326, 519-20, 582; μ 70, 85; ν 96, 259; ξ 327.
PSI 1173 (Pack[2] 1209)—Cod. pap., IIIp.

Ed. pr. G. Coppola, *PSI* 10 (1932), 131-40; cf. R. Pfeiffer, *Philologus* 92 (1937), 14-6 = *Ausgew. Schr.*, München 1960, 37-9; Turner 1977, nr. 207

λ 321, 322, 326, 519-20, 582: v. 001.

002. λ 308, 576 (?).
P.Vindob.Gr. 29784 (Pack[2] 2447)—Vol. pap., IIIp.
Ed. pr. H. Gerstinger, *MPER.* N.S. 1 (1932), 130-1; cf. R. Pfeiffer, *Philologus* 92 (1937), 16 n. 25 = *Ausgew. Schr.*, München 1960, 39-40 n. 25.

μ 70, 85: v. 001.

ν 96, 259: v. 001.

ξ 327: v. 001.

BIBLIOGRAPHY

Arrighetti, G., Il POx 1611: alcuni problemi di erudizione antica, *SCO* 17 (1968), 76-98.

———, Fra erudizione e biografia, *SCO* 26 (1977), 13-67.

———, Hypomnemata e Scholia: alcuni problemi, *MPhL* 2 (1977), 49-67.

———, *Poeti, eruditi e biografi. Momenti della riflessione dei Greci sulla letteratura*. Biblioteca di Studi Antichi 52. Pisa 1987.

Bethe, E., *Quaestiones Diodoreae mythographae*. Diss. Göttingen 1887.

Erbse, H., *Scholia Graeca in Homeri Iliadem (Scholia Vetera)*, voll. I-VII. Berolini 1969-88.

———, review of Van der Valk 1963-4 vol. I, *Gnomon* 36 (1964), 549-57.

Haslam, M.H., A New Papyrus of the Mythographus Homericus, *BASP* 27 (1990), 31-6.

———, The Homer Lexicon of Apollonius Sophista I. Composition and Constituents; II. Identity and Transmission, *CPh* 89 (1994), 1-45; 107-118.

Janko, R., The Shield of Heracles and the Legend of Cycnus, *CQ* 36 (1986), 38-59.

Lünstedt, P., *Untersuchungen zu den mythologischen Abschnitten der D-Scholien.* Diss. Hamburg 1961.

Maass, E., Die Iliasscholien des Codex Leidensis, *Hermes* 19 (1884), 534-68.

Montanari, F., *Studi di filologia omerica antica, I.* Biblioteca di Studi Antichi 19. Pisa 1979.

———, Gli Homerica su papiro: per una distinzione di generi, in: *Ricerche di filologia classica, II.* Biblioteca di Studi Antichi 45. Pisa 1984, 125-38.

———, Revisione di P. Berol. 13282. Le Historiae fabulares omeriche su papiro, in: *Atti XVII Congr. Papirol., Napoli 1983.* Napoli 1985, 2.229-42.

———, Filologia omerica antica nei papiri, in: *Proceed. XVIII Congr. Papirol.—Athens 1986.* Athens 1988, 2.337-44.

———, Note sulla tradizione manoscritta degli Scholia D in Iliadem. Un caso di errore da archetipo, in: *Storia, Poesia e Pensiero nel mondo antico. Studi in onore di Marcello Gigante.* Napoli 1994, 2.475-81.

Moretti, A.F., Revisione di alcuni papiri omerici editi tra i P. Mil. Vogl., *Tyche* 8 (1993), 87-97.

Panzer, I., *De Mythographo Homerico restituendo.* Diss. Greifswald 1892.

Schimberg, A., Zur handschriftlichen Ueberlieferung der scholia Didymi: I, *Philologus* 49 (1980), 421-56; II-III, *Wiss. Beilage z. Progr. K. Ev. Gymnasiums zu Ratibor* 1891/2. Ratibor 1891-2.

Schmidt, M., *Didymi Chalcenteri Gramm. Alex. Fragmenta.* Lipsiae 1854.

Schmidt, M., *Die Erklärungen zum Weltbild Homers und zur Kultur der Heroenzeit in den bT-Scholien zur Ilias.* Zetemata 62. München 1976.

Schwartz, E., Apollodoros, *RE* I 2 (1894), 2856-86.

———, De Scholiis Homericis ad historiam fabularem pertinentibus, *NJPhP* Suppl. 12 (1881), 405-63.

Schwarz, I., *De scholiis in Homeri Iliadem mythologicis capita tria.* Diss. Vratislaviae 1878.

Snipes, K., Literary Interpretation in the Homeric Scholia: the Similes of the Iliad, *AJPh* 109 (1988), 196-222.

Turner, E.G., *Greek Papyri. An Introduction.* Oxford 1968, 1980[2] (*Edizione italiana* a cura di M. Manfredi, Roma 1984).

———, *The Typology of the Early Codex.* Philadelphia 1977.

Valk, M. van der, On Apollodori Bibliotheca, *REG* 71 (1958), 100-68.

———, *Researches on the Text and Scholia of the Iliad*, I-II. Leiden 1963-4.

Wilamowitz, U. von, Die griechische Heldensage, *Sitz. Preuß. Akad. Wissensch.* 1925, 41-62 = *Kleine Schriften* V 2, Berlin 1971, 54-84.

Protreptic in Ancient Theories of Philosophical Literature

S.R. Slings

'Protreptic' is perhaps the term most often used in discussions of ancient philosophical literature.[1] Yet after Hartlich's indispensable but antiquated *farrago* of analyses of extant protreptic texts, reconstructions of lost ones and renderings of ancient theoretical statements concerning protreptic (1889), no comprehensive study has been published.[2] Of course much energy has been devoted to the reconstruction of lost *Protreptics* by Aristotle and (rather less energetically during the last fifty years) Posidonius.[3] There are two studies on the early stage of protreptic.[4] But other than that, surprisingly little work has been done on this important issue.

In this paper, I will give an overview of ancient theories concerning protreptic. As I have already treated fourth-century protreptic at some length in my book on the *Clitophon* (1981), I will only touch on that period here. I start with two extracts from Epictetus' *Diatribe* *Πρὸς τοὺς ἀναγινώσκοντας καὶ διαλεγομένους ἐπιδεικτικῶς* (3.23.30-1; 27-8):

---

[1] With the possible exception of 'diatribe', which has been shown by Schmeller 1987 to be a ghost-word as an ancient term for a philosophical genre, and to have limited usefulness as a tool of analysis. By contrast, 'protreptic' has acquired a firm status as a title or sub-title for a whole range of texts from the fourth century BCE onwards, and term and genre alike are the topic of reflection by philosophers as early as Plato's *Euthydemus* and Pseudo-Plato's *Clitophon*.

[2] Jordan's paper offers some salutary methodical remarks but no analysis. The problems he has with protreptic as a genre I had tried to solve by distinguishing between implicit and explicit protreptic (1981, 70-3).

[3] Of these, Gerhäusser 1912 is still indispensable as a collection of material.

[4] Gaiser 1959—see the sensible remarks of de Strycker 1962; Slings 1981, 70-199.

(1) *'Ιατρεῖόν ἐστιν, ἄνδρες, τὸ τοῦ φιλοσόφου σχολεῖον· οὐ δεῖ ἡσθέντας ἐξελθεῖν ἀλλ' ἀλγήσαντας. ἔρχεσθε γὰρ οὐχ ὑγιεῖς, ἀλλ' ὁ μὲν ὦμον ἐκβεβληκώς, ὁ δ' ἀπόστημα ἔχων, ὁ δὲ σύριγγα, ὁ δὲ κεφαλαλγῶν. εἶτ' ἐγὼ καθίσας ὑμῖν λέγω νοημάτια καὶ ἐπιφωνημάτια, ἵν' ὑμεῖς ἐπαινέσαντές με ἐξέλθητε, ὁ μὲν τὸν ὦμον ἐκφέρων οἷον εἰσήνεγκεν, ὁ δὲ τὴν κεφαλὴν ὡσαύτως ἔχουσαν, ὁ δὲ τὴν σύριγγα, ὁ δὲ τὸ ἀπόστημα; ...*
φιλόσοφος δ' ἐπ' ἀκρόασιν παρακαλεῖ; ... ποῖος ἰατρὸς παρακαλεῖ ἵνα τις ὑπ' αὐτοῦ θεραπευθῇ; καίτοι νῦν ἀκούω ὅτι καὶ οἱ ἰατροὶ παρακαλοῦσιν ἐν 'Ρώμῃ· πλὴν ἐπ' ἐμοῦ παρεκαλοῦντο. "Παρακαλῶ σε ἐλθόντα ἀκοῦσαι ὅτι σοι κακῶς ἐστι καὶ πάντων μᾶλλον ἐπιμέλῃ ἢ οὗ δεῖ σε ἐπιμελεῖσθαι, καὶ ὅτι ἀγνοεῖς τὰ ἀγαθὰ καὶ τὰ κακὰ καὶ κακοδαίμων εἶ καὶ δυστυχής." κομψὴ παράκλησις· καὶ μὴν ἂν μὴ ταῦτα ἐμποιῇ ὁ τοῦ φιλοσόφου λόγος, νεκρός ἐστι καὶ αὐτὸς καὶ ὁ λέγων.
'Folks, the philosopher's school is a doctor's surgery: you're not supposed to have enjoyed yourselves when you come out, but to have suffered. For you don't come in sane men, but this man's got his shoulder dislocated, that one has an abscess or a cyst, the other suffers from migraine. Should I, then, make you sit down and deliver to you some nice conceit or flourish, so you'll praise me and come out, this man taking out his shoulder as he'd brought it in, the other with his head in the same condition, and likewise the man with the abscess or the cyst? ...
Does a philosopher invite people to come and listen to him? ... What kind of doctor is that, who invites his patients to his surgery so they can be cured by him? True, I hear that in Rome nowadays doctors do invite their patients to their surgery, but in my time they were invited to make house-calls. "I invite you to come and hear that you're not at all well: you take care of everything except for what you should take care of, you can't tell good from evil—in short, you're wretched and miserable." A charming invitation indeed! Yet if the philosopher's speech does not have this effect, it's a dead thing, and so is its speaker.'

The moral of these passages is clear. If a philosopher wishes to speak in public, he must not aim at pleasing his audience with rhetorical tricks, but at accusing them of not having their priorities in order. Epictetus is clearly criticising the more philosophically-minded representatives of the Second Sophistic, for example Dio Chrysostom, who is mentioned twice in this diatribe (17; 19).

But these opponents have one argument left; it is voiced, as so often in Epictetus, by a fictitious objector (3.23.33-4):

> (2) - Τί *οὖν, οὐκ ἔστιν ὁ προτρεπτικὸς χαρακτήρ;*
>
> - Τίς *γὰρ οὐ λέγει; ὡς ὁ ἐλεγκτικός, ὡς ὁ διδασκαλικός. τίς οὖν πώποτε τέταρτον εἶπεν μετὰ τούτων τὸν ἐπιδεικτικόν; τίς γάρ ἐστιν ὁ προτρεπτικός; δύνασθαι καὶ ἑνὶ καὶ πολλοῖς δεῖξαι τὴν μάχην ἐν ᾗ κυλίονται, καὶ ὅτι μᾶλλον πάντων φροντίζουσιν ἢ ὧν θέλουσιν. θέλουσι μὲν γὰρ τὰ πρὸς εὐδαιμονίαν φέροντα, ἀλλαχοῦ δ' αὐτὰ ζητοῦσι.*
>
> '"But wait a minute, isn't there a thing called protreptic genre?"—Who says there isn't? Like the refutative, like the didactic. Who has ever introduced as a fourth class the epideictic genre? What does protreptic consist of? The ability to show either a single person or a crowd the contradiction they're rolling around in, to show that they take care of everything except what they really wish. They wish that which leads to happiness, but they're looking for it some place else.'

Epideictic does not have a place in philosophical discourse; to a philosopher it makes no difference whether he is addressing a single person or a crowd, whereas for epideixis an audience of more than one is a logical prerequisite. However, in this period there were evidently philosophical orators who disguised their epideictic speeches as protreptic. Elsewhere in this diatribe, Epictetus gives us an idea of their subject-matter: Pan and the Nymphs (11), the death of Achilles (35), Xerxes and the battle of Thermopylae (38).

Evidence for this use of the term *protreptic* to cover epideictic oratory with a philosophical veneer is plentiful. In another diatribe, Epictetus says when addressing people who have not yet internalised their philosophical views (3.16.7):

> (3) *διὰ τοῦτο ἄτονά ἐστι καὶ νεκρά, καὶ σικχᾶναί ἐστιν ἀκούοντα ὑμῶν τοὺς προτρεπτικοὺς καὶ τὴν ἀρετὴν τὴν ταλαίπωρον, ἣ ἄνω κάτω θρυλεῖται.*
>
> 'That's why your words are out of tune and dead [the same strong language, indeed the same word, as in (1)] and one has to puke if one

listens to your protreptic speeches, your wretched virtue which you kick around all the time.'

The emperor Marcus Aurelius is grateful to his Stoic teacher Rusticus, who prevented him from (M.Ant. 1.7)

(4) Παρὰ 'Ρουστικοῦ ... καὶ τὸ μὴ ἐκτραπῆναι εἰς ζῆλον σοφιστικὸν μηδὲ τὸ συγγράφειν περὶ τῶν θεωρημάτων ἢ προτρεπτικὰ λογάρια διαλέγεσθαι ἢ φαντασιοπλήκτως τὸν ἀσκητικὸν ἢ τὸν εὐεργετικὸν ἄνδρα ἐπιδείκνυσθαι·

'going astray and imitate the sophists or to write about philosophical tenets or to deliver little protreptic speeches or to extol in an imaginative way the man of self-discipline or the benefactor;'

It comes hardly as a surprise that it is the same Rusticus who introduced him to the diatribes of Epictetus (*καὶ τὸ ἐντυχεῖν τοῖς 'Επικτητείοις ὑπομνήμασιν, ὧν οἴκοθεν μετέδωκεν, ib.*). The parallels between this passage and Epictetus prove that *ἄνδρα ἐπιδείκνυσθαι* means 'to extol a man in an epideictic speech'.[5] If so, the protreptic speeches that Marcus did not write were laudatory, whereas Epictetus wanted them to be critical.

This epideictic form of protreptic has its roots in long-standing rhetorical precepts. Xerxes and the battle of Thermopylae remind us of the treatment of Funeral speeches in the *Techne* ascribed to Dionysius of Halicarnassus, where we are told (Ps.-D.H. *Rh.* 6.4, 2.280 U.-R.) that after the treatment of the deceased's country, forefathers, character, conduct and accomplishments

(5) μετὰ ταῦτα δὲ ... ἐπὶ τὸ προτρεπτικὸν μεταβησόμεθα, προτρέποντες ἐπὶ τὰ ὅμοια τοὺς ὑπολειπομένους· καὶ πολὺς ὁ τόπος οὗτος.

'we should proceed to protreptic, namely by exhorting those left behind to similar things, and that part is very important.'

Protreptic is followed by consolation. Marcus' little speeches extolling great men go straight back to Isocrates, who writes (9.77):

---

[5] Not, as it is usually taken, 'to show myself off as a man who practises self-discipline or as a benefactor'; the more so since Marcus goes on to thank Rusticus for his renunciation of rhetoric, poetry and ἀστειολογία (*καὶ τὸ ἀποστῆναι ῥητορικῆς καὶ ποιητικῆς καὶ ἀστειολογίας, ib.*).

(6) *τοὺς μὲν γὰρ ἄλλους προτρέπομεν ἐπὶ τὴν φιλοσοφίαν ἑτέρους ἐπαινοῦντες, ἵνα ζηλοῦντες τοὺς εὐλογουμένους τῶν αὐτῶν ἐκείνοις ἐπιτηδευμάτων ἐπιθυμῶσιν.*

'We exhort people to philosophy by praising others, so that they will imitate those who have been praised and wish to possess the same virtues as they.'

In the year 369 CE, Themistius wrote a *Protreptikos* for the three-year-old consul Valentinianus, which is nothing but a lengthy eulogy of the young dignitary's father, the emperor Valens. Certain declamations of the exhorting type were called *προτρεπτικοί*.[6] From Aristotle onwards, exhortation had come under the heading of political oratory, praise under epideixis, but the more level-headed theorists were aware that the two are closely related.[7]

However, I am not so much interested in the rhetorical origins of the phenomenon which Epictetus wishes to criticise, but in the argument he uses to deny it a place in philosophical discourse altogether, in other words in the trichotomy of this discourse (2): protreptic, elenctic, didactic. The trichotomy recurs in a slightly different form in *Diatribe* 3.21. If you want to be a teacher of philosophy, you need some specific qualities (3.21.18-20):

(7) *καὶ πρὸ πάντων τὸν θεὸν συμβουλεύειν ταύτην τὴν χώραν κατασχεῖν, ὡς Σωκράτει συνεβούλευεν τὴν ἐλεγκτικὴν χώραν ἔχειν, ὡς Διογένει τὴν βασιλικὴν καὶ ἐπιπληκτικήν, ὡς Ζήνωνι τὴν διδασκαλικὴν καὶ δογματικήν. σὺ δ' ἰατρεῖον ἀνοίγεις οὐδὲν ἄλλο ἔχων ἢ φάρμακα, ποῦ δὲ ἢ πῶς ἐπιτίθεται ταῦτα μήτε εἰδὼς μήτε πολυπραγμονήσας.*

'and above all god must have called you to take up this position, as he called Socrates to take up the elenctic position, Diogenes the royal,

[6] For instance the military ones by Lesbonax and the 'protreptic for the athletes' in the same pseudo-Dionysian *Techne*. Athenian inscriptions have taught us that at ephebic games one of the ephebes used to deliver a protreptic speech, and fragments of two such speeches have been preserved (*IG* ii/iii^2 2119.231; 2291a and b).

[7] We find statements to that effect in Quintilian (3.8.28), Clement of Alexandria (*Paed.* 1.10.89.3-4) and Origen (*Philocalia* 18.16).

critical position and Zeno the didactic, theoretical position. But you open a doctor's surgery while having only medicines, but where or how these are applied you neither know nor care.'

The vocation of teacher is here combined with a trichotomy which is identical to the one in (2): there is an elenctic and a didactic slot, and the protreptic is called 'royal and critical'. The quotations under (1) and (2) make it clear enough why protreptic should be equalled with critical—royal is a clear reference to the Cynic ideal of the king.[8] In *Diatribe* 3.22, which is devoted to the Cynic's vocation, Epictetus actually quotes a protreptic speech with verbal similarities to the definition of protreptic as given in (2). This speech opens with an echo of the speech of Socrates in the Platonic or, as I prefer to believe, pseudo-Platonic *Clitophon* (407b1 ff.) which we know from other sources (D.Chr. 13.14-7; Ps.-Luc. *Cyn.* 18, 4.145.11-2 Macleod) was a favourite among the Cynics of this period.

We also observe in (7) that typical representatives of each of the genres have been added, just as in rhetorical theory each of the *genera dicendi* has its own typical exponent in oratory, historiography and even mythology. The scheme as presented by Epictetus is taken over and extended by the Roman orator Fronto (*Epist. ad Ant. de Eloqu.* 134.7-12 Van den Hout):

(8) *Quid? philosophi ipsi nonne diverso genere orationis usi sunt? Zeno ad docendum planissimus, Socrates ad coargendum captiosissimus, Diogenes ad exprobrandum promptissimus, Heraclitus obscurus involvere omnia, Pythagoras mirificus clandestinis signis sancire omnia, Clitomachus anceps in dubium vocare omnia.*

'Don't the philosophers themselves use various types of discourse? Zeno is the clearest teacher, Socrates the shrewdest refuter, Diogenes the most fanatic reprover; Heraclitus the dark makes everything complicated, Pythagoras the sorcerer makes everything certain by secret signs, Clitomachus the fence-sitter makes everything doubtful.'

[8] The Cynic's beggar's staff was called 'Diogenes' sceptre' (3.22.57, cf. 4.8.30); cf. Billerbeck 1978, 123. For the idea in general, see Höistad 1948.

It is interesting to observe that both trichotomies are accompanied by comparisons of the philosopher with the doctor. This analogy was considered a Stoic platitude by Cicero, himself no mean dealer in platitudes,[9] but it is interesting to see it used, as twice in Epictetus, by the Academician Philo of Larisa, in another division of philosophy, in which protreptic plays, again, an important part (fr. 2 Mette (*Lustrum* 28-9 (1986-7), 9-24), Stob. 2.39.20-40.15 Wachsmuth).

> (9) ἐοικέναι δή φησι τὸν φιλόσοφον ἰατρῷ. καθάπερ οὖν ἔργον ἰατροῦ πρῶτον μὲν πεῖσαι τὸν κάμνοντα παραδέξασθαι τὴν θεραπείαν, δεύτερον δὲ τοὺς τῶν ἀντισυμβουλευόντων λόγους ὑφελέσθαι, οὕτως καὶ τοῦ φιλοσόφου. κεῖται τοίνυν ἑκάτερον τούτων ἐν τῷ προσαγορευομένῳ προτρεπτικῷ λόγῳ· ἔστι γὰρ ὁ προτρεπτικὸς ὁ παρορμῶν ἐπὶ τὴν ἀρετήν. τούτου δ' ὁ μὲν ἐνδείκνυται τὸ μεγαλωφελὲς αὐτῆς, ὁ δὲ τοὺς ἀνασκευάζοντας καὶ κατηγοροῦντας ἢ πως ἄλλως κακοηθιζομένους ἀπελέγχει. δεύτερος δὲ ὁ πρὸς τὴν ἰατρικὴν ἀναλογίαν δευτέραν ἔχων τάξιν. ὡς γὰρ ἰατροῦ μετὰ τὸ πεῖσαι παραδέξασθαι τὴν θεραπείαν τὸ προσάγειν ἐστὶ ταύτην ... οὕτως αὖ κἀπὶ τῆς ἐπιστήμης ἔχει.
>
> 'The philosopher is similar to a doctor. As it's the doctor's task first to persuade the patient to undergo treatment, second to refute the arguments of those who give contrary advise, so too with the philosopher. Both these tasks are contained in the so-called protreptic speech: protreptic incites to virtue. Of protreptic, one part demonstrates her great usefulness, the other refutes those who try to demolish virtue and slander her or mistreat her in any other way. Second after this comes the part that according to the medical analogy takes second position. For as it is the doctor's task after having persuaded patients to undergo treatment to start the treatment..., so it is with knowledge.'

I don't intend to quote the rest of the passage, but an overview of Philo's divisions is necessary:

1. προτρεπτικός	a. ἐνδείκνυται τὸ μεγαλωφελὲς αὐτῆς
	b. ἀπελέγχει

[9] *Tusc.* 4.23; for more parallels see Hartlich 1889, 330.

2. *θεραπευτικά* a. *ὑπεξαιρετικὸν τῶν ψευδῶς γεγενημένων δοξῶν*
b. *τῶν ὑγιῶς ἐχουσῶν ἐνθετικόν*
3. *περὶ τὴν εὐδαιμονίαν*
4. *παραγγέλματα*
λόγος περὶ βίων a. *ἴδιος*
b. *κοινός, πολιτικόν*
5. *τὸν ὑποθετικὸν λόγον, δι' οὗ τὰς πρὸς τὴν ἀσφάλειαν καὶ τὴν ὀρθότητα τῆς ἑκάστου χρήσεως ὑποθήκας ἐν ἐπιτομαῖς ἕξουσιν.*

1. protreptic a. demonstrates its great usefulness
b. refutes
2. therapeutic a. removes false opinions
b. puts in sound opinions
3. happiness
4. prescripts,
conduct of life a. private
b. public (politics)
5. advice, 'by means of which they will have in a nutshell precepts for safety and for the correct use of everything'.

(5 is intended for those who lack the time for going through the process of 2 through 4.)

What Philo and Epictetus have in common is first the ethic orientation of protreptic: it exhorts to virtue, not as one might have supposed to philosophy. In an age when it was customary to define philosophy as 'the study of virtue' (Sen. *Ep.* 89.8) this is not surprising—still it deserves notice that the Aristotelian type of exhortation to philosophy is ignored. Of course, the whole point of the analogy between doctor and philosopher is precisely this reduction of philosophy to ethics; Philo ignores physics and logic altogether.

It is, besides, interesting to see protreptic and elenctic brought together under one head. This, too, can be parallelled from Epictetus (2.26.1; 4):

(10) *Πᾶν ἁμάρτημα μάχην περιέχει. ἐπεὶ γὰρ ὁ ἁμαρτάνων οὐ θέλει ἁμαρτάνειν ἀλλὰ κατορθῶσαι, δῆλον ὅτι ὃ μὲν θέλει οὐ ποιεῖ. ...*

> Δεινὸς οὖν ἐν λόγῳ, ὁ δ' αὐτὸς καὶ προτρεπτικὸς καὶ ἐλεγκτικὸς οὗτος ὁ δυνάμενος ἑκάστῳ παραδεῖξαι τὴν μάχην καθ' ἣν ἁμαρτάνει. καὶ σαφῶς παρίσταται πῶς ὃ θέλει οὐ ποιεῖ καὶ ὃ μὴ θέλει ποιεῖ.
>
> 'Every wrong action entails a contradiction. Since the wrongdoer doesn't want to do wrong but to do right, clearly he isn't doing what he wants to. ... So that man is an impressive speaker, good at protreptic and elenctic at the same time, who is capable of showing everyone the contradiction through which he does wrong, and of making clear how he isn't doing what he wants and is doing what he doesn't want.'

What unites the two in Epictetus is the notion of μάχη, contradiction, which recurs in the definition of protreptic in (2). The idea that refutation is the most effective way of exhortation is already set out in the famous description of ἔλεγχος in Plato's *Sophist*, where contradiction is also a key-issue (Slings 1981, 149-58). As Epictetus goes on to mention Socrates (cf. 2.12.6) in this context, who as we saw delivered the speech in the *Clitophon* that inspired the critical, Cynic idea of protreptic, it is possible that with 'the man who is good at protreptic and elenctic at the same time' Epictetus actually means Socrates.

However that may be, there is a close similarity, although a similarity in form rather than content, between Epictetus' trichotomy and Philo's more intricate scheme. Protreptic and elenctic are preparatory to the main part of philosophical discourse, which in Philo is split up into four parts, whereas in Epictetus it is simply 'didactic' as in (2), or 'didactic and theoretical' as in (7). Leaving elenctic aside for the moment, it is important to note that the concept of philosophical protreptic, throughout antiquity, never stands alone: protreptic is always protreptic to something else. This is already the case in Xenophon (*Mem.* 1.4.1) and Pseudo-Isocrates (1.3-4), and it is the whole point of the *Clitophon*, which can be subsumed in the words τί τοὐντεῦθεν; 'What next?' (408e1-2; cf. Plu. 798b). This is precisely the reason why Epictetus and Marcus Aurelius are so critical of rhetorical protreptic λογάρια: they don't lead up to anything—there isn't anything that logically does come next.[10]

Anyway, despite the similarities on the surface between the schemes of Philo and Epictetus, the differences between them are much more important than the similarities. Philo's protreptic and elenctic are general, not *ad hominem*, as they are in Epictetus (and in Plato). Protreptic and elenctic take up the same position in the scheme, but they can't be identified, as they can in Epictetus (and as they must in Plato). Elenctic is not to convict someone of the contradiction that leads to wrongdoing, but to refute counter-arguments to the pursuit of philosophy. As for protreptic, it is a far cry from Epictetus' Cynic-inspired fundamental criticism of people who have their priorities wrong—in Philo, it actually consists of the type condemned by Epictetus and Marcus Aurelius: praise of the usefulness of virtue, in the words of Epictetus (3), 'your wretched virtue which you kick around all the time'.

There are good grounds for thinking that when Philo divides protreptic into praising virtue and elenctic he is thinking of Socrates, as is perhaps the case with Epictetus as well. Philo was the last leader of the Middle Academy, and praising virtue and refuting others are the two activities that converge in Socratic speech as analyzed in a passage from Cicero's *Academica* I, which presents a typical Middle-Academy view of Socrates (*Ac.* 1.16; cf. Slings 1981, 97 f.).

> (11) *hic in omnibus fere sermonibus qui ab iis qui illum audierunt perscripti varie copioseque sunt ita disputat ut nihil adfirmet ipse, refellat alios, nihil se scire dicat nisi id ipsum ...*
> *quae cum diceret constanter et in ea sententia permaneret, omnis eius oratio tam in virtute laudanda et in hominibus ad virtutis studium cohortandis consumebatur, ut e Socraticorum libris maximeque Platonis intellegi potest.*

[10] It is also for this reason that we find the adjective προτρεπτικός contrasted with such words as διδασκαλικός (Origen *Fr. Comm. Ephes.* 21; Vettius Valens 2 *prooem.*, 54.3 Pingree), ὑφηγητικός (Galen, *De propr. animi* 6.19, p. 23,14-5), λογικός (Eusebius *DE* 10.4.7).

'His method in all the discussions which have been written down so differently and so completely by his listeners consists in not making any statements himself and refuting others, and in saying that he knows nothing except just that. ... As he persevered in this attitude all his speech consisted in praising virtue and exhorting others to pursue it, as one may infer from the books of the Socratics, especially Plato.'

It may sound strange that Plato is brought in as a witness for a protreptic Socrates, but there is in fact good authority for this. In the *Apology*, a work which presents Socrates' elenctic activities as brought about by the Delphic oracle, Socrates says at one point (30a7-b2, cf. Slings 1981, 162-7):

(12) *οὐδὲν γὰρ ἄλλο πράττων ἐγὼ περιέρχομαι ἢ πείθων ὑμῶν καὶ νεωτέρους καὶ πρεσβυτέρους μήτε σωμάτων ἐπιμελεῖσθαι μήτε χρημάτων πρότερον μηδὲ οὕτω σφόδρα ὡς τῆς ψυχῆς ὅπως ὡς ἀρίστη ἔσται, λέγων ὅτι "Οὐκ ἐκ χρημάτων ἀρετὴ γίγνεται, ἀλλ' ἐξ ἀρετῆς χρήματα καὶ τὰ ἄλλα ἀγαθὰ τοῖς ἀνθρώποις ἅπαντα καὶ ἰδίᾳ καὶ δημοσίᾳ."*

'For I go about doing nothing else but persuading both the young and the old among you not to care either for their bodies or their possessions prior to or to the same extent as for the best state of their souls, saying: "From wealth doesn't come virtue, but from virtue comes wealth and all the other good things to men, both privately and publicly."'

It is not so much the combination of Socrates' elenctic and protreptic activities that is un-Platonic in Cicero (and Philo), nor indeed the eulogy of virtue, and to quote Philo once more, 'its great usefulness' (*τὸ μεγαλωφελὲς αὐτῆς*), but the absence of the care for the soul, which is central to Socrates' protreptic in the *Apology*, as it is in Epictetus' definition of protreptic: 'to show that people take care of everything except what they really wish' ((2); cf. (1)). The importance of caring is one more argument for my thesis that when Epictetus combines elenctic and protreptic in one person, as he does in (10), he is really thinking of Socrates.

There are several more divisions of philosophy that are relevant here, two of them trichotomies like the one found in Epictetus. I'll leave out entirely one found in Xenophon (to which I alluded briefly above), and I'll be as brief as possible about one in Pseudo-Demetrius *On Style* (296-8), since I've already discussed them extensively in my book on the *Clitophon*.

(13) Καθόλου δὲ ὥσπερ τὸν αὐτὸν κηρὸν ὁ μέν τις κύνα ἔπλασεν, ὁ δὲ βοῦν, ὁ δὲ ἵππον, οὕτως καὶ πρᾶγμα ταὐτὸν ὁ μέν τις ἀποφαινόμενος καὶ κατηγορῶν φησιν ὅτι δὴ "ἄνθρωποι χρήματα μὲν ἀπολείπουσι τοῖς παισίν, ἐπιστήμην δὲ οὐ συναπολείπουσιν τὴν χρησομένην τοῖς ἀπολειφθεῖσι". τοῦτο δὲ τὸ εἶδος τοῦ λόγου 'Αριστίππειον λέγεται.

ἕτερος δὲ ταὐτὰ ὑποθετικῶς προοίσεται, καθάπερ Ξενοφῶντος τὰ πολλά, οἷον ὅτι "δεῖ γὰρ οὐ χρήματα ...".

τὸ δὲ ἰδίως καλούμενον εἶδος Σωκρατικόν, ὃ μάλιστα δοκοῦσιν ζηλῶσαι Αἰσχίνης καὶ Πλάτων, μεταρυθμίσει ἂν τοῦτο τὸ πρᾶγμα τὸ προειρημένον ὧδέ πως· "ὦ παῖ, πόσα σοι χρήματα ...;" ἅμα γὰρ καὶ εἰς ἀπορίαν ἔβαλεν τὸν παῖδα λεληθότως καὶ ἠνέμνησεν ὅτι ἀνεπιστήμων ἐστί, καὶ παιδεύεσθαι προετρέψατο· ταῦτα πάντα ἠθικῶς καὶ ἐμμελῶς, καὶ οὐχὶ δὴ τὸ λεγόμενον τοῦτο ἀπὸ Σκυθῶν.

εὐημέρησαν δ' οἱ τοιοῦτοι λόγοι τότε ἐξευρεθέντες τὸ πρῶτον, μᾶλλον δὲ ἐξέπληξαν τῷ τε μιμητικῶι καὶ τῷ ἐναργεῖ καὶ τῷ μετὰ μεγαλοφροσύνης νουθετητικῷ.

'Speaking more generally, just as the same bit of wax is moulded by one man into a dog, by another into an ox, by a third into a horse, so with regard to the same subject-matter one man will state as an accusation "people leave their wealth to their children, yet they don't leave with it the knowledge how to use their legacy"; this type of discourse is called Aristippean.

Another will express the same thought as an advice, as normally in Xenophon: "People must not ...".

The Socratic type in the stricter sense of the phrase, one which was apparently adopted especially by Aeschines and Plato, will reformulate the same matter as a question, for example "My boy, how much wealth ...?" In this way the speaker has brought the boy into apory without the latter realising it and has reminded him that he is ignorant, and at the same time he has exhorted him to have himself instructed. And all this in a personal and harmonious manner, not as the saying goes "in the Scythian mode".

> This type of speech met with great success when it was first invented, and they made a deeper impression than the others through their truth to life, their vividness and their man-of-the-world criticism.'

I may be allowed to state some points dogmatically (cf. Slings 1981, 96-102). This is not a trichotomy of philosophical genres; rather, one and the same subject-matter (*πρᾶγμα*), which happens to be protreptic (as a matter of fact it is derived from the *Clitophon*), is formulated as three different speech-acts, one 'declarative and accusing', the other 'as an advice', the third as a question, which is protreptic and leads into aporia, and is therefore, presumably, elenctic; those are the *εἴδη τοῦ λόγου*, and obviously they cannot be identified with the three *χαρακτῆρες* of Epictetus (2).[11] Epictetus' critical protreptic of the Cynic type (7) is identical to the first form here, the protreptic-elenctic of (10) to the third. The second speech-act recurs as a separate part of philosophical literature in Philo and elsewhere, but is absent from Epictetus. Vice versa, the latter's 'didactic, theoretical' genre doesn't correspond to anything in this text, which is not about parts of philosophical literature, but about philosophical styles.

The remarks on the third style are interesting: the exhortation takes place *ἠθικῶς καὶ ἐμμελῶς*, 'in a personal and harmonious manner'; these texts made an enormous impression 'by their man-of-the-world criticism' (*τῷ μετὰ μεγαλοφροσύνης νουθετητικῷ*). This looks like the opposite of Epictetus' idea of strongly reproving protreptic.[12]

Before discussing the third trichotomy, found in Clement of Alexandria, we'll have to plod our way through the most intricate of the div-

---

[11] This claim was made by E.G. Schmidt (1962). The link with the *Clitophon* was made by Carlini (1968).

[12] In point of fact, the word *προτρεπτικός* is coupled once or twice with *πρᾷος* as in the famous scene from Lucian's *Dream*, where the poor boy has ruined a piece of marble and is beaten up by his uncle *οὐ πράως οὐδὲ προτρεπτικῶς*, 'in an unfriendly and un-protreptic way' (2.136.16 MacLeod). The same juxtaposition is found in Eusebius (*DE* 4.10.14). The Christian sect which published its tracts under the pseudonym Macarius, notorious champions of the free will, emphasise time and again that the force of sin, as the force of God's grace, is protreptic, not anancastic.

isions of philosophy that were ever made—I mean the one made by Eudorus of Alexandria and preserved, like the fragment of Philo of Larisa, by Arius Didymus, who in his turn was excerpted by Stobaeus (Eudorus Alex. fr. 1 Mazzarelli (*Riv. Filos. Neo-scol.* 77 (1985), 197-209; 535-55), Stob. 2.42.7-45.6). I suppose we must count our blessings that only Eudorus' divisions of ethic philosophy were excerpted by Arius Didymus—we can only guess at the rarefied heights of pure partition that must have inspired his breakdown of physics and logic, which I'm sure we would never be able to understand. Although Eudorus is not a fool, his work is a perfect illustration of Seneca's dictum that philosophy should be split up, not shattered (*dividi enim illam non concidi utile est*, *Ep*. 89.2).

(14) *ἠθικόν*:
1. *θεωρητικόν*
2. *ὁρμητικόν*
3. *πρακτικόν*:
   a. *περὶ τῶν οἰκειούντων πρός τινας πράξεις*:
      i *ὁ ὑποθετικός*, ii *ὁ προτρεπτικός*
   b. *περὶ τῶν ἀλλοτριούντων (ἀποτρεπόντων) ἀπό τινων πράξεων*: *παραμυθητικός* = *παθολογικός*
   c. *ὁ τῶν αἰτίων ἀποδοτικὸς τῶν ἐπιτελούντων τινὰς σχήσεις ἢ κινήσεις*
   d. *περὶ ἀσκήσεως*
   e. *περὶ τῆς ἰδίως λεγομένης πράξεως*:
      περὶ τῶν καθηκόντων, περὶ τῶν κατορθωμάτων, περὶ τῶν χαρίτων, περὶ βίων, περὶ γάμου

Ethics is divided into a theoretical, hormetical and practical part; this tripartition is also found in Seneca (*Ep*. 89.14). I will ignore here the subdivisions of (1) and (2), although protreptic occurs under (1) as well as under (3), but in a highly obscure, corrupt and lacunose context. The masculine article in the subdivisions under (3) refers to *λόγος*. So we find successively (3a) a logos that attracts one to certain actions, (b) another that estranges one from them, (c) a logos that gives the causes of mental states or movements, (d) a logos about ascesis, and (e) one about praxis in the stricter sense of the word. Clearly the verbs *οἰκειόω* and *ἀλλοτριόω* are used in (3ab) for what is normally called *προτρέπω* and *ἀποτρέπω* respectively. Eudorus gives this away when in (3b) he substitutes *ἀποτρεπόντων* for *ἀλλοτριούντων*. Eudorus introduced this terminology obviously in order to bring protreptic and practical advice under one head, and I suspect he wanted to do so because they are monitory, as is consolation, as opposed to the other subtypes, which are analytical or prescriptive, as the part *περὶ βίων*, which we found already in Philo (9, 4a), certainly is: this has to do with concrete rules for life, especially marriage (which is mentioned by both Philo and Eudorus); it is therefore identical to the part called *παραινετική* by Posidonius (fr. 176 E.-K. = Sen. *Ep*. 95.65):

> (15) *Posidonius non tantum praeceptionem* [*παραινετική*] ... *sed etiam suasionem* [*ὑποθετικός*] *et consolationem* [*παραμυθητικός*] *et exhortationem* [*προτρεπτικός*] *necessariam iudicat; his adicit causarum inquisitionem, aetiologian* ... *Ait utilem futuram et descriptionem cuiusque virtutis; hanc Posidonius ethologian vocat, quidam characterismon appellant* ...
>
> 'Posidonius regards not only precepts as necessary, but also advice, consolation and exhortation. He adds research of causes, *αἰτιολογία*. He further says that a description of virtues may be useful—this he calls *ἠθολογία*, others *χαρακτηρισμός*'.

Seneca translates *παραινετικός* as *praeceptiva* and *praeceptio*; he devotes two letters (94 and 95) to this genre; the first example he gives is 'how a married man should behave towards his wife'.

It will be obvious that Eudorus, although nominally an Academician, is heavily indebted to Stoic terminology. As I said, his general tripartition recurs in Seneca. His theoretic division (1) has numerous points of contact with a Stoic division of ethics preserved in Diogenes Laertius 7.84. This part of his work is closely related to Posidonius, and probably heavily inspired by him, as will be seen when one compares (14, 3) to (15). In addition to prescripts, protreptic, advice, consolation and theory of causes all put in an appearance. Eudorus has Posidonius' *characterismos* as a part of his (1), and he adds the doctrine of *ἄσκησις*, *καθῆκον* and *κατόρ-*

θωμα here; we don't know where Posidonius placed these topics. Seneca, and probably Posidonius and Eudorus as well, thought of protreptic not in terms of the Cynic-critical protreptic of Epictetus, since in another passage (*Ep*. 94.39) *adhortatio* and *obiurgatio* are actually contrasted.

When we compare Eudorus and Philo, one thing that strikes us, apart from the former's greater complexity, is that paradoxically enough Eudorus is more practical, or rather more interested in finding a pigeon-hole for existing philosophical genres. This can be observed in the final section of (14), 3e. Here he first states that it is *περὶ τῶν καθηκόντων* and *περὶ τῶν κατορθωμάτων*; since some of these exist by themselves, while others have to do with the relationship to our fellow-men, the *τόπος περὶ τῶν χαρίτων* 'came into being' (*συνέστη*); this genre is represented for us by Seneca's *de Beneficiis*. Eudorus goes on (*ib*.; 2.44.24-45.2):

> *πάλιν δ' ἐπεὶ τῶν καθηκόντων καὶ τῶν κατορθωμάτων ἃ μὲν λέγεται σύνθετα ἃ δὲ ἀσύνθετα, συνέστη ἐκ τοῦ κατὰ τὰ σύνθετα ὁ περὶ βίου λόγος, οὗ μέρος ὢν ὁ περὶ γάμου κατ' ἰδίαν ἐτάχθη διὰ τὸ πλῆθος τῶν ἐν αὐτῷ ζητημάτων.*
>
> 'Again, since some *καθήκοντα* and *κατορθώματα* are compound and others not, out of the compound ones came into being *ὁ περὶ βίων λόγος* [which we also saw in Philo]. *ὁ περὶ γάμου* is a part of this but it received a place of its own because of the great number of problems involved'

'Ο *περὶ γάμου* is, of course, another genre, exemplified by Plutarch's *Γαμικὰ παραγγέλματα*.

Before moving on to my final text, I have to mention two problems connected with the divisions of Eudorus and Posidonius. One is the difference between *ὑποθετικός* 'advising' and *παραινετικός* 'prescriptive', which is also present in Philo. All three texts make the distinction in one form or another, but it seems more a matter of type of speech-act than anything else. As Seneca remarks with regard to *παραινετικός* and *χαρακτηρισμός*, they're really the same: if you want to give precepts you say 'you must do this if you want to be self-controlled', if you describe a virtue you say 'the self-controlled man is he who does this and abstains from that' (*Ep*. 95.66).[13]

A second point is the exact meaning of παραμυθητικός. This seems to fit Seneca's *consolatio* well enough, and of course it's what the word means. If my diagnosis of Eudorus' method is correct, he created his section (3b) with the express aim of finding a place for a venerable philosophical genre, the consolation. Yet elsewhere Seneca couples *consolationes* and *dissuasiones* (*Ep*. 94.39); the Stoic division in Diogenes Laertius couples προτροπαί and ἀποτροπαί, and so, of course, does rhetorical theory. For lack of data for Seneca's *dissuasiones* as a separate genre, I must leave this problem alone here.

And finally, where better to end this overview of the history of protreptic theory than with the literal apotheosis of the λόγος προτρεπτικός! It is found at the beginning of the *Paedagogus* of Clement of Alexandria (1.1.1.1-2.1):

> (16) Τριῶν γέ τοι τούτων περὶ τὸν ἄνθρωπον ὄντων, ἠθῶν πράξεων παθῶν, ὁ προτρεπτικὸς εἴληχεν τὰ ἤθη αὐτοῦ ... πράξεών τε ἁπασῶν λόγος ἐπιστατεῖ ὁ ὑποθετικός, τὰ δὲ πάθη ὁ παραμυθητικὸς ἰᾶται, εἷς ὢν ὁ πᾶς λόγος οὗτος ... Ὁ γοῦν οὐράνιος ἡγεμών, ὁ λόγος, ὁπήνικα μὲν ἐπὶ σωτηρίαν παρεκάλει, προτρεπτικὸς ὄνομα αὐτῷ ἦν ... νυνὶ δὲ θεραπευτικός τε ὢν καὶ ὑποθετικὸς ἅμα ἄμφω, ἑπόμενος αὐτὸς αὐτῷ παραινεῖ τὸν προτετραμμένον, κεφάλαιον τῶν ἐν ἡμῖν παθῶν ὑπισχνούμενος τὴν ἴασιν. κεκλήσθω δ' ἡμῖν ἐνὶ προσφυῶς οὗτος ὀνόματι παιδαγωγός ... καίτοι καὶ διδασκαλικὸς ὁ αὐτός ἐστι λόγος, ἀλλ' οὐ νῦν· ...
>
> 'There are three things in man, his way of life, his actions, his πάθη. Of these, the protreptic has as its domain his way of life ... all the actions are governed by the advisory, while his πάθη are healed by the παραμυθητικός. This is one and the same logos ... When the heavenly guide, the logos, called us to our salvation, his name was protreptic ... now he is at the same time therapeutic and advisory, and succeeding himself he gives precepts to the converted and to cap it all

---

[13] There is also an obvious relationship between ὑποθετικός and θετικός, for which cf. Schmeller 1987, 14-7.

he promises us healing of our πάθη. Let us call him by one apt name pedagogue ... True, the same logos is also didactic, but not now.'

The three domains ἦθος πρᾶξις πάθος, of which the last two vaguely recall ὁρμή and πρᾶξις in Eudorus and Seneca, coincide with a very surprising text, namely Aristotle about the dance in the first chapter of the *Poetics* (1447a28).[14] The three functions of the logos, who is at the same time a literary genre and the second person of the trinity, are all found in Posidonius; the didactic was found in Epictetus. In this work Clement doesn't need the didactic function of the logos—he needs him as a pedagogue only. This is why he says: 'the same logos is also didactic, but not now.' In the past, scholars have identified the διδασκαλικός with Posidonius' παραινετική (15),[15] but this is refuted already by the verb παραινεῖ, and by the description a little further on of the pedagogue (1.1.2.1-2.2):

> ἤδη δὲ καὶ εἰς τὴν τῶν δεόντων ἐνέργειαν παρακαλεῖ, τὰς ὑποθηκὰς τὰς ἀκηράτους παρεγγυῶν καὶ τῶν πεπλανημένων πρότερον τοῖς ὕστερον ἐπιδεικνὺς τὰς εἰκόνας. ἄμφω δὲ ὠφελιμώτατα, τὸ μὲν εἰς ὑπακοήν, τὸ παραινετικὸν εἶδος, τὸ δὲ ...
>
> 'Now he calls us to do our duties by handing down unassailable precepts and by showing mankind the examples of those who have erred in the past. Both are highly useful, the one, the paraenetic, leading to obedience ...'

This shows that Clement uses παραινετικός as an equivalent of ὑποθετικός. As I said, the distinction made between these two in Philo, Eudorus and Posidonius was a little problematic—Clement disposes of the problem by using one as a synonym for the other.

Similarly, he uses θεραπευτικός as an alternative for παραμυθητικός; this is more restricted than Philo's use of the term, because Philo had used it as a consequence of the medicine analogy, whereas for Clement healing is only one half of the pedagogue's task. As for παραμυ-

---

[14] Clement may have been inspired by Arius Didymus, whose epitome starts with strings of definitions of ἦθος and πάθος (Stob. 2.38.3-39.9; cf. Long. 9.15 and Russell's note).

[15] Discussed by Marrou 1960, 11-13.

θητικός, this has little or nothing to do with consolation, as the description shows, nor is it ἀποτροπή in general, as maybe in Eudorus: here it is encouraging by means of examples. Doubtless the alternative name παθολογικός, mentioned by Eudorus, encouraged Clement to use παραμυθητικός in this way.

And with this divine status of protreptic I end this overview of ancient theories. Let me summarise the main results. (1) Protreptic invariably comes first in systematic divisions. (2) Protreptic is invariably treated as ethic protreptic, even by Posidonius, whose own *Protreptikos* seems to have had a more general scope, namely to exhort to philosophy, like Aristotle's. (3) There are at least two different views of protreptic, one argumentative and praising virtue, the other criticising men for not caring about virtue. (4) There is relatively little overlap between the divisions that have come down to us and hardly ever identity; attempts to harmonise them have frequently hampered the progress of scholarship. This goes for Wendland's identification of Clement's four *logoi* with Posidonius' views as preserved by Seneca, and also for the attempt, made as late as the sixties of this century by Ernst Günther Schmidt (1962) and Carlini (1968), to identify Epictetus' trichotomy with Demetrius' εἴδη τοῦ λόγου. There is much work to be done, but the way it should be done is by patient examination of the texts, not by advancing speculative hypotheses.

BIBLIOGRAPHY

Billerbeck, M., *Epiktet, Vom Kynismus, herausgegeben und übersetzt mit einem Kommentar*. Leiden 1978.

Carlini, A., Osservazioni sui tre εἴδη τοῦ λόγου in Ps.-Demetrio, De eloc. 296sg., *RFIC* 96 (1968), 38-46.

Gaiser, K., *Protreptik und Paränese bei Platon*. Stuttgart 1959.

Gerhäusser, W., *Der Protreptikos des Poseidonios*. München 1912.

Hartlich, P., De exhortationum a Graecis Romanisque scriptarum historia et indole, *Leipziger Studien* 11 (1889), 209-336.

Höistad, R., *Cynic Hero and Cynic King. Studies in the Cynic Conception of Man*. Uppsala 1948.

Jordan, M.D., Ancient Philosophic Protreptic and the Problem of Persuasive Genres, *Rhetorica* 4 (1986), 309-33.

Marrou, H.-I., *Clément d'Alexandrie, Le Pédagogue*, vol. 1. Paris 1960.

Russell, D.A., *'Longinus', On the Sublime*. Oxford 1964.

Schmeller, Th., *Paulus und die 'Diatribe'. Eine vergleichende Stilinterpretation*. Münster 1987.

Schmidt, E.G., Die drei Arten des Philosophierens. Zur Geschichte einer antiken Stil- und Methodenscheidung, *Philologus* 106 (1962), 14-28.

Slings, S.R., *A Commentary on the Platonic Clitophon* (Dissertatie Vrije Universiteit). Amsterdam 1981.

de Strycker, E., [review of Gaiser 1959], *Gnomon* 34 (1962), 13-21.

Wendland, P., *Quaestiones Musonianae*. Berlin 1886.

The Poetics of Medicine[*]

Ineke Sluiter

One morning, a long time ago, Diogenes the Cynic woke up to an unusual noise outside the barrel in which he lived. When he popped out his head to find out what was going on, he saw people running to and fro, carrying arms, brandishing spears and bringing stones to reinforce the wall. The general buzz of activity told him that the Corinthians were obviously preparing for war. And all of a sudden, Diogenes felt very useless and left out of it all. To remedy this, he hoisted up his tunic and started with all his might to roll his barrel up and down Kraneion hill. When asked by one his friends what on earth he thought he was doing, he explained this remarkable display of psychological self-help *avant la lettre* as follows: 'I, too, am rolling my barrel; I do not want to give the impression that I am the only lazybody among so many hard workers!'.

The anecdote can be found in Lucian's *On How to Write History* (§ 3) and applies directly both to the subject and the occasion of this paper. Obviously, I owe it to my teacher and mentor Dirk Schenkeveld at least to try my hand at rolling my barrel, if at nothing more constructive, in the field of ancient literary criticism. And fortunately, I find myself in good company: for the author who will be in the centre of attention in the following pages, Galen, was not averse to barrel-rolling in this area (or almost any other) either, even though we do not usually associate such interests with a doctor.

As a matter of fact, by Galen's time, philology had become firmly established as a legitimate activity for the more ambitious exponents of the medical profession. In the third century BCE, the Ptolemies had founded the Museum and the Library as a part of their cultural policy.

---

[*] Professor Geoffrey Lloyd kindly read and commented on an earlier draft of this paper.

The great literary heritage from the Greek past was studied there by philologists who enjoyed the support, financially and otherwise, of the monarchs. In this way, the Ptolemies gave off a clear signal that they claimed to be the legitimate heirs to Greek culture and Greek *paideia*, traditionally embodied in literature. As a result of the active interest shown by the Ptolemies, the social and intellectual status of philology rocketed and became something of an intellectual trend. Contemporary doctors, too, suddenly developed a taste for the lexicographical and exegetical study of the Hippocratic corpus, sometimes slightly to the detriment of their surgical and anatomical interests. The change occurred between the generation of Herophilus and that of Bacchius.[1] From this time onward, Hippocratic exegesis was definitely on the medical agenda. In that sense Galen stood in a clearly defined tradition when he devoted more than a little interest to the most authoritative source of the medical profession, Hippocrates.[2]

A language-oriented approach to an authoritative text in any field was also stimulated by the nature of ancient education at large. The language disciplines, grammar, rhetoric and logic,[3] had always been the nucleus of the ancient school system, where they were applied to the study of the poets, Homer in particular. Homer's authority was approached through philology, so when people encountered an authoritative text in their later walk of life, linguistic analysis would impose itself as a natural approach to the study of such texts. This phenomenon may be labeled the 'philological paradigm' of Antiquity.

Moreover, Galen's interest in linguistic and literary matters also fit in very well with the general tendencies of his age, the second century CE, and especially with the interests of the 'movement', if that is the proper word, of the Second Sophistic.[4] Although Galen was no sophist

---

[1] Cf. Von Staden 1989, 427 ff.; 454 ff.

[2] Cf. for Galen's strategy in using Hippocrates' authority, Lloyd 1991.

[3] The ancient terms are not coextensive with the modern ones.

[4] Cf. Bowersock 1969, 59 ff.; Kollesch 1981.

himself, his education, status and taste for travel corresponded to what we know of the acknowledged representatives of the Second Sophistic. Even if his Commentaries on Hippocrates reveal a Galen extremely critical of the exaggerated attention paid by his predecessors and contemporaries to form and style instead of content, it is still significant that he feels obliged to enter into the discussion at all. Galen himself was proud of the fact that he had had a thorough training in grammar and rhetoric. He is very much opposed to a trend he claims to discern in his own day, viz. to skip this educational basis and to proceed directly to philosophy and medicine. As he points out, this procedure produces the kind of ignoramuses who will uncritically believe that they have bought an authentic work by Galen, when anyone without any schooling in medicine, but with basic philological training would be able to undeceive them at the very first glance (*De libris propriis* 19.8 f. Kühn). His general philological interests stand out quite clearly from the list of his works (*De libris propriis*, 19 K.), which features, among other items, a commentary on Aristotle's Περὶ ἑρμηνείας, works on the correctness of names, on homonyms, on the question whether philology is useful for ethics, and a number of lexicographical studies on Attic authors and the comedians.

The superman Hippocrates, the ultimate authority in medical matters, who emerges from Galen's work, is very much Galen's own construction, intended first and foremost to boost and bolster Galen's own reputation. A lot of exegetical and lexicographical work had been done already, as I just pointed out, but the sheer volume of Galen's work on Hippocrates tended to absorb all previous scholarship. The picture that emerges from Galen's work—and I will, of course, focus on the literary aspects in this paper—is the following: Hippocrates is a model of medical perfection *and* a remarkable author at the same time. In fact, Galen has to adapt the current grammatical and rhetorical ideals of his day to make Hippocrates fit, but he manages to do so without breaking the boundaries set by the philological paradigm: he never discards the norms imposed by grammar and rhetoric as irrelevant to a medical man. Galen rearranges the rhetorical virtues, stressing brevity and clarity while downgrading the importance of grammatical correctness. He connects this move with the concept of a separate genre, namely the ἐπιστημονικὴ διδασκαλία, the genre of scientific (scholarly) instruction. In this genre, the effectiveness of the message is always more important than its linguistic form.[5]

Now, Hippocrates was not the kind of author that would be studied by the 'real' literary critics in antiquity. There is, however, one remark in Demetrius *On Style* (§ 4) which quotes the beginning of Hippocrates' *Aphorisms* (without the name of the author) as an example of a so-called ξηρὰ σύνθεσις, an 'arid composition', the negative counterpart of the plain (ἰσχνός) style. Since Galen, too, has something to say (well actually, a lot) about this aphorism, let us compare their findings. Demetrius explains why exceedingly brief members are equally out of place in discourse as long ones: they produce the so-called 'arid' composition. He adds the following comment on his example ὁ βίος βραχύς, ἡ τέχνη μακρά, ὁ καιρὸς ὀξύς ('life is short, art long, opportunity fleeting', Hipp. *Aph*. 1.1; *Eloc*. 4):

> κατακεκομμένῃ γὰρ ἔοικεν ἡ σύνθεσις καὶ κεκερματισμένῃ, καὶ εὐκαταφρόνητος διὰ τὸ μικρὰ σύμπαντα ἔχειν.
>
> 'The composition here seems to be minced fine, and may fail to impress because everything about it is so minute' (tr. W. Rhys Roberts).

Although here the overdose of μικρά is judged negatively, elsewhere in the same treatise Demetrius allows scope for brevity as a virtue, for instance in § 7 where he acknowledges the relationship between brevity and the forceful style (δεινότης).[6] And he goes on to comment on brevity as follows (*Eloc*. 9):

---

[5] Galen's views on Hippocrates' linguistic and rhetorical merits are discussed at length in Sluiter 1994 (forthc.); for a more general overview see Pearcy 1993.

[6] *Eloc*. 7: τῶν δὲ μικρῶν κώλων κἂν δεινότητι χρῆσίς ἐστι· δεινότερον γὰρ τὸ ἐν ὀλίγῳ πολὺ ἐμφαινόμενον καὶ σφοδρότερον, διὸ καὶ οἱ Λάκωνες βραχυλόγοι ὑπὸ δεινότητος: 'Short members may also be employed in vigorous passages. There is greater vigour and intensity when much meaning is conveyed in a few words. Accordingly it is just because of their vehemence that the Lacedaemonians are chary of speech' (tr. W. Rhys Roberts).

> ἡ δὲ τοιαύτη βραχύτης κατὰ τὴν σύνθεσιν κόμμα ὀνομάζεται [cf. κατακεκομμένη, *ib.* § 4] ... ἔστι ... καὶ ἀποφθεγματικὸν ἡ βραχύτης καὶ γνωμολογικόν, καὶ σοφώτερον τὸ ἐν ὀλίγῳ πολλὴν διάνοιαν ἠθροῖσθαι, καθάπερ ἐν τοῖς σπέρμασιν δένδρων ὅλων δυνάμεις· εἰ δ' ἐκτείνοιτό τις τὴν γνώμην ἐν μακροῖς, διδασκαλία γίνεταί τις καὶ ῥητορεία ἀντὶ γνώμης.
>
> 'From the point of view of composition such brevity is termed a "phrase" ... brevity suits apophthegms and maxims; and it is a mark of superior skill to compress much thought in a little space, just as seeds potentially contain entire trees. Draw out the maxim at full length, and it becomes a lecture or a piece of rhetoric rather than a maxim' (tr. W. Rhys Roberts, adapted).

In fact, what Galen does in his commentary on Hippocrates' *Aphorisms* is just this, viz. to draw out the pithy sayings to full-length pieces of instruction. And he seems to react to those who draw a distinction between aphorisms and teaching in his very commentary on the first aphorism (17b.345-56 K.; esp. 351). In this part of his commentary—which stretches over eleven pages in Kühn's edition—he analyses the first aphorism as the proem of the work (as had become traditional in ancient exegesis of *Aphorisms*; 17b.346 K.); this proem is then interpreted as a programmatic statement. The text of *Aphorisms* 1.1, which Galen treats as a single unit, reads:

> ὁ βίος βραχύς, ἡ δὲ τέχνη μακρή, ὁ δὲ καιρὸς ὀξύς, ἡ δὲ πεῖρα σφαλερή, ἡ δὲ κρίσις χαλεπή. δεῖ δὲ οὐ μόνον ἑωυτὸν παρέχειν τὰ δέοντα ποιέοντα, ἀλλὰ καὶ τὸν νοσέοντα καὶ τοὺς παρέοντας καὶ τὰ ἔξωθεν.
>
> 'Life is short, art long, opportunity fleeting, experiment tricky, judgement difficult. One should not only prepare oneself to do what one should, but also the patient and those present and the external circumstances.'

Galen reads this aphorism as a coherent whole: life is short only in comparison with the enormousness of art, which in turn is apparent from the fact that 'opportunity is fleeting': this means that it is fiendishly difficult to know exactly when to act, because bodies are in a state of constant flux. There are two procedures regulating medical action: one is experience, πεῖρα, which is tricky, because the material on which it

after *ἡ δὲ τέχνη μακρά* serves only as an explanation (17b.348 K.), while the second part of the aphorism is a piece of advice to the prospective readers. According to Galen, what this first aphorism[7] tries to convey is the *τρόπος τῆς διδασκαλίας* and the *χρεία τῶν συγγραμμάτων*: the 'method of teaching' and the 'use of Hippocrates' writings' (Gal. *in Hipp. Aph.* 1.1, 17b.351 f. K.):

> Τό *τε γὰρ ἀφοριστικὸν εἶδος τῆς διδασκαλίας ὅπερ ἐστὶ τὸ διὰ βραχυτάτων ἅπαντα τὰ τοῦ πράγματος ἰδία περιορίζειν, χρησιμώτατον τῷ βουλομένῳ μακρὰν τέχνην διδάξαι ἐν χρόνῳ βραχεῖ· τό τε ὅλως διὰ τοῦτο συγγράφειν ὅτι ὁ βίος βραχύς ἐστιν ὡς πρὸς τὸ τῆς τέχνης μέγεθος εὐλογώτατον.*
>
> 'For the aphoristic type of instruction, i.e. defining as briefly as possible everything essential to the matter in hand, is the most useful type for someone wishing to teach a long art in a short time. And, generally, it stands to reason that one's motivation for writing treatises is the fact that life is short in comparison with art's magnitude.'

Galen expatiates on this latter point explaining that each individual can only hope to contribute a little bit to the perfection of medicine over a single lifetime. And at the end of his extensive discussion, he summarises his interpretation of the first aphorism as follows (17b.355 K.):

> Ἡ *μὲν τέχνη μακρὰ γίνεται ἑνὸς ἀνθρώπου παραμετρουμένη βίῳ. χρήσιμον δὲ τὸ καταλιπεῖν συγγράμματα καὶ μάλιστα τὰ σύντομά τε καὶ ἀφοριστικά. εἴς τε γὰρ αὐτὴν τὴν πρώτην μάθησιν καὶ εἰς τὴν ὧν ἔμαθέ τις [ὠφεληθῆναι] μνήμην καὶ εἰς τὴν ὧν ἐπελάθετό τις μετὰ ταῦτα ἀνάμνησιν ὁ τοιοῦτος τρόπος τῆς διδασκαλίας ἐπιτήδειος.*
>
> 'Art is long when measured against the life of an individual human being. And it is useful to leave behind writings and especially brief and aphoristic ones. [NB this phrase has nothing whatsoever in the aphorism of which it could be considered a paraphrase; however, it is essential to Galen's view of function and purpose of the aphorisms.] For such a style of teaching is suitable for the very first introduction

---

[7] It is Galen's belief that this first aphorism must necessarily fit in with what follows (17b.351 K.).

to a subject, and in order to remember what one has learned, and to bring back to mind afterwards what one has forgotten.'

In this way, the first aphorism becomes a *leçon par exemple*: it is a programmatic statement explaining that, and how, aphorisms fulfill their didactic task, and the explanation itself takes the form of an aphorism. There is no true difference between aphorisms and teaching, as in Demetrius' observation, nor does Galen share the negative view of the first aphorism advocated by Demetrius. On the contrary, he qualifies the production of treatises necessary to counter the negative effects of the shortness of life as (17b.352 K.):

ὅσα τις ἔγνω τοῖς μετέπειτα καταλιπεῖν ἐν συγγράμμασιν, ἀκριβῶς τε ἅμα καὶ ταχέως καὶ σαφῶς ἅπασαν τὴν τῶν διδασκομένων πραγμάτων φύσιν ἑρμηνεύοντα.

'leaving all one's knowledge behind for the next generations, expressing the nature of what needs to be taught with precision, brevity and clarity'.

There is nothing εὐκαταφρόνητος, nothing of Demetrius' *quantité négligeable*, about this kind of work.

As far as I know, the passage from Demetrius is the only example of 'official' literary criticism being extended to include Hippocrates. So in a sense, Galen was left a free hand to demarcate Hippocrates' position among the acknowledged literary classics and to establish the genre of the ἐπιστημονικὴ διδασκαλία; the exclusion of scholarly writing from the domain of literature, which had become tradition ever since Aristotle's verdict on Empedocles' 'poetry', did not bother him.[8]

The genres that Galen uses as a foil for Hippocrates are poetry, especially Homer,[9] and historiography. Both the poets and the historians of the classical period may also be quoted as linguistic parallels to

[8] Ar. *Po*. 1, 1447b17 f. Οὐδὲν δὲ κοινόν ἐστιν Ὁμήρῳ καὶ Ἐμπεδοκλεῖ πλὴν τὸ μέτρον.

[9] Galen's views on and use of the poets have been studied before by DeLacy 1966 and Moraux 1987.

Hippocrates, in matters of vocabulary, idiom or syntax.[10] But even in these linguistic matters, Galen sometimes differentiates quite subtly between poetic work and Hippocrates, for example when he insists that the theory of the *epitheta ornantia* should not be extended to Hippocratic texts:[11] in explaining Hippocrates, Galen says, it is not acceptable to deny an adjective its full force and to put it on a par with a phrase like *γάλα λευκόν* in Homer. Generally speaking, however, the poets' and historians' status of *παλαιοί* guarantees the legitimacy of using them as sources of linguistic comparison. But when it comes to their use as sources of knowledge, it is a different story altogether.

Not surprisingly, the age-old criterion of adherence to truth, or reality versus fiction, was especially important to Galen. In Hellenistic and Roman doctrine, literary forms could be distinguished in accordance

---

[10] Parallels from Herodotus: *σφακελίζεσθαι*, *in Hipp. Aph.* 50 (18a.156 K.); *μετεξετέρην*, *in Hipp. Art. comm.* 3 (18a.599 K.); from Homer: e.g. *in Hipp. Aph.* 43 (18a.147 K.), see further Moraux 1987, 26 ff.; from Pindar: e.g. *in Hipp. Prorrhet. I comm.* 3.118 (16.763 K.); from Thucydides: e.g. *in Hipp. Epid. VI* 12 (17b.167 f. K.); from Demosthenes and the orators: e.g. *in Hipp. de art.* 1.50 (18a.384 K.), cf. *in Hipp. Prognost.* 3.2 (18b.237 K.).

[11] In *De Comate sec. Hipp.* 3 (7.656 K.), Galen wonders what Hippocrates means by *καταφορὰ νωθρά*. He thinks it imperative to find an explanation: *οὐ γὰρ ἦν τῶν ματαίως τὰ ὀνόματα ἐπιτιθέντων οὗτος ὁ ἀνὴρ οὔτ' ἀνοήτως πρόσκειται τῇ καταφορᾷ τὸ νωθρά, οὔτέ φησιν ὥσπερ Ὅμηρος, ὕγρον ἔλαιον καὶ γάλα λευκὸν μηδενὸς ἕνεκα διορισμοῦ. καὶ γὰρ πᾶν γάλα λευκὸν καὶ ἔλαιον ὑγρόν· ἀλλ' ἑκάστη λέξις καὶ συλλαβὴ πᾶσα πρᾶγμά τι σημαίνει παρ' αὐτοῦ.* Cf. *ib.* 657 *ἐπιμέλειαν περὶ τὰς λέξεις*. Galen concludes that the *νωθρὰ καταφορά* is a subtype of the *ἄγρυπνος καταφορά*, the attack of *κῶμα* that comes on without sleep being one of the symptoms.

The second text which discusses this phenomenon is *In Hipp. Epid. VI* 6 (17b.339 f.): *τὸ δὲ ἐπὶ τοῦ σπληνὸς εἰρημένον "ἀριστερὸς σπλὴν μέγας", οἱ μὲν οὕτως προσκεῖσθαι νομίζουσιν ὡς τῷ γάλα τὸ λευκὸν ὁ ποιητὴς προσέθηκε καὶ τῷ σύες τὸ χαμαιευνάδες, οὐκ ὄντος οὔτε γαλακτός τινος ὃ μὴ λευκόν ἐστιν, οὔτε συῶν αἳ μὴ χαμαιευνάδες εἰσίν. τάχα δὲ κτλ.* (Galen then proposes an emendation: he submits that *ἀριστερός* forms part of the previous aphorism, 'there comes no blood from the left nostril', thus eliminating the combination *ἀριστερὸς σπλήν*.)

with their assumed degree of factual truth.[12] Roughly speaking, there was a threefold division: in declining order of truthfulness they were ἱστορία (*fama*, *verum*); πλάσμα (*fictum argumentum*, *verisimile*); and μῦθος (*fabula*, *falsum*). There was some variation in the application of this triad: Asclepiades of Myrlea, for instance, takes the three degrees of truthfulness as subspecies of ἱστορία, with ἀληθὴς ἱστορία coming out 'on top'.[13] Of course, it was precisely Hippocrates' superior command of the facts, his insight into reality, that was to make us forgive him his minor flaws in expression. The truth criterion separates Hippocrates' work from poetry. That is not to say that the poets can never be right in medical matters. But the nature of their work makes truth an entirely accidental feature. This is why Galen is so fiercely opposed to Chrysippus in *De placitis Hippocratis et Platonis*: Chrysippus used the authority of the poets as an argument, that is to say, he replaced scholarly argument with quotations from the poets, instead of using the poets merely as additional illustrative material. In Galen's eyes, this was unacceptable. In his ranking of types of argument there is only one scientific type, and three unscientific ones.[14] Among these latter types, the one based on authority takes second position, after the dialectical type; it is styled 'rhetorical', and just barely precedes the sophistic type, that degrades itself even to the point of using worthless etymologies. According to Galen, quotations from the poets are in order only when one's position has already been proven to be correct by other means, or when one is proposing a generally accepted statement.

Let me give two practical illustrations of this attitude to the relevance of poetry, both dealing with fantasy figures: Centaurs and the Cyclops. In the third book of *De usu partium*, Galen discusses the functionality of hands, a virtually unique feature of human beings that explains why we

---

[12] See Brink's commentary on Hor. *Ars* 338-42; Meijering 1987, 76 ff.; 84 ff.

[13] See Sextus Empiricus *M.* 1.252 f.

[14] DeLacy 1966; for Galen's epistemology, see Frede 1981.

walk on only two legs. We can do without the speed that four legs would have given us, and use our hands to execute clever things that we have thought out (3.169 K.). Then Galen stops and wonders whether a combination of four legs *plus* two hands, like the Centaurs have, would not have been even better, but rejects the idea as an impossible combination of two types of bodies. Even if human beings and horses could couple, it is unthinkable that a viable embryo could result from it. And then Galen chides Pindar for describing exactly this (Gal. *De usu partium* 3.1, 3.169 K.):

> Πίνδαρος δ' εἰ μὲν ὡς ποιητὴς προσίεται τὸ τῶν Κενταύρων μυθολόγημα, συγχωρητέον αὐτῷ· εἰ δ' ὡς σοφὸς ἀνὴρ καί τι περιττότερον τῶν πολλῶν ἐπίστασθαι προσποιούμενος ἐτόλμα γράφειν
>
> ... ὅς
> ἵπποισιν Μαγνητίδεσσιν ἐμίγνυτ' ἐν Παλίου
> σφυροῖς. ἐκ δ' ἐγένοντο στρατὸς
> θαυμαστός, ἀμφοτέροις
> ὅμοιοι τοκεῦσι, τὰ μα-
> τρόθεν μὲν κάτω, τὰ δ' ὕπερθε πατρός
>
> ἐπιτιμητέον αὐτῷ τῇ προσποιήσει τῆς σοφίας.
>
> 'If Pindar accepts the story of the Centaurs in his capacity of a poet, he should be forgiven for it. But if he dared to write the following as a knowledgeable person, claiming to know more than the masses, he should be taken to task for his pretension to knowledge: "... and he coupled with the Magnesian mares on the spurs of Pelion; and a weird breed was engendered, in the favor of either parent: the mare's likeness in the parts below, and the manlike father above [Pi. *P.* 2.46 ff., tr. Lattimore]"'.

And after some further discussion of the problem, Galen continues (*De usu partium* 3.1, 3.170 f. K.):

> ἀλλ', ὦ Πίνδαρε, σοὶ μὲν ᾄδειν τε καὶ μυθολογεῖν ἐπιτρέπομεν εἰδότες τὴν ποιητικὴν μοῦσαν οὐχ ἥκιστα τῶν ἄλλων τῶν οἰκείων κόσμων καὶ τοῦ θαύματος δεομένην· <u>ἐκπλῆξαι</u> γὰρ οἶμαι καὶ <u>κηλῆσαι</u> τοὺς ἀκροατὰς, οὐ <u>διδάξαι</u> βούλεσθαι, ἡμεῖς δ', οἷς <u>ἀληθείας</u>, οὐ <u>μυθολογίας</u> μέλει, σαφῶς ἴσμεν οὐσίαν ἀνθρώπου τε καὶ ἵππου παντάπασιν ἄμικτον ὑπάρχουσαν.

> 'But, Pindar, we will leave the singing and story-telling to you. For we know that the Muse of poetry needs her own apparel and wonder as much as any of the Muses. I think she wants to astonish and entrance her audience, not to instruct them. We, however, who are concerned with truth, not story-telling, know very well that the natures of human beings and horses do not allow crossing in any way.'

In the first passage quoted, the poet is opposed to the *σοφὸς ἀνήρ*, but his poetic license, alluded to by *συγχωρητέον*, is respected; in the second, the functions of *ἐκπλῆξαι* and *κηλῆσαι* are opposed to *διδάξαι*, as *μυθολογία* is to *ἀλήθεια*. It goes without saying that this terminology has a long-standing pedigree in literary criticism.[15]

So, as we saw, Centaurs were relegated to the world of poetical fiction, but the story of the Cyclops is used very differently in the next book of *De usu partium* (4.14, 3.313 K.). There, Galen has just described the position of the liver and the importance of the vena cava. A wound in these parts is always lethal. And to corroborate this point Galen adduces the story of Odysseus' vengeance on the Cyclops: if it had not been for the fact that Odysseus and his companions could never have escaped from the cave by themselves, Odysseus would surely have executed his original plan: to stab the Cyclops in the area of the liver and the vena cava, thus ensuring his instantaneous death. It was only because the entrance to the cave was blocked by an enormous boulder that Odysseus had to resort to burning out Polyphemus' eye: the Cyclops had to remain alive to remove the blockade.[16]

The mythological character of the narrative is completely discounted here, and the story is, for once, taken at face value. On the other hand, Galen does stick to his own principles. Homer is not put forth as proof of how vital this part of the human body is, but rather to the contrary: the vulnerability of the liver area explains the relevance of Odysseus' deliberations. Galen's views on the relevance of poetry to scientific work are

---

[15] Cf. Meijering 1987, 62 ff. (on poetic license); 6 ff. (*ψυχαγωγία*), cf. the table of opposites 10 f. (from Polybius).

[16] Galen quotes *Od.* 9.361 (*ὅθι φρένες ἧπαρ ἔχουσιν*).

fairly traditional; the passages just quoted may be compared with the discussion between Strabo and Eratosthenes as reflected in the first book of Strabo's *Geographica*.[17]

Obviously, claiming a position for the genre of the scholarly treatise distinct and autonomous from *poetry* was not the main challenge Galen had to face. The real problem was to differentiate the genre from the only serious competitor as a literary prose genre, historiography. The need for differentiation may have been reinforced by the name ἱστορία itself: for 'history', the results of previous research, had always been one of the epistemological pillars of medicine. And as a literary genre, it was historiography that ever since Aristotle derived its uniqueness as a genre precisely from its particular claim to truthfulness and correspondence to reality.[18] In the period between Thucydides and the second century CE, the notion of the usefulness of history had changed: Thucydides considered history useful because of the rational insight it provided into the mechanisms of past events, but he did not claim that history had a predictive value.[19] He realised that the absence of fiction may make the genre less entertaining, but accepted this consequence. On the other hand, Polybius did stress the prognostic possibilities provided by history[20] (and, incidentally, the connection of prognosis with history brought the genre into even closer proximity to medicine). Thus, usefulness for theoretical purposes gave way to usefulness in given situations. And

---

[17] Cf. Schenkeveld 1976.

[18] Arist. *Po*. 9, 1451a36 ff.; see Brink 1960, 17 for the incidental role of history in this section of Arist. *Po*.

[19] See Th. 1.22; the absence of τὸ μυθῶδες is considered ἀτερπέστερον there. Thucydides aims at τὸ σαφές *and* τέρψις.—While Thucydides at least acknowledges that a lack of τὸ μυθῶδες may diminish the entertainment aspects of historiography, he still thinks this effect entirely secondary. Cf. for the interpretation of the use of history, de Romilly 1954.

[20] See Verdin 1973, 548 n. 28 for references. E.g. 6.57.4 προειπεῖν ὑπὲρ τοῦ μέλλοντος; 3.31.13. Note that Polybius is not the first to express this thought. It had been voiced before by orators, see Walbank 1967, 392.

where the entertainment aspect of historiography is concerned, Polybius states that its absence is what distinguishes historiography from tragedy.[21] In the second century CE, however, historiography underwent a decisive change, at least if we may believe Lucian.

Lucian—a slightly younger contemporary of Galen's—is the author of the only ancient monograph dedicated exclusively to the theory of historiography, *On How to Write History*—as one will see, it was no coincidence that my opening anecdote was derived from this treatise. In it he complains about the incompetent historians that were mushrooming in Rome at the time. Instead of devoting themselves to writing useful histories—to Lucian, *τὸ χρήσιμον* is the only legitimate purpose of writing history at all, while *τέρψις* is secondary at best[22]—they utterly confuse the genre of historiography with encomiastic literature and poetry. Lucian tries to redress this uncalled-for striving after amusement by stressing the traditional relationship between historiography and usefulness and truthfulness.[23] As far as I know, Galen nowhere refers to contemporary developments in historiography, nor does he need to. For him, the only relevant material for comparison with Hippocrates lies in the classical historians, Herodotus, Thucydides and Xenophon. But his approach to historiography is necessarily the very opposite of Lucian's: in order to make the criterion of *ἀλήθεια* more exclusively relevant for the genre of the scholarly treatise, Galen had to downgrade its relevance for the genre of historiography.

---

[21] Plb. 2.56.11-2: *τὸ γὰρ τέλος ἱστορίας καὶ τραγῳδίας οὐ ταὐτόν, ἀλλὰ τοὐναντίον. ἐκεῖ μὲν γὰρ δεῖ διὰ τῶν πιθανωτάτων λόγων ἐκπλῆξαι καὶ ψυχαγωγῆσαι κατὰ τὸ παρὸν τοὺς ἀκούοντας, ἐνθάδε δὲ διὰ τῶν ἀληθινῶν ἔργων καὶ λόγων εἰς τὸν πάντα χρόνον διδάξαι καὶ πεῖσαι τοὺς φιλομαθοῦντας· ἐπειδήπερ ἐν ἐκείνοις μὲν ἡγεῖται τὸ πιθανόν, κἂν ᾖ ψεῦδος, διὰ τὴν ἀπάτην τῶν θεωμένων, ἐν δὲ τούτοις τἀληθὲς διὰ τὴν ὠφέλειαν τῶν φιλομαθούντων*. Meijering 1987, 10; 46.

[22] Lucian. *Hist. Conscr*. 9; 13; 42. Cf. Schmitt 1984; Korus 1986, 35. Lucian also stresses the prognostic value of history, cf. Verdin 1973, 547.

[23] Cf. Kessler 1982, 50 ff.

This explains why he stresses on various occasions that historians (especially Herodotus) are read for pleasure only, but that the students of medicine should display a different attitude towards their reading (*In Hipp. Epid. VI Comm.* 3, 17b.33 K.):

> ... ἐάν τέ τις μὴ καθάπερ Ἡροδότου καὶ Κτησίου μόνον ὡς ἱστορίαν ἀναγινώσκῃ τὰ βιβλία τῶν παλαιῶν ἰατρῶν, ἀλλ' ἕνεκα τοῦ πλεῖόν τι ἔχειν εἰς τὰ τῆς τέχνης ἔργα.
>
> '... at least if one does not read the books by the ancient doctors just like those by Herodotus and Ktesias, merely as history, but in order to become more proficient in the exercise of one's art.'[24]

Herodotus' companion in this text is significant: Ctesias, a contemporary of Thucydides, was 'popular precisely for the story-telling element' in his work (τὸ μυθῶδες). His work 'is full of fanciful details, pathetic episodes elaborately narrated, elements of biography and romance side by side with political and military narrative' (Connor 1985, 459).

In the case of Thucydides there is an extra complication, for this historian actually ventured into the field of medicine in his description of the plague. Here, Galen has to resort to another tactic to show Hippocrates' superiority. He adduces the criterion of the audience, something he also did to defend the need for writing his own commentaries: Hippocrates wrote for specialists, Galen explained his work for students.[25] In the case of the plague, the argument runs that Thucydides wrote as a layman for laymen, while Hippocrates wrote as a specialist for his colleagues. This explains why Thucydides' account is flawed in its selection of details: since Thucydides did not have a clue as to which details were relevant and which were not, he just presented everything

---

[24] Cf. *De anatom. adm.* 3.9 (2.393 K.), where Galen claims that the histories of Herodotus are read ἕνεκα τέρψεως only.

[25] Cf. Sluiter 1994 (forthc.).

pell-mell. Hippocrates, on the other hand, eliminates everything that is not strictly relevant to the medical side of the story.[26]

Seriousness and usefulness, reliability of the facts and an intelligent account of the underlying causes: it would seem that Hippocrates' literary virtues were all on the side of *docere* and *τὸ χρήσιμον*, with nothing to balance them on the side of *delectare* and *τέρψις*.[27] However, Galen manages to make Hippocrates score even on this latter count. In fact, the story from Hippocrates' *Epidemics* that I am referring to so appealed to his fancy that he quotes from it on four different occasions.[28] Here, I will discuss the most extensive version (*De semine* 1.4, 4.524 K.). The issue is the membrane that is said to encompass the embryo right from the moment of conception. Its presence could be demonstrated by dissecting animals. However, says Galen,

> *Ἄμεινον δὲ Ἱπποκράτους ἀκοῦσαι περὶ τῶν αὐτῶν λέγοντος ἐν τῷ περὶ φύσεως παιδίου γράμματι· παιδεύσει τε γὰρ ἡμᾶς τῷ τῆς θεωρίας ἀκριβεῖ, καὶ τέρψει, κεράσας οἵᾳ δὴ λέξει τὴν διήγησιν, ὥστ' ἐπανιέναι τε βραχὺ τὸ σφοδρὸν τοῦ λόγου, καὶ διαναπαύεσθαι σὺν ὠφελείᾳ τερπόμενον, ἵν' ἑξῆς νεανικώτεροι γενόμενοι συντείνωμεν ἡμᾶς αὐτοὺς ἀκμαιότερον ἐπὶ τὸ κατάλοιπον τοῦ λόγου. καὶ τοίνυν ἤδη ἀκούσωμεν τοῦ Ἱπποκράτους.*

---

[26] Gal. *De diff. resp.* (7.854 K.): *Θουκυδίδης μὲν γὰρ τὰ συμβάντα τοῖς νοσοῦσιν ὡς ἰδιώτης ἰδιώταις ἔγραψεν, Ἱπποκράτης δὲ τεχνίτης τεχνίταις*. Thucydides himself also envisages a select audience, cf. Th. 1.22.4 and Montanari 1984, 116 (comparing Lucian, Polybius and Strabo).

[27] Combining instruction and entertainment becomes a characteristic feature of great literature at least from the second century BCE onwards (Neoptolemus of Parium *apud* Phld. *Po.* V, col. xiii 8-15 Jensen); Hor. *Ars* 343; Strabo 1.2.9, cf. Meijering 1987, 6.

[28] Complete: *Sem.* 1.4 (4.524 ff. K.); incomplete: *In foet. form.* 1 (4.653 ff. K.); *Nat. fac.* 2.3 (2.86 K.); *Adv. Lycum* 7.3 (18a.236 K.). The original story is in Hipp. *Nat. puer.* 13.1-4 (7.488 ff. Littré). A good paraphrase plus discussion in Weisser 1983, 194 f.; cf. further Lonie 1977 and 1981.

'It is better to listen to Hippocrates when he discusses these same issues in his '*On the Nature of the Child*'.[29] For he will instruct us by the precision of his theory, and amuse us by mixing his narrative with a certain quality of speech.[30] This entails a brief relaxation of the power of his style, and resting awhile, and entertainment accompanied by profit, in order that we may subsequently be rejuvenated and exert ourselves even more energetically in absorbing the rest of his argument. Well now then, let us listen to Hippocrates'.

The relevant opposition is the one between *παιδεύειν* and *τέρπειν*, to educate and to entertain. The value of the instruction is guaranteed by Hippocrates' precision (*τὸ ἀκριβές*), and his ability to entertain by his style (λέξις). The relaxation of his usual forcefulness does not, however, lead to mere amusement, but to a combination of entertainment and instruction: *σὺν ὠφελείᾳ τερπόμενον*, which influences the attitude of his audience in a positive and stimulating way. Horace would approve!

Although strictly speaking the story itself is irrelevant here, it would be unfair to deprive you of it, if only because that would also mean denying you the opportunity to judge Hippocrates' λέξις for yourselves. So here it is, in Galen's version (*De semine* 1.4, 4.525 f. K.): Hippocrates reports how he came to see a six-day old embryo, a *γονή* 'seed'![31]

Ὡς δὲ εἶδον τὴν γονὴν ἑκταίην ἐοῦσαν, ἐγὼ διηγήσομαι. γυναικὸς οἰκέτις μουσουργὸς πολύτιμος ἦν, παρὰ ἄνδρας φοιτέουσα, ἣν οὐκ ἔδει λαβεῖν ἐν γαστρί, ὅκως μὴ ἀτιμοτέρη ἔη.

---

29 For the construction *ἀκούω τινος λέγοντος*, cf. Schenkeveld 1992.

30 Or: 'by the kind of speech with which he mixes his narrative'. Cf. Strohmaier 1981, 192 f., who mentions Benedict Einarson's emendation *ἡδείᾳ* for *οἵᾳ δή*, which seems to be confirmed by the Arabic version: 'because he mixed it with a talk which contains a lovely story'. However, as Strohmaier rightly stresses, this translation is by Hunayn, who had a solid knowledge of Greek, knew his Homer, and had enjoyed thorough philological training at Constantinople. Therefore, the possibility cannot be excluded that Einarson and Hunayn arrived at the same conjectural emendation independently.

31 Cf. Weisser 1983, 167 f.: in the Arabic tradition, too, the embryo could be called 'a seed' during the first couple of days after the conception.

ἠκηκόει δὲ ἡ μουσουργὸς, οἷα γυναῖκες πρὸς ἀλλήλας λέγουσιν, ὅτι, ἐπὴν γυνὴ μέλλῃ λήψεσθαι ἐν γαστρί, οὐκ ἐξέρχεται ἡ γονή, ἀλλ' ἔνδον μένει. ταῦτα ἀκούσασα συνῆκε, καὶ τοῦτο ἐφύλασσεν ἀεί. καί κως ὡς ᾔσθετο οὐκ ἐξιοῦσαν τὴν γονήν, ἔφρασε τῇ δεσποίνῃ. καὶ ὁ λόγος ἦλθεν ὡς ἐμέ. κἀγὼ ἀκούσας ἐκελευσάμην αὐτὴν πρὸς τὴν γῆν πηδῆσαι. καὶ ἑπτάκις ἐπειδὴ ἐπεπήδητο, ἡ γονὴ κατερρύη ἐπὶ τὴν γῆν, καὶ ψόφος ἐγένετο, κἀκείνη ἰδοῦσα ἐθεᾶτο αὐτὴν καὶ ἐθαύμαζεν. ὁκοῖον δ' ἦν, ἐγὼ ἐρέω· οἷον εἴ τις ᾠοῦ ὠμοῦ τὸ ἔξω λεπύριον περιέλοι, ἐν δὲ τῷ ἔνδον ὑμένι τὸ ἔνδον ὑγρὸν διεφαίνετο. ταυτὶ μὲν Ἱπποκράτης μαρτυρεῖ περὶ τοῦ μένειν ἔνδον τὴν γονὴν καὶ ἔχειν ὑμένα.

'How I came to see a six-day-old seed, I will recount. A lady acquaintance had a valuable slave, a singing girl, who served the gentlemen. On no account should she become pregnant, lest it diminish her value. The singing girl had listened to the kind of talk women have among each other, namely that when a woman is about to conceive, the seed does not leave again, but remains inside. She had understood this well and was always checking whether this happened. When she somehow noticed that the seed did not leave again, she informed her mistress. And word was given to me. When I had heard what was the matter, I ordered her to jump to the ground. And when she had jumped seven times, the seed flowed down to the earth, and there was a sound. She saw it and looked at it intently and with wonder. I will say what it was like: it was as if someone had peeled off the outer shell of a raw egg and the moisture inside was shining through the inner membrane. This is Hippocrates' testimony on the fact that the seed remains inside and that it has a membrane.'[32]

---

[32] The story is reported only this far because it is the point about the membrane that Galen is interested in here. Note how an egg-like object is being observed, simply because that is what the 'seed' was expected to look like. Note the number seven. The story has been trivialised in that in Hippocrates' version the girl is made to jump *πρὸς πυγήν*. She hits her buttocks with her heels while jumping. This is related to some kind of Laconic dance, which fits in with the girl's profession, but it also accounts for the abortive effect in a better way than does the reading *γῆν*. Is *γῆν* an intrusion from p. 526?; cf. Weisser 1983, 194 f.

I suppose a male doctor in the second century may well have been charmed by this story.

Now, where stylistic theory was concerned, Galen had demonstrated that Hippocrates' style coincided with the ideal style, *and*—not by coincidence—with that of Galen himself.[33] Galen is not in the habit of calling attention to the entertaining aspects of Hippocrates, and neither does he stress his own frivolous side. Nevertheless, he can parallel Hippocrates on this point too: In his *Ad Pisonem de theriaca* 8 he recounts the story of the death of Cleopatra, who killed herself by means of a poisonous snake, after having tried out the effectiveness of the poison on her two faithful lady-servants. It worked. Whatever one may think of this, I will restrict myself to noting Galen's comment on his own performance (*Ad Pisonem de theriaca* 8, 14.237 K.):

> ᾿Αλλὰ τοῦτο μὲν οὐκ ἀτερπῶς ἱστορείσθω διὰ τὴν σὴν ἐν πᾶσι τοῖς λόγοις φιλοτιμίαν, καὶ ἵνα διὰ τούτου τὴν ὀξύτητα πρὸς τὸ ἀποκτεῖναι τούτων τῶν θηρίων ὦμεν εἰδότες.
>
> 'But let this not unamusing account be reported because of your eager interest in all manner of stories, and in order that it may make us knowledgeable about how quickly these creatures can kill.'

Here, too, the serious part of the work is not forgotten. The story is told at least as much to serve a didactic purpose as to please Galen's addressee. Sheer amusement plays no part in an ἐπιστημονικὴ διδασκαλία.[34]

It is time to sum up. In this paper I have drawn attention to one aspect of what may be called 'the philological paradigm' in Galen, namely his use of poetical theory in delineating Hippocrates' position as an author and in

---

[33] Cf. Sluiter 1994 (forthc.).

[34] On the other hand, Galen does at times get carried away by his own sense of humour, although a modern (and possibly an ancient) audience may fail to be equally impressed by it. The long digression about the problems Centaurs may encounter in living the life of an ordinary human being (*De usu partium* 3.1, 3.171 ff. K.) is a case in point. I can find no didactic or instructive point in the digression whatsoever.

and in conquering a place for the ἐπιστημονικὴ διδασκαλία as a literary genre. The literary critics of the first centuries BCE and CE had paid little, if any, attention to Hippocrates. This left Galen a more or less free hand to create his own self-constructed super author and super authority, conveniently labeled 'Hippocrates'.

We have seen how Galen applied the criterion of truth or fiction to distinguish scholarly work from poetry. For Galen to think it at all necessary to define the relationship between medicine and poetry is, in itself, revealing. Historiography, medicine's main competitor as a serious prose genre, was traditionally opposed to poetry by this very truth criterion. In order to create a clear distinction between historiography and scholarly writing, the relevance of the truth criterion to the former had to be watered down, while its entertainment value and the lack of erudition in its intended audience were stressed. This went against the grain of contemporary theory about historiography, that tended to keep it strictly separated from encomiastic and poetical works by applying this very truth criterion. However, Galen may have felt justified in taking this attitude by contemporary historical practice.

On the other hand, Galen did not go so far as to deny outright that Hippocrates, too, could be entertaining. On the contrary, there is at least one occasion on which he explicitly ascribes this characteristic to Hippocrates. And it is particularly relevant to our concept of the philological paradigm that in the story concerned he is especially charmed by Hippocrates' *style*.

As a result, Galen has earned himself a place in a symposium on Ancient Literary Criticism: this is what comes from rolling your barrel.

BIBLIOGRAPHY

Bowersock, G.W., *Greek Sophists in the Roman Empire*. Oxford 1969.

Brink, Ch.O., Tragic History, *Proceedings of the Cambridge Philological Society* 6 (1960), 14-9.

Connor, W.R., Historical Writing in the fourth century BC and in the Hellenistic Period, in: P.E. Easterling and B.M.W. Knox (eds.), *Cambridge History of Classical Literature I.* Cambridge - New York 1985, 458-71.

DeLacy, Ph., Galen and the Greek Poets, *GRBS* 7 (1966), 259-66.

Frede, M., On Galen's Epistemology, in: Nutton 1981, 65-86.

Kessler, E., Das rhetorische Modell der Historiographie, in: R. Kosselleck, H. Lutz and J. Rüsen (eds.), *Formen der Geschichtsschreibung*. München 1982, 37-85.

Kollesch, J., Galen und die zweite Sophistik, in: Nutton 1981, 1-11.

Korus, K., Funktionen der literarischen Gattungen bei Lukian, *Eos* 74 (1986), 29-38.

Lloyd, G.E.R., Galen on Hellenistics and Hippocrates: Contemporary Battles and Past Authorities, in: G.E.R. Lloyd, *Methods and Problems in Greek Science. Selected Papers*. Cambridge 1991, 398-416.

Lonie, I.M., De natura pueri, ch. 13, in: *Corpus Hippocraticum. Actes du Colloque hippocratique de Mons 1975*. Mons 1977, 123-35.

———, *The Hippocratic Treatises 'On Generation', 'On the Nature of the Child', 'Diseases IV'. A Commentary* (= Ars Medica 2. Abt. Bd. 7). Berlin/New York 1981.

Meijering, R., *Literary and Rhetorical Theories in Greek Scholia*. Groningen 1987.

Montanari, Fr., Ekphrasis e verità storica nella critica di Luciano, *Ricerche di filologia classica II: Filologia e critica letteraria della grecità*. Pisa 1984, 111-23.

Moraux, P., Homère chez Galien, in: J. Servais et alii. (eds.), *Stemmata. Mélanges de philologie, d'histoire et d'archéologie grecques offerts à Jules Labarbe*. Liège-Louvain-la-Neuve 1987, 25-37.

Nutton, V. (ed.), *Galen: Problems and Prospects. A Collection of Papers submitted at the 1979 Cambridge Conference*. London 1981.

Pearcy, L.T., Medicine and Rhetoric in the Period of the Second Sophistic, in: W. Haase (ed.), *ANRW* II 37.1, Berlin-New York 1993, 445-56.

Romilly, J. de, L'utilité de l'histoire selon Thucydide, in: *Entretiens sur l'antiquité classique* 4 (1954), 39-81.

Schenkeveld, D.M., Strabo on Homer, *Mnemosyne* 29 (1976), 52-64.

Schenkeveld, D.M., Prose Usages of AKOYEIN 'To Read', *CQ* 42 (1992), 129-41.

Schmitt, W.O., Bemerkungen zu Lukians Schrift 'Wie man Geschichte schreiben muss', *Klio* 66 (1984), 443-55.

Sluiter, I., The Embarrassment of Imperfection. Galen's Assessment of Hippocrates' Linguistic Merits, in: P.H. van der Eijk, H.F.J. Horstmanshoff, P.H. Schrijvers (eds.), *Ancient Medicine in its Socio-Cultural Context, Papers read at the Congress held at Leiden University, 13-15 April 1992*. Amsterdam/Atlanta 1994 (forthcoming).

Staden, H. von, *Herophilus. The Art of Medicine in Early Alexandria*. Cambridge - New York etc. 1989.

Strohmaier, G., Galen in Arabic: Prospects and Projects, in: Nutton 1981, 187-96.

Verdin, H., Lucianus over het nut van de geschiedschrijving: in: *Zetesis, album amicorum aangeboden aan E. De Strijcker*. Antwerpen 1973, 541-8.

Walbank, F.W., *A Historical Commentary on Polybius (vol II, comm. on books vii-xviii)*. Oxford 1967.

Weisser, U., *Zeugung, Vererbung und Pränatale Entwicklung in der Medizin des arabisch-islamischen Mittelalters*. Erlangen 1983.

Allegory, Aenigma, and Anti-Mimesis: A Struggle Against Aristotelian Rhetorical Literary Theory

Peter T. Struck

1. Introduction

I begin with two well-known statements for the study of literary theory in antiquity. The D-scholion on *Iliad* 5.385 attributes to Aristarchus the following opinion (ed. Lascaris, Rome 1517, fol.i iv v.24-6):

> *'Αρίσταρχος ἀξιοῖ τὰ φραζόμενα ὑπὸ τοῦ ποιητοῦ μυθικώτερον ἐκδέχεσθαι, κατὰ τὴν ποιητικὴν ἐξουσίαν, μηδὲν ἔξω τῶν φραζομένων ὑπὸ τοῦ ποιητοῦ περιεργαζομένους.*
>
> 'Aristarchus thought that readers ought to take things told by the poet as more like legends, according to poetic license, and not bother themselves about what is outside the things told by the poet.'

In contrast Porphyry begins his essay *On the Cave of the Nymphs* this way (*Antr*. 4):

> *Ὅτι ποτὲ αἰνίττεται 'Ομήρῳ τὸ ἐν 'Ιθάκῃ ἄντρον*
>
> 'What on earth does the cave in Ithaca mean for Homer...'

And a page later he continues (*Antr*. 4):

> *τοιούτων ἀσαφειῶν πλήρους ὄντος τοῦ διηγήματος πλάσμα μὲν ὡς ἔτυχεν εἰς ψυχαγωγίαν πεποιημένον μὴ εἶναι*
>
> 'Given that the description is full of obscurities, it is not, in fact, a casual fiction created for our amusement.'

The two attitudes here embodied are emblematic of different (though rarely separate) traditions of literary theory in antiquity, what I am here calling the allegorical and the Aristotelian rhetorical. I claim that we can usefully distinguish these two stances toward the text as the ancients themselves did, by their different attitudes toward the problems and possibilities of literary *mimesis*. As an indication of these different stances, I will concentrate more on the questions that these authors ask of the texts they examine than on the answers they give.

I follow a series of modern critics in situating Aristarchus within a generally peripatetic tradition. His technical terminology, his presuppositions, and the kind of criticism he engages in all reinforce this view. What I mean by rhetorical is generally the stance toward the work of literature that the best tools for understanding whatever meanings it might contain are those developed for analyzing and reproducing good speeches, and secondly that the meanings in the poem will entirely surrender themselves by the use of these tools.

As the secondary literature on the allegorists is not widely established, a few preliminaries might be helpful. Allegory, until Martianus Capella, is a system of reading, not writing. Earlier poets had probably taken into account the theory behind allegorical criticism, notably Virgil and Ovid, but this is perhaps best understood as one manifestation of a common phenomenon, the diffuse and unsystematised movement of ideas from literary theory to literary practice. Allegory, understood as a coherent genre of writing, where personifications of abstract qualities are important characters in the action, is a later development. Aside from some older articles by Tate,[1] thorough but unique treatments by F. Buffière (1956) and J. Pépin (1958), and a few recent monographs, the allegorical tradition of reading has been understudied. And the most widely current opinion is very out of date indeed; we have to go all the way back to Cicero to find it. In the *de Natura Deorum* Cicero understands allegory as the systematic practice of bad reading (1.41). It reads into a text what is not there, which in anybody's book, including the allegorists', is the mark of bad interpretation.

I will suggest in this paper, first, that the allegorical critics, for whom I admit to taking Porphyry as a metonymy, have a more or less cohesive theoretical framework for their stance toward the text, based on

[1] Tate, J., On the History of Allegorism, *CQ* 28 (1934), 105-14; id., Plato and Allegorical Interpretation [1], *CQ* 23 (1929), 142-54; [2], *CQ* 24 (1930), 1-10; id., The Beginnings of Greek Allegory, *CR* 41 (1927), 214-5.

a particular understanding of literary *mimesis*. I will try to clarify it by contrasting it with the notion of *mimesis* that follows in the wake of Aristotle. Secondly, I suggest that understanding the allegorists' position will help to illuminate some of the assumptions behind the more familiar Aristotelian tradition. Re-examining the allegorists can give us a place to stand, outside of the Aristotelian mainstream, from which we may be able to gain a critical distance from that tradition, and better understand it, as well as the allegorists. I will begin by looking from Aristotle toward Aristarchus.

2. The wake of Aristotle

Pre-Aristotelian theories of language included Gorgias'. If we are to judge from the prominent place Plato gives him among the sophists, his theory of the magical power of words was influential. In the *Encomium of Helen*, he calls language 'a great master, who with the tiniest and least visible body achieves the most divine works' (*λόγος δυνάστης μέγας ἐστίν, ὃς σμικροτάτῳ σώματι καὶ ἀφανεστάτῳ θειότατα ἔργα ἀποτελεῖ*, *Hel.* 8). It is a drug which can drive the humors and end either illness or life. It has the power to 'drug' (*φαρμακεύσω*, *Hel.* 10b (=14)) and 'bewitch' (*μετέστησεν γοητείᾳ*, *Hel.* 10).

As Jacqueline de Romilly (1975, 69-88) has shown, Aristotle in the *Rhetoric* can be seen as in great measure resisting this view of words, which he was the first to recognise as being perhaps too seductive to the professional word smith, whose faith in his own power would be confirmed by a mystified understanding of the way language works. He replaces it with what has since become our common sense: that words mirror the world, in a more or less adequate way. They are no longer tiny bodies. Their substance, to which magical power was attributed by Gorgias, is dissolved, and they become images. But Aristotle will not follow Plato's devaluation of representations in general. Words maintain a power, but a wholly intellectualised one. Their affective power must be understood through their arrangement into logically convincing *μιμήματα*, under the controlling hand of a speaker following rules that make up the *techne* of rhetoric: grammar and lexis. The words are then understood by a reader who also knows the *techne*, and uses it to decode the words back into the πράγματα they point to. The value that guides the mimetic process is clarity.

If Gorgias was trying to give the orator the power attributed to poetic speech, Aristotle implicitly suggests that the poet should strive to be more like the orator. The issue of the meaning (*dianoia*) of a work of literature for Aristotle becomes, provocatively, a rather bland one of his six basic elements of poetry, the analysis of plot structure being by far more interesting for him. In the *Poetics* Aristotle refers the *dianoia* entirely to his treatise on rhetoric (1456a35). We can see in this an attempt to fix the focus of literary criticism away from questions about *dianoia* (let alone *hyponoia*, a term well-established in Aristotle's time) and towards identifying and categorising the various species of the literary genus. Issues that come under the heading of meaning do not belong to poetics but to the rhetorical art.

As was the case for rhetoric, in the *Poetics* the greatest value for language (*lexis*) is clarity, here with the proviso that the language is not base (1458a18, cf. *Rh.* 1404b). But this caution against being base is quickly qualified. The poet should also be careful not to be too lofty. If he or she overuses rare words or metaphors, or other things that tend to produce dignity in speech, the poem will be incomprehensible. It will become an *aenigma*, Aristotle says, which he puts on the level of nonsense or a foreign language, βαρβαρισμός (1458a24). At the level of plot, too, the value of clarity, here organised around a concept which Aristotle organises around the word Homer uses for epiphanies (ἐνάργεια), is the guiding value for the poet (1455a24). So clarity is a central value governing the literary work, with a tolerance for occasional unclarities in order to produce dignity.

Clarity in language for Aristotle is definitionally the use of common words in their common meanings (1458a19, 33). That the κύριον, the stabilising power of common usage, can anchor a one-to-one correspondence between word and thing is never in question for Aristotle. There are of course some complicating factors, most prominently in homonyms and metaphorical language. But with homonyms, Aristotle assures us in the *Categories* (1a1-6), the same word has simply been agreed upon for two different essences. And if one is asked to give a definition of one or the other of the essences, one simply understands the essence that is asked for. As for metaphor, Aristotle's definition of it in the *Poetics* (1457b)—as displacement of the proper sense for another sense that the context creates—reinforces the notion that there is a proper sense for a particular word in the first place. A word naturally, by the κύριον (usage and nature begin to blur here), means one particular thing. A metaphor displaces it for another thing, which, to the extent that it is a successful metaphor, is made clear by the context surrounding it.

If Aristotle reacts against Gorgias on the rhetorical side of his notion of *mimesis*, he clearly reacts against Plato on the philosophical side. Despite Plato's thorough critique of the Gorgianic view of language in the *Gorgias*, language still has the power to act as a *pharmakon* for Plato (Asmis 1992). If poetic language was a drug for Gorgias, Plato wants to ensure that it is a prescription drug, carefully regulated and controlled by the state, because of its power to produce delusions by shaping a weak soul. The Pre-Aristotelians, Gorgias and Plato, had seen the word as a phonetic substance, which produces its effect by entering the ear and then shaping the soul of the listener (Asmis 1992, 341-8). In his notorious banishment of the poets in book 10 of the *Republic*, Plato articulates a philosophical position that captures the anxiety of *mimesis* in language apparent among less sophisticated thinkers who view language as a magic spell, The poets' work is third from the truth because it makes a phantom image of the phenomenal world, itself already an image of what is real truth, the Forms. *Mimesis* through language puts truth in the balance. We add to this Plato's understanding in the *Cratylus* that the name-giver engages in an epistemologically loaded task; the notion of truth is at stake here not just with the larger constructions of language but down to the individual word. We should be careful to note that in the *Cratylus* he treats the issue of the truth (ἡ ἀλήθεια) of names separately from what is at stake in the dialogue, the correctness (ἡ ὀρθότης) of names. The latter issue is the question of whether the sound of a word can match the essence of what it represents; and in the end, Plato is dubious about it. But the issue of truth is raised (twice) by the argument that true statements must be made up of true elements. He leaves uncontroverted in the dialogue the claim that truth, if it is to exist, must begin at the level of the individual word (385c, 430d).

We get a sense of what this means for Plato's claim that the individual units of language are tools for cutting up the world and teaching (388a-c). The individual word becomes a tool, an *organon*, that must be shaped by the rarest of artisans, the lawgiver, under the guidance of the all-important dialectician, whose tool it is (390d). If a person does not know the world well, presumably, he or she will make faulty tools, and introduce words for things that do not exist, leave unnamed things that do exist, or name things falsely by grouping too many or too few things under a particular word. A single word, then, does work, it makes a claim about the way things are by cutting at one place rather than another. We might contextualise this understanding of language by comparing it with a statement Plato makes in the *Phaedrus* in regard to what the dialectician does, using, we may assume, the word as an *organon*. The good dialectician brings things together (ἄγειν εἰς μίαν ἰδέαν) and cuts things apart (τέμνειν) where the natural seams are. A person who does not understand the world well will not cut along the joints (κατ' ἄρθρα) and will be like a bad butcher (265d-e). I suggest that here we see fleshed out, so to speak, Plato's concern over the power of the individual unit of meaning to which we attach a word. For example, by making four cuts (μαντική, τελεστική, ποιητική, ἐρωτική) of what we claim to be a single thing 'madness' (μανία, 265b) rather than making five or three, we make claims about the way the world is.

If for Plato truth is at stake in language down to the single word, Aristotle says precisely the opposite at the very beginning of the *de Interpretatione*. The notion of truth, he says, is only relevant to words in combination, and using a single word is not, he says explicitly, an act of combination or division (16a10-20). In sharp contrast with Plato, the word for Aristotle is a benign name, a label that we give to an essence that is more or less straightforward in its autonomy. The process of *mimesis* as it happens with a word does not place truth in the balance. So it is not the fraught affair that it was for Plato. A single word, being only a label, does not in itself make any claim about the world, it does no cutting. For Aristotle, the world is more cooperative to our attempts to name it than it was for Plato. The interesting problems begin to arise only when we string words together, in Aristotle's thinking, and predicate claims about the separate essences that (it seems) we all know to be out there in the world. There is a certain trust in Aristotle of the words we use, in order that we may get on with the task of classifying and categorising the various essences that present themselves to us. In Aristotle, individual words are not interrogated, as they consistently are in Plato, especially in the Socratic dialogues. They are more or less adequate mirror images of essences whose separate and autonomous existence, if not their precise properties, are apparent to most observers. For Aristotle, in general, the base units of meaning in language are not to be approached with the same distrust with which Plato approaches linguistic representations.

The degree of Aristotelian scepticism toward a belief in the special (and for most of his predecessors, with the exception of Plato, mystified) representational status of language is without precedent, as far as I know, and enormously influential. It is he and not Plato who solidifies the notion of the user of language as picture painter for a whole line of literary critics, through Horace and beyond, who take clarity as the guiding value in poetry. (The comparison of the poet with the picture painters occurs 7 times in the *Poetics* 1447a, 1448a twice, 1450a, 1450b, 1454b, 1460b).) Of course Aristotle allows for pictures of reality that deviate from the way things are, either in the direction of the way things should be or the way they are said to be (1460b10). But what the poet produces are still primarily pictures, clear ones if the poet is good, whether of things that really happen or that might happen. And if we follow Aristotle's wake into the rhetorical tradition, *mimesis* ceases completely to be a problem of linguistic representation. It becomes at least by the time of Demetrius the name for a rhetorical training exercise, which becomes *imitatio* for Cicero and Quintilian, the mimicking of earlier literary and oratorical models.

Aristotle seems to have successfully drained out all the epistemological anxiety that Plato placed in the term.

As Roemer (1924, Chapt. iii), Van der Valk (1964, 84), and more recently Roos Meijering (1987) have shown, it appears clear that Aristarchus' work as represented in the Greek scholia stands in a Peripatetic tradition of literary theory. Accepting this premise, it appears that Aristotle's central value for great poetry, clarity, is part of the Alexandrian's inheritance. But Aristarchus made use of this principle in a more rigid manner than Aristotle.

In the *Poetics*, clarity is a goal that a poet should strive for. In Aristotle's estimation, Homer seems to have achieved clarity in some places, but in other places he has not. In the case of Odysseus' landing at the cave of the nymphs, for example, it seemed absurd to Aristotle that Odysseus should not have woken up when the ship ran aground and the Phaeacians carried him ashore. Aristotle forgives the unclarity, ironically enough because Homer makes it unclear, he obscures the absurdity (ἀφανίζει τὸ ἄτοπον), 'by the charm of his other merits', as the Loeb translates (1460b). By the time we reach Aristarchus, however, Aristotle's ideal goal for a poet becomes internalised and taken as an indicator for what counts as being truly Homeric. Unclarity, now in the form of an apparent sense that poses problems, is a mark that a line is un-Homeric, and worthy of deletion or emendation. Anything unclear must have sneaked into the text during the process of redaction and it is the central task of the critic to take it out.

The most characteristic aspect of Aristarchus' literary critical activity is the clarifying through textual emendation of the sometimes irrational elements of the text. When Ares bellows with the voice of 9000 soldiers at *Iliad* 14.148 (ἐννεάχιλοι), Aristarchus suggests that we read: like people having nine lips (ἐννέα χεῖλη ἔχοντες). When the men who hear the Sirens are said by Homer to starve on the spot at *Odyssey* 12.43 Aristarchus adds for us that this is because of a lack of provisions (Van der Valk 1949, 112). At *Odyssey* 1.320, he adds a possible reading for ἀνόπαια as a kind of bird, so that Athena might not seem to fly through a small roof opening. For if we take the word as from ἀν' ὀπήν, meaning that she flew up through a smoke vent, it appears clear that Athena has actually taken the form of a bird, in order to fit through the small hole, rather than that she flies bird-like. We might find evidence for understanding Aristarchus' commentary this way by comparing it with a similar comment by an anonymous scholiast whom Van der Valk believes to be Aristarchus. When Hermes moves across the waves resembling a seagull at *Odyssey* 5.55, we are told that this refers only to the god's speed, not to his figure (Van der Valk 1949, 118).

Here the Aristotelian preference for clarity can be seen as teaming up with Aristotle's caution against using the marvellous. The result is that the Aristotelian tolerance of the marvellous is overrun. We arrive at a strict demand for *mimesis* in a narrower sense than Aristotle had intended it. The poet is held even more closely to the goal of imitating things as they are, and is not allowed to represent things as they are said to be or might be. Aristotle's guiding value of clarity has become Aristarchus' absolute rule.

We can see the foregrounding of the value of clarity in Aristarchus' injunction not to bother oneself with what the poet does not say. What the poet does 'say', or perhaps we are better off translating 'show' (the verb in the D-scholion is φράζειν, which Aristarchus insists Homer never uses to mean simply say or tell, but more emphatically as show or point out (LSJ, s. v.))—what the poet does show, then, should be self-evident. It can be expected to be plain. The meaning of the text can be assumed to be clear to one who has mastered the *techne*, the knowledge of the scheme of grammar and lexis that renders Homer's language transparent and his meaning plain.

The D-scholion I began with is an attempt to make clear one of the thorniest ἄτοπα facing the Homeric critic: the binding of a god. The commentary tells us not to bother ourselves about the binding (δέω) of Ares by Otus and Ephialtes. We can compare Aristarchus' treatment of the offending verb δέω in another instance where it appears, during the tryst of Ares and Aphrodite, in *Odyssey* 8. At line 352, Aristarchus offers εὐθηνοῖμι for δεοῖμι, for no other apparent reason than that δεοῖμι would paint a picture dissonant from Aristarchus' view of the way things are. For the Alexandrians, giants do not bind gods. So the D-scholion on the

Iliad seems to serve the same purpose as the textual emendation in the *Odyssey*. At *Iliad* 5.385, it appears, Aristarchus could not locate a satisfactory textual solution, and so falls back on the poetic license argument. We are right then to understand the poetic license position, at least as it appears in Aristarchus in this instance, as defensive in nature. I find it difficult to understand this, as Aristarchus himself does, as the marking out of a realm of pure *poiesis*.

I draw from this brief survey of Aristotle's theory and Aristarchus' inheritance of it the following general conclusions: First, *mimesis*, for these critics, takes place through the transparent medium of language. One can assume clarity when reading a poet skilled in the poetic art. We should not read with the expectation of semantic trouble that is insoluble by recourse to the knowledge of lexis and grammar. Mastery of the *techne* of poetry is equivalent to rendering transparent the medium of language, and making words point to things-as-they-are without dissonance or obscurity. Second, the poet creates as the fully sovereign, independent master, unsullied by what is *outside*. He has full control over what comes into his poem. He chooses precise words that point without undue complication to stable and obvious things in the world. So the poet is a solitary master practising a pure art.

3. The allegorical tradition

Our earliest record of sustained literary criticism, a commentary on an Orphic poem found at Derveni, presents a very different picture of poetics indeed. I follow Walter Burkert in dating the text of the papyrus from Derveni to the era before Plato (1970, 443). The allegorical method found here stands near the head of a tradition that had a vogue among the Pre-Socratics, and representatives in all the major periods to follow.[2]

[2] That Plato found the need to disagree with them in the *Republic* is evidence for readings of *hyponoia* by critics of the classical period. In the Hellenistic period we find Chrysippus and Crates; the Early Roman, Cornutus, Artemidorus and Heraclitus; and the Late Roman, Plotinus, Porphyry, and Proclus, among many others.

Any firm conclusions of the details of the Derveni papyrus must be hedged until the long-awaited publication of a scientific edition of the text. But a few preliminary statements can be made. If the provisional reconstruction of the text as it appeared in the *ZPE* (47 (1982), appendix) turns out to be correct, the *aenigma* appears here also, but not at all as Aristotle's nonsense or *βαρβαρισμός*. It is rather the focus of critical energy for the text's interpreter. It appears twice as an adverb in col. 4,[3] and I follow Jeffrey Rusten's reading of it in a variant verb form[4] in col. 10 (which also appears in col. 14):

> *ὅτι μὲμ πᾶ[σ]αν τὴμ πόησιν περὶ τῶμ πραγμάτων αἰνίζεται κ[α]θ' ἔπος ἕκαστον ἀνάγκη λέγειν*
>
> 'Since he [the poet] puts hidden ideas about reality [*ainizetai*] into all his poem, it is necessary to speak line by line [or word by word]'.[5]

The line reveals a stance toward the poem that is wholly different than the one I am claiming to exist in the wake of Aristotle. Rather than expecting clarity from a poet and being suspicious of unclarity, this commentator expects that the poet has been unclear. Aristotle might tolerate this type of writing, in moderation, to produce dignity; Aristarchus will not allow that a great poet would ever make his or her meaning unclear. It is certainly not the case that either critic would see this murkier mode of representation as a central feature of poetic writing or interpretation.

The repeated appearance of the *aenigma*, the riddle, in the Derveni papyrus adds precious information to our sometimes hopelessly fragmentary evidence of the Presocratic context for Aristotle's literary work. I suggest that based on the Derveni papyrus, we can locate more precisely, within the technical term *aenigma*, what was surely a central feature of

---

[3] I am following M. L. West's numeration of the columns. He takes 'Unplaciertes Fragment A', as it is designated in the *ZPE*, as column I. Each column number then is one higher than in *ZPE*.

[4] And not from *αἰνέω*.

[5] Translation from Rusten 1985, 133.

Aristotle's reaction against earlier theories of poetic language.[6] Aristotle's foregrounding of clarity, as we saw earlier, was formulated specifically as opposed to this term. Whereas earlier critics saw murky riddles hinting at higher truths, Aristotle, characteristically, saw murky nonsense. These different visions of what counts as being poetic lead the critic to ask different questions of the text.

When the Derveni commentator engages the poem, we can see this different vision at work. I will look at 2 examples that Rusten has treated. In col. 7, we have 10 lines that are devoted to teasing out the meaning of the word *πανομφεύουσαν*, the sense of which remains difficult. The commentator claims that *ὀμφή* is the same as *φωνή*, and *λέγειν* is the same as *φωνεῖν*, and the idea of teaching, *διδάσκειν*, is contained in the idea of *λέγειν*, therefore *πανομφεύουσαν* is equivalent to *πάντα διδάσκουσαν*. Secondly, later in the commentary, in col. 10, we are offered a reading of *αἰδοῖον* as carrying the hidden sense of *ἥλιον* (see also 13.1). The commentator tells us that, as is the case with the sun, without the genitals there is no *genesis*. The commentator tells us that the poet saw this fact and made use of this state of affairs in the world to convey a hidden meaning.[7]

By Aristarchus' lights I think we could safely conjecture that this type of reading would be judged *ἔξω τῶν φραζομένων ὑπὸ τοῦ ποιητοῦ*. If we venture to reconstruct the Derveni commentator's judgement on this issue, can we say that he would see his own interpretation as *outside* the poem? Or did he not consider that the poet placed inside the poem the notion of *ὀμφή* and thereby brought to the inside *φωνή*, *λέγειν*, and *διδάσκειν*? Or similarly, with *αἰδοῖον* comes inside the poem the notion of generation and all its attendant manifestations, including the sun.

---

[6] Aristotle's distaste for using omen-language to describe what the poet does can also be seen at *Poetics* 1453b9, where he says that one ought to produce pity and fear and not something portentous (*τερατῶδες*).

[7] West (1983, 85) has made the conclusion that the Derveni interpreter was working from a corrupt text, and *αἰδοῖον* here cannot be the noun for sexual organ, but must be the adjective meaning 'reverend'.

Though I see no evidence to conclude that the Derveni commentator was a sophisticated philosopher, the stance toward the text that he takes is less puzzling if we understand his commonsense vision of the way language works to be closer to the one Plato articulates than the one Aristotle does. The categories of language for the Derveni commentator do not appear to be simple labels of obvious and discrete entities in the world out there. They are rather categories with unstable boundaries, which makes them more like the sometimes inaccurate cuts of Plato's reality than Aristotle's labels. A word pulled to the inside of a poem by a poet will itself pull at the other words that surround it; our attempt to cut apart these aspects of reality by making different words for them may or may not be successful. The process by which *πανομφεύουσαν* brings in *πάντα διδάσκουσαν* does not appear to me to be subsumable under a scheme of lexis and grammar. Whether, in the end, we find the Derveni commentator's particular reading to be convincing—and without a better understanding of the context in which he wrote it would be difficult to conclude that it is—I think we can at the very least conclude that the commentator enacts a different notion of what counts as the literary critic's task than Aristotle does. For the Derveni commentator the poem is a riddle to be solved, for Aristotle, it is the masterwork of a craftsman to be appreciated.

As we will see in more detail below, the notion *mimesis* will become so fraught within the allegorical tradition, especially when the Neoplatonists find Platonic roots for it, that the allegorists will try to find a way to displace it altogether. For them the logic of the riddle, the *aenigma*, takes over from the *μίμημα*. The *aenigma* and its derivatives are one in a series of challenges to *mimesis* in the allegorists' technical vocabulary. With its attendant senses of riddle, omen, and oracle, this term suggests an obliqueness of signification, situated after one has taken account of grammar and lexis. As for example in the famous sayings of the Sphinx, the words may make perfect sense in relation to themselves, but how to map them onto the world is left in doubt. The study of lexis, such as the *grammatikoi* and *rhetores* emphasise, may be important, but usually as a preliminary step[8] to what they see as the central task of the literary critic, rooting out deep meanings that are understood to be underneath the mimetic surface of the poem.

Among the other technical terms introduced by the allegorists are the more familiar *hyponoia* and *allegoria*. The very propositions of *under*-meaning and *other*-speaking, by the negativity in their formulation, tell us that the *dianoia* we have found will never be sufficient. I would like to pause briefly at another less familiar term that will be important for understanding Porphyry's interpretation. The *symbolon*, which has very little use within the study of literature until Chrysippus identifies it with allegory, is developed as a literary category from within the allegorical tradition. It becomes the central notion by which the later allegorists attempt to displace *mimesis*. Chrysippus is followed by a long succession of allegorical critics—including Philo, Cornutus, Clement of Alexandria, Heraclitus, probably Numenius, and certainly Porphyry, Iamblichus, and Proclus—who use the symbol as a technical term for more murky and oblique, or especially charged images, for which *mimesis* appears to them an inappropriate category. As it becomes more elaborated in the later allegorical tradition, the symbolic mode of indication is consistently defined as being identical with allegory and as being opposed to *mimesis*.[9]

---

[8] Philo *De conf. ling*. 143, cited in J.I. Porter, Philo's Confusion of Tongues, *QUCC* 24 (1986), 55-74; Porphyry, *Quaestionum Homericarum*, liber 1, ed. A.R. Sodano, 1.22-8 (see below). Proclus differentiates his allegorical commentary from (presumably) something like what I am here calling Aristotelian rhetorical theory. In an inversion of Aristarchus' rhetoric, he contrasts what he does with those who merely trouble themselves about style (*τὴν περὶ τὴν λέξιν πολυπραγμοσύνην*, *In R*. 1.164.8). The simple arrangement of the books in Pseudo-Plutarch's *Life of Homer*, with lexical issues coming first, followed by allegorical ones, is a straightforward example of the attitude.

[9] The bluntest formulation of the position must await Proclus (*In R*. 1.198.9-24; cf. 1.86.15-18; 1.77.13-30).

4. Porphyry and the Cave of the Nymphs

When Odysseus lands at the cave of the nymphs in Phorcys, Homer includes 11 lines describing it in some detail. The cave contains kraters and amphoras of stone that bees use to store honey, stone looms where nymphs weave purple cloth, and two gates, one for mortals and one for immortals. After briefly describing these features, Homer continues on with his story as though what he had just described were a perfectly normal setting. Whereas, we remember, Aristotle's curiosity was piqued because Odysseus did not wake up when the ship landed here, Porphyry seems to feel that the elements within the cave are in need of explanation. As was noted earlier, he opens *On the Cave of the Nymphs* with a question using the verbal form of *aenigma*, *ainittetai*: What on earth does Homer mean by the cave? (Ὅτι ποτὲ αἰνίττεται Ὁμήρῳ τὸ ἐν Ἰθάκῃ ἄντρον.) We are forced, Porphyry tells us, to trouble ourselves with (πολυπραγμονεῖν ἀναγκάζοντα) a number of bothersome questions (*Antr.* 3). For example: 'What is a gate of men and one of gods?' (τίς μὲν ἀνθρώπων πύλη, τίς δὲ θεῶν), 'What is the use of the kraters and amphoras?' (τίς δὲ καὶ ἡ τῶν κρατήρων καὶ ἀμφιφορέων παράληψις), and 'Who could remain credulous when told that the goddesses go around weaving sea-purple cloaks on stone looms in murky caves...?' (τίς γὰρ ἂν πιστεύσαι θεὰς ἁλιπόρφυρα ἱμάτια ὑφαίνειν ἐν σκοτεινοῖς ἄντροις ἐπὶ λιθίων ἱστῶν). Porphyry's πολυπραγμονέω is a close synonym of Aristarchus' περιεργάζομαι.

Given Porphyry's familiarity with and apparent respect for Aristarchus' work, I think we would not be bothering ourselves too much to read an answer to Aristarchus in Porphyry's words. We are forced to ask these questions, he says, and the answers are not to be found in lexis or grammar alone. As we know from his *Homeric Questions*, Porphyry considered analysis by the tools of grammarians and rhetoricians to be one possible λύσις, or solution, for a troublesome spot in the text. But in that work he reserved the possibility of finding a solution by allegory.[10] He tells that the first method is a kind of warm-up or preliminary exercise for the real contest, which is the kind of interpretation he ventures into in the *On the Cave of the Nymphs*.[11]

The best way to get a sense of how Porphyry understands his interpretation based on allegory to differ from his analysis based on the tools of grammarians and rhetoricians is through his category of symbolic speech. In his *Life of Pythagoras* Porphyry makes the move of a full break with *mimesis* that seems to me is a logical extension of the allegorical frame of mind. He equates the symbol with allegory and *aenigma*, and specifically defines these terms as opposed to *mimesis*. He tells us that Pythagoras had three ways of speaking (γραμμάτων τρισσὰς διαφοράς), which he learned from the Egyptians (*V.P.* 12):

> ἐπιστολογραφικῶν τε καὶ ἱερογλυφικῶν καὶ συμβολικῶν, τῶν μὲν κυριολογουμένων κατὰ μίμησιν, τῶν δ' ἀλληλογορουμένων κατά τινας αἰνιγμούς.
>
> 'epistolographic and also hieroglyphic and symbolic, the first being ordinary speech according to *mimesis*, and the others allegorising according to certain riddles.'

In what we have of Porphyry's writing, as far as I know, he does not say this explicitly of poetic language. But it appears to me clear that he has some such distinction in mind when he envisions solutions according to lexis and those according to allegory. Porphyry repeatedly calls Homer's cave a *symbolon*, using the word and its variants over 25 times in his short treatise. Though Porphyry also uses the language of *mimesis* in the cave commentary, it is far outweighed by the density of symbol, *aenigma*, and allegory derivatives. Taking into account the *Life of Pythagoras* passage together with the *Homeric Questions*, I consider this balance of terminology weighted toward what Porphyry opposes to the mimetic to be significant.

---

[10] Porphyry, *Quaestionum Homericarum ad Iliadem pertinentium reliquiae*, Iliad book 19, section 221 ff., line 38; book 20, section 67 ff., line 4.

[11] Porphyry, *Quaestionum Homericarum*, liber 1, ed. A.R. Sodano, 1.22-8.

In order to find out what the cave means *in* Homer's text, Porphyry feels it necessary to explore what caves in and of themselves are. He surveys the opinions not only elsewhere in the Homeric corpus, but also of the Presocratics, Plato, the Persians, and his own scientific sense of what caves are and what they do in the world. He nowhere suggests that Homer had in mind a particular traditional belief when he constructed the cave. His position is closer to the following: Caves have certain configurations with respect to the world. These can be researched by examining and evaluating the available opinions on caves from all sources. This is equivalent to finding and evaluating all the possible semantic affiliations of *τὸ ἄντρον*. Homer, possessing an acute understanding of the world, knew about caves also, and constructed his cave in the poem in accordance with particular aspects of caves as they exist in the world. The referent of the word is a bothersome issue for Porphyry. It is not clear and plain, but he considers it part of his work as a literary critic to investigate it. The cave in Homer, Porphyry suggests in the end, is a crystallisation of the material cosmos, the world subject to generation and decay. Each of the elements inside of it adds to this aspect, highlighting particular parts of the world that comes into being and passes away.

Porphyry is not uninterested in whether there was a real cave in the harbour of Phorcys. He takes up the question by way of introduction to his analysis. But he soon leaves it. After examining briefly the evidence for and against a historical cave, Porphyry tells us (*Antr*. 4):

> *εἴτε δ' οὕτως ἔχον ἀφηγήσατο εἴτε καὶ αὐτός τινα προσέθηκεν, οὐδὲν ἧττον μένει τὰ ζητήματα <τῷ> τὴν βούλησιν ἢ τῶν καθιδρυσαμένων ἢ τοῦ προσθέντος ποιητοῦ ἀνιχνεύοντι, ὡς ἂν μήτε παλαιῶν ἄνευ συμβόλων μυστικῶν τὰ ἱερὰ καθιδρυσαμένων μήτε Ὁμήρου ὡς ἔτυχε τὰ περὶ τούτων ἀφηγουμένου.*
>
> 'This said, whether Homer described it as he did because it was like that or embellished it, for anyone trying to trace the intentions of either the people who made the shrine or for the poet who described it that way the aforementioned problems [the questions he felt forced to consider] remain. Neither would the ancients have established a shrine without mystical symbols, nor would Homer have described them randomly.'

The judgement that a representation has no particular object in the world toward which it points is not the end point of the literary critic's work, as it was for Aristarchus, but the starting point. Porphyry's position highlights one of the premises in Aristarchus' taking poetic license as an end point of critical activity. If we find that a poet has fabricated something, and has not imitated a real state of affairs in the world, Aristarchus' theory does not admit the possibility that the poet had in mind to convey some significance.[12] To search for meanings from such places in the poem is to pull to the inside of a poem what should be left on the outside.

The kind of criticism that Porphyry engages in in the Cave of the Nymphs essay has traditionally been considered to be at odds with what he does in the *Homeric Questions*. This misunderstands what allegorical criticism attempts to do. An allegorical critic as skilled as Porphyry will not dismiss close reading of the text, that is lexical and grammatical analysis. But this will not be the end point of his work. He carries on following what I have claimed is the distinctive feature of allegorical criticism, the belief that the text's relationship to the world may sometimes be something other than a straightforward representation; that the reality it points to in the world may itself have signifying power, and bring along with it, to the inside of the poem, a whole host of attendant significations. The urge to go on with interpretation emerges from a belief that the poem signifies in a way that is more akin to riddles and oracles than to what the picture painter does. The riddle metaphor indicates a different understanding of how poetry works, and a different vision of the role of the literary critic, who now feels forced to tease on meanings understood to be hidden, even after he has used all available knowledge of the *techne* of poetic language.

It is perhaps then not so surprising that the same critic who produces the best surviving allegorical exegesis from antiquity also preserves what

---

[12] We do Aristarchus better justice by putting the issue in his terms: the poet seeks to entertain, not to teach. As is clearer in Eratosthenes, this position is part and parcel of the poetic license argument. Only with this premise will the concept be invoked as a closure of interpretive activity.

has been understood to be the motto of the critics who follow in the wake of Aristotle. Aristarchus' principle that we should interpret Homer from Homer survives from a citation in Porphyry's *Homeric Questions*. I suggest that both in the *Homeric Questions* and in the essay on the Cave of the Nymphs, Porphyry believed that he was being faithful to what Homer said, that he was reading Homer from Homer. Porphyry closes his essay on the Cave of the Nymphs by an appeal against what he anticipated to be an objection from the kind of theory that Aristarchus engages in his work: 'This sort of exegesis should not be considered forced or the product of a credulousness or exuberance to find things', he tells us (*οὐ δεῖ δὲ τὰς τοιαύτας ἐξηγήσεις βεβιασμένας ἡγεῖσθαι καὶ εὑρεσιλογούντων πιθανότητας*, *Antr*. 36). Aristarchus would clearly think that Porphyry, by going deeply into the question of what caves themselves might mean, was reading into Homer what was not there. It seems that for Aristarchus a cave will always be just a cave. Would Porphyry agree? I think the answer is clearly no. So Aristarchus' opinion as we have it in the D-scholion, that we should not bother ourselves with what is outside the text, as well as Cicero's judgement that the Stoics read into a poem what is not there, seem to me to beg the question, as the allegorists see it. The questions we should be asking, according to them, are: What counts as being the inside and the outside of the text? Are these two regions stable, and may the rules of *lexis* and grammar decide the boundary between them? Or does a signification through language always carry the possibility of meaning more than what *lexis* and grammar say it means?

BIBLIOGRAPHY

Asmis, E., Plato on Poetic creativity, in: R. Kraut (ed.), *Cambridge Companion to Plato*. New York 1992, 338-64.

Buffière, F., *Les Mythes d'Homère et la pensée grecque*. Paris 1956.

Burkert, W., La genèse des choses et des mots, *Les études philosophiques* 25 (1970), 443-55.

De Romilly, J., *Magic and Rhetoric in Ancient Greece*. Cambridge, MA 1975.

Meijering, R., *Literary and Rhetorical Theories in the Greek Scholia*. Groningen 1987.

Pépin, J., *Mythe et allégorie*. Paris 1958.

Roemer, A., *Die Homerexegese Aristarchs in ihren Grundzügen dargestellt*. Paderborn 1924.

Rusten, J.S., Interim Notes on the Papyrus from Derveni, *HSPh* 89 (1985), 121-40.

van der Valk, M., *Textual Criticism of the Odyssey*. Leiden 1949.

———, *Researches on the Text and Scholia of the Iliad*, part 2. Leiden 1964.

'Εκ τῶν μύθων ἄρξασθαι. *Greek Fable Theory after Aristotle: Characters and Characteristics*[*]

J.G.M. van Dijk

1. Introduction

Exceptionally, comprehension of a particular text is hampered, not facilitated, by its context. This seems to be the case with the above Greek quote, which is taken from the chapter on *μῦθος* in the *Progymnasmata* by Aelius Theon. As Theon repeatedly used the word *μῦθος* to mean 'fable' in the preceding and following pages, one is naturally inclined to translate, say, 'to start with the fables'. This inclination will be even more irrepressible when this expression figures in the title of a paper on Post-Aristotelian Fable Theory that is read at the start of the day. Nevertheless, this is not what Theon meant. The phrase indicates something which Theon recommends teachers to accustom their pupils to put into practice 'after a fable has been told in its entirety'.[1] He exemplifies this by quoting the incipit of Hesiod's fable in which a hawk addresses a

---

* This is a revised and enlarged version of a paper read at 'Greek Literary Theory after Aristotle. A Symposium in Honour of Professor Dirk M. Schenkeveld', Amsterdam, Vrije Universiteit, 8 April 1994. Prof. dr. A.H.M. Kessels and Drs. S.H.C.M. Otten rapidly and kindly corrected the interpretation of the Greek and the English, respectively. Throughout this paper, the abbreviation '*Aes.*' refers to Perry 1952.

[1] *Prog.* 3 (p. 74 Sp.): *χρήσιμον δὲ καὶ τὸ ὁλοκλήρου τινὸς εἰρημένου μύθου ἐθισθῆναι τὸν μανθάνοντα χαριέντως ἐκ τῶν μύθων ἄρξασθαι, ὥσπερ Ἡσίοδος* [*Op.* 202-12 (*Aes.* 4a)]. Reche Martínez (1991, 75) does not translate *ἐκ τῶν μύθων* when rendering: 'Es útil también que, después que sea contada una fábula completa, el alumno se acostumbre a comenzar las fábulas con elegancia, como Hesíodo: ...'!

nightingale right from the start. In the end, the context does provide a clue for the interpretation. The clause could be rendered by 'to start with direct speech, *oratio recta*'. The present paper has already been following Theon's advice for some time.

Nowadays, the literary genre of the fable is somewhat controversial, in more than one sense. First, its heterogeneity is elusive. Ironically, this observation reproduces one of the few scholarly *communes opiniones*.[2] Secondly, fables seem to have lost their *quondam* reputation. Fable books were among the first to be printed but are often disregarded now. This may be explained by a combination of, on the one hand, the common misconceptions that all fables are about animals, plants, or inanimate objects[3] and have a moral purpose,[4] and, on the other hand, the equally universal aversion to everything which smacks of didacticism—the use of fables in education has a long history. However, any fable collection will show the untenability of a reduction of the fable characters to animals, plants, and objects. La Fontaine's first book of Fables, for example, contains both the immortal Cicada and the Ant and the Old Man dismissing Death. Of course, one can, as some do, exclude fables like the latter from the discussion. But several objections may be raised. First, one would thus be compelled to eliminate more than half of the fable collections.[5]

---

[2] Perry 1959, 18; Nøjgaard 1964, 47; Adrados 1979, 57; Leibfried 1982, 16; cf. Josifovic 1974, col. 24-5; Lindner 1978, 17; Van Rooijen-Dijkman 1984, 7.

[3] E.g. Dodsley 1764, lxviii-lxx; McMahon 1927, 2-3; Leibfried 1982, 22 (contra: Lindner 1978, 39; cf. Nøjgaard 1964, 66; Adrados 1979, 31; Dithmar 1984, 110); Georgopapadakos 1989-1990, s.v. *μῦθος* 3. '*αλληγορική διήγηση που αναφέρεται στα ζῷα ή τα φυτά*'.

[4] E.g. McMahon 1927, 2-3; García Gual 1978, 12; Looij 1988, 13: 'het dierenverhaaltje-met-een-les, de fabel dus'; Leibfried 1989, 15-7 (contra: *ib.* 17-20); many dictionaries and encyclopaedias, s.v. (e.g. Hanks 1986: 'a short moral story, esp. one with animals as characters').

[5] Dover (1966, 42 n. 9) seems to advocate this draconian measure. Applying Aphthonius' classification (see below, under 1.2.3) *avant la lettre*, the fable collections can be subdivided as follows. 'Rational': Babr. 2, 10, 15, 18, (20), 22, 30, (34), 47, 49, 54, 57-8, (59), 61, 63, 66, 68, 70, 75, 116, 119, 126-7,

Secondly, even such a reduction is not a nostrum, because aetiologies[6] and present tense descriptions of animal behaviour[7] will remain odd ones out. Thirdly, this method separates what the author or the tradition explicitly presents as belonging together, either by a reduction to a common denominator 'fable' and/or by a connection with the name of Aesop, the legendary fabulist. Finally, and conversely, fables may differ in terms of the type of characters involved, but they share other, and more important, characteristics, notably a metaphorical element and particular (persuasive, satirical, or illustrative) functions, one of which

(136); Phaedr. 1.14, 18; 2.2, 5; (3.1), 5, 8-11, (14), (19); 4.5, (7), (10-11), 12, (18), 22-3, 26; 5.1-2, 5-7; *App.* 2, (3), 4-10, 13, 15-7, 20, 27, 29; *fab. aes.* (ed. Hausrath) (5), 8, 13, (28), 29-35, (36), 40, 42, 46, (47), 53, (55), 56-7, 60-1, 65, 67, (68), 69, (72), 80, 90-1, 96-7, 101, (102), 104-6, 110-3, 116, (121), 123, 170, 180, 183-4, (188), 214, 216, 220-1, (229), 230, 253, 274, 278, (279), 282, (284), 289, 299-301, 304-6; Av. 1, 4, 10, 12, 22-3, 25, 29. 'Moral': Babr. 5, 12, 14, 17, 19, (21), (24), 25, 28, 29, 31, 35-6, 39-41, 44, 46, 53, 60, 62, 64-5, 67, 69, 73-4, 77, (78), 79, 81-2, 84-5, (86), 87, 89-90, (91), 93-6, (97), 99-103, 105-7, 109, 112, 115, (118), 120-2, 130, (132), 133-4, 140; Phaedr. 1.1, 3-5, 7, 8-13, 16-7, 19-21, 24-6, (27), 28-31; 2.4, 6, 8; 3.12-3, (15), 16; 4.2-3, 6, (8), 9, 14, 21, 24-5; 5.9; *App.* 1, 14, 18-9, 22, 25-6, 30-2; *fab. aes.* (ed. Hausrath) 4, 7, 9-10, 12-7, 19-20, (27), 41, 43, 45, 48, 70-1, 73, 75-6, 81-6, 92, 98-100, 114-5, 118, 125-6, 128, 130-2, 135-6, 138-40, 143-4, 146-8, 150-6, 158-62, 164, 166-7, 169, 174, 176-7, 181-2, 191, 194-5, 198-9, 201-3, 206, 211-2, 218, 231, 233-4, 236-7, 239-46, 249, 251-2, 254-9, 263, 265-71, 273, 275, 280, 285, 287, 291, 293, 295-6, 302; Av. 2-3, 6, 11, 13, (15), 16, 18-9, 26-7, 31, 34-5, (37), 40-1, (42). All fables not listed above belong to Aphthonius' 'mixed' category (including perhaps the items bracketed above). In view of the above lists, I really do not understand Handford's computation (1964, p. xix) that '[n]early three-quarters of the extant fables are stories about animals, ...' nor García Gual's calculation (1978, 14 n. 4): 'En las colecciones griegas supera [sc. el porcentaje de fábulas con personajes animales] a los dos tercios.'

[6] E.g. Babr. 74 (*Aes.* 105); *fab. aes.* 181 (*Aes.* 171).

[7] Phaedr. *App.* 22 (*Aes.* 550); *ib.* 30; *fab. aes.* 120 Hausrath (*Aes.* 118); Babr. 35; *fab. aes.* 243 Hausrath; Av. 35 (*Aes.* 218).

(e.g. the moral or sociological[8] function), however, must not be proclaimed the only one.

This introductory sketch of the situation—a rough draft—may serve as promythium. Whoever seeks to retrieve the content of the notion of 'fable' in antiquity finds a valuable supplementary tool in extant ancient theoretical passages on fables from various literary genres. Obviously, these testimonies are of paramount importance, as they provide external contemporary information on the genre. Their study might minimise, if not altogether preclude, both the lurking danger of imposing modern ideas on ancient texts and that of the vicious circle one inevitably enters when sticking to the fable collections. This paper proposes to take a close look at several ancient, as well as a few Byzantine, Greek theoretical testimonies by investigating and comparing their views on the fable as a literary genre. It confines itself to the characters of fable, but will not confine them. The contemporary universality of the aforesaid misconception may justify the attention given to this aspect. The testimonies have been ordered by genre, since their provenance and ensuing line of approach may be responsible for an emphasis on some aspects or a neglect of others.

2. Rhetoricians

2.2 Rhetorical Prose

Aristotle, Rhetoric *2.20, 1393a23-1394a18 (*Aes. *T 94)*

First, theoretical passages from rhetorical and oratorical prose will be discussed. Of course, the section from Aristotle's *Rhetoric* dealing with fables—the oldest one extant—has to be considered first: a discussion of Greek Fable Theory after Aristotle cannot evade starting with him. Aristotle does not make any statement on the characters of fables, but he does narrate two fables *in extenso* to exemplify the genre. His first example (1393b8-22; *Aes*. 269a) is a fable which was allegedly told by

---

[8] Pro: e.g. Crusius 1913, p. ix; Meuli 1954, 73. Contra (rightly): Perry 1959, 23-5. For an introductory discussion of the locus classicus (Phaedr. 3.Prol.33-7 (*Aes*. T 57)) and some pros and cons, see Leibfried 1982, 25-37.

Stesichorus (fr. 104 (a) *PMG* = TA 8 *PMGF*), about a horse which was willing but unable to take revenge on a stag which had intruded, and destroyed, his private meadow. The horse summoned the aid of a man, who stipulated that the horse took a bit and allowed him to mount armed with javelins. The horse met his demands, and thus had his revenge at the price of[9] his own freedom. Aristotle's second example (1393b22-1394a1; *Aes*. 427) is a fable put into Aesop's mouth, about a fox who got stuck in a ravine and was vexed by parasites. Yet he declined the offer of a pitiful hedgehog to remove them. The fox thus explained his refusal: 'These are satiated, but if you remove these, others will come instead and drink the remainder of my blood.' The characters in Aristotle's examples are mainly, but obviously not exclusively (as has been upheld by La Fontaine and Adrados),[10] animals: a human being does play quite a large part in the first fable, an aetiology of the domestication of the horse by man.[11]

2.2 Progymnasmata

Theon, Progymnasmata *1-3 (cf.* Aes. *T 65, 85, 103)*

As the fable was one of the preparatory rhetorical exercises (Clark 1957, 177 ff.), the extant chapters on μῦθος in the *Progymnasmata* by various rhetoricians constitute a significant part of Post-Aristotelian Fable Theory. First comes Theon's discussion of the fable—the longest one extant. Theon's liberal attitude towards possible fable characters is apparent in four different ways. To begin with, the fact that no characters are mentioned in his definition—the oldest and, according to some,[12] best one

---

[9] 1393b17-18 ἀντὶ τοῦ τιμωρήσασθαι, misinterpreted by Nøjgaard 1963, 5 and Karadagli 1981, 15.

[10] De La Fontaine 1668, 37: 'Aristote n'admet dans la fable que les animaux; il en exclut les hommes et les plantes. Cette règle est moins de nécessité que de bienséance, puisque ni Ésope, ni Phèdre, ni aucun des fabulistes, ne l'a gardée—...'; Adrados 1979, 37-8.

[11] In its turn, the domestication of the horse serves as an aetiology for man's temper in *fab. aes.* 107 (*Aes.* 105).

[12] Perry 1959, 22, and, in his wake, Blackham 1985, p. xi, 7, 252.

extant: 'A fable is a fictitious story that gives the semblance of reality'[13]—is a telling argumentum e silentio.

Then, while discussing different ethnic fable varieties, listing Libyan, Sybaritic, Phrygian, Cilician, Carian, Egyptian, and Cyprian, besides Aesopic ones, Theon slightingly opposes anonymous rival theoreticians who restrict the *fabulae personae* of one variety to irrational animals and those of another to human beings: all characters occur in all varieties.[14] Theon's stand betrays the existence of a contemporary debate on whether or not the aforesaid variants represent essentially different kinds of fables (cf. Reichel 1909, 51). One can only speculate about the identity of Theon's antagonists.

Further, in order to exemplify various aspects of the genre, Theon adduces eight fables in which different kinds of characters occur. In a kind of general introduction, Theon alludes to four fables from classical historiographers as examples of examples worthy of imitation and memorising: Herodotus' fable of the fisherman who played flute to the fish; Philistus' fable of the horse, which is lost but might be equated with that from Aristotle discussed above (1.1.1); Theopompus' fable about War and Violence, which has not been preserved either but might be roughly identical with a Babrian aetiology about the gods being paired off; Xenophon's fable about the sheep complaining to the shepherd about his preferential treatment of the sheep dog.[15] In the chapter on fable proper, Theon exemplifies four of the nine exercises pupils have to do: retelling, declining, connecting with a context, elaborating, abridging,

---

[13] *Prog.* 1 and 3 (pp. 63 and 72 Sp.): *μῦθός ἐστι λόγος ψευδὴς εἰκονίζων ἀλήθειαν*. For this interpretation of *ἀλήθεια*, see Van Dijk 1993c, 175-6 and 1993d, 26. Reche Martínez 1991, 73: 'una verdad'.

[14] *Prog.* 3 (p. 73 Sp.): *οἱ δὲ λέγοντες τοὺς μὲν ἐπὶ τοῖς ἀλόγοις ζῴοις συγκειμένους τοιούσδε εἶναι, τοὺς δὲ ἐπ' ἀνθρώποις τοιούσδε ..., εὐήθως μοι ὑπολαμβάνειν δοκοῦσιν: ἐν πᾶσι γὰρ τοῖς προειρημένοις εἰσὶν ἅπασαι αἱ ἰδέαι.*

[15] *ib.* 2 (p. 66 Sp.); Hdt. 1.141 (*Aes.* 11a); Philist. *FGrH* 556F6 (*Aes.* 269a); Theopomp. *FGrH* 115F127, Babr. 70 (*Aes.* 367); X. *Mem.* 2.7.13-4 (*Aes.* 356). Van Dijk 1993a, 28-9.

providing with or making up in accordance with a given epimythium, disproving and proving fables. Theon quotes two verses from Hesiod's animal fable—one of which has already been dealt with before—, to illustrate the retelling of fables in a charming style. Two other citations, this time from a fable by Phaedo, a pupil of Socrates', show how the grammatical cases in which the characters are put can be alternated. Phaedo's fable was about a lion's cub which was a prince's pet, thus uniting royal scions of different realms. It is tempting to speculate about a similarity between Phaedo's fable and that told by the chorus in Aeschylus' *Agamemnon* about the immutability of nature—a favourite fable theme.[16] Regrettably, Theon's quotes are the only fragments of Phaedo's fable to survive. Next, Theon summarises the aetiological fable of the camel imploring Zeus—a typical character in aetiological fables[17]—for horns but getting deprived of his ears instead. This paraphrase serves to illustrate how to connect a fable to a context. Theon compares the camel to Croesus, in all probability hinting at the latter's Persian campaign. Theon's eighth example is the fable of the dog carrying a piece of meat in his mouth, that is to say, until he snapped at a larger, but imaginary, one (*Aes*. 133). This fable exemplifies the construction of an epimythium matching the preceding fable.

Finally, when explaining another exercise—how to disprove fables composed by others—Theon (p. 77 Sp.) mentions gods and animals as possible fable characters: Prometheus, but not 'another of the gods', is the traditional creator of man, an ass is never wise, a fox never senseless; fabulists should not deviate from these data. Both the short list in itself and its order are significant: it shows that fable characters are flat characters, although one might object that the matter is somewhat more compli-

---

[16] Phaedo, Zopyr. *ap*. Theon. *Prog*. 3 (p. 75 Sp.; tentative textual criticism by Von Wilamowitz-Möllendorff 1879, 476); A. *A*. 717-36; neither is listed as fable in *Aes*., but see Van Dijk 1994.

[17] E.g. *fab. aes*. 3, 105, 107-11, 119, 172, 196, 228 Hausrath (*Aes*. 3, 103, 105-9, 117 (Theon l.c.), 163, 185, 240).

cated: in some fables the ass *is* smart[18] and in others the fox is outfoxed (Schwarzbaum 1969, 125-31). Further, and more importantly in this connection, Theon apparently has no objections to combining Prometheus with, and even mentioning him before, typical characters like the ass and the fox, the Aesopic character *par excellence*. To put it more clearly, Prometheus is as typical a fable character as the fox. Prometheus is a character in many, particularly aetiological, fables indeed.[19]

To sum up, Theon explicitly allows both irrational and rational characters in fables, which is also apparent from his examples: only two out of eight examples are pure animal fables (Hesiod's, Dog), four combine (an) animal(s) with a human being (Herodotus', Philistus', Xenophon's, Phaedo's), one with a god (Camel), whereas one even has only gods as characters (Theopompus'); besides, Theon appears to consider gods to be just as typical as animals in fables. In fact, Theon does not consider the quality of characters to be an essential characteristic of fables; otherwise he would have referred to this issue in his definition of the genre.

Hermogenes, Progymnasmata *1 (*Aes. *T 101)*

Hermogenes is the next author to discuss fable in his *Progymnasmata* and to be discussed here. He made the fable the first exercise because of its educational value.[20] Hermogenes actually started with the fable, unlike Theon, who relegated it to the second place, after the *χρεία*. Hermogenes

---

[18] E.g. Babr. 122, *fab. aes.* 198, 257 Hausrath, Rom. 52 Thiele, *Pa. Bodl.* 106 Knöll, Ign. Diac. 1.21 (*Aes.* 187).

[19] E.g. Call. *Iamb.* 2, fr. 192 Pfeiffer (*Aes.* 431); *Vit. Aesop.* 94G (*Aes.* 383; Van Dijk 1995); *fab. aes.* 102 Hausrath (*Aes.* 100); *fab. aes.* 228 Hausrath (*Aes.* 240); Phaedr. 4.15-6 (*Aes.* 515ab); Phaedr. *App.* 5-6 (*Aes.* 535); Babr. 66, *fab. aes.* 229 Hausrath (*Aes.* 266); Ach. Tat. 2.21, *fab. aes.* 292 Hausrath (*Aes.* 259); Them. *Or.* 32, 359d, Stob. 3.1.122 (*Aes.* 430).

[20] *Τὸν μῦθον πρῶτον ἀξιοῦσι προσάγειν τοῖς νέοις, διότι τὰς ψυχὰς αὐτῶν πρὸς τὸ βέλτιον ῥυθμίζειν δύναται· ἔτι οὖν αὐτοὺς ἁπαλοὺς ὄντας ἀξιοῦσι πλάττειν.* Baldwin's translation (1928, 23-4) of *μῦθος* by 'myth' is unfortunate.

does not make any direct statement on the nature of fable characters. His examples, however, can be analysed. They are threefold. First, Hermogenes refers to two archaic animal fables by mentioning their respective authors and one of their protagonists: Hesiod's Nightingale and Archilochus' Fox. To these Priscian (*Praeex.* 1) adds an allusion to Horace's (Country or City) Mouse (*S.* 2.6.79-117; *Aes.* 352) in his Latin translation of Hermogenes. It is unclear to *which* Archilochean fox fable Hermogenes (and Priscian) are referring, the one in which the fox was outfoxed by the eagle or the one in which the fox outsmarted the ape.[21] Then, Hermogenes exemplifies the need for a fabulist to use particular characters to illustrate a particular type of behaviour: use a peacock to depict someone involved in a beauty contest, a fox for a smart number, and apes for apers. These examples again show a stock characterisation of animals in fables. Finally, Hermogenes seems to have been more considerate towards his pupils than Theon, for he reduces the latter's nine exercises to two, consisting in elaborating and reducing a fable. This *gymnasma* is exemplified by two versions of one fable, which show that the use of direct speech is the major device to elaborate fables. Hermogenes' example is about apes who are dissuaded by an aged congener from building a city (*Aes.* 464). The old age of a wise counsellor is typical in fables.[22] Prima facie, rational characters are totally absent from Hermogenes' examples. However, human beings do play a part, though somewhat distantly and indirectly, in the elaborated version of the ape fable: the apes compare themselves to mankind, and it is from this that their wish to found a city originates—men have houses, assemblies and theaters, so why not apes? This goes beyond the common anthropomorphism of animal characters in fables.

---

[21] Archil. fr. 172-181 (*Aes.* 1) and 185-187 West (*Aes.* 81) respectively. See Huschke 1810, p. ccxxviii.

[22] Cf. e.g. Babr. 21 (*Aes.* 290); Aphth. 23, Nicol. 10 (*Aes.* 138); Phaedr. 3.3 (*Aes.* 495); *fab. aes.* 13 Hausrath (*Aes.* 13).

Aphthonius, Progymnasmata *1* (Aes. *T 102)*

A landmark in Post-Aristotelian Fable Theory is Aphthonius' tripartition of fables, which uses characters as a criterion. After having borrowed Theon's definition of the genre, Aphthonius distinguishes fables about human beings, fables about irrational animals, and fables composed of both. He terms these three categories, respectively, rational, moral, and mixed.[23] Lessing[24] criticised the absence of gods and personifications, which, however, probably belong to the rational group; likewise, the moral group is likely to comprise plants and objects. Aphthonius exemplifies moral fables by the classic of the Cicada*s* and the Ant*s* (*Aes.* 373)—varying a particular theme by changing the grammatical number of the protagonists is common in fables (Van Dijk 1994). This example opens Aphthonius' (like La Fontaine's) private small fable collection, in which moral and mixed fables amply outnumber the rational category.[25] Byzantine scholiasts (see Kustas 1973, 23-6) add examples of the other two categories: thus, Doxapater and John of Sardes paraphrase the aforesaid fable of the Old Man dismissing Death,[26] to which Doxapater adds the fable of the middle-aged man who had two mistresses and went bald through their fault, because the younger pulled out his grey hairs and the older his young hairs (*Aes.* 31). These are examples of rational fables; however, Doxapater's substitution of the middle-aged man by an old man is somewhat irrational because the old woman is likely to be idle (Van Dijk 1994). Besides, Doxapater and John of Sardes add an allusion to the

---

[23] Τοῦ δὲ μύθου τὸ μέν ἐστι λογικόν, τὸ δὲ ἠθικόν, τὸ δὲ μικτόν· καὶ λογικὸν μέν, ἐν ᾧ τι ποιῶν ἄνθρωπος πέπλασται, ἠθικὸν δὲ τὸ τῶν ἀλόγων ἦθος ἀπομιμούμενον, μικτὸν δὲ τὸ ἐξ ἀμφοτέρων, ἀλόγου καὶ λογικοῦ. Nadeau (1952, 265) terms the first category 'verbal'.

[24] Lessing 1759, 117: '...wo bleiben diejenigen Fabeln, die aus Gottheiten und allegorische Personen bestehen?'

[25] Rational: 6. Moral: 1, 3, 8-9, 11-2, 16-7, 21-5, 28-9, 35-7, 40. Mixed: 2, 4-5, 7, 10, 13-5, 18-20, 26-7, 30-4, 38-9.

[26] Doxap. *in Aphth. Prog.* 2.173 Walz; Jo.Sard. *in Aphth. Prog.* 1.11 (p. 8 Rabe); *Aes.* 60.

sad fable of the race horse ending his days in the service of a miller to exemplify Aphthonius' mixed category.[27] Rather stylishly, Doxapater compares the way in which this category is composed of the other two to the way in which a mule is a crossbreed of a horse and an ass (2.169 Walz).

Sopater Rhetor Progymnasmata

Byzantine scholiasts on the chapter on fable from the *Progymnasmata* by Aphthonius have transmitted fragments from those by Sopater. Sopater rewords and elaborates Theon's definition, without adding any remark on fable characters. Sopater seems to equate fable and animal fable when reporting that a fabulist can make his fables reliable by keeping to 'the nature or reputation of each *animal*', which is exemplified by a lion, who is royal, a fox, who is wicked, and a stag, who is coward and silly. However, to exemplify the illustrative and hortatory functions of fables, Sopater subsequently alludes to four fables, two (perhaps even three) of which combine animals with human beings: the aforesaid dog with the piece of meat; the lion who fell in love with a girl and naively (and fatefully) complied with his future father-in-law's malicious request to have his teeth and claws extracted lest he bruise his supposed fiancee's skin (*Aes.* 140); the fowler who judged a cicada by the sound it produced and thought it a good catch;[28] and the Ass in the Lion's Skin, in many versions of which human beings (farmers, shepherds, children) occur to chase off or, even worse, club to death the exposed impostor (*Aes.* 188, 358). Sopater's very examples show that the characterisation of animals in fables is not as stereotypic as he stated a few lines before: the lion's behaviour is not exactly regal.

---

[27] Doxap. *in Aphth. Prog.* 2.173 Walz, Jo.Sard. *in Aphth. Prog.* 1.14 (p. 9 Rabe; both absent from Adrados 1987, 341); Babr. 29, Aphth. 13 (*fab. aes.* 320 Hausrath; *Aes.* 318); cf. Phaedr. *App.* 21 (*Aes.* 549).

[28] Aphth. 4 (*fab. aes.* 316 Hausrath; *Aes.* 397).

Nicolaus, Progymnasmata *1 (cf.* Aes. *T 104)*

Nicolaus is the last author of *Progymnasmata* which contain a chapter on fable to be discussed here. Nicolaus opens his lengthy chapter with a slight elaboration of Theon's definition of the genre. Curiously enough, Priscian's Latin translation of Hermogenes starts with Nicolaus' version of Theon's definition. Although the constitution of the text calls for some prudence, it is nevertheless clear that in the next paragraph Nicolaus is doing something which Theon had condemned firmly: assigning particular kinds of characters to particular kinds of fables. Sybaritic fables, says Nicolaus, have only rational characters, Lydian and Phrygian fables only irrational characters. These, and similar, restrictions[29] meet with two principal objections. First, they are supported by too little evidence, if any: there are only two extant specimens of Sybaritic fables—those told by Philocleon in Aristophanes' *Wasps*[30]—, whereas examples of Lydian and Phrygian fables are simply lacking.[31] Secondly, even these few examples are not in perfect accordance with Nicolaus' restriction: in one Sybaritic fable an anthropomorphised object occurs (just like in Aesopic fables).[32] Therefore, Theon's policy on this subject remains preferable. On the other hand, Nicolaus admits both irrational and rational characters in Aesopic fables. He adds that some theorists discriminate between fables (*μῦθοι*) and myths about the gods, which they term *μυθικὰ διηγήματα*. It is unclear whether or not Nicolaus endorses this distinction. Next, like Hermogenes and Sopater, Nicolaus stresses the required plausibility of fables, which can be achieved in four ways: by depicting the animal

---

[29] Nicol. *Prog.* 1 (p. 7 Felten): *εἰσὶ δὲ οἱ <μὲν> Συβαριτικοὶ <οἱ ἐκ μόνων λογικῶν ζῴων, Αἰσώπειοι δὲ> οἱ ἐξ ἀλόγων καὶ λογικῶν συγκείμενοι, Λύδιοι δὲ καὶ Φρύγιοι οἱ ἐκ μόνων ἀλόγων*. Cf. Schol. in Ar. *Av.* 471 (*Aes.* T 5); Isid. *Etym.* 1.40 (cf. *Aes.* T 64).

[30] 1427-32 (*Aes.* 428); 1435-40 (*Aes.* 438).

[31] Contra Keller 1861-67, 350-61. Cf. Hausrath 1909, col. 1719-23; West 1984, 114-6.

[32] Ar. *V.* 1436 ἐχῖνος 'pot' (not 'tortue' (contra Nøjgaard 1964, 457)); Adrados 1979, 30.

characters in their natural (1) habitats and (2) seasons and attributing natural (3) words and (4) acts to them. The two devices last mentioned are exemplified in chiastic order: a mouse must not be said to aspire to kingship, nor a lion to be caught by the smell of cheese; a fox must speak cleverly, and sheep must talk nonsense. Nicolaus goes on: a fabulist may have an eagle, but not a jackdaw, carry off fawns and lambs. Should a fabulist feel obliged to deviate from what is natural, say, when sheep talk friendly with wolves, this has to be arranged before and explained in the fable itself. Nicolaus' last two examples are not as absurd as the first two: there *are* fables about a jackdaw imitating an eagle[33] and about sheep negotiating on peace with wolves.[34] Not surprisingly, in view of the aforesaid predominance of the motif of the immutability of nature, neither deviation from nature proves to be successful. Nicolaus' mentioning eight different animal species could, on the face of it, suggest that he thinks of fable as animal fable. The penultimate sentence of the chapter, however, subtly but unmistakably shows once again that he is not. Nicolaus prescribes that fables should be told in a simple and natural style, which matches the characters, '*especially when*'[35] it is an animal fable.

2.3 Oratorical prose

Maximus of Tyre, Oratio *32.1 (cf.* Aes. *T 4 ?)*
Beside the chapters on fable in the *Progymnasmata* discussed above, general remarks on fable characters occasionally occur in orations, in

---

[33] Babr. 137; *fab. aes.* 2 Hausrath; Aphth. 19; *Pa. Bodl.* 110 Knöll; Ign. Diac. 1.55 (*Aes.* 2); in Synt. 9 the jackdaw is replaced by a raven.

[34] Babr. 93, Vit. Aesop. 97GW (Van Dijk 1995), Aphth. 21 (Nicol. 5), Lib. *Prog.* 1.1, *fab. aes.* 158 Hausrath, Rom. 63 Thiele, *Pa. Bodl.* 80 Knöll (*Aes.* 153).

[35] *Prog.* 1 (p. 11 Felten): ..., *ὥστε ... τὰ λεγόμενα μὴ μείζω τῆς τῶν ὑποκειμένων προσώπων ποιότητος φαίνεσθαι, καὶ μάλιστα ὅταν ἐξ ἀλόγων ζῴων ὁ μῦθος ὑπάρχῃ συγκείμενος*. To attribute causal force to *ὅταν* (cf. LSJ s.v.) is inconsistent with Nicolaus' restrictions discussed above.

connection with a particular embedded fable. Thus, Maximus of Tyre opens his treatise *On pleasure* by reporting that 'Aesop ... represents in a fable modes of life of animals and their conversations; in Aesop, even the trees and the fishes talk, the one with the other and pell-mell with humans'.[36] Thus, Maximus mentions, to apply Aphthonius' classification discussed above (1.2.3) *avant la lettre*, moral and mixed fables. The subsequent fable comes under the latter heading and comprises a parenthesis on the immutably smart nature of the fox in fables. In this case, the fox blames a shepherd who had feigned to protect a stag, his refugee, against a lion but tried to betray him by sign language. It might be noted here that Maximus suggests that the fable might have been used by Epicurus to depict men who feign to repudiate pleasure while secretly longing for it.[37]

Himerius, Oratio *66*

Himerius, when narrating a lengthy fable about gods and mountains (*Aes.* 432), inserts two parentheses in which the occurrence of these characters in Aesop's fables is defended by comparing, and preferring, fables to epics: as to the gods,[38] Aesop paints a nobler, and therefore more trustworthy, picture of them than, alas, Homer does; regarding mountains, if we allow Hesiod (*Th.* 22-3; cf. Him. *Or.* 47.9) to have the Helicon make poets out of shepherds, Aesop must not be denied the right to grant it the faculty of speech.

---

[36] Αἰσώπῳ τῷ Φρυγὶ πεποίηνται λόγῳ δίαιται θηρίων καὶ συνουσίαι· διαλέγεται δὲ αὐτῷ καὶ τὰ δένδρα, καὶ οἱ ἰχθύες, ἄλλο ἄλλῳ καὶ ἀνθρώπων ἀναμίξ (p. 367 Hobein).

[37] Maximus' vagueness perhaps explains the absence of the passage under consideration from modern editions of the fragments of Epicurus (Van Dijk 1993d, 30).

[38] *Or.* 66.4 (p. 235 Colonna): παρακαλεῖ γὰρ καὶ θεοὺς αὐτοὺς ἐπὶ τὸν μῦθον ὁ Αἴσωπος καὶ εἰς οὐρανοὺς ἀναβιβάζει τὸν ἔλεγχον· ...

Themistius, Oratio *22, 278c*

Themistius observes that in Aesop's fables the fox always tricks stronger animals, as is exemplified by his subsequent beast fable (278d-279a; *Aes.* 372), in which a fox serves a ravenous lion well by driving apart two bulls. The obvious conclusion that Themistius considers fables animal fables is refuted by other fables of his ascribed to Aesop, in which gods and human beings[39] occur, often even exclusively.

2.4 Second Sophistic

Philostratus, Imagines *1.3 (*Aes. *T 52)*

Remarks on fable characters can occasionally be found in writings from the so-called second sophistic movement, which may be discussed here, following on the rhetorical and oratorical prose. Philostratus' *ἔκφρασις* of an allegorical painting unmistakably witnesses the presence of human characters in fables: '... the painting is clever in representing the persons of the Fables. For it combines animals with men to make a chorus about Aesop, composed of the actors in his fables' (Fairbanks 1931, 13).[40] Previously, Philostratus had remarked that Aesop grants animals the faculty of speech (λόγος) 'in order to point a moral' (λόγος; Fairbanks 1931, 12).[41] This play with the polysemy of *λόγος* is somehow reminiscent of the ambiguity of *μῦθος* in Theon discussed before. Philostratus exemplifies animal characters by mentioning lion, fox, horse, and tortoise. Obviously, the first two are typical protagonists in fables, which is—at least, regarding one of them—also apparent from Philostratus'

---

[39] Only gods: *Or.* 16, 208a (*Aes.* 46). Only human beings: *Or.* 21, 262b (*Aes.* 266); *Or.* 32, 359bc (quoted by Stob. 3.1.122; *Aes.* 393). Only gods and human beings *Or.* 32, 359d (quoted by Stob. *ib.*; *Aes.* 430). Human beings and animals: *Or.* 21, 245ab (*Aes.* 358).

[40] *Φιλοσοφεῖ δὲ ἡ γραφὴ καὶ τὰ τῶν μύθων σώματα, θηρία γὰρ συμβάλλουσα ἀνθρώποις περιίστησι χορὸν τῷ* Αἰσώπῳ *ἀπὸ τῆς ἐκείνου σκηνῆς συμπλάσασα.*

[41] ... λόγου *τοῖς θηρίοις μεταδέδωκε* [sc. Αἴσωπος] λόγου *ἕνεκεν.*

ἔκφρασις: '... the fox is painted as leader of the chorus, since Aesop uses him as a slave in developing most of his themes ...' (Fairbanks 1931, 13).[42] The last couple of Philostratus' examples, however, are less typical. It is tempting, but speculative, to assume that Philostratus is here alluding to a common, but less felicitous (because less paradoxical) variant of a widespread fable, in which a horse, not a tortoise, beats a hare.[43] Supposing that this assumption is reasonable, one might be inclined to believe that Philostratus is at the same time alluding at a *particular* fox-lion fable, just as he (or another Philostratus) does elsewhere.[44]

Philostratus, Vita Apollonii *5.14-6 (cf.* Aes. *T 62, 100, 105)*

Philostratus' namesake confronts Menippus and Apollonius, reviling and adoring Aesop, respectively, when comparing fable and myth. It is curious that both opponents fight with the same arguments. One of these consists in the occurrence of animal characters in fables. Menippus exemplifies these by frogs and asses. These examples can be taken to express his disdain of the genre because in fables neither usually plays the hero's part.[45] Menippus, however—much to the present writer's relief—, is silenced by Apollonius, who, among other things, argues that fables evoke respect for animals by showing the regal, naive, smart, and guileless character traits of each species. A comparison with the *Progymnasmata* (and the fables themselves) shows that the first three epithets probably belong to lions, sheep, and foxes, respectively, but the prov-

---

[42] ... *κορυφαία δὲ τοῦ χοροῦ ἡ ἀλώπηξ γέγραπται, χρῆται γὰρ αὐτῇ ὁ Αἴσωπος διακόνῳ τῶν πλείστων ὑποθέσεων, ...*

[43] Tortoise: e.g. *fab. aes.* 254 Hausrath (*Aes.* 226); horse: e.g. Lib. *Prog.* 1.2; Adrados 1987, 242-3.

[44] *VA* 7.30 (*Aes.* 142). For the ascription of the different works to the Philostrati, see e.g. Anderson 1986, 291-7.

[45] Frogs: e.g. *Aes.* 138. Ass: e.g. *Aes.* 91. Ass and Frogs: *Aes.* 189.

enance of the fourth one is uncertain.[46] Apollonius' argument does not legitimate the conclusion that he equates fable and animal fable, although Menippus may. For Apollonius subsequently relates how Hermes granted Aesop the art of fable-telling (μυθολογία) because, on the one hand, he had already distributed all other arts and, on the other, retained good memories of the genre since a *fable*, in which a cow talked to a man, incited him to steal Apollo's cattle. This aetiology is noteworthy because it is a fable about fable in more than one sense: the fable is about the origin of fable—it could be termed an autoreflective fable—, and the larger fable serves as a frame for the inner fable;[47] this occurrence of a fable-within-a-fable is unique in Greek (if not in Indian)[48] literature. On a different level, it might be noted that the special meaning of the compound μυθολογία is not included in LSJ.

3. Paroemiography

3.1 Paroemiographers

Luci(ll)us Tarrhaeus fr. 1 Linnenkugel

Because of the close, but problematical, relationship between proverbs and fables,[49] some paroemiographers discuss fable in the prefaces to their collections of proverbs. Thus, Pseudo-Ammonius and Eustathius

---

[46] βασιλικός: cf. Sopat. Rh. *Prog. ap.* Jo. Sard. in Aphth. *Prog.* 1.6 (p. 6 Rabe); εὐήθης: cf. *ib.* 1.13 (p. 9 Rabe); κομψός: cf. other epithets of the fox in fables: πανουργός (Jo. Sard. *ib.*; Attic. fr. 2 Des Places *ap.* Eus. *PE* 15.4.4-5), δριμύς (Attic. *ib.*), σοφός (Max. Tyr. 32.1; see above), δολερός (Them. *Or.* 22, 278c; see above, under 1.3.3), ποικίλος (e.g. Pl. *R.* 365c; Opitz 1891, 19), κερδαλέος (Pl. *ib.*; Archil. fr. 185 West) and, of course, κερδώ (e.g. Babr. 19.3); in the fable collections ἀκέραιος occurs only in *fab. aes.* 107.15, Aphth. 25.8, and 36.8 Hausrath, where it is applied to man, a crane's head, and reed, respectively.

[47] Neither is listed as fable in *Aes.*, but see Van Dijk 1994.

[48] Kalilah wa Dimnah, translated into Greek by Simeon Seth, ed. Sjöberg 1962.

[49] Cf. Quint. 5.11.21 and see e.g. the papers collected by Carnes 1988.

have preserved Luci(ll)us Tarrhaeus' definition of fable in which he confines its characters to animals and plants.[50] Luci(ll)us subsequently exemplifies these two subgenres by quotations of the incipits of the oldest extant Greek animal and plant fables, the former by Hesiod's only and both of Archilochus' animal fables referred to above (1.2.2), the latter by Callimachus' plant fable in which a bramble ventures to intervene in a dispute between a laurel and an olive tree (*Iamb.* 4, fr. 194 Pfeiffer; *Aes.* 439).

Pseudo-Diogenian Praefatio *(cf.* Aes. *T 85, 89)*

In the preface to his collection of proverbs, Pseudo-Diogenian seems to just borrow Luci(ll)us Tarrhaeus' definition and examples, although he omits the citation from Hesiod. However, there is more to it. First, Pseudo-Diogenian, like Theon, flatly turns down the existence of any difference between the various geographical fable variants: 'they are different in name, but similar in meaning'.[51] Curiously enough, however, all but one of the paroemiographer's subsequent examples of these indigenous variants have human characters, one of them even exclusively, which is in flagrant contradiction to his previous restriction of fable characters to animals and plants. All examples are from archaic and classical poets, from Timocreon and an *epinikion* by Simonides the Carian fisherman's dilemma to dive or not to dive for an octopus, from Aristophanes' *Wasps*[52] the unhorsed Sybaritic horseman derided by a friend, again from Timocreon the Cypriots' pigeons literally flying out of the

[50] Fr. 1 Linnenkugel *ap.* Ps.-Ammon. *Diff.* p. 18 Nickau; Eust. *Il.* 11.430 (855.3), *Od.* 14.508 (1768.58): ... *ὁ μὲν αἶνος λόγος ἐστὶ μυθικὸς ἐκφερόμενος ἀπὸ ἀλόγων ζῴων ἢ φυτῶν πρὸς ἀνθρώπων παραίνεσιν.*

[51] Οἱ *δ' ἄλλοι τῶν κατειλεγμένων ὀνόματι μὲν διαφέρειν, δυνάμει δ' εἰσὶν ἐμφερεῖς*. For the constitution of the text, see Leutsch - Schneidewin (*CPG* 1.179).

[52] The examples of the Sybaritic and Cyprian fable from Aristophanes and Timocreon, respectively, by Anon. Περὶ *αἴνου* (*PSI* 1221) might be part of a lost treatise on fable and proverb similar to Pseudo-Diogenian's *Preface*; see Bartoletti *ad loc.*

frying pan into the fire, and from Aeschylus the Lybian fable of the eagle hit by an arrow equipped with its own wings.[53]

3.2 Grammarians

Herennius Philo. fr. 32 Palmieri
Some grammarians discuss fable and proverb under one heading in their lexicons of synonyms and antonyms. Thus, again according to Pseudo-Ammonius and Eustathius, Herennius Philo borrows both Luci(ll)us Tarrhaeus' definition and his examples.

(Pseudo-?)Ptolemaeus Ascalonita. s.v. αἶνος καὶ παροιμία
Like Herennius Philo, Ptolemaeus borrows Luci(ll)us' definition discussed above (2.1.1), but, unlike Herennius, not his examples.

4. Philosophy and science

4.1 Philosophy
Plutarch 152d, 162b-c, 871d
Stray remarks on fable characters occur also in philosophical and related literature. Thus, Plutarch three times refers to Aesop's fables by mentioning two animal species. These three passages can best be discussed together. In the *Banquet of the Seven Sages* (*Mor.* 152d) Aesop, who is a guest at the symposium, is said by Solon, with a ring of mockery, to be 'clever in understanding ravens and jackdaws' (Babbitt 1928, 383). Later on (162b-c), Aesop defends himself against Solon's mockery by comparing the dolphin who could speak to Arion. In another treatise, *On the Malice of Herodotus* (*Mor.* 871d), Plutarch compares the way in which the challenged historiographer uses various barbarians as his mouthpieces to the way in which Aesop uses 'ravens and apes'. These passages do not prove that according to Plutarch Aesop's fables are always animal fables,

---

[53] Timocr. fr. 8 *PMG*, Simon. fr. 9 *PMG* (*Aes.* 425); Ar. *V.* 1427-32 (*Aes.* 428); Timocr. fr. 4 *PMG* (not in *Aes.*, nor in Van Dijk 1994); A. fr. 139 Radt (*Aes.* 276a; see Van Dijk 1993b).

since elsewhere in his *Moralia* Plutarch ascribes two fables which have only gods as characters to Aesop,[54] whereas human characters occur in a fable narrated by Aesop, nota bene in the *Banquet* (*Mor.* 156a; *Aes.* 453).

4.2 Oneirocritic

Synesius, De Insomniis *19, 154d-155a*

Synesius derives the faculty of speech granted to the characters in fables from dreams. He exemplifies these by a peacock, a fox, and the sea.[55] The first two examples are the same as Hermogenes', the third constitutes the only extant mention of the possibility that elements are fable characters (beside Himerius' Helicon). It is true that the sea speaks in only one extant fable, but of course it is only a guess that Synesius has this particular fable on his mind.[56] If so, he implicitly admits human characters in fables too, since in this particular fable the sea addresses a farmer (or a shipwrecked sailor).

5. Fabulists

5.1 Babrius

Prooemium *1* (Aes. *T 95)*

Some programmatical passages, not to mention the fables themselves, in the fable collections deal with the characters of the genre. In the proem to the first volume of his fable collection Babrius describes the paradisaical condition of the Golden Age reflected in Aesop's fables. Babrius' description shows that the characters in Aesop's fables are heterogeneous: 'Even the pine tree talked, and the leaves of the laurel. The fish swimming

---

[54] 609f (*Aes.* 462; absent from Adrados 1987, 392; elsewhere (*Mor.* 111f-112b) Plutarch relates the same fable without mentioning Aesop), 645b (*Aes.* 100).

[55] *'Εγὼ μὲν γὰρ οἶμαι καὶ τοὺς μύθους ἐξουσίαν παρὰ τῶν ἐνυπνίων λαβεῖν, οἷς καὶ ταῶς καὶ ἀλώπηξ καὶ θάλαττα φθέγγονται.*

[56] Farmer: Babr. 71, *Pa. Bodl.* 54 Knöll; shipwrecked sailor: *fab. aes.* 178 Hausrath (*Aes.* 168); cf. *fab. aes.* 223 Hausrath (*Aes.* 207).

about in the sea chatted with the friendly sailor, and quite intelligibly, too, the sparrows conversed with the farmer ... and good fellowship prevailed between gods and mortals.' (Perry 1965, 3).[57] Thus the Bouriant papyrus. The Athos Codex, among other things, replaces the pine with a rock and adds a ship as interlocutor of the fish. These variant readings constitute the only extant mentions of inanimate objects as fable characters in Greek literature.[58]

119.11-12

The epimythium of a Babrian fable (*Aes.* 285) about a pious craftsman who dashed an ungrateful Hermes idol to pieces and was astonished to find a hidden treasure, observes that 'Aesop brings even the gods into his fables in the course of cautioning us one against another' (Perry 1965, 157).[59]

These final choliambs constitute the last passage to be discussed in this paper. In the end, this paper thus appears not to have started with the fables but ended with them.

To conclude in a brief epimythium, only few of the above theoretical testimonies (Paroemiographers and Grammarians) confine fable characters to animals and plants; one of these is contradicted by his very examples

[57] 1.*Prooem.* 9-16: ἐλάλει δὲ πεύκη καὶ τὰ φύλλα τῆς δάφνης, | καὶ πλωτὸς ἰχθὺς συνελάλει φίλῳ ναύτῃ, | στρουθοὶ δὲ συνετὰ πρὸς γεωργὸν ὡμίλουν. | ... | θνήτων δ' ὑπῆρχε καὶ θεῶν ἑταιρείη. | μάθοις ἂν οὕτω ταῦτ' ἔχοντα καὶ γνοίης | ἐκ τοῦ σόφου γέροντος ἡμῖν Αἰσώπου | μύθους φράσαντος ... Perry (1965, 2) prints the text of *P.Bour.* 1., whereas Jagoda Luzzatto-La Penna (1986, 2) prefer the text of *Cod. Athous Mus. Brit. Addit.* 22087: 9 πέτρῃ, 10 νηί; on 14-16, see Vaio 1982.

[58] Besides, in Latin literature: Aug. *c. mend. ad Consent.* 28; Isid. *Etym.* 1.40 (*Aes.* T 64).

[59] Καὶ τοὺς θεοὺς Αἴσωπος ἐμπλέκει μύθοις, | βουλόμενος ἡμᾶς νουθετεῖν πρὸς ἀλλήλους. The authenticity of the epimythium is vindicated by Hohmann 1907, 83. Nevertheless, it is bracketed by Perry (1965, 156), but not by Jagoda Luzzatto-La Penna (1986, 118; see the apparatus criticus ad loc.).

(Pseudo-Diogenian). Attempts to extend this minority by interpreting others (Themistius, Plutarch) to imply a similar restriction are unsuccessful. Elements (Himerius, Synesius) and objects (Babrius var. lect. *bis*) are each mentioned only twice as fable characters. Most theoretical testimonies either explicitly (Theon, Aphthonius, Nicolaus, Maximus, Himerius, Philostratus *Im.*, Babrius) or implicitly (Aristotle, Hermogenes, Sopater, Philostratus *VA*, Synesius?) allow rational fable characters too. Their point of view is recommended by the Aesopic tradition.

BIBLIOGRAPHY

Adrados, F.R., *Historia de la fábula greco-latina*, I: *Introducción y de los orígenes a la edad helenística*. Madrid 1979.

———, III: *Inventario y documentación de la fábula greco-latina*. Madrid 1987.

Anderson, G., *Philostratus*. London - Sydney - Dover, N.H. 1986.

Babbitt, F.C., *Plutarch's Moralia*, II, London - Cambridge, MA 1928.

Baldwin, C.S., *Medieval Rhetoric and Poetic*. New York 1928.

Blackham, H.J., *The Fable as Literature*. London - Dover 1985.

Carnes, P. (ed.), *Proverbia in Fabula. Essays on the Relationship of the Proverb and the Fable*. Bern - Frankfurt am Main etc. 1988.

Clark, D.L., *Rhetoric in Greco-Roman Education*. New York 1957.

Crusius, O., Aus der Geschichte der Fabel, in: C.H. Kleukens (ed.), *Das Buch der Fabeln*. Leipzig 1913, i-lxiii.

Dijk, J.G.M. van, Fables in Ancient Historiography, *Bestia* 5 (1993), 27-42. [1993a]

———, Intertextualiteit in de Griekse literatuur. De functie van een fabel van Aeschylus tot Eustathius, *Kleio* 22 (1993), 141-57. [1993b]

———, Theory and Terminology of the Greek Fable, *Reinardus* 6 (1993), 171-83. [1993c]

———, De theorie van de fabel in de Griekse Oudheid, in: W.L. Idema et al. (eds.), *Mijn naam is haas. Dierenverhalen in verschillende culturen*. Baarn 1993, 22-36. [1993d]

———, *Addenda ad Aesopica.* Unnoticed and Neglected Themes and Variations of Greek and Latin Fables, *Bestia* 6 (1994), forthc.

———, The Fables in the Greek *Life of Aesop*, *Reinardus* 8 (1995), forthc.

Dithmar, R., *Die Fabel. Geschichte. Struktur. Didaktik.* Paderborn 1984^6.

Dodsley, R., *An Essay on Fable.* Birmingham 1764 (repr. Los Angeles 1965).

Dover, K.J., Aristophanes' Speech in Plato's *Symposium*, *JHS* 86 (1966), 41-50.

Fairbanks, A., *Philostratus, Imagines.* London - Cambridge, MA 1931.

García Gual, C., Acerca de las fábulas griegas como género literario, in: P. Bádenas de la Peña - J. López Facal (eds.), *Fábulas de Esopo. Vida de Esopo. Fábulas de Babrio.* Madrid 1978, 7-26.

Γεωργοπαπαδάκος, A. et al., Τό *μεγάλο λεξικό της νεοελληνικής γλώσσας μονοτονικό.* Athina 1990^5.

Handford, S.A., *Fables of Aesop.* Melbourne - London - Baltimore 1964.

Hanks, P. et al. (eds.), *Collin's Dictionary of the English Language.* London - Glasgow 1986^2.

Hausrath, A., Fabel, Pauly - Wissowa, *Realenzyklopädie* 6.2 (1909), 1704-36.

Hohmann, E., *De indole atque auctoritate epimythiorum Babrianorum.* Diss. Königsberg 1907.

Huschke, I.G., Dissertatio de fabulis Archilochi, in: F. de Furia (ed.), *Fabulae Aesopicae quales ante Planudem ferebantur....* Lipsiae 1810, cciv-ccl.

Jagoda Luzzatto, M. - La Penna, A., *Babrii Mythiambi Aesopei.* Leipzig 1986.

Josifovic, S., Aisopos und die Aisopische Fabel, in: Pauly - Wissowa, *Realenzyklopädie*, Suppl. 14, 15-40.

Karadagli, T., *Fabel und Ainos: Studien zur griechischen Fabel.* Diss. Königstein 1981.

Keller, O., Untersuchungen über die Geschichte der griechischen Fabel, *NJPhP* Suppl. 4 (1861-67), 307-418.

Kustas, G.L., *Studies in Byzantine Rhetoric.* Thessaloniki 1973.

La Fontaine, J. de, Préface, *Fables.* Paris 1668. (ed. J. Giraudoux - J. Lupin. Paris 1964, 33-8)

Lessing, G.E., *Abhandlungen über die Fabel.* Berlin 1759. (ed. H. Rölleke. Stuttgart 1987)

Leibfried, E., *Fabel.* Stuttgart 1982^4.

———, *Fabel.* Bamberg 1989.

Lindner, H., *Fabeln der Neuzeit. England, Frankreich, Deutschland.* München 1978.

Looij, M., *Van fabeldier tot wrekend beest.* Utrecht 1988.

McMahon, A.L., *The Origin of the Fable and its Development in Classical Literature*. Diss. Lincoln, NE 1927.

Meuli, K., Herkunft und Wesen der Fabel, *Schweizerisches Archiv für Volkskunde* 50 (1954), 65-88.

Nadeau, R., The Progymnasmata of Aphthonius in Translation, *Speech Monographs* 19 (1952), 264-85.

Nøjgaard, M., Le cerf, le cheval et l'homme. Étude sur la transmission des fables antiques, *C&M* 24 (1963), 1-19.

———, *La fable antique*, I: *La fable grecque avant Phèdre*, København 1964.

Opitz R., Über den 'Weiberspiegel' des Semonides von Amorgos, *Philologus* 50 (1891), 13-30.

Perry, B.E. (ed.), *Aesopica*, I: *Greek and Latin Texts*. Urbana, IL 1952.

———, Fable, *Studium Generale* 12 (1959), 17-37.

———, *Babrius and Phaedrus*. London - Cambridge, MA 1965.

Reche Martínez, M.D., *Teón, Hermógenes, Aftonio. Ejercicios de retórica*. Madrid 1991.

Reichel, G., *Quaestiones progymnasmaticae*. Diss. Leipzig 1909.

Rooijen-Dijkman, H.W.A. van, Fabels: tot nut en vermaak, *Hermeneus* 56, 1984, 6-15.

Schwarzbaum, H., The Vision of Eternal Peace in the Animal Kingdom (AA-Th 62), *Fabula* 10 (1969), 107-31.

Sjöberg, L.-O., *Stephanites und Ichnelates*. Stockholm - Göteborg - Uppsala 1962.

Vaio, J., The First Prologue of Babrius: Lines 14-16, *ICS* 7 (1982), 233-8.

West, M.L., The Ascription of Fables to Aesop in Archaic and Classical Greece, in: F.R. Adrados (ed.), *La Fable*, Genève 1984, 105-36. Wilamowitz-Möllendorff, U. von, Phaidon von Elis, *Hermes* 14 (1879), 187-93, 476-7.

Menander Rhetor on Hymns

J.M. Bremer

1. Introduction

Two personal remarks by way of introduction. First: that I have known and appreciated D.M. Schenkeveld since about 35 years. Having read Classics at the same time in Amsterdam at two different universities, we share many experiences: first as undergraduates, then as teachers—first in secondary school and then at our several universities. It is a privilege to have been his *collega proximus* for so long. Second: that my interest for the topic of this paper stems from my current research. Together with William Furley of Heidelberg University, I am preparing a book which will be entitled *Greek Hymns*; this book will offer a substantial selection from Greek religious poetry with a commentary and accompanying essays.

Epideictic oratory came into its own with Gorgias in the last decades of the 5th century BCE. Before him there was a tradition of speeches commemorating and praising the heroic war-dead (the ἐπιτάφιοι λόγοι). Gorgias wrote a funeral speech himself, but he opened the field for speeches praising mythical personalities (Helen, Palamedes). Plato followed this up with Agathon's praise of Eros in his *Symposion*. Isocrates and Xenophon composed encomiastic obituaries of great kings: Euagoras (± 370) and Agesilaos (± 350). By way of provocation and display some non-conformist prose-writers selected even trivial realities as object of their *enkomia*: did not Polycrates praise 'salt' and 'mice', 'pots' and 'pebbles'? (Radermacher 1952, 130-2).

It is surprising that for more than seven centuries after this 'discovery' of epideictic oratory, prose-writers abstained from devoting their talents to the praising of *gods*. It is not difficult to find an explanation for this fact of literary history. Hymns functioned in the context of religious festivals: their form (poetical) and performance (song, and in some cases dance) was firmly anchored in the oral tradition. Therefore the Greeks felt that the composition of hymns was the exclusive business of poets. There is an indication for the truth of this hypothesis: when in the second half of the second century CE the orator Aristides, propelled by his highly personal religious feelings, started writing prose hymns, he felt the need for an elaborate apology.[1] Sticking to the old adage that attack is the best form of defense, he spent the first four pages of his hymn to Sarapis in criticizing the liberty and irresponsibility of poets in making their hymns, and in justifying his own enterprise. I quote a few phrases from the proem of this speech (45.1-4 Keil). 'Poets behave as if they are tyrants of the themes and subject-matter: *ὥσπερ τύραννοί τινες τῶν νοημάτων ὄντες*' (1). 'There is no limit to their daring and invention': *οὐδὲν αὐτοῖς ἀτόλμητον οὐδ' ἄπορόν ἐστιν* (2). 'When making hymns to the gods they behave as if they were easy-living Olympians themselves': *εὐδαίμονές τε καὶ κατ' αὐτὸν τὸν Ὅμηρον ῥεῖα ζώοντες ἐπειδὰν ποιῶσι τοὺς ὕμνους καὶ παιᾶνας τοῖς θεοῖς* (3). 'In our naiveté we respect the poets to the point of abstaining from making hymns ourselves and leaving this task to them as if they were truly the privileged interpreters in relation to the gods': *οὕτω δὲ σφόδρα αὐτοὺς σεμνύνομεν ὥστε καὶ αὐτοὶ τοῦ ποιεῖν τοὺς ὕμνους τούτοις παρακεχωρήκαμεν ὥσπερ προφήταις ὡς ἀληθῶς οὖσι τῶν θεῶν* (4).—Orators, on the other hand, have been trained to say 'the appropriate thing', *τὸ προσῆκον*, and to say it 'in the proper fashion', *ὀρθῶς* (4). Aristides even proclaims that in poetry the power of *measure*, *μέτρον*, 'extends its rule only over the separate lines': *ἐκεῖ μὲν γὰρ τὸ ἔπος ἢ τὸ ἰαμβεῖον μετρεῖ μόνον*, but that 'in oratory it rules over the entire speech': *ἐνταῦθα δὲ ὅλον καταμετρεῖ τὸν λόγον καὶ διὰ παντὸς ὡς ἀληθῶς δίεισιν* (10). And he composed hymns himself, not only to Sarapis, but

[1] This apology was recently discussed by D.A. Russell in his own contribution to Russell 1990, 201-6.

also to Zeus, Poseidon, Athena, Dionysus, Heracles, Asclepius, the Asclepiads and even one to the Aegean Sea!

But Aristides' example was not followed by others. As far as we can see, poets kept dominating the field and went on composing hymns;[2] nothing like a productive tradition of prose hymns did ever develop. Two centuries would pass before another eccentric religious person, the emperor Julian, produced new prose hymns, one addressed to the Sun, another to the Mother of the Gods.

To this marginal position of the *writing* of prose hymns corresponds a marginal position of Hymns in the *rhetorical treatises*. In his *Rhetoric* (1.9) Aristotle defines the *enkomion* as the praise of excellence, excellence being the English equivalent of τὸ καλόν or ἀρετή. And he explains that a presumption of excellence is given in the birth and ancestry of the *laudandus*; certainty about it can be found in his deeds which allow conclusions as to his character and nature (1367b30-3). This simple scheme (γένος, φύσις, ἔργα) might have provided him with a basis for constructing a simple and effective theory of praising the gods. But in Aristotle's *Rhetoric* there is no trace of such a theory.[3]

---

[2] The number of poetical hymns of the second to the fourth century CE which have been preserved is not impressive, Mesomedes being the most fertile poet. But there is some evidence of a continuing production of new poetical hymns for cultic purposes (cf. my observations in Versnel 1981, 201-3).

[3] It is true that in 1366a28-30 Aristotle says συμβαίνει ... ἐπαινεῖν πολλάκις οὐ μόνον ἄνθρωπον <u>ἢ θεὸν</u> ἀλλὰ καὶ ἄψυχα κτλ. but in the rest of this chapter (1.9) he does not at all discuss praise of the gods.

Menander Rhetor is the first to give a full-blown theory[4] about the composition of hymns; at the end of the second treatise he[5] also offers an elaborate specimen of a prose hymn (the Σμινθιακός). Russell and Wilson suggest that he should be dated in the reign of Diocletian; if that is correct,[6] the theoretician comes just about half way between the two practitioners Aristides and the emperor Julian! My contribution to this symposion consists of two complementary parts; first I shall sketch what I think are the most interesting parts of Menander's theory, and then discuss his Σμινθιακός.

2. The theory of writing hymns at the beginning of Menander's first treatise

On the very first page Menander mentions the different *species* of the *genus* hymn: paeans, dithyrambs, hyporchemes etc.[7] But in his own

---

[4] It is true that he has two predecessors, but their contribution is very limited. In his *Institutiones* Quintilian has one paragraph on 'how to praise a god' (3.7.7-9). And in a fragment of a rhetorical treatise by Alexander, son of Numenios, an author who flourished under Hadrian, we find two pages (*Rhet. Graeci* 3.4-5 Spengel) in which he gives a list of items a writer should deal with in praising a god: birth, identity, power, crafts & inventions, location(s).

[5] For the sake of convenience I shall speak about Menander as the one and only author of the two treatises which go under his name. Russell - Wilson 1981 argue that the two parts of the treatise have been written by different authors, but they acknowledge that 'these arguments do not amount to formal proof of different authorship' (p. xxxviii).

[6] Introduction, p. xl. In his review of Russell - Wilson, *Mnemosyne* 37 (1984), 193-9, Schenkeveld argues that *if* the first treatise is by Genethlius (this name is offered as an alternative for Menander in the title of codex P), a date under the reign of Aurelian is more probable.

[7] Russell - Wilson (1981, xxix-xxx) discuss the passage 331.20-37 which contains this classification; they observe that it is forgotten or at least not used in the rest of what M. says; and as this same passage is omitted in M and W, two of the three MSS, they conclude: 'almost certainly it should be deleted'. Even so, one has to take into account that codex P has it. This codex is the venerable

theory he has no use at all for this traditional classification and he comes up with a classification of his own. Why? I suggest the following explanation: the traditional names were deeply rooted in religious worship as it was practised in the archaic period and probably even before that. In their recent monographs Zimmermann (1992) and Käppel (1992) have presented the evidence for this view, and argued that in both cases the 'literarische Gattung' can only be explained in terms of the religious 'Sitz im Leben'. Between the archaic period and the time in which Menander wrote his treatise, almost a millennium had passed, and one can be sure that in this long period the festivals and rituals had changed beyond recognition. There was no 'Sitz im Leben' any more for paeans and dithyrambs; the old names did no longer make sense, except as labels for texts from a period long past which a *γραμματικός* occasionally had to explain to his pupils.

Menander's own classification is a new and functional one. He distinguishes eight different kinds, and offers them in couples (four times *οἱ μέν* ... *οἱ δέ*). Hymns serve either the purpose of invoking and inviting a god (*ὕμνοι κλητικοί*), or of saying farewell to the god when he leaves (*ἀποπεμπτικοί*); either of explaining the nature of the god (*φυσικοί*), or of offering a narrative of his deeds (*μυθικοί*); they present the birth and provenance of the god (*γενεαλογικοί*) or they 'make and posit' the god when an abstract concept is made into a divinity (*πεπλασμένοι*); and finally there are hymns which serve the purpose of praying that something may happen or be granted (*εὐκτικοί*) or of praying that something may *not* happen (*ἀπευκτικοί*).

Menander is too good a teacher to confine himself to such a skeleton: he enlivens his classification by adding an example here and there, such as that *ὕμνοι κλητικοί* are found among the poems of Sappho and Anacreon (333.9), and that Plato, in the series of *enkomia* on Eros in his *Symposion*, gives a genealogical hymn to Phaidros and to Aristophanes a mythological one, while Socrates' speech approaches the type of a *ὕμνος φυσικός* when he explains the essence of Eros, but also shows

---

Parisinus graecus 1741, important for the text of Aristotle's *Poetics* and *Rhetoric*.

traces of a *ὕμνος πεπλασμένος* in the narrative about the birth of Eros from Poros and Penia (334.10-6). And the bulk of his theory is a sketch of the topoi for the different kinds of hymns.

There is another aspect of Menander's theory which is more important than this matter of classification. You will remember that Aristides accused the poets of going too far in using their privilege of liberty. Menander, who is not a proud performer but a practical professor of rhetoric, says simply: *λογιστέον ὡς ἐξ ἐλάττονος ἐξουσίας μέτεστι τῇ συγγραφῇ* (334.21): 'We must be aware that prose enjoys licence to a smaller degree'. What does this 'smaller degree of licence' mean in practice? I shall give two examples of Menander drawing the line for prose-writers. In their *ὕμνοι κλητικοί* poets indulge in enumerating the various locations of the gods, *ὡς παρὰ τῇ Σαπφοῖ καὶ τῷ 'Αλκμᾶνι πολλαχοῦ εὑρίσκομεν. ὁ μὲν γὰρ Ἄρτεμιν ἐκ μυρίων ὀρέων, μυρίων δὲ πόλεων, ἔτι δὲ ποταμῶν ἀνακαλεῖ κτλ* (334.29-30): 'We find this practiced often by Sappho and Alcman. When he[8] summons Artemis to come, he invites her to come from countless mountains and cities and rivers'. And not content with that, poets even takes time to describe all these locations. A well-known example of this poetical practice is the hymn to Dionysus in Sophocles' *Antigone*: the first two stanzas of this song present a list of the various localities of the god, viz. Italy (Icaria?), Eleusis, Thebes, and Delphi. Sophocles describes these sites according to the *Gesetz der wachsenden Glieder*: in 2, 5, 12, and 14 words respectively (1115-30). In this matter of elaborate descriptions Menander is strict: *τοῖς δὲ συγγραφεῦσι βραχυτέραν τὴν περὶ ταῦτα διατριβὴν ἀναγκαῖον γίνεσθαι· οὔτε γὰρ ἐκ πολλῶν τόπων καὶ χωρίων ἀνακαλέσουσιν, οὔτε ἐφ' ἑκάστου μετὰ διαγραφῆς* (335.6-8). 'Prose-writers must necessarily abridge the time spent on these topics: they will not summon

[8] There is a textual problem here on which see Russell - Wilson *ad loc.*—In Sparta the cult of Artemis Orthia was very important, and Alcman will probably have composed hymns in her honour; but in the extant fragments of Alcman one finds no trace of any such elaborate invocation of Artemis. It is strange that the recent editors of testimonia about Alcman (Calame, Campbell, Davies) do not present or refer to this passage in Menander.

divinities from many places and countries, nor give a description of each place'.

Another example of the limited possibilities of prose-writers is the following. Menander acknowledges that 'the freedom of poets to present mythical narratives at leisure and to wrap them up in poetical ornament and elaboration produces no satiety or disgust in the audience': *ἡ ἐξουσία καὶ τοῦ κατὰ σχολὴν λέγειν (τοὺς μύθους) καὶ τοῦ περιστέλλειν τοῖς ποιητικοῖς κόσμοις καὶ ταῖς κατασκευαῖς οὔτε κόρον οὔτε ἀηδίαν παρίστησι*. 'But the possibilities of prose-writers and orators are extremely limited, because myths, when presented nakedly, pain and distress the audience: they should therefore be dispatched as briefly as possible': *συγγραφεῦσι δὲ ἢ λογοποιοῖς ἐλαχίστη ἐξουσία· γυμνοὶ δὲ οἱ μῦθοι τιθέμενοι σφόδρα λυποῦσι καὶ ἐνοχλοῦσι τὰς ἀκοάς. δεῖ τοίνυν ὅτι βραχυτάτοις ἀπαλλάττεσθαι* (338.29-339.3). This statement implies that prose-writers can present mythical narratives only in a naked way, the statute of prose leaving them no room for poetical ornament. Menander goes on to explain how even in these circumstances, i.e. within these professional limitations, a clever prose-writer can present a brief mythical narrative to good effect if he is prepared to follow some rules: *τὰ μὲν παραλείπειν λέγοντα, τὰ δὲ κατὰ συμπλοκὴν εἰσάγειν, τὰ δὲ προσποιεῖσθαι ἐξηγεῖσθαι, τὰ δὲ μὴ πιστεύειν μηδὲ ἀπιστεῖν* (339.6-9): 'in his narration he should omit some elements, and select and combine others; he should adopt the pose of giving a commentary, and of neither believing nor disbelieving the stories he tells'.[9]

A third example of what a poet can allow himself, as opposed to a prose-writer, is found in Menander's discussion of the genalogical hymn. He observes that—although the birth of a god is a frequent element in hymnic praise—there are not many hymns which concentrate on the birth

---

[9] In Greek hymns which were used in cult or composed in a semi-liturgical style, we do not find very extensive narratives. When Menander emphasises here the liberty of poets to compose long narratives, he is perhaps thinking of the Homeric hymns or those composed by Callimachus.—During the discussion S.L. Radt pointed out that Pindar, in his treatment of myth, is as it were following the advice given here by Menander (apart from its last item, the suspension of belief—JMB).

of a god. But sometimes poets have undertaken to do precisely that, and they get away with it (one thinks of course of the famous Homeric hymns to Apollo and Hermes, and Callimachus' hymn to Delos). Menander: *ποιητῇ μὲν καθ' αὐτὸ μόνον τὸ εἶδος χρήσιμον, συγγραφεῖ δὲ οὐδέποτε, ὁ μὲν γὰρ καὶ Χάριτας μαιουμένας καὶ Ὥρας ὑποδεχομένας καὶ τὰ τοιαῦτα πραγματεύεται, ὁ δ' ἐπαναγκὲς ὅτι βραχύτατα ἐρεῖ* (340.19-23): 'This type of hymn, if practiced in isolation from other types, is of use to poets; but to prose-writers never. For it may be the poet's business to present Charites acting as midwives, and Horae as taking care of the baby when it has been born, and so on and so forth; the prose-writer, however, must be as brief as possible'.

According to Menander there is a type of hymn which does offer a wider scope to the prose-writer. That is the *ὕμνος πεπλασμένος*, when by way of fiction, *πλάσις*, something new is offered to the audience, either by the fabrication of a new divinity (often a personification of an abstract concept), or by giving to an existing divinity a new birth-story or a new family tie. This category of Menander is nothing new at all: the Greeks[10] had showed themselves extremely inventive from the beginning, Hesiod's *Theogony* being the most obvious example: this poem brims with abstractions accorded a divine identity and pedigree. Menander here declares for the first time: *ἥκει καὶ αὕτη ἡ ἐξουσία παρὰ τῶν ποιητῶν τοῖς συγγραφεῦσιν* (341.11-2): 'this specific licence comes from the poets to the prose-writers'. Menander points to the Homeric examples of Fear and Panic as sons of the war-god Ares (*Iliad* Λ 37, Ν 299, Ο 119) and of Sleep and Death as twin brothers (Ξ 231 and Π 672); and he proudly adds: *ἤδη δὲ καὶ ἡμεῖς τὸν Λόγον Διὸς ἀδελφὸν ἀνεπλάσαμεν ὡς ἐν ἠθικῇ συνόψει* (341.12-7): 'I myself have invented Logos to be Zeus' own brother as in an ethical synopsis'. Russell - Wilson note: 'We can do little more than raise the question what the allegory means and what the *ἠθικὴ σύνοψις* might be.' But even so it is a telling

---

[10] They were well aware of this tendency: *καινολογία τίς ἐστιν ὁ μῦθος, οὐ τὰ καθεστηκότα φράζων ἀλλ' ἕτερα παρὰ ταῦτα*. Strabo 1.1.19.

example of the direction in which Menander wants to stimulate his pupils and his readers.

A proof of Menander's preference for this type is found in the fact that here he is most detailed in his advice to the would-be writer of hymns (341.18-342.20). The presentation of the new 'theology' should in the first place be all of a piece, and not consist of isolated and disconnected elements: *μὴ ἀπηρτημένως ἀλλὰ συνεχῶς πλάττειν*. To reach that effect, the fiction should not be far-fetched: *πλάσις ... μὴ ἀνακεχωρηκυῖα*. Second, one should make up the story not in a repellent but in a smooth and pleasing fashion: *μὴ ἀηδῶς, ἀλλὰ στωμύλως καὶ γλαφυρῶς ἀναπλάττειν*. It is a symptom of the long distance between the archaic period and Menander when he tells us that the story of Athena's birth from the head of Zeus—one of the most venerable and momentous pieces of *μυθοποιία* of the Greeks!—is such an unpleasant product. He sees the possibility of this story having an allegorical meaning, *ὑπόνοια*,[11] but in itself—he repeats—it is a most unpleasant figment: *ἀηδῶς πέπλασται*. Third: we should create a basis in reality especially for those parts which we make up: *πίστεις λαμβάνειν ἐκ τῶν ἀληθῶν, ἐν οἷς ἂν ψευδώμεθα*. Only in this way will the hymn be acceptable. Again Menander adds that he has given an example of this: *ὡς καὶ ἡμεῖς πεποιήκαμεν* (one can only guess what this may have been). Fourth precept: hymns which offer a 'new construction' should be internally consistent and not contain or imply elements which are mutually exclusive: *ἔτι δὲ καὶ τοὺς πεπλασμένους ὕμνους ἑαυτοῖς εἶναι συμφώνους, καὶ μὴ ἐναντιούμενα ἢ μαχόμενα ἐφέλκεσθαι*.

He concludes this already long section by saying explicitly that this is the most promising way for a prose-writer who wants to write hymns: *χρὴ δὲ εἰδέναι, ὅτι γονιμώτατος καὶ ἐπινοίας ἐστι σημεῖον*

[11] In *SVF* II 908 we find an allegorical interpretation of this myth by Chrysippus.

ὁ τοιοῦτος ὕμνος (342.19-20): 'You should realise that this type of hymn is [for prose-writers] very creative and a sign of inventiveness'.[12]

At the end of his theoretical discussion of hymns, Menander comes back to the fundamental difference between poets and prose-writers as far as the topics and types of hymns are concerned: *τῷ μὲν ποιητῇ ἐξαρκεῖ καὶ μέρος τι ἀπολαβόντι καὶ κατακοσμήσαντι τῇ ποιητικῇ κατασκευῇ πεπαῦσθαι, ὁ δὲ συγγραφεὺς πειράσεται διὰ πάντων ἐλθεῖν. χαριέστατον δὲ τὸ τοιοῦτον μέρος παρέσχηται ἐν τοῖς Μαντικοῖς Ἀριστείδης* (343.30-344.2): 'For a poet it is sufficient to pick and choose one particular part (i.e. a type of hymn, or an element out of the entire range of topics): once he has fitted it out with the poetical apparatus, his task is over and done with. But the prose-writer shall attempt to cover all the ground. In his *Speeches commanded by Prophecy* Aristides has provided a most delightful example of how one can fulfil such a task.' This is a clear indication how Menander has operated so far: he has taken Aristides as his example and derived his theory from him.

3. The *Σμινθιακός* at the end of the second treatise

In the first half of this paper we have been in a position to observe theoretically the quandary of the prose-writer who attempts to write hymns to the gods. For he cannot avoid following the massive tradition which invites him to reach poetical heights, but as a pedestrian who finds himself in the plain, a practitioner of prose—*πεζὸς λόγος*—, he does not have the proper shoes for feats of poetical alpinism; or to use a more apt image, he cannot soar to the clouds on wings of fancy. All he can do is to use his strong points to good advantage: (1) a rational and full treatment of the available topoi, especially those of the *ὕμνος πεπλασμένος*; (2) clarity of style; (3) a pleasing proportion between the parts of his *λόγος*.

[12] For other cases of *ἐπίνοια* meaning 'original idea', 'conceit' see LSJ s.v. I 3.

Let us now trace how this theory is put into practice, by following the course of Menander's *Σμινθιακός*. This is a prose hymn addressed to Apollo Smintheus; the hymn is going to be part of a festival in honour of Apollo. The festival will take place in Alexandria, a city founded by Alexander the Great in the Troad (444.4-10). It will include a contest (*ἀγῶνα τὸν ἱερὸν τοῦτον* 444.17) in which Menander's addressee is supposed to participate with this very speech. What we read is not the full text of a speech but a series of practical tips interspersed with long pieces to show how Menander would do it himself.

The very first paragraph already offers a proof of the quandary which I sketched above. For the proem Menander offers two topoi, (1) the law of reciprocity requests that one should praise Apollo in speech as it is from him that mankind has received speech, *ἀποδοῦναι λογίῳ θεῷ χάριτας διὰ τῶν λόγων οὓς δι' αὐτὸν κεκτήμεθα*, and (2) Apollo is the protector and helper of our city, not only now but from time immemorial, *προστάτης καὶ συνεργὸς τῆς ἡμετέρας πόλεως οὐ μόνον νῦν ἀλλὰ καὶ ἀνέκαθεν* (437.7-11). A quick glance at these two topoi suffices to perceive that here philosophical theology and poetical mythology are rubbing shoulders. The first topos echoes Cleanthes' hymn: from Zeus we have received speech and reason (4),[13] let us therefore praise Zeus in return: *τιμηθέντες ἀμειβώμεσθά σε τιμῇ ὑμνοῦντες τὰ σὰ ἔργα* (36-7). One is also reminded of the dictum of another Stoic philosopher Epictetus: *λογικός εἰμι· ὑμνεῖν με δεῖ τὸν θεόν.* (*Diatrib.* 1.16.21).[14] The second topos refers directly to the tradition of Apollo worshipped in the

---

[13] The MS here has *ἤχου μίμημα λαχόντες* which will not do. Scholars agree that one expects here a phrase referring to man being 'from Zeus' (*ἐκ σοῦ*) by having a share of the divine *λόγος*. Powell (*Coll.Alex.*) and Hopkinson (*Hell.Anthol.*) read *ϑεοῦ μίμημα*. I prefer to combine two suggestions (by Meineke and Wachsmuth respectively) and to read *λόγου τίμημα λαχόντες*.

[14] In his Hymn to Sarapis Aristides uses the same topos to express his indignation that we do not use our *λόγος* (he means rhetorical prose!) to praise the gods: *πρὸς πάνθ' ... ἡμῖν ἔπεισιν ὁ λόγος, πρὸς δὲ τοὺς θεοὺς αὐτοὺς τοὺς δόντας ἡμῖν αὐτὸν οὐ παντάπασιν ἀξιοῦμεν χρῆσθαι τούτῳ* (45.4).

Troad according to Homer: κλῦθί μευ, ἀργυρότοξ' ... Σμινθεῦ. (*Iliad* A 37-9).

When the orator has to start the hymn proper, there is the traditional embarrassment 'how shall I address thee?' τίνα σε χρὴ προσειπεῖν· This problem is solved in a philosophical way: Apollo is the Sun, source of the splendour of the heaven; he is the Mind, going through[15] heavens,ether and earth; he is the Creator, δημιουργός, of the universe; his light is the Power which dispels chaos and gives its definite place to everything (438.12-25).—But then the orator interrupts himself: ἀλλὰ ταῦτα μὲν σοφῶν παισὶ φιλοσοφεῖν παραλείπω, ἣν δὲ ἀκήκοα μυθολογούντων γένεσιν, ταύτην καὶ δὴ πειράσομαι λέγειν (438.25-7): 'We shall leave this to scholars to discuss; I shall attempt to tell you the story of Apollo's birth which I have heard from the people who deal with mythology'. Then he tells the story about Apollo's birth, in which the orator simulates another perplexity: 'was it on Delos that Leto gave birth to Apollo, or in Lycia?' (439.8-9). Homer's authority helps to decide the matter, for he uses the phrase Λυκηγενέι κλυτοτόξῳ (Δ 101, 119). The orator is now in a position to suggest that on his way to Delphi Apollo had to travel through Asia Minor and came to the Troad. Conclusion: he can be called Σμίνθιος as well as Πύθιος. It is our own local Apollo. *Quod erat demonstrandum.*

In this way the orator has to navigate. On one hand the poetical tradition of the Greeks in general and local pride more in particular, require him to adhere to, at least to touch upon, the traditional mythological elements: his audience would be disappointed if he gave them nothing of that kind. On the other, there are the promising possibilities of a more rational discourse which bring him time and again to a philosophical approach. Popularised philososophy of course, but even so.

The speech continues with an exposition of the four principal powers (δυνάμεις) of Apollo: archery, prophecy, music, and medicine.

---

[15] This is the thoroughly Stoic δόγμα of God (= Logos) *going through* the universe: τὸν θεὸν διὰ πάσης οὐσίας πεφοιτηκέναι (*SVF* I 158, cf. *ib.* 153, 155, 159, 161, 162). Russell - Wilson (p. 353) point out that 'Menander's "solar religion" gathers to itself the ideas of Plato and the Stoics'.

As far as the archery is concerned, the orator cannot deal with it in any other way than according to the tradition—a tradition which we can follow all the way from the Homeric *Hymn to Apollo* via a stasimon in Euripides' *IT* (1234-57) to the Delphic paean by Limenios: with his bow and arrows Apollo kills the serpent Python because it occupies and ravages the area of the future oracle, and he kills Tityos for attempting to rape Leto. Prophecy is dealt with in the same traditional way.

As for the treatment of Apollo's third accomplishment, music, Menander recommends reminding the audience briefly of the Olympic scene familiar to all of us from the last lines of the first book of the *Iliad*—Apollo striking his lyre accompanied by the company of the Muses—but then to take a chance for an interesting development: *καὶ φιλοσοφήσεις μετρίως ἐνταῦθα· εἰ δὲ δεῖ καὶ τὸν ἀπορρητότερον λόγον εἰπεῖν, ὃν φιλοσόφων παῖδες πρεσβεύουσι, λέγουσιν αὐτὸν ὄντα τὸν ἥλιον μουσικῇ μὲν κινεῖσθαι, κατὰ μουσικὴν δὲ περιδινεῖν περὶ αὐτὸν τὸν πόλον, καὶ δι' ἁρμονίας ἅπαντα τὸν κόσμον διοικεῖν.* (442.28-33): 'On this point you should administer a moderate dose of philosophy, and say: "If you allow me to utter a doctrine which is rather secret, a piece of learning highly esteemed by the philosophers: they proclaim that Apollo, being the sun, moves himself by the sweet force of music—that he swings the heavens around him according to music—that he conducts the entire cosmos harmoniously"'. Again we see the prose-writer coming into his own: in such a passage he can show off his philosophical learning,[16] his didactic talents and the clarity of his style. But having suggested this, Menander makes the orator switch back to myth: ENTER the Muses, Orpheus, Amphion, and Arion. The orator should mention and praise them, focusing on Apollo: they receive their superb music from him, all of them: *ἀνοίσεις δὲ τὰ ἐγκώμια ἐπὶ τὸν μουσηγέτην, ὡς παρ' ἐκείνου λαμβανόντων τὴν μουσικήν* (443.10-2).

[16] In *Cra.* 405a-e Plato explains the name 'Apollo' in relation to the four arts of the god (archery, prophecy, music and medicine) and ends with an elaborate discussion of Apollo's musical accompaniment to the motion of the universe. This must have been in Menander's mind here. I thank Ineke Sluiter for reminding me of this connection.

Having thus dealt with Apollo's four powers (I pass over the treatment of medicine), the orator has to take in the full impact of the situation in which he is performing: there is the city, the festival, the temple and Apollo's statue to praise. Of course the city derives splendour from its Founder, Alexander the Great. It was he who brought it about—according to the orator—not only that the site of Troy was enriched with a new city but also that the age-old cult of Apollo Sminthios was re-introduced.

Coming to this point of the speech—the relation between the city and its god—the orator seems to strike a chord of a still vital religious sentiment: *ἡμεῖς πειρώμενοι ἀεὶ τῆς τοῦ θεοῦ προνοίας τε καὶ εὐμενείας οὐ ῥᾳθυμοῦμεν τῆς περὶ αὐτὸν εὐσεβείας, καὶ ὁ μὲν διατελεῖ καρπῶν ἀφθόνων διδοὺς φορὰν καὶ ῥυόμενος κινδύνων, ἡμεῖς δὲ ὕμνοις ἱλασκόμεθα* (444.12-7): 'As we experience always the providence and benevolence of the god, we are not careless in worshipping him. He goes on giving plentiful crops and rescuing us from perils, we keep propitiating him with hymns.'

For the praise of temple and statue the young orator is told to use rhetorical questions: 'What walls were built like this at Thebes? What temple at Athens? What Phidias fashioned such an image? Perhaps this statue fell from heaven!' (445.10-1; 18-9). All this is tradition; this time not poetical tradition, but the stock-in-trade of epideictic rhetoric.

The speech comes to its finale. Menander has written it out in full. The penultimate part of the speech corresponds to the second part of its beginning, and the very last with the very first. The before-last part repeats the 'embarrassment': 'how shall I address Thee?' The answer is given by an avalanche of traditional epithets (445.28 ff.). So close to the finish the orator cannot go into any deep philosophical waters, but in the series of names suggested by Menander one is struck by the syncretism which is characteristic of religious speculation of late antiquity: 'O Apollo, the Persians call you Mithras, the Egyptians Horos, the Thebans

Dionysus', Μίθραν σε Πέρσαι λέγουσιν, Ὧρον Αἰγύπτιοι, Διόνυσον Θηβαῖοι (446.3-4).[17]

The last sentence is a short prayer for the prosperity of the city and for the speaker himself: σὺ μὲν ἀκμάζειν ἀεὶ ταῖς εὐδαιμονίαις τὴν πόλιν τήνδε δίδου, νεῦσον δὲ καὶ χάριν τοῖς λόγοις· παρὰ σοῦ γὰρ καὶ οἱ λόγοι καὶ ἡ πόλις (446.9-13). Menander had started with underlining the connection between Apollo, giver of λόγοι, and the λόγοι to be pronounced in his honour. He ends with the same topos.

By now it will have become clear what I have wanted to point out as the critical line which runs through Menander's discussion of the prose hymn, both theory and practice. A central fact of the cultural situation in Menander's time was that the production of great poetry had dried up almost entirely. The Greek language was still exploited intensively by practitioners of oratory in combination with erudition displayed by grammarians and teachers of rhetoric. Incidentally, at occasions like the Apollo festival in Alexandria Troas, which required a celebration of a divinity, young and promising orators wanted to rise to the occasion, and senior professors like Menander Rhetor were prepared to show them the way. But there was no way back to the old inspiration. The old religious tradition with the accompanying songs belonged to the irrevocable past. There was enough of religion in the air, but it was of a new kind, more personal and more philosophical. Menander did his best, and tried to combine the old and the new, myth and philosophy, poetry and prose. He must have been a clever and a careful man. But his treatise did not result in a new and creative wave of prose hymns. We should not blame him for that. Even Aristotle's *Poetics* did not result in a new era of tragedy.

---

[17] Cf. the 2nd-century CE *Carmen in Attinem* (= Hippol. *Haer.* 5.9.8; p. 99 Wendland): σὲ καλοῦσι μὲν Ἀσσυρίοι τριπόθητον Ἄδωνιν, ὅλη δ' Αἴγυπτος Ὄσιριν, Σαμόθρᾳκες Ἀδάμνα κτλ; cf. Nock 1961, 150-1 and Nilsson 1961, 477-8, 573-6.

BIBLIOGRAPHY

Käppel, L., *Paian, Studien zur Geschichte einer literarischen Gattung*. Untersuchungen zur antiken Literatur und Geschichte 37. Berlin - New York 1992.

Nilsson, M.P., *Geschichte der griechischen Religion* II. München 1961.

Nock, A.D., *Conversion, the Old and the New in Religion from Alexander the Great to Augustine of Hippo*. Oxford 1961.

Radermacher, L., *Artium Scriptores*. Wien 1952.

Russell, D.A. (ed.), *Antonine Literature*. Oxford 1990.

Russell, D.A., - Wilson, N., *Menander Rhetor*. Oxford 1981.

Velardi, R., Le origini dell' inno in prosa tra V e IV secolo AC: Menandro Retore e Platone, in: A.C. Cassio - G. Cerri (eds.), *L'inno tra rituale e letteratura nel mondo antico*. Roma 1991, 205-31.

Versnel, H.S., (ed.), *Faith, Hope and Worship, Aspects of Religious Mentality in the Ancient World*. Leiden 1981.

Zimmermann, B., *Dithyrambos, Geschichte einer literarischen Gattung*. Hypomnemata 98. Göttingen 1992.

Late Platonist Poetics:
Olympiodorus and the Myth of Plato's Gorgias

Robin Jackson

The sixth-century-CE Platonist scholarch Olympiodorus of Alexandria pays considerable attention to myth in his *Commentary on Plato's Gorgias*. His comments provide a useful illustration of the way Platonic texts were read in late antiquity. They address the myth with which the *Gorgias* concludes (*Grg*. 523a-527e), and also the relation between Platonic myth and Greek myth in general. Olympiodorus' treatment of myth is the clearest pointer to his version of late Platonist poetics[1].

Olympiodorus' analysis of the *Gorgias* myth is largely traditional, with frequent references to the lectures of his teacher Ammonius, and relies heavily on Proclus, especially the extended discussion of Socrates' critique of the poets in the *Republic* and the myth of Er, with which the *Republic* ends.[2] What makes Olympiodorus' comments of particular interest is the absence of any other Platonist *Gorgias* commentary. No fragments survive of the commentary by Iamblichus, for example, assuming there was one, and from Proclus we have only a few scattered remarks. So it is in Olympiodorus' comments that we have our best evidence for the reconstruction of late Neoplatonic interpretation of the

---

[1] References without title are to Olympiodorus *in Grg*. by lecture and section (if necessary by page and line number in Westerink's Teubner), or to Plato (usually the *Gorgias*) by Stephanus page and section.

[2] *R*. 2-3; 10, 614b-621d; Proclus *in R*., especially Essays 5 & 6. Olympiodorus' use of divine etymologies doubtless draws on Proclus' commentary on the *Cratylus*. Olympiodorus refers to a tradition of interpretation on the *Gorgias* myth (e.g. 48.4).

Gorgias and its myth.[3] But although Olympiodorus is faithful to his sources, he is also prepared on occasion to challenge them.

Olympiodorus attempts to elucidate the text of Plato as best he can for his students, focussing on its utility for moral development. In common with other Alexandrian commentators, he shows only modest interest in the abstract speculation characteristic of the fifth-century Athenian Platonists. His comments, admittedly often pedestrian and superficial, are nevertheless honest efforts which need to be read in historical and pedagogic context.

The *Gorgias* is an extended portrait of the Socratic *elenchus*, featuring a sharp critique of the intellectual pretensions of rhetoric and of the attractions of power and pleasure as elements in the good life. The *Gorgias* myth, one of several that conclude Platonic dialogues, caps the dialectical exercises with an imaginative tale of the fate of the human soul after death. An inescapable *post mortem* rewarding of virtue and punishment of vice—with emphasis on the punishment of tyrants, the heroes of Socrates' interlocutors—takes place before judges who are immune to the blandishments of rhetoric. The myth's eschatological themes give it an obvious appeal for Platonist commentators. Indeed for Olympiodorus, the *Gorgias* myth is the coping-stone of the whole dialogue, not so much an appendix as a climactic revelation of the theme of the dialogue.

Nevertheless, myth is officially a secondary concern for Olympiodorus: 'our proper concern is not the myths, but the best constitution', he says, as if myth is a temptation to be resisted (44.7). In support, he refers to the *Phaedrus*, where Socrates puts off mythology in favour of research into human nature, and also to Socrates' lack of enthusiasm for poetic analysis in the *Republic*.[4] But in fact, in a characteristically Neo-

[3] On Iamblichus' commentaries see Dillon (1973, Introduction). Proclus refers to his commentary on the *Gorgias* myth, e.g. at *in R.* 2.178, which will have been a major source for Olympiodorus. Even the *Gorgias* scholia derive largely from the school of Olympiodorus.

[4] *Phdr.* 229-30; *R.* 378d. Olympiodorus concludes: 'Hence we should disregard myths, and instead pursue truth and the good life' (44.7).

platonic way, Olympiodorus attends closely to myth. His extended discussion of the *Gorgias* myth—with excursuses on the nature of myth in general and the significance of familiar Greek myths—occupies a substantial part of his commentary, and involves a rare departure from his usual strict procedure of general lecture (*θεωρία*) and specific line-by-line comments (λέξις).

Olympiodorus' analysis of myth is crucial for his reading of Plato and of the Greek poets. As a Platonist, he of course maintains official respect for Plato's views, including Socrates' criticism of Homer and the poets in the *Republic*. But, unlike Plato, he also seeks to foster respect in his pupils for the Hellenic tradition in general, in which the Homeric poems play a major part. Hence Olympiodorus acknowledges an opposition between philosophy and poetry, while nevertheless upholding the intellectual significance of poetry. For in his time Olympiodorus has to defend Homer and pagan culture in general against a sceptical if not outright hostile audience. Plato's notorious attacks on Homer and the poets therefore demand clarification from a commentator who wishes to remain a loyal Platonist but also to defend the Greek tradition.

Olympiodorus begins his analysis of the *Gorgias* myth with a general outline of the function of myth. 'The ancients employed myths', he says in scholastic manner, 'for two reasons: with a view to nature and to the soul' (46.2). In the first case, nature, the working of myths resembles our understanding of our world. For from 'the seen' (such as the visible order of the heavenly bodies) and 'the bodily' (such as the cessation of bodily motion at death) we infer the existence of invisible and incorporeal motive powers (presumably the world-soul and individual soul). Myths work in a similar way, offering a route from the visible to the unseen. As examples Olympiodorus offers myths of divine adultery or violence (Socrates' examples from the *Republic*): 'in these instances we do not pursue the surface meaning, but proceed to what is unseen and seek the truth' (46.2).

For Olympiodorus, myth fits our intellectual make-up. A creature of pure intellect, unreliant on appearances, would have no need of myths, and an irrational creature would rely entirely on myth, as on appearance. Myths are thus to the faculty of imagination as proofs are to intellect, and the views of persons of sound judgment are to opinion (46.6). Myths are images (*eikones*, 46.3). As Olympiodorus says of divine statues (doubtless with christian criticism in mind): 'Do not think that philosophers honour representations (εἴδωλα) in stone as divine. It is because we live in the sensory world and are not able to attain the bodiless and immaterial power, that we conceive of representations as a reminder (*anamnesis*) of those things, so that by seeing and respecting them we might arrive at a notion of those bodiless and immaterial powers' (47.5). Olympiodorus' first function of myth, as nature-allegory, reflects the oldest approach to the allegorising of myth in the Greek tradition, a practice going back a thousand years to the Presocratics and most fully developed in the hands of the Stoics. By nature, of course, Olympiodorus means Platonist metaphysics rather than the material universe, and metaphysics located within the technical context of a Platonist psychology.[5]

Olympiodorus' second function for myth elaborates on this psychological aspect. Myth is related to the imagination (*phantasia*), the non-rational faculty of soul 'that deals with such things as shapes and forms' (46.3). This part of the soul is most active in children, and is also that in which the passions are active.[6] Hence Olympiodorus' definition of myth as 'nothing other than a false statement imaging the truth' (46.3).[7] Hence too our enjoyment of myth: 'if myth is an image of truth, and the soul is an image of what is before it, then it is likely that the soul enjoys myth as image to image' (46.3). There is thus a natural link between the

---

[5] For Olympiodorus as for other Platonists it is the allegory of divine figures that is most important. But there is little sign of the allegorical presence of, e.g., the Proclan divine henads in the guise of the traditional deities.

[6] Hence the connection between myths and childhood (46.3, 'myths are familiar from childhood'). Myths disturb the passions with their horrific stories, but divine sayings (= myths?) are useful for putting the passions to sleep (20.3). Similarly Olympiodorus regards the *Phaedo* myth as useful in soothing the lower soul (presumably concerning the fear of death), just as arguments are directed to the higher levels of soul.

[7] The definition is traditional, cf. Damascius *in Phd.* 198.29-30, 237.27-8.

soul (at least at its lower levels) and myth, which explains why myth brings us enjoyment but is also potentially dangerous.

Myth, then, has a dual function. It also has two forms, poetic and philosophical (46.4). Poetic myths are the traditional myths told by poets such as Homer, and philosophical myths are those we find in Plato.[8] The philosophical category also includes 'Orphic' and 'Pythagorean' myths.[9] From the *Gorgias* Olympiodorus cites Socrates' myth of the leaky vessels (493a1-c5) as a Pythagorean myth.

According to Olympiodorus, again in schematic style, philosophical and poetic myth each has its own advantages and disadvantages (46.4).[10] The advantage of poetic myth is its manifest absurdity and inconsistency, so that almost no-one could believe that what it says is literally true. 'What man of sense could believe', he says of Zeus, 'that he wanted to lie with Hera on the ground, without bringing her into the chamber?', or of a hero like Achilles, 'that he called a king "wine-sack" and so forth or wept unrestrainedly for a mere girl?' (46.4).[11]

---

[8] Contrast Proclus' more elaborate distinction of types of poetry into inspired (especially Homer, non-mimetic, corresponding to the highest level of soul), didactic or mimetic (appealing to the lowest soul, emotions and phantasia), itself based, Proclus tells us, on Syrianus' comments on *Phaedrus* 245. The nearest point of contact appears to be that by 'poetic myth' Olympiodorus refers only to what Proclus calls inspired poetry, particularly that of Homer and Hesiod, and particularly concerning the gods. See Proclus *in R.* 1.177 f., and Lamberton 1992, 120-1.

[9] Olympiodorus refers to one of Socrates' arguments against suicide as 'mythical and Orphic', and says that Plato cites 'Orphic myths everywhere', *in Phd.* 1.1, 5.10. 'Orphic' myths also include myths such as the dismemberment of Dionysus by the Titans, *in Phd.* 1.5. Olympiodorus does not seem to include the Chaldaean oracles as myths.

[10] Olympiodorus' distinction echoes the contrast drawn, in somewhat different terms, by Proclus, *in R.* 1.71-86, 159-63.

[11] Olympiodorus also cites contradictions between Homer's description of one hero (Bellerophon) as wise and another (Achilles) as the opposite, and between the gods' eternity and paternity (47.1). Olympiodorus' familiarity with poetic myth has the feel of traditional school examples rather than direct personal

Olympiodorus also cites an anecdote from the Platonic biographical tradition. Plato is supposed to have said to Dionysius concerning Heracles: 'if the myths (of Heracles' sufferings) are true, then Heracles was not a son of Zeus nor was he happy; but if he was a son of Zeus or was happy, then the myths are false' (41.7). This must mean *literally* false, for as he says in a related story about Theseus: 'if (Theseus' myths) are true, he is base; but if he is a hero, then it is clear that certain other things are symbolically conveyed by (the myths)' (44.7).[12]

This is the advantage poetic myth has over philosophical myth: because its surface meaning is patently objectionable or absurd (*ἄτοπον*), it obliges us to look for how it might be saying 'something different', and thus to seek a concealed truth within. This use of the evident absurdity of a text regarded as authoritative to motivate reading myths other than literally is a traditional justification of the turn to allegorical interpretation.[13]

So the solution to the surface absurdity of myth lies in its allegorical decoding. Myth is thus a 'false statement' in the sense that it is false at a literal level, but is 'an image of truth' in that its concealed meaning expresses what is true. In extracting a concealed meaning from traditional myths consistent with the demands of Platonist philosophy, Olympiodorus is working within a long allegorical tradition. It goes back to at least middle-Platonist speculation, and draws on Stoic and even earlier Presocratic speculation, and involves the decoding of traditional texts into the

---

acquaintance.

[12] Olympiodorus makes Heracles' labours signify various things. One of them makes him a Socratic hero: the myth of his descent to Hades and abduction of Cerberus (not, incidentally to be rationalised as the conquest of one Dog, a brutal man) signifies how Heracles, who was happy and very great, saved everyone from refutation (44.6).

[13] See Pépin 1958, *passim*.

terms of Neoplatonic metaphysics and psychology.[14] Seen at its peak in Porphyry's analysis of the Cave of the Nymphs or the interpretations of Proclus, it involves the treatment of Homer and the other poets as inspired authors, whose texts can yield insights into the mysteries of Platonist eschatology.[15]

Olympiodorus is familiar with perhaps the most celebrated example, the violence and castration of Ouranos in the divine succession myth of Hesiod (46.2).[16] In the hands of the Platonists Hesiod's narrative of conflict, deceit and mutilation among the earliest gods becomes an account of the sublime procession of transcendent being from the highest principle.[17] The new reigns of Kronos and Zeus do not represent changes at the divine level, but different dispositions of the human soul. What gives Olympiodorus' handling of it particular relevance to the *Gorgias* is that at the opening of the *Gorgias* myth Socrates refers to Zeus, Poseidon and Pluto apportioning the inherited kingdom from Kronos. There is no mention of violence, and Socrates' laconic and euphemistic account of the divine succession is itself an early episode in the rationalising of Hesiod's myth—which Olympiodorus is rightly able to bring to bear in this context to supplement the traditional Platonist analysis (47.1).

When Olympiodorus says poetic myth is incredible—'not even cursory hearing accepts it' (46.4)—he presumably means incredible to the

---

[14] So, for example, Plotinus allegorised Odysseus' wanderings as a symbolic account of the travails of the soul on the route to the intelligible world (1.6.9). Olympiodorus in fact is less complimentary: Odyssseus is someone who taught himself but lost his companions (44.6). Olympiodorus prefers Theseus, and discourages belief in any stories which might appear to make Theseus (and the Spartan Lycurgus) less than successful (44.1-8).

[15] See Lamberton 1986, Whitman 1987, Sheppard 1980, Coulter 1976. It is noteworthy that Olympiodorus does not speak of poetic inspiration, nor of the poets as witting allegorists.

[16] *Th*. 154-206, 453-506.

[17] On Plotinus' version see Hadot 1981, on Proclus', see Pépin 1976, 203-6.

mature and sensible person of good character (or the relevant level of the soul operative in such a person). For he points out that the disadvantage of poetic myth is that it deceives the young, who are unable to grasp that it is allegorical or proceed to discover the hidden meaning (46.5). Owing to their inexperience they need to be protected from the harm that putting their belief in the surface meaning will lead to (44.7).[18] Olympiodorus does not say, but that harm presumably consists in intellectual and moral damage caused by belief in the false and indecent, as well as the loss consequent upon separation from the truth to be found within the allegory.[19]

But it cannot simply be just the young who fail to allegorise. For Olympiodorus complains at length about those who persistently misread myths as factual accounts. Against such opponents he constructs a polemic on the necessity of reading myths allegorically, rebutting Euhemerist and other historicist readings (44.3-8).[20] He rejects, e.g., reading the myth of Erichthonius' birth from Hephaestus' seed when in pursuit of Athena as a literal account of Athenian autochthony. Instead he urges that it be read in Platonic terms, as a 'Phoenician falsehood', 'a noble lie of origins' (*R.* 414a-b), useful for motivating citizens to love their city (44.3). And he criticises the Cretans for cognitive as well as moral error:

---

[18] Here Olympiodorus follows Proclus' interpretation of Socrates' critique of poetry in *Republic* 2-3, namely that Socrates was not condemning the poets in general but only from the point of view of educating the young (*in R.* 1.159 f.). As Olympiodorus puts it: 'Plato did not concede to the young the benefit of grasping allegorical meaning (*hyponoia*), for the young are not receptive of allegory, since they cannot judge what is and what is not allegory, and what they take in is "hard to cleanse"' (46.5, citing *R.* 378d).

[19] Cf. Marinus, *Procl.* 12-3: 'I would suffer to be current, out of all ancient books, only the *Timaeus* and the oracles, for people suffer actual injury from their undirected and uncritical reading.'

[20] Olympiodorus nevertheless calls historicising interpretations ἀλληγοροῦντες (i.e. 'giving an account of the other meaning' sc. than the surface meaning). The error, as Olympiodorus sees it, lies not in allegorising (for he takes such interpretation as natural) but in locating the wrong referents for the allegory.

in defending their indulgence in homosexual pleasures by reference to the myth of Zeus and Ganymede, they treat a myth, he says, as a factual account (*logos*) and thus reveal their failure to understand the necessity of proceeding beneath the surface of a myth to its concealed meaning (40.3, 46.5).[21]

Another celebrated example is Theseus' slaying of the Minotaur (44.5). This is not a historical account of the slaying of Taurus, the general of Minos, but 'symbolically signifies something different': the Minotaur represents our bestial passions, Ariadne's thread is the divine power that we depend on, and the Labyrinth is the complex nature of life.[22] This polemic against historicist interpretation goes back ultimately to Stoic sources—it is interesting to suppose that its attraction in the sixth century is as a covert rebuttal of Christian attacks, which often used arguments from within pagan polemic.[23] Olympiodorus' historicists interestingly include his predecessor as Alexandrian scholarch, Ammonius, for according to Olympiodorus Ammonius had (by implication, approvingly) given a historical account of Theseus' opponent Sciron (44.4, 44.6).

---

[21] Olympiodorus' allegorical interpretation of Ganymede is a soul that succeeds in raising itself into a close association with the divine. Olympiodorus' attack doubtless reflects prevailing values shared with Christianity, and is invited by Plato's dismissal of homosexual acts as unnatural at *Lg.* 6, 636c—he makes no reference to *Smp.* or *Phdr.* There is a problem with Olympiodorus' use of the phrase 'treating a myth as a factual account', for this is Socrates' description of his own view of the *Gorgias* myth (523a2, cf. 47.1).

[22] Olympiodorus' source for the historicist interpretation of the Minotaur is Plutarch, reporting an idea attributed to the Cretans by Philochorus (*Thes.* 16.1, 19.2). Olympiodorus says that Socrates puts off interpretations of myths about 'Minotaurs and other monsters', about which he has doubts, in favour of self-examination (44.7, with reference to *Phdr.* 229-30). In this passage Socrates does not mention the Minotaur, but his remarks about other monsters counsel against excessive rationalisation of myths into a plausible historical record, and imply that mythical monsters are better understood in terms of hybrid forces within the soul, an invitation to allegorical interpretation.

[23] See Fuhrmann 1990.

So the absurdity of the surface meaning of poetic myth both justifies and requires inquiry into its concealed significance. Philosophical myth, by contrast, has the advantage that 'even if you stay with the surface meaning, you are not harmed' (46.6). Sometimes Olympiodorus implies a stronger claim, such as when he says that philosophical myth, in contrast to poetic myth, 'benefits the wise' (30.2). But he does not say why poetic myths, after allegorical decoding, are not also beneficial to the wise. The effect is to muddy his contrast by an implied preference for philosophical myth.[24]

As examples of philosophical myth Olympiodorus cites punishments or the existence of rivers beneath the earth (clearly with the *Phaedo* myth in mind): 'if you believe that these literally take place, no harm follows'. Why? Because it is reasonable to believe 'either that these things are true, or if not these, then something of the sort' (46.9). Olympiodorus thus relies upon the generalising defence of the truthfulness of myth used by Socrates himself in the *Phaedo*.[25] So philosophical myth, like poetic myth, bears inconsistency and impossibility on its surface. But to a lesser extent, perhaps: Socrates describes his short myth of the leaky vessels as 'bordering on the absurd' (ἐπιεικῶς ... ὑπό τι ἄτοπα, 493c5). Olympiodorus paraphrases this as 'not completely absurd' (οὐ πάνυ ἀτόπους, 30.2, 155.27 Westerink), inferring that philosophical myths are *less* absurd, even at the surface level, than poetic myths.

Socrates' myth of the leaky vessels (493a1-c5) is a crucial passage for Olympiodorus, giving him a justification for his exegetical principles

[24] Similarly, Olympiodorus sometimes recommends that the young, in order to avoid the influence of indecorous poetic myths, should learn 'other myths' (46.5). But he does not explain how these differ from philosophical myths (are they the relics of Proclus' third category of myth, didactic myths?).

[25] 'It would not be fitting for a person of sense to insist that all this is just as I have described it; but that this or something like it is true ... he may properly venture to believe' (114d1-4). Olympiodorus would interpret Socrates' description of the Gorgias myth being as a *logos* (i.e. a truthful account?) not just a *mythos* (a fanciful narrative) along similar lines.

within the *Gorgias* itself.[26] Socrates relates a myth told by 'a wise man, a Sicilian or Italian', who said that we are dead and that the body is our tomb. He named the desiderative part of the soul, easily swayed and persuaded, a jar (with a pun, worthy of Socrates himself, on πίθος and πιθανός, 493a5). The foolish resemble the uninitiated, and the desiderative part of their soul—uncontrolled and non-retentive—resembles a leaky jar. In Hades these uninitiated souls are most unhappy, as they carry water in a perforated sieve to pour into a perforated jar. Socrates points out that his mythographer used the image of a sieve to stand for the souls of the foolish, because it is perforated 'and through lack of belief and forgetfulness unable to hold anything'.

Olympiodorus identifies Socrates' 'wise man' as Empedocles, and thus as a Pythagorean (30.5).[27] So this is clearly a philosophical myth. The context, to do with the soul and the mysteries, is of obvious relevance for Neoplatonist eschatological interests, and Socrates' own explication offers an invitation to allegorising. The principal contrast is between fanciful surface details (talk of carrying water in leaky sieves and jars) and serious concealed references to the soul and its destiny. So Olympiodorus can claim that here in the text of the *Gorgias* itself he has a primer on how to read a philosophical myth, such as the one that Socrates subsequently delivers at the end of the dialogue. It is therefore not surprising that Olympiodorus regards it as a key passage (29.4, 44.7). We do not know to what extent this is simply tradition, and to what extent Olympiodorus' own work on the *Gorgias* has prompted the view.

In any event, unlike poetic myth, the surface meaning of philosophical myths is harmless—it lacks the indecency or other moral problems of poetic myth.[28] The *disadvantage* of philosophical myth follows from its very advantages: just because trust in the surface meaning is not harmful,

---

[26] On this passage of the *Gorgias*, see Linforth 1944.

[27] Olympiodorus consistently claims that Empedocles was a Pythagorean (cf. *Proem.* 9) and that he was Gorgias' teacher.

[28] Cf. *Anon. Prol.* 7.15 f.: Plato is superior to the poets in the propriety (τῷ εὐσχήμονι) of his myths. Cf.Proclus *in R.* 1.27-41, 1.73 f.

the hearer is tempted to remain at the surface level and not to seek the deeper truth concealed within (46.6). Callicles, for example, rejects the *Gorgias* myth as ridiculous and fails to appreciate that it has a concealed meaning (47.1). You have to be philosophically disposed, it seems, even to sense the need to delve into the deeper meaning of philosophical myth. Hence an important use of philosophical myths is not stimulation or revelation, but masking, concealing the truth from the uninitiated, like screens in temples (παραπετάσματα), 'so as not to transmit doctrines indiscriminately (46.6).[29]

We should note what Olympiodorus' distinction between poetic and philosophical myth is *not*. We might have expected that poetic myths would suffer from being entertaining, perhaps, but not stimulating. They might seduce us into staying with their surface allurement, that is to say, but not prompt us to the further reflection and inquiry necessary to detect their concealed meaning. Philosophical myths, on the other hand, we might expect, might suffer from being less entertaining, but for that very reason would encourage us to concentrate on their content, free from the distracting lures of surface entertainment. But Olympiodorus' contrast is the inversion of this: for him poetic myth clearly invites, indeed requires, decoding, whereas philosophical myth can be taken at face value. Remaining satisfied with the surface exposition of *post mortem* judgement, while it will lead to no harm—presumably it will encourage moral behaviour—will not however lead to philosophical insight.

So what prompts deeper interpretation of philosophical myth? Philosophical myths are philanthropic, Olympiodorus says, offering a helping hand by including a clue at the surface level about their concealed meaning. Take, for example, the temporal dimension: myths necessarily represent as sequential what is in reality timeless and eternal. This reflects a traditional principle of analysis, namely that myths represent in the

[29] On myths as 'screens' (an idea clearly taken from the mysteries) cf. Olympiodorus *in Cat.* 11-2, Proclus *in R.* 1.73, Sallustius *De Diis* 2-3.

language of sequence and fragmentation what is in reality simultaneous, indivisible, eternal and universal.[30]

Thus in the *Gorgias* myth, Olympiodorus reminds us that references to individual gods and to changes within the divine world are not to be taken literally (48.8). The relevance of myths to philosophy derives from the poverty of discursive reason and language to give an account of transcendent reality. In the *Gorgias* myth Socrates observes that there was in the time of Kronos a law that after death the just depart to the Isles of the Blessed and the unjust descend for punishment to Tartarus (523a4 f.). Olympiodorus fastens on Socrates' parenthetical observation about this law, that 'it holds to this very day among the gods' (*καὶ ἀεὶ καὶ νῦν ἔτι ἐστὶν ἐν θεοῖς*, 523a4), explaining it as a helpful hint at the surface of the myth that its concealed reference is to an eternal state of affairs and that the whole myth is to be understood non-temporally (47.8).[31]

Philosophical myths are also more comprehensive than poetic myths, because they incorporate proofs or demonstrations (*apodeixeis*) in the course of the myths, like the morals (*epimythia*) of Aesop's fables

---

[30] 'The myth, proceeding the way a myth does, does not preserve the simultaneity of things that are always together, but divides them into a former and a latter, and says first things that are imperfect and then things that are perfect' (48.2-3). Cf. Plotinus 3.5.9. Olympiodorus also counsels his students not to be disturbed by the 'poetic names' of the gods (47.1-3), which imply that the gods are plural individuals, capable of indecorous passions and acts, rather than aspects of a single abstract principle to which their names allegorically refer.

[31] Similarly, when Pluto reports that judgements have been erroneous, Zeus replies that he already knew (523e6): for Olympiodorus this is a sign to us at the surface of Zeus' real divine nature, and thus an invitation to pursue it further at the concealed level (49.1). Cf. how Proclus too holds that a Platonic myth bears some sign on its face of being a representation of divine reality, though we need instruction before we can grasp exactly what (*in R.* 1.73).

(49.3).[32] So the surface absurdity is balanced by the meaning's being made explicit, just as a moral is explicitly drawn in Aesopian fables.

Nevertheless there is obviously room for argument over the relation between surface and allegorical meaning in a philosophical myth. Take, for example, Zeus' removal of humans' foreknowledge of death, one of the most striking details of the *Gorgias* myth. Olympiodorus says: 'This is a problem at the surface level: for if foreknowledge is a good thing, why does Zeus remove it? and if foreknowledge is a bad thing, why did Zeus grant it originally?' (48.4). Olympiodorus' predecessors had disagreed: some said (presumably in defence of the view that foreknowledge of death was bad) that Zeus removed it because it encouraged vice, facilitating late in life rehabilitation. But Olympiodorus believes the puzzle cannot be resolved at the surface level (he does not say why), and its solution must therefore lie in its symbolic meaning. That turns out to involve ignorance: foreknowledge of death carries with it the idea of our being rid of our current life (*τὴν ἐνταῦθα ἀπαλλαγήν*) and implies, Olympiodorus suggests, that the only judgements to be feared are earthly judgements. But, as the myth tells, in truth the soul is immortal and judgements follow our death here. Foreknowledge of death thus amounts to ignorance of the most important sort, the removal of which is a blessing (48.4). Apparent knowledge symbolically standing for ignorance displays a characteristically Platonist inversion, but one notes that, despite earlier raising the question, Olympiodorus does not seem to have explained why Zeus granted foreknowledge in the first place.[33]

---

[32] *Anon. Prol.* 7.15 f. also refers to Plato's myths containing proofs, and the perspicuity of their good purpose, 'without having to wait for the drawing of the moral, as in Aesop'. Cf. Proclus *in R.* 1.71-86, Ammonius *in Int.* 249.1-25. It is not clear, however, what form these demonstrations are supposed to take, and a puzzling reference to fire in the *Phaedo* myth is little help. Elsewhere Olympiodorus uses 'moral' to describe the concealed meaning of the myth itself: e.g the myth of Hera's feet being bound to an anvil signifies the heaviest two elements, etc. (34.4, cf. 4.3): the problem is that this is a *poetic* myth.

[33] Neither here, nor elsewhere, does Olympiodorus employ the distinction, systematically developed in Proclus, between images (*εἰκόνες*) that represent by similarity and symbols (*symbola*) that represent indirectly or by opposites (cf.

Likewise the abrupt, dramatic opening of the *Gorgias* myth ('hearken to a perfectly fine account', 523a1) is for Olympiodorus a covert declaration of its character as a philosophical myth and therefore its superiority to poetic myths. The latter are 'merely fine' (47.1), that is, presumably, fine only after allegorical decoding, not on the surface too. Similarly Olympiodorus fastens on Socrates' unusual claim about the veracity of the *Gorgias* myth, that it is a factual account (*logos*), not simply mythical, as it seems to Callicles, who is unable to grasp its concealed meaning (523a1, 47.1). This is a useful illustration of Olympiodorus' practice of locating a significant textual reference in support of a Platonist interpretation.

A related, decisive advantage, of philosophical myths is this. The significance of a poetic myth can be disputed (44.6-7). Of course, notoriously, philosophers also dispute. But unlike poets, philosophers follow certain general moral and metaphysical principles, the 'common notions' (κοιναὶ ἔννοιαι), and so their myths are trustworthy. The common notions are a set of basic truths, the most basic insights available, supplying premises for demonstration (3.1, 48.5, *in Alc.* 18). Even in technical areas, such as the basic stuff of the universe or the nature of the soul, Olympiodorus believes that we may safely follow whatever position most closely accords with the common notions (44.7).[34] Plato's myths, for example, symbolically express important common notions, such as 'God is good' or 'honour one's parents' (41.2).

Proclus *in R.* 1.71-96, etc., Dillon 1991, 251).

[34] Olympiodorus' confidence in the common notions as the foundations of knowledge is perhaps also reflected in the assumption that similar ideas can be expressed in very different language: e.g. the treatment of the names of the pagan gods (4.3, 47.2-4) and cf. his discussion of Socrates' daimonion (*in Alc.* 21-3).

'But in the case of poetic myths, there are no common notions to teach us. So first you need to explicate them' (44.6-7).[35] This 'first' must mean that there are no common notions visible in poetic myths *before* allegorical decoding. But Olympiodorus does not say why the common notions should remain invisible *after* the symbolic meaning has been revealed, and indeed has already shown how poetic myths allegorically express truth. So it seems unlikely that he would want to say that even after decoding the concealed meaning of poetic myth is not in accord with the common notions. His meaning is probably the weaker thesis that the surface meaning of poetic myths does not accord with the common notions, but they can be revealed by allegorical decoding. But then his contrast with philosophical myths in terms of accord with the common notions disappears. The problem seems to be that Olympiodorus vacillates between condemning poetic myth as false, and explicating it as a symbolic expression of truth. Perhaps an enthusiasm to privilege philosophical myth, using his favourite device of the common notions, has led him to focus on a surface contrast between poetic and philosophical myth, rather than the similarity between their revealed meanings. If it is true that for Olympiodorus philosophical myth remains superior to poetic myth, even after the latter has been subjected to allegorical decoding, then there is a contrast with other Platonists, for whom the inspired Homer, properly interpreted, is as authoritative as Plato himself.[36] Yet Olympiodorus realises that poetic myths can treat the same material as philosophical

---

[35] Olympiodorus says 'Hence we should first explicate the myths—for indeed Plato explicates them'. But the example given is the myth of the leaky vessels (493a), not very helpfully, since this is a philosophical myth.

[36] Contrast Hermeias: 'Mythology is a sort of theology (*θεολογία τις*) and the characteristic mistake of the uninitiated is to fail to grasp with wisdom the intention of the mythoplasts but rather to follow the apparent sense' (*in Phdr.* 73.18-21).

myths, e.g. that an underworld myth such as the *Phaedo* (or *Gorgias*) myth has the same subject as poetic myths of the underworld (46.9).[37]

Within the category of philosophical myth Olympiodorus draws a further distinction, into those that are underworld myths (*nekuiai*) and those that are not. Non-underworld philosophical myths include the myth of the movement of the heavens in the *Statesman* (269c-274a), or the birth of Eros in the *Symposium* (203-4), or the myth of the leaky vessels in the *Gorgias* (493a-c). 'Only those myths that are about the soul are underworld myths', he says (46.9). In practice, that means three myths: the *Gorgias* myth, the *Phaedo* myth and the myth of Er in the *Republic*. But it is more than this, for the myth of the leaky vessels in the *Gorgias*, which Olympiodorus gives as an example of a non-underworld myth, is also a tale about souls and the underworld. So what Olympiodorus precisely means by *nekuia* is presumably an eschatological myth of judgement set in the underworld, a myth of serious theological import, concerning the divine realm, the good, the soul and its fate. Perhaps because of his focus upon philosophical myth, Olympiodorus fails to observe that there can also be *poetic* underworld myths, such as *Odyssey* 11.

Olympiodorus follows a traditional schematisation of the world of the dead myths: they contain judges, places of judgement and victims, with emphasis in the *Phaedo* on the places of judgement, in the *Republic* on the souls who undergo judgement, and in the *Gorgias* on the judges.[38] The classification seems not to be Iamblichan, however, for Olympiodorus says that Iamblichus recognised only two Platonic myths as underworld myths, excluding the *Gorgias* myth from the category (46.9). It is interesting that the reference is to a letter, rather than to a commentary by Iamblichus. Olympiodorus' resolution is characteristic: he wants to follow

[37] A philosophical myth can be a restatement of a related poetic myth, with its concealed meaning made clearer: 'Callicles knew these (sc. underworld) myths (sc. as poetic myths), but had not penetrated to their deep meaning, so Socrates expounds the nature of those judges there (in a philosophical myth?)' (49.4).

[38] Cf. Procl. *in R.* 1.168, 2.128.

the traditional line, but also seeks to preserve the reputation of a great figure like Iamblichus. So he explains away Iamblichus' apparent heterodoxy in terms of the local demands of his context: Iamblichus' correspondent must have asked only about the *Phaedo* and *Republic* (46.9).

Iamblichus had brought the *Gorgias* back into the Platonist mainstream, including it within a revised curriculum, which subsequently became canonical.[39] That curriculum takes the student from concern for well-being through self-knowledge (so begins with the *Alcibiades 1*, which taught that a human being is primarily a soul),[40] to knowledge of the physical universe and ultimately knowledge of divine metaphysics. By assigning to the *Gorgias* the position of second dialogue in his curriculum, Iamblichus seems to have taken it to be about the physical universe as much as, even more than, its more evident subject of ethics and politics.

Now we are told that Iamblichus, however improbably, identified the subject (*skopos*) of Plato's *Sophist* as the demiurge.[41] A similar interpretation may have been advanced concerning the *Sophist's* companion dialogue, the *Politicus*, whose myth of the helmsman who controls the motions of the heavens could easily yield an interpretation which identifies the helmsman (and the statesman of the dialogue's title?) with a demiurgic power. The *Gorgias* too concerns the statesman, for Socrates criticises contemporary politicians and describes himself as possibly the only citizen truly aiming at statesmanship (521d3). Like the *Politicus*, the evident concern of the *Gorgias* is with a human rather than a divine statesman. But Socrates argues in the *Gorgias* that the correct management of one's own and the state's constitution (*politeia*) reflects the order

---

[39] See *Anon. Prol.* 26, with the discussion *ad loc.* of Westerink (1962).

[40] Iamblichus *in Alc.* fr. 2.8-9 Dillon; the view recurs in Proclus' and Olympiodorus' own *Alcibiades* commentaries.

[41] Scholiast on the opening line of Plato's *Sophist*. The scholiast also speaks of Iamblichus' demiurgic triad and of his 'Father of Demiurges'. *Anon. Prol.* 21-2, on the other hand, refers to a theory according to which the *skopos* of the Sophist is the sophist rather than division or non-being.

of the universe itself (507e-508a). It is not difficult therefore to see how Iamblichus could have identified the artificer of the universe's constitution in the *Gorgias*, on whom human statesmen are modelled, with the demiurgic creator of the *Timaeus*. So, however strange at first sight such an interpretation of the *Gorgias* might seem, Iamblichus may likewise have seen the *Gorgias* as essentially about demiurgic powers. The idea would be perhaps that dialogues about the physical universe had the ultimate aim of promoting awareness of a higher power operative within it.[42]

Here the *Gorgias* myth plays an important part, because for an Iamblichan approach the divine narrative was doubtless a primary clue to the *skopos* of the whole dialogue.[43] Olympiodorus mentions Iamblichus by name only when interpreting the myth (46.9), and specifically links the demiurge interpretation of the *Gorgias* with its myth, though without mentioning Iamblichus by name (*Proem*. 4). Proclus too seems to have endorsed a demiurgic analysis of the *Gorgias* myth, describing a triad of demiurges and a pre-demiurgic force above them, and with a Zeus-demiurge as the myth's key figure.[44] Olympiodorus only mentions *one* demiurge, a reflection perhaps of his general economy and reluctance to indulge explicitly the more prolific forms of Neoplatonic polytheism.

The *Gorgias* myth describes the inheritance of the world from Kronos and its subsequent division between Zeus, Poseidon, and Pluto/Hades (523a-b). Olympiodorus cites the Platonist association of

---

[42] *Anon. Prol.* 22 seems to be referring to a similar interpretation when speaking of those who thought the *skopos* of the *Gorgias* was 'the intellect which contemplates itself'. The Aristotelian ring suggests that the latter description is a less accurate description of the Iamblichan view, influenced by the Platonic-Aristotelian syncretism of the Alexandrian school.

[43] It is worth noting that the Iamblichan corpus includes all the dialogues with a lengthy myth: *Gorgias*, *Phaedo*, *Politicus*, *Phaedrus*, *Symposium*, *Timaeus*, *Republic*.

[44] E.g. *Theol.Plat.* 9, 18.25-7 Saffrey-Westerink; cf. 13, 26.17-8. Zeus is in a sense a member of this demiurgic triad which the *Gorgias* is supposed to hint at, but in another sense he is prior to it (e.g. *in Ti.* 1.315.8-11).

these last three with a threefold division of material things: the heavens, the sub-lunary world of fire, air, and water, and the earthly realm (47.4).[45] Olympiodorus identifies Kronos, a higher power, with pure intellect, and Zeus, a lower power, as a life-giving power (47.2-4). The identification of Zeus as the demiurge is standard Neoplatonism, an illustration of the injection of the traditional Greek gods into Platonist metaphysics.[46] For Olympiodorus Zeus is the central figure of the myth: he is the power of judgment, he has the sceptre to indicate his control of judgments and he is responsible for installing the judges, his agents (47.4, 48.2). Justice is of course the original, along with statesmanship (463d), of which earlier in the dialogue Socrates presented rhetoric as an image (465c). The system of judgment instituted by Zeus explains in mythic guise why the values of the orator, the power-seeker and the hedonist are inadequate, thereby crowning the work as a whole.

One wonders whether Iamblichus excluded the *Gorgias* myth from the group of underworld myths because in his view it was not about the souls who are being judged but about the powers of judgment. If the judges, for Iamblichus, represent the demiurge, the cosmic statesman who constitutes the universe in accordance with the principles of justice, then perhaps the *Gorgias* myths belongs not with eschatology but to with a demiurgic grouping.[47] Olympiodorus *officially* rejects the Iamblichan

---

[45] On the poets making Zeus, Poseidon and Pluto represent three different strata of the sublunary world, with Kronos the deity responsible for the realm beyond, see *in Phd.* 1.3-4, and cf. Procl. *Theol.Plat.* 368.16-24.

[46] See for example Iamblichus ap. Hermeias *in Phdr.* 136.17-9 (cf. 45.13, 94.6, 256.5) and in Proclus *in Ti.* 1.308.17-8; 1.315.15-31, 316.12-6.

[47] We do not know exactly what Olympiodorus said about the *Phaedo* myth: our Olympiodorus *Phaedo* Commentary does not include the section on the myth, although Olympiodorus' *Commentary on Aristotle's Meteorology* contains a digression on the subterranean geography of the *Phaedo* myth (*in Mete.* 141-50). But the *Gorgias* on the civic virtues is preliminary to the *Phaedo* on the higher, purificatory virtues (23.3). Hence the punishment described in the *Gorgias* myth makes the soul more temperate and prepares it for purification, but does not purify it, however, for that depends on its 'return to itself and to virtue' (50.4).

view. But his commentary contains evidence, incompletely reconciled, of the two competing classifications of the Gorgias myth. For he defines an underworld myth as concerned with souls, and thus includes the *Gorgias* myth among the *nekuiai*, but he goes on to make the powers of judgement (rather than the souls judged) the main topic of the myth.

Olympiodorus makes it clear that he does not himself subscribe to the demiurgic interpretation of the *Gorgias* as a whole (*Proem.* 4), in favour of a less esoteric notion of 'constitutional well-being' (πολιτικὴ εὐδαιμονία).[48] The myth displays the 'paradigmatic cause' (παραδειγματικὸν αἴτιον) of constitutional well-being, its relation to the orderliness of the universe itself.[49] Hence Olympiodorus' emphasis, in his treatment of the myth, on the underworld judges and their judgments. He holds that the myth tells of the existence of 'universal' rulers to judge souls, who in contrast to earthly judges are beyond the influence of rhetoric (46.7). The existence of judgements implies freedom of choice: so the myth underlines the Platonist thesis of the soul as a self-mover, and the good as something in our power for which we can be held responsible (48.5).

The judges are the sons of Zeus, Rhadamanthys and Minos (523e5). Here we have an instance of the impossible at the surface of a philosophical myth, for gods do not beget humans, and if they did there would have been no judges of those who lived before them (49.2). So in the allegory being a son of Zeus stands for being a real, divine judge (49.2), and Rhadamanthys and Minos are souls who love god, not human souls, but

---

[48] The translation 'constitutional' for πολιτικὴ reflects Olympiodorus' use of *politeia* for both soul and city, based on the parallel between *psyche* and *polis* in the *Republic*.

[49] The myth thus complements other sections of the dialogue: the discussions with Gorgias and Polus reveal that constitutional well-being rests on knowledge not rhetoric (its 'productive cause', ποιητικὸν αἴτιον). The discussion with Callicles reveals that constitutional well-being aims at the good, not pleasure (its 'final cause', τελικὸν αἴτιον). The notion of paradigmatic cause doubtless reflects the observation in *R.* 9, 592b3, that the ideal state exists as a παράδειγμα ἐν οὐρανῷ for the one who wishes to constitute himself as its citizen.

divine powers of rational soul who have learned of the wrongdoing of other souls (48.7).

Other features of the underworld are just as straightforwardly allegorised: the meadow represents the sublunary world, for wetness represents becoming (49.3). Of Homer's villains, Tityus represents appetite being moderated, Sisyphus is spirit, Tantalus is the life in accordance with appearances. The Isles of the Blessed do not stand for not real islands ('as the geographers say'—presumably a jibe against rationalising geographers) but 'a psychic constitution that is elevated and despises becoming' (47.6). And so on.

The main action of the *Gorgias* myth concerns Zeus' altering of the *post mortem* judgements. Plato's myth begins with a whimsical episode about judgements at first going astray, with victims being sent to wrong destinations. As a result Zeus, prompted by Pluto, makes both judges and judged naked, rather than embodied, and instructs Prometheus to end the victims' foreknowledge of their death (523d-e).[50] Olympiodorus fastens on the problematic implication that divine judgements might be faulty. His line is surprising, making the myth refer *simultaneously* to the divine and the human (48.8): 'in reality, as I shall demonstrate, the judges are always naked and always embodied, and the judgements are always bad and always very fine' (47.6). Divine judgements are of course always

[50] Olympiodorus seizes the opportunity of the mention of his name for an excursus on the allegorical significance of the Prometheus myth. Prometheus is the overseer of the descent of rational souls, whose striving for self-knowledge is symbolised by the upwards tendency of fire. He opposes the will of Zeus only at the literal level: in fact both Zeus and he want soul to remain on high, but its fall is necessary, and so the inferior figure brings it down, despite the unwillingness of the superior. Similarly, Epimetheus oversees the irrational soul (he understands when struck, not before) represented by Pandora, who links the rational soul and the body. Epimetheus' receipt of the gift of gods shows how the lowest dregs of the universe are necessary if it is to be perfect: it has to have a bottom, and the life of (irrational) soul has to have the passions (48.6-7). The analysis, which removes conflict from the divine world, goes back via Damascius and Proclus as far as Plotinus (4.3.14).

correct (Olympiodorus does not allow any error into the divine).[51] By erroneous judgements Socrates refers to human judgements, distorted by the influence of the body, which like a veil obscures our sight (48.2).[52] There is possibly some aspect here of Olympiodorus' thesis whereby philosophical myths include at the surface level some reference to their deeper meaning. But Olympiodorus does not explain on what principles some references in the myth are to be taken as simultaneously about our life here as well as about the divine, so leaving himself open to the criticism that the option is arbitrarily used to disarm difficult sections. Nevertheless the idea that the faulty judgements are human not divine is obviously important for him, and he claims that his sources have failed to preserve it in their allegorical interpretations (48.3).

Similarly Olympiodorus is shocked at the thought of the myth's sentence of eternal punishment for the great sinners. 'Certainly we are not punished for all time', he says. 'It would be better to say that the soul is mortal than to maintain this. For if the soul is punished for all time and never enjoys the good, then it is for all time in a state of vice. And yet above all punishment aims at some good' (50.2). He insists on the principle, supported within the Gorgias itself (e.g. 477a), that all punishment is ultimately beneficial. 'So if punishment brings us no benefit and does not lead us toward what is better, then it is imposed in vain, but neither god nor nature does anything in vain'. His solution is the traditional one, that by punishment 'for all time' Plato means punishment for a 'great year', a complete revolution of the heavens (50.2-3).[53] This is one

---

[51] Similarly Zeus make the changes only at Pluto's suggestion, in order to demonstrate that the inferior always turns towards the superior (48.2).

[52] 'Socrates signifies our judgement on our life here, for sometimes we say of a bad man who has died, "What a divine chap, may he go to the Blessed Isles", perhaps because he did us some service, or we are simply in error about him' (48.2-3).

[53] Olympiodorus repeats his point at *in Phd.* 63.18 f., *in Mete.* 146.9 f.; it recurs in numerous late Platonist contexts, most relevantly Procl. *in R.* 2.178-9, *in Ti.* 3.277-8.

of the most obvious places where Platonists adjust the plain meaning of Plato. The bitter mood of the *Gorgias* has often attracted attention, and the severity of the punishment in its myth is somewhat softened in other contexts. Some have supposed that Plato mellowed over time.[54] But Olympiodorus as a unitarian Platonist looks for a consistency of outlook, and employs other Platonic texts to construct an account that is consistent, if not literal.

Similarly the *Gorgias* myth makes no explicit mention of reincarnation of souls after a period of punishment or reward. But Olympiodorus, again in a unitarian way on the basis of the *Phaedo* and *Republic* myths, assumes that the doctrine of reincarnation is to be read into the *Gorgias* myth. From the cross-roads where the judges sit some souls are sent down to the world below, while others proceed 'to a place in the middle, i.e. to be born again' (49.3).[55] This is not a senseless move, and it is arguable that the *Gorgias* myth needs a background of reincarnation: the hanging up of the flayed souls of villains as an example to other souls (525d), for instance, makes little sense if the others never return to life.[56] In constructing a consistent, if not exactly literal, interpretation of Platonic eschatology Olympiodorus is reflecting the Platonists' strikingly distinctive approach to the interpretation of Plato.

There is little doubt that Olympiodorus' place in the history of literary interpretation in antiquity is a modest one. His commentary is more significant for the tradition that he is a witness to than for any insights of his own. But through the accident of survival, we can see in his commentary on the *Gorgias* and the *Gorgias* myth in particular evidence of the continuity of Greek philosophical speculation.[57]

---

[54] Cf. Dodds 1959, *ad loc.*

[55] Once again the position is traditional, cf. Procl. *in R.* 2.132-3.

[56] Dodds 1959, *ad loc.*

[57] My work on Olympiodorus has been supported by the University of Melbourne and the Australian Research Council. I should like to express gratitude to Cambridge University, the University of East Anglia, Norwich, and to

BIBLIOGRAPHY

Coulter, J.A., *The Literary Microcosm: Theories of Interpretation of the Late Neoplatonists*. Leiden 1976.

Dillon, J., Image, Symbol and Analogy: Three Basic Concepts of Neoplatonic Exegesis, in: J. Dillon, *The Golden Chain: Studies in the Development of Platonism and Christianity*. Aldershot 1990, 247-55.

———, *Iamblichi Chalcidiensis in Platonis Dialogos Commmentariorum Fragmenta*. Leiden 1973.

Dodds, E.R., *Plato Gorgias*. Oxford 1959.

Festugiere, A.-J., *Proclus In Rem Publicam*. Paris 1970.

Fuhrmann, M., Die Antike Mythen im christlich-heidnischen Weltanschauungskampf der Spätantike, *A & A* 36 (1990), 67-81.

Hadot, P., Ouranos, Kronos and Zeus in Plotinus' Treatise Against the Gnostics, in: M.J. Blumenthal et al. (ed.), *Neoplatonism and Early Christian Thought*. London 1981, 124-37.

Lamberton, R., *Homer the Theologian: Neoplatonist Allegorical Reading and the Growth of the Epic Tradition*. Berkeley 1986.

———, The Neo-Platonists and the Spiritualization of Homer, in R. Lamberton - J.J. Keaney (eds.), *Homer's Ancient Readers: The Hermeneutics of Greek Epic's Earliest Exegetes*. Princeton 1992, 115-33.

Linforth, I. M., Soul and Sieve in Plato's Gorgias, *Univ. Calif. Publ. Class. Phil.* 12 (1944), 295-314.

Pépin, J., *Mythe et Allégorie*. Paris 1958 (new ed. 1976).

Sheppard, A., *Studies on the Fifth and Sixth Essays of Proclus' Commentary on the Republic*, (*Hypomnemata* 61). Göttingen 1980.

Westerink, L.G., *Anonymous Prolegomena to Platonic Philosophy*. Amsterdam 1962.

———, *The Greek Commentaries on Plato's Phaedo*. Amsterdam 1976; 1977.

———, *Olympiodorus In Platonis Gorgiam*. Lipsiae 1970.

Whitman, J., *Allegory: Ancient and Medieval*. Cambridge, MA 1987.

Professor D.M. Schenkeveld and his colleagues at the Free University of Amsterdam. In particular I am indebted to my colleagues Harold Tarrant and Kimon Lycos.

Practice to Theory: Byzantine 'Poetrics'

Thomas Conley

In the popular view, Byzantine literature and philosophy are held to be stagnant, imitative, theologically and ideologically and formally hide-bound. I imagine the popular view of Byzantine poetry—of which, if I may begin with a bold understatement, there is no shortage—would see it as even more mindlessly derivative and boring. But there is considerable diversity in the poetry that has survived, and if Byzantine poetry is derivative, it is often hard to see what in classical or late classical poetry it is derived from. The range of poetic possibilities allowed even by what appear to be strict rules of prosody, line-construction, formal structure, subject-matters, propriety, and of the uses to which poetry might be put is, in fact, nothing short of enormous. Given the present constraints, we can hardly expect to do justice to that diversity; but I hope the brief survey here will be sufficient to give at least a rough idea of its dimensions and implications.

A 'poetics' I take to be a set of standards governing the production and evaluation of poems, properly (if there be such a thing) speaking. Byzantine writers were pretty sure what a 'poem' is, or ought to be; and of how to compose and evaluate one. There are no treatises on the subject from the Byzantine millennium, however;[1] so we will have to extrapolate some of those standards from the scattered remarks made about poetry in scholia to poets, from commentaries on rhetorical handbooks, from the large collection of grammatical works on metrics, and from the poems themselves, some of which are themselves 'critical' in nature, others of

---

[1] Aristotle's *Poetics* is one of the texts in *Par.gr.* 1741, from the mid-tenth century; but there is no evidence that any Byzantine reader either cared for or comprehended what Aristotle said in it.

which reveal underlying presumptions that might be jerry-built into a set of generalisations that might be called a 'poetrics'.

A number of such generalisations, as one might expect, can be gleaned from the sorts of things that seem to have been proscribed. One common proscription is directed at vulgarity, particularly as regards meters and diction. These were taken seriously, it seems. Mauropous writes as though the decline in attention to proper prosody is equivalent to the decline of civilisation itself: 'Lack of measure anywhere is a mighty evil / especially that which corrupts nature's meters' (*ἀμετρία γὰρ πανταχοῦ κακὸν μέγα / μαλίστα δ' ἡ φθείρουσα τὴν μέτρου φύσιν*), he says (Mauropous, *Poem* 34.11-2, in de Lagarde - Bollig 1882). About the same time Mauropous wrote those words—mid-eleventh century or so, so quite far along—Isaak I Komnenos had Michael Keroularios arrested for a threat he made, which, Skylitzes tells us was not only impudent in itself but badly written, to boot (*δημῶδες ... καὶ καθημαξευμένον*).[2] A century later, John Tzetzes can barely contain his fury against those who used dichronics 'like buffaloes (*βούβαλοι*)' (*Chil.* 3.61, p. 562). Perhaps a more accurate idea of how vitriolic Tzetzes could be may be seen in *Chil.* 12.233 ff. (p. 476 f.), where he accuses his opponents of *κοπροφιλία*; and in his attacks against those whose diction was nothing short of heretical when it was not simply barbarous.[3] And still later, toward the end of the thirteenth century, Maximos Planudes complains of the rubbish

---

[2] Cedrenos-Skylitzes 2.643.11 f. In the threat itself—*ἐῶ σε ἔκτιστα, φοῦρνε· ἐῶ ἵνα σε χαλάσω*—'*φοῦρνε*' surely does not really mean 'oven', as in Jeffreys' (1974, 162) 'I set you up, you oven, and I shall pull you down', but is a calque—therefore something like the vulgar English 'fucker'). Stephanus, s.v. *φουρνοπλάστης*, demurs: 'omittimus alia nominis Latini *φοῦρνος* composita et derivata', and refers us to DuCange. DuCange (*Glossarium* 3.637) records *furnus* = *furneus* = '*stercus, fimus.*' So perhaps *φοῦρνε* could also be translated equally well by another English appellation: 'you shit'. Either way, Keroularios' goose is cooked.

[3] See Tzetzes *Schol. Ar.* 1.73.9-18 and 304 Positano: references to *βλάσφημος / βλασφημακάτοι*; 71.6 f.: *ἀλλ' εἰς θατεριστὰς ἀχαρίστους ἀδιαφοροδιχρόνους κουτουρβιτζίως* (from a Turkish word); 105.14 f.: *κἂν οὐκ ἀρέσκῃ βαρβάροις τοῖς ἐν λόγοις τοῖς θετερίσταις μισοδιχρονωτάτοις*.

being passed off as poetry that is in fact poetic prevarication, full as it is of spurious meters, and probably borrowed from Anatolian popular chant instead of the canon of famous Greek poets. 'The evil practice' of attending only to stress accents instead of proper quantities—a practice far worse than simply fudging with 'dichronics' opportunistically—results only in unmetrical words strung together with no real connection to *metron*. 'Such poetry is just like a corpse—for the soul of a line is its meter (*ψυχὴ γὰρ στίχου τὸ μέτρον*)—wrapped in grave clothes' (*An.Bachm.* 100.21 f.).

Attention to the rules of correct prosody is of course fundamental, if only because of the apparently unanimous conviction that a poem (*poiema*) is, by definition, a complex locution that is not prose because of the presence of meter (e.g. Schol. Heph. 166.14 f.). To get an idea of how serious Byzantine critics and writers were—at least officially—we need only look at the huge body of literature on prosodics[4] that embodies the rules to which they continually appeal both in their explanations of, e.g., what makes poetry different from rhythmic prose and in their critical remarks on individual poets or poems, rules for composition sometimes themselves expressed in poems—for example, the verses attributed by Gigante (1974, 35) to George Ammiraglio, which begin:

> *πρῶτον μὲν οὖν καὶ τρίτον ἢ πέμπτον πόδα*
> *ἴαμβον ἢ σπονδαῖον εὐτρέπιζέ ποι·*
> *λοιπόν στοίχιζε, καὶ στίχους ὅλους γράφε. . .*
>
> 'First, set up the first and third and fifth feet in iamb or spondee, and then fill in the rest, and write whole lines ...'

Rigour in metrical matters was admired in grammarians as much as was rigorous adherence to metrical schemes by poets—or so we hear in

---

[4] Many of these can be found in Studemund 1886. For Hephaistion, see Consbruch's preface, which includes also some of the fragmenta as they appear in scholia to Hermogenes composed from before the tenth century to well into the fourteenth: e.g. Markellinos' *Prolegomenon* (4.6.21 f. Walz); Schol. Heph. *Poem.* 166.14 f. Consbruch; Schol. in Hermogenes *Id.* 2.892 ff. W (from *Par.gr.* 1983 and 2977, both 10th-11th); *ib.* 2.936.26 W, quoted also by Planudes, 5.474.7 ff. W; *ib.* 983.15, with a reference to 'Longinus philologos', etc. On the identity of this Longinus, see Mazzucchi 1990.

various eulogies pronounced at their funerals (e.g., Guglielmino 1974, 454, 456, etc.). At the same time, however, the history of the variations on the most common Byzantine line, the dodecasyllabic, is remarkably complex. I will not go into any of that complexity here, except to say that there are so many 'rules' about when or whether one may use a barytone or oxytone or paroxytone to begin or end a line (*στίχος*), or where to put any of those in relation to the caesura, that one begins to suspect that the 'rules' were all after the fact. Rigorous adherence to some constant pattern in placing those, or indeed of breaking the line into its sense-units by means of *anapausis*, seems so much the exception that it became a sort of stylistic signature for some poets, for example George of Pisidia (fl. 635), who was widely and frankly imitated, and Manuel Philes (d. 1345), who was not. In Prodromos (d. c. 1160), for instance, the placement of a caesura in the middle of each hexameter verse seems to be peculiar to him. Enjambment is avoided with particular care by Theodoros Studites (d. 826). On the whole, careful attention to metrical quantities is uncharacteristic of Byzantine poets. This will come out in some of the quotations I will provide; and is, I think, only partly because of changes in pronunciation. The main reason lies elsewhere.

Byzantine critics were also serious about the matter of properly poetic, and properly Greek, diction, in combination with criticism of the handling of meters. So, in the epigram by Geometres (# 7, Sajdak 1930/31, 530):

ὦ γραμμάτων ἄπειρε, κομπάζεις μέγα.
Τί τὴν σόλοικον καὶ βεβαρβαρωμένην
γλῶτταν παρορμᾷς εἰς ἄμυναν τῶν λόγων.

'Ignorant of letters, what a great racket you make! Do you think you come to the rescue of writing with mistakes and barbarous words?'

Good meter and proper diction, like good style in prose, was seen as a mark not only of technical skill but of character as well. It is not entirely clear why the author of *AP* 11.274 called Callimachus a 'blockhead' (*ὁ ξύλινος νοῦς*), but it is clear why the **J** editor of *AP* 15 (probably Konstantinos Rhodios, himself a talented poet) had little patience with the pretensions of Kometas. Of *AP* 15.40, Kometas' 'Lazarus' poem, he writes in the margin, 'words full of crap' (*τὰ κοπρίας γέμοντα σαθρίαν* ἔπη); and of Kometas' claims in 15.38 to have repaired the text of Homer, 'Kometas, this is all quite unbearable', (ταῦτα δυσκόμιστα πάντ' ἔπη). And, of course, there are the scathing criticisms of the hapless Leo Choirosphaktes that Konstantinos Rhodios cast in such Aristophanic *makrologia* as (Matranga 1850, 624.12-15):

ὀλεθροβιβλοφαλσογραμματοφθόρε,
σολοικοβαττοβαρβαροσκυτογράφε,
καὶ ψευδομυθοσαθροπλασματοπλόκε,
ἑλληνοθρησκοχριστοβλασφηματοφθόρε κτλ

—and so he goes on for more than two dozen lines. The severity of such judgements will not be fully appreciated unless one is aware that, on the whole, poets were allowed a great deal of freedom in their choice of diction, compared to orators. The scholia to Theokritos, for instance, are full of assurances that many of those odd and irregular words are proper as *poetic* locutions. These include obscure dialectal words and archaic forms, *perittologia* (in the grammatical sense), and even epic diction in non-epic contexts.[5] Johannes Sikeliotes notes the option available to poets of using τερατολογία ('monsterwords', 6.490 f. W). Eustathios, too, notes many 'poetic' usages in Homer that might not seem right to one brought up on 'Attic' prose, alluding once even to a poetic *autonomia* that operates in such cases (Eustathios 4.1110.5, *ad* Il. 17.366).[6] That autonomy in form did not, however, extend to improper pronunciation, which had to be avoided no matter if the poet in question may have a speech impediment: so, perhaps, the fun made at the expense of a poet who lisps or stutters in the epigram ascribed to Leo Choirosphaktes (Sternbach 1900, 297 f.) that begins ὦ τραυλορῆμον τραυλεπίτραυλε γνάθε, or in another, composed by John Geometres (# 4, Sajdak 1930/31, 531 f.):

Κρίσιν κριταὶ κρίνουσιν ἐν κριτηρίῳ
ἀεὶ τὸ ῥῶ λέγοντες ἠκριβωμένως.
Κριτὴς δ' οὐ γνοὺς ἀσφαλῶς τὸ ῥῶ λέγειν

[5] Schol. Theoc. (Kiessling 1819) includes the *argumenta vetera* as edited by Zacharaias Kallierges (who added some observations of his own): see e.g. p. 844, *ad Id.* 1.123; 911, *ad* 7.45; 912, *ad* 7.59; 925, *ad* 8.33, etc.

[6] See also Van der Valk's discussion in the preface to vol. 2, pp. xxxiv ff.

ὀρθῶς προσειπεῖν οὐκ ἂν ἰσχύσῃ λόγον,
ἀλλὰ κλιτὴν μὲν τὸν κριτήν, τὴν δὲ κρίσιν
κλίσιν προσείποι, πάντα λοξὰ καὶ νόθα.
῾Ο γοῦν ἑαυτὸν μὴ σθένων ὀρθῶς λέγειν
πῶς ἄλλον ἰσχύσειε μὴ λοξὰ κρίνειν;
'Critics criticise with criticism based
upon criteria, always saying 'r' most carefully.
But a critic who doesn't know
very well how to say his 'rho'
won't be able to speak his piece successfully;
for he'll say 'clitic', not 'critic'
and 'cliticism' for 'criticism', all of it
sideways and bastardised.
One who knows he cannot speak correctly,
How could he be able to CRiticise directly?'

Poets should sound like nightingales or swallows, but not like nightingales or swallows who cannot properly pronounce their 'r's'. And if it seems unduly harsh to criticise someone for having a speech defect, we might remember that stuttering and stammering were thought to indicate wickedness of soul and ugliness of body (e.g., Arethas 1.228.8 f.).

If poets were allowed more license than orators in their word-choice, they were even less constrained as regards the other part of *lexis*, *schemata.* I know of no explicitly stated 'grant of permission' in the scholiastic literature, but surely no prose author would be allowed the sort of paranomasia one finds in a poem by Kasia (Krumbacher 1897, 359.71 ff., ascribed to Theodoros Studites in *Cod. Laur. Acquisti e doni* 341 (16th cent.), f. 166^{r}):

Εἰ τὸ φέρον φέρει σε, φέρου καὶ φέρε·
εἰ δὲ φέρον φέρει καὶ σὺ οὐ φέρει,
σαυτὸν κακώσεις, καὶ τὸ φέρον σε φέρει.

or the extended anaphora we see in another epigram by Geometres (the same severe Geometres we saw earlier; *An.Par.* 4.320.6 ff.):

<u>σοὶ</u> πάντα τἀμά, <u>σοὶ</u> πνοήν, <u>σοὶ</u> τοὺς λόγους
<u>σοὶ</u> χειρὸς ἄρσιν, <u>σοὶ</u> πορείαν, <u>σοὶ</u> στάσιν
᾿Ιωάννης δίδωσι, <u>σοὶ</u> τὰ πάντά μοι,
φύλαξ, ὁδηγός, σύμμαχος γένοιο μοι.

We simply do not see in prose, even the most elevated, the anaphoric constructions that we see in, e.g., Philes or Holobolos.[7] Or take asyndeton, as in the opening lines of Philes' poem about the elephant (in Lehrs - Dübner - Ameis):

Ζῷον τὸν ἐλέφαντα τετράπουν σκόπει,
εὐρὺ, σθεναρὸν, ἐμβριθὲς, μέλαν, μέγα,
κεκυφὸς, ὀξύφωνον, ἀμβλύ τι βλέπον,
ἰταμὸν, ἀπρόσιτον ἐξ ἐρημίας,
ἱλαρὸν, εὐάγωγον ἐκ παροικίας ... (vv. 17-21)

'Behold the elephant, a four-footed beast, broad, powerful, stately, dark, immense, lumbering sharp of voice, dull of sight, fierce, unapproachable in the wild, [but] cheerful and docile when tamed ...'

or in the description of the only creature the elephant fears, the Indian *δράκων* (probably a cobra):

τίς γὰρ ἢ δράκων
ὀξὺς, πονηρὸς, ἐμβριθὴς, γλίσχρος, μέγας,
φθορεὺς, ἰταμὸς, ἀνθρακῶδες ἐμβλέπων,
ψυχρὸς, πλαδαρὸς, ἐνδακεῖν ἠπειγμένος,
ἕρπων, συρίττων, ἐξεμῶν, ἀντιπνέων ... (247-51)

'What beast more than this serpent is so quick, wicked, fearsome, slick, immense, deadly, fierce, glaring black-eyed, coldblooded, shiny, quick to strike, slithering, hissing, stomach-turning, writhing, quick to twist and strike ...'

The figure *klimax* is not uncommon in high Byzantine prose; but nowhere will we find anything on the order of Tzetzes' iambics addressed to Manuel I Komnenos, which begin

Ἄναξ βασιλεῦ, σοῦ πεσόντος οὐ φέρω,
καὶ μὴ φέρων, τὸ πάθος αὐτὸς δακρύω,
καὶ δακρύων, τὸ φίλτρον εἰς σὲ δεικνύω,
καὶ δεικνύων, τὴν πίστιν αὖ ἐκτυννύω ...

---

[7] For Philes, see *Carm.* 2.306 (#90: 'Against a Dirty Old Woman': Ἀ *μιαρὰ / γραῦς* ... repeated five times in seven lines; lines 24-9: Οὓς ... Ὡς ... Ὦ ... Ὦ ... Ὦ, *κτλ*; 2.122: ten lines of twelve (vv. 75-86) begin with *καὶ*, etc. For Holobolos, see e.g. #18, in Boissonade 1833, 179.3-180.7.

and continue that way for over ninety lines (text in Matranga 1850, 619-22).

As for poetic form, in the sense both of 'structural' form and 'generic' form, there, too, Byzantine poets were both constrained and free. In the matter of poetic structure, once we get beyond the constraints of proper metrical form and length of a single *stichos* (maximum, we are told, 32 syllables per line), there do not seem to be any categorical expectations about how a poem should be structured. Epigrams, of course, should be short or relatively short, at least short enough to fit onto whatever they were inscribed upon. But like most eighteenth-century British poetry, much Byzantine poetry is 'little more than prose versified, and bad prose at that'. A glance at, for instance, poems by Mauropous or Philes suggests that there are no formal rules about how long, or short, a poem may be. The *Synopsis* by Konstantinos Manasses in 6733 political verses comes to an end, quite reasonably, when he gets to the present. But why the introduction to astrology (Miller 1872) composed for the *sebastokratorissa* Eirene by John Kamateros (who was, incidentally, the boon drinking companion of the emperor Manuel I Komnenos) should extend over 1351 verses is not clear.

There are seldom, moreover, any notable movements in thought in Byzantine poetry. The expectation that a good poem will contain a *volta* of some kind, for instance, does not seem to have been part of Byzantine poetrics. We do occasionally see such movement of thought, of course, in the occasional appearance of a priamelic opening, as in the opening lines of Mauropous *Poem* 34 (after Pindar); and some of Philes' poems come surprisingly close to sonnet-form—e.g. the lament for Simonide (Philes *Carm* 2.144).[8] But examples of this sort of thing are few and far be-

[8] See also, e.g., #173, *Carm.* 1.194 f. (volta at v. 10); #134, 1.169 f. (volta at v. 10); and #93, 1.144 f.: a sixteen-line poem ending with a rhymed couplet (!). The Simonide in the 'sonnet' is probably Simonide, daughter of Andronikos II Palaiologos, who gave her in marriage to the Serbian emperor Milutin when she was six years old. Milutin consummated the marriage immediately. Her portrait, as a grown woman, can be seen in the Church of the Annunciation in Gracanica. Her face, in this painting, has about it a deathly pallor. The poem needn't refer to her actual death, but may simply refer to her removal to the

tween. Outside of the expectations generated by a title that announces 'this is an anacreontic' or 'this is an epitaph', there is not much in Byzantine poetry that arouses expectations in any obvious predictable way and then fulfills them (which any good periodic sentence will do, of course; which is why I said 'bad prose' before).

As for generic constraints, once we get out of church, where the constraints were quite rigid (Moran 1986, chapter 3), these seem quite feeble. That is, there are liturgical poetic forms that were established early on and which remained pretty consistent: the *kanon*, for instance. The most common 'secular' genres used by Byzantine poets, however, were not themselves very demanding as poetic forms (as compared to *terza rima*, for instance, or the villanelle): thus, 'anacreontics' and 'elegies' were defined more by metrical considerations, line-by-line or couplet-by-couplet, than by considerations of structural form; and the only constraint on an epigram appears to be that it be short. For poems of mid-length (say 20 or 30 lines) there does not seem to be even a name, beyond some indication of their meters; and so we get poem after poem with the superscript 'στίχοι ἰαμβικοί', or sometimes just 'στίχοι'. In general, moreover, Byzantine genres do not seem to have been constrained even in regard to subject-matter. It is to be expected that erotic matters, for instance, will appear in anacreontic poems—e.g., one attributed to Markos Angelos (14th century; Nissen 1940, 76-80), which is well within the φέρ' ὕδωρ φέρ' οἶνον tradition of Anacreon himself (fr. 51 *PMG*). But we often find liturgical subjects treated in anacreontics (e.g. Elias Synkellos, 'Ανακρεόντειον κατανυκτικὸν ᾀδόμενον εἰς ἦχον ..., Matranga 1850, 2.641 ff. (the ἦχοι are, in addition, arranged alphabetically)); and in the *opuscula* of the philosopher from the Nicaean interlude, Nikephoros Blemmydes, we find some treatises on urinalysis composed in the liturgical *kanon*-form (Koutzes 1944/48, 60-63). I shall have more to say about such matters later.

Byzantine poets had at their disposal a rather different kind of resource for 'structuring' their poems than we usually think of when we

Serbian court, which might be viewed as worse.

hear the phrase 'poetic form'. I refer, of course, to the visual devices of acrostic or abecedarian construction and to related phenomena such as the *karkinoi* and *technopaignia* we find occasionally in manuscripts. These are employed for the most part without regard for subject-matter or even 'mood'. For example: in an epigram attributed to Theodoros Studites, dedicated to Irene Patrikia, we find:

> **Ε**ὔχρηστον ὄντως σκεῦος ἡγιασμένον
> ἰσοστατοῦν γε χρυσοκολλήτῳ στέφει
> ῥαντοῖς καλοῖσι μαργάροις ηὐγασμένῳ
> ἡ τῇδε θεῖσα τὸ τρισόλβιον δέμας·
> νέου γὰρ ἀνδρὸς ἐκτομὴν ὑποστάσα,
> ἥρωος ἄλλου τῷ σθένει καὶ τῷ κλέει ... (Studites # 113.1-6, p. 298 Speck)

Another good example can be found in a much longer dedication composed by Manuel Holobolos in Oxford *Barocc.* 125, f. 237^r (Treu 1896, 539), the initial letters of which spell out his name and long list of titles. There is also, however, a long tradition of liturgical acrostics, hundreds of which were inventoried by Krumbacher a century ago. The most famous example is perhaps the Pentecostal *kanon* by John Damascene (text in *PG* 96.832-6), where the first letters of each successive line spell out the initial verse: Θειογενὲς Λόγε, Πνεῦμα παράκλητον πάλιν ἄλλον. This poem, and others like it but even more complex in acrostic design, were admired by Eustathios, who devoted considerable attention to them in his commentary (see especially *PG* 136.508-9, 512). Poems laid out in such a way obviously provided for many possibilities for spiritual meditation.

Abecedarian poems can be about almost anything, from polemic to 'elegiac' lament (see, e.g., Anastasijevic 1907). One such poem composed by Nikephoros Kallistos Xanthopoulos (#2, Papadopoulos-Kerameus 1902, 42 f.) is a vague paraenesis exhorting an unknown adressee to lead a holier life. A more memorable—and more 'poetic'—example that comes to mind is the poem by Konstantinos Sikeliotes ('ἀπὸ μουσικῶν μελαθρῶν', Matranga 1850, 689-92), who flourished around the turn of the ninth century, in anacreontics and arranged alphabetically in its quatrain-stanzas, on the loss of his family members in a storm at sea. This, too, is unfortunately too long to reproduce here.

Karkinos, or 'crab'-poetry, is an elaborate acrostic kind of poetry. Each line is a palindrome; and the initial letters—as well as the terminal letters, obviously—of each verse spell out the first line, thus giving vertical palindromes on either side, as well. There is a rather remarkable specimen printed in Sternbach (1900, 298 f.), too long to reproduce here. But there is a good example from an Athonite manuscript (*Kavsokalyvion* 10 (14th cent.) of 'Theognostos' (Munitz 1979, xxxix f.):

ΣΟΣ ΕΙΜΙ ΤΙΜΙΕ ΣΟΣ
῾Ο βιβλίον σοι Τοῦτ**Ο**
Συνθεὶς ἅμα καὶ γράψα**Σ**
Εἰκὼν θεοῦ πάντιμ**Ε**
῾Ιλαρὲ τῷ βλέμματ**Ι**
Μιμητὰ τοῦ ᾿Αβραα**Μ**
᾿Ιωσὴφ τῷ σώφρον**Ι**
Τῷ φυγοσοδόμῳ Λώ**Τ**
᾿Ιδοὺ προσάγω δή σο**Ι**
Μῦρον καθὼς Μαριὰ**Μ**
᾿Ιησοῦ τῷ Σωτῆρ**Ι**
᾿Εμοῖς λόγοις τιμῶν σ**Ε**
Σὺ δ' ἀντίδος σὰς εὐχὰ**Σ**
Οὗ κρεῖττον οὐδὲν ἄλλ**Ο**
ΣΟΣ ΕΙΜΙ ΤΙΜΙΕ ΣΟΣ

Poetry like this is obviously the creature of a manuscript culture, for none of the acrostic features can be apprehended by the ear. It is well represented in idiorhythmic monastic settings, clearly since it, too, provides iconic material for contemplative use, as Eustathios tells us. This is especially true in the case of poems that include *versus intertexti*, such as the one printed by Hörnandner (1990, 33):

Ιαταταιὰξ τῆς ἐμῆς ἀτυχίας·
πᾶς ἀδικεῖ με· πῶς ἔχεις, **δίκη**, στέγειν;
οὐδεὶς **μαλαγμὸς τῆς** φθονούσης καρ**δίας**:
σῆς ἔργα **ταῦτα**, Χριστέ, μακροθυ**μίας**;

The embedded verse here is, of course, Ἴαμα ταῦτα τῆς ἐμῆς ἀκηδίας. ('These [lines] are a remedy for my laziness'). But as we saw, such visual devices were also used in dedications and super-scriptions, as a sign, perhaps, of the technical virtuosity of either the poet or the scribe.

This brings us to settings and subject-matters and the poetic forms they demanded—or, rather, seem *not* to have demanded. Grammarians and rhetoricians from the earliest stages of the Byzantine tradition (and no doubt before) seem to have agreed that certain meters were appropriate to certain subject-matters: one did not compose iambics about the gods, but dactyls. So, for instance, John Geometres, in the trimeters he appends to his hymns to the Virgin (at *PG* 106.865D), explains the appropriateness of his using 'strong' meters for divine matters, weak for human; and Niketas Eugenianos (d. 1190?), in an *epithalamion* found in *Cod.Laur* 341 offered 'for nighttime enchantments' (*εἰς θελξιθύμους ἐννύχους*, Gallavotti 1935, 233 ff., #5, vv. 17-21), observes that Homer carefully chose his diction and solemn meters when singing about sublime and mysterious matters. But no such rules seem to have held rigidly or for long. If it is possible to write on urines in *kanon*-form and about the death of a loved one in anacreontics, it seems, almost any 'form' can be used of any subject, depending on the occasion and audience.

This should not surprise us. There is a persistent tradition that makes of poetry a subdivision of rhetoric. Homer, we find in texts from Hermogenes to Planudes, wrote panegyrics *ἐν ἐμμέτρῳ λόγῳ* (Hermogenes *Id.* 2.10, 389.21 f. Rabe; and see Planudes 5.556 W). The chief difference, Sikeliotes (among others) tells us, is that poets write about 'nonexistents' (*μὴ ὄντων*) (6.486.27-487.2 W); but the poets he has in mind are the so-called *πλαστουργοί*. It is also common knowledge that rhetorical writers from Aristotle on cited passages in prose or poetry rather indifferently to exemplify their point Gregory of Corinth (7.1153.17 ff. W) does not hesitate to use examples from Sappho and Thucydides side-by-side to illustrate methods of stylistic virtuosity (*δεινότης*). Devices from the 'species', too, could be appropriated to the needs of the 'genus': Kastoros of Rhodes, for instance, writes at some length about the adaptability of various metrical feet to various Hermogenean *ideai* (3.712 ff. W; see also 7.875.5 ff. W, from *Par.gr.*1983+2977 (10th- 11th cent.)). Poets and rhetors, the anonymous 'On the four parts of a perfect *logos*' tells us, draw on the same parts of the art (3.575.2 ff. W); and 'recent' [prose] writers use poetic diction that the ancients would have deemed inappropriate, but it appears anyway (3.579.2 ff. W, 581.26 [Demosthenes!]; 582.26-583.27 W). It should therefore come as no surprise that Rhakendytes' *Synopsis rhetorikes* includes a chapter (15) devoted to iambs (3.359.13 ff. W)—or, for that matter, that Gregory of Corinth could assure his readers that ἰαμβεῖα λογογραφία τις (Donnet 1967, 323.277 f.).

But there are rhetorical aspects of poetry and of the criticism of it that go beyond considerations of the mere presence of, or the utility of, meter. I think, for instance, of Psellos' observation (Dyck 1986, 48.93 ff.) that, for all his poetic virtues, Euripides occasionally departs from τὸ πρέπον, surely a rhetorical consideration.[9] When I refer to the rhetorical aspect of poetry, what I have in mind in particular is the fact that most, if not all, Byzantine poetry is occasional. The lament of Konstantinos of Sicily may be viewed as an exception, unless we read it not as a lyric poem in the modern sense but as an *ethopoiia*-exercise (τί ἂν εἴποι ...;), in which case it, like all the other examples of such poems, would have been meant to demonstrate 'poetic' proficiency in a chancellary-bureaucratic setting.[10] Only by paying attention to the occasional settings of Byzantine poetry can we begin to explain the astonishing variety of mixtures of rhetorical genres and poetic forms. From very early in the period, we find, for instance, two instances of *ethopoiia* by John the Grammarian and George the Grammarian in anacreontics (Matranga 1850, 633 ff., 638 ff.; 648 ff.); and, at almost the other end of the Byzantine

[9] A recent editor of this text thinks—and he may be right—that πρέπον here refers only to the appropriateness of the three elements that delight the ear: μέλος, ῥυθμός, and μεταβολή, citing as support Dionysius of Halicarnassus *Comp.* 38—which is, of course, about prose composition. Psellos makes it clear, however, in a poem on poetry (Sternbach 1900, 318 f.; see also Psellos, p. 463, #91) that the function of those elements is in the end rhetorical.

[10] On some of the connections betwen literary production and its institutional settings, see my 'Byzantine Criticism and the Uses of Literature', forthcoming in *The Cambridge History of Literary Criticism*, vol 2 (ed. A. Minnis).

period, *ethopoiiai* in the 'traditional' dodecasyllables by John Grasso, one of the Otranto poets of the 13th century, some of which are in dialogue form (Cantarella 1948, 108-17, nos. ix-xii). These are called πεπλασμένοι ('fictions') in their superscripts. And there are many other examples. Philes composed an *ethopoiia dramatike* over nine hundred verses long, in which 'Philes' conducts a dialogue with his 'Νοῦς' and the stock virtues; and which turns out to be an 'encomium' addressed to one of the Kantakouzenoi (Philes *Carm.* 1.143-84). There are numerous ἐπιτάφιοι / ἐπιτύμβια / θρῆνοι and ἐπιθαλάμια in anacreontics as well as in political *stichoi*. In anacreontics, we have, e.g., Elias Synkellos 'To himself' (Matranga 1850, 2.645 ff.); George the Grammarian's *Epithalamia*, (Matranga 1850, 573 ff.); and Leo Magister on the marriage (it is not clear which) of Leo VI. In political verse, we find an *epithalamion* by Theodoros Prodromos on the occasion of the marriage of Manuel I Komnenos and Irene-Bertha. Prodromos also composed epinikia in verse—both in the lofty hexameter (e.g. nos. 2, 68, 77-9, etc. in Hörandner's edition, 1974) and in the more pedestrian political verse (nos. 4, 5, 10, etc.; and see n.9, called a ὕμνος); and Manuel Holobolos composed nineteen poems in political verse (Boissonade 1833, 159-82), all 18-20 lines long, which are nothing if not *prooimia* to the sorts of *basilikoi logoi* one finds in, e.g., Regel's *Fontes Rerum Byzantinarum*. These contain all the conventional *topoi* of that genre (light, fire, sun, the traditional catalogue of imperial virtues, etc.) and even make traditional epithets into poetic formulae—e.g., the frequent insertion after the caesura of such phrases as καὶ τῷ πορφύρας γόνῳ. Such mingling of rhetorical genre and poetic forms appears to go back a long way in the tradition. It has been argued recently that Romanos' *kontakion* for Palm Sunday (#16) contains all the *topoi* recommended in the handbooks for *basilikoi logoi,* and can in effect be read as a metrical sermon, meant to be chanted (Carafigliou-Topping 1977, 67). And, of course, there is also Philes' elephant poem, which I quoted earlier, a long dodecasyllabic *ekphrasis* on an animal that seems to have fascinated Byzantine writers, clearly inspired by the *physiologus* tradition, but in fact a 'Mirror for Princes' addressed to the emperor. The formal possibilities, in short, seem almost endless.

The degree to which Byzantine poets felt free to mix and match subjects, metrical schemes, and poetic forms depending on the demands and resources of situation and audience brings out the true extent to which poetry was seen as a mode of rhetoric. If this is true, then more can be learned about this poetry by looking at occasion and appropriateness than by genre analysis.But it should at the same time be noted that the poetry seems far less bound by such considerations than the prose rhetoric does, perhaps with the understanding (as in, e.g., Psellos, Sternbach 1900, 318 f.) that the aim, above all, was delight (*ἡδύς ... θέλγουσα καὶ τέρπνουσα καὶ νοῦν καὶ φρένας*), however much moving and instructing there might be as well. At times I am tempted to think that the principal 'demand' to which Byzantine poets responded was the famous one made by the jaded lady to her chef: '*étonnez-moi*!' There is in Byzantium no poetic of the ideal poem Mallarmé dreamed of, in short.

As a final note on the rhetoric of Byzantine poetry: one of the more intriguing features found in some of the poems I have talked about is a sort of rhetoric of disclosure: what might be called an 'enigma to enlightenment' structure. One good example of this is yet another poem by Philes (Baldwin 1985, 228):

> *Τί τοῦτο; καὶ πῶς καὶ παρὰ τέχνης τίνος*
> *εἰκὼν ἀμυδρὰ καὶ σκιώδης εὑρέθης*
> *εἰς εὐτελοῦς ὕφασμα ληφθεῖσα κρόκης;*
> *καὶ πῶς ὁ κηρὸς ἐγχεθεὶς ὑπὸ φλόγα,*
> *κἂν εἰς ὕλην εὔπρηστον οὐκ εἶχε φλέγειν,*
> *ἔγραψα τὸν σὸν πλαστικῶς τοῦτον τύπον;*
> *Βαβαί, Μαριάμ, ἐξαμείβεις τὰς φύσεις·*
> *καὶ γὰρ σεαυτὴν ἐκ πυρὸς ξένου γράφεις*
> *αὖθις φανεῖσα τοῦ πυρὸς κρείσσων βάτος,*
> *οὗ Χριστὸς αὐτὸς πρὸς τὸ πῦρ τῆς λαμπάδος*
> *τὴν μυστικὴν ἄνωθεν ἐκβλύζει δρόσον,*
> *ὡς ἂν ὁ πιστὸς τὴν γραφὴν ταύτην βλέπων*
> *τὴν φασματώδη τῶν παθῶν φεύγῃ φλόγα.*
> 'What is this? And how and by what artful means
> did you, a faint and shadowy image, find yourself
> soaked into a fabric with so cheap a woof?
> And how did the wax, melted by flame as it was,

not scorch the flammable cloth,
but pictured true to life this image?
O Mary! You have changed the very natures of these things;
for you portray yourself by the means of a strange flame.
Once before, you appeared as a bush more
fiery than fire. Here, Christ, from above, scatters
a mystic dew on the flame of the lamp;
so that the believer, seeing this image,
might escape the morbid flame of passion.'

This is another of the poems I have found that contains a *volta* (interesting also for the high incidence of enjambment, not very frequent in Byzantine poetry). At that point (v. 7), the questions leading up are answered, the riddle, if you will, solved. Here we see what I think may be an important rhetorical feature of much Byzantine poetry, a pattern of expectation and fulfilment that might be paraphrased as 'from enigma to enlightenment'. This fondness for enigmas undoubtedly goes back on the literary side to the popularity of such devices in the *Palatine Anthology*; but it has something to do also with a rather more profound tendency to see everything in those terms: the world and the texts that it includes are all equally mysterious at first, and then brought into clarity by the efforts of those who are skilled with words. It is certainly a conscious pattern not only in poems that contain a *volta*; it is also true in some respect or other of, e.g., the *makrologia* lines of Konstantinos Rhodios, the acrostic and *karkinos* and *versus intertexti* poems we saw before. It seems also to be at work as a 'minor form' in the long runs of anaphora and rhetorical questions we often (more often than in prose) find in Byzantine poems.

The apparent crossovers between rhetoric and poetry and the criticism of both brings up a number of related issues that make as much difference to one as to the other. So, for instance, it may be true that the savage remarks made by the **J** editor of *AP* or by Tzetzes might be ascribed to sheer nastiness in addition to technical scruples. In some cases—Tzetzes is the most prominent, I think—there is another motive: namely, social and professional anxiety, as many of his remarks were competitive in nature, meant to show how much better he was as a critic and poet and therefore more deserving of patronage during the rough and tumble years of the mid-twelfth century. At the same time, it should probably be added that technical judgements were often more than just technical in the Byzantine tradition, from Photios (who has hardly anything to say about poetry) on. It seems a commonplace of Byzantine criticism that good style is not just a technical matter, but an ethical one, as well. Indeed, by the mid-14th century, we see evidence of a conviction among Byzantine scholars that bad style may be the cause of political decay.[11] In this area, what holds for the criticism of prose holds as well for poetry.

Poetry in Byzantium was not simply a knack of getting one's lines to scan but—at least at its best—a way of coming to grips with things, part of the equipment for living (as Kenneth Burke once put it) in both the city of men and the city of God. This side of poetry has been touched on infrequently, unfortunately , and usually in connection with the theme of Byzantine mysticism (e.g. Beck 1969, 91 ff.). But 'mystical' is not a very accurate label to apply to the vast corpus of Byzantine poetry. I prefer to see the Byzantine way of coming to grips with things by means of poetry as quite deeply realistic, looking not to the heavens or to the Past but to the *hic et nunc*, permitting the poet to deploy the technical resources available with the freedom needed to establish the precise location of the convergence of permanence and change. That is, far from being stagnant and hidebound, there is something peculiarly contemporary about it—one is almost tempted to say 'post-modern', except that seems an awfully strange thing to say about Byzantine poetry. On the other hand, there is one other feature of Byzantine poetry that I have not talked about here that may make the post-modern label stick. I refer of course to the frequency with which Byzantine poets wove into their own verse fragments, verses, even longer units of other, earlier poetry. Byzantine

[11] See, e.g., Demetrios Kydones *Apologia* (ed. S. Mercati, *Notizie di Procuro e Demetrio Cidone* ... Vatican City 1931), 370.52 ff.; Chortasmenos, *Letters* 10 and 19; Gennadios Scholarios, *Oeuvres*, 8 vols. (ed. Petit et al., Paris 1928-32), 4.406.22 ff.

poetry, it has been said, is excessively—perhaps suspiciously—allusive.[12] The obvious and persistent Byzantine practice of allusion, internal quotation, and partial or full cento composition should probably, however, be viewed not from the vantage point of the post-Romantic critic looking for original genius, but from the viewpoint of the audiences for which that poetry was composed. There is, in short, a great deal in Byzantine poetry that reminds one of Borges' dictum, *hablar es incurrir en tautologías*. But, clearly, what we are looking at in these allusions and centones is not merely display—even less, slavish *tautología* —but a matter of cultural definition and formation.

Where has all this gotten us? Well, we have gotten to a point where we are saying that, far from being an indulgence in archaism, Byzantine poetry—and therefore the poetrics behind it—is 'post-modern'! Unlike a great deal of contemporary post-modernism, however, the motive seems to have been an effort to construct what Kenneth Burke once called a 'frame of acceptance', wherein poetry becomes a literary strategy for preserving what political or theological strategies could not—viz., the sense of being connected, with the Past, to be sure, but also with one another. And that—if you will permit me to end with a timid overstatement—is what poetry is for, is it not?

BIBLIOGRAPHY

Anastasiejevic, D., Alphabete, *ByzZ* 16 (1907), 449-501.

[12] That this is common across all the Byzantine centuries is clear from a glance at any critical apparatus that provides *fontes* for a Byzantine text: e.g., George of Pisidia at *Exp.Pers*. 227-38 (allusions to Aeschylus and *Psalms* alike); Leo the Philosopher (*AP* 9.361); Theodoros Prodromos *Poem* 17 (almost in its entirety); and Johannes Chortasmenos' poem consisting in great part of verses from one by Prodromos! (no. 6, drawing on Prodromos 45). See also, e.g., Hörandner 1976. Sometimes, of course, editorial zeal turns up phantom *fontes*, as is the case with, e.g., Monaco.

Baldwin, B., *An Anthology of Byzantine Poetry*, London Studies in Classical Philology 14. Amsterdam 1985.

Beck, H.-G., Antike Beredsamkeit und byzantinische Kallilogia, *A & A* 15 (1969), 91-101.

Bekker, I., *Georgius Cedrenus Historiae* 2 [CSHB 35]. Bonn 1839.

Boissonade, J., *Anecdota Graeca* vol. 5. Paris 1833; repr. Hildesheim 1962.

Cantarella, R., *Poeti bizantini*, 2 vols. Milano 1948.

Carafigliou-Topping, E., Romanos On the Entry into Jerusalem: a Basilikos Logos, *Byz*. 47 (1977), 65-91.

Donnet, D., *Le traité* Περὶ συντάξεως λόγου *de Grégoire de Corinthe*, Études de ... l'Institut historique belge de Rome 10. Roma 1967.

Dyck, A., *Psellos, Essays on Euripides and George of Pisidia and On Heliodorus and Achilles Tatius*, Byzantina Vindobonensia 16. Wien 1986.

Gallavotti, G., Novi Laurentiani codices analecta, *RSBN* 4 (1935), 203-36.

Gigante, M., *Poeti bizantini di Terra d'Otranto nel seculo XIII*, Byzantina et Neoellenica Neapolitana 7. Napoli 1974.

Guglielmino, A., Un maestro di grammatica a Bisanzio nell'XI secolo e l'Epitafio per Niceta di Michele Psello, *SicGym* 27 (1974), 421-63.

Hörandner, W., *Theodoros Prodromos: Historische Gedichte*, Wiener Byzantinische Studien 11. Wien 1974.

———, La poesie profane au XIe siècle, *Travaux et Memoires* 6 (1976), 245-63.

———, Visuelle Poesie in Byzanz, *JÖB* 40 (1990), 1-42.

Hunger, H., *Johannes Chortasmenos ... Briefe, Gedichte und kleine Schriften*, Wiener Byzantinische Studien 7. Wien 1969.

Jeffreys, M., The Nature and Origins of Political Verse, *DOP* 28 (1974), 141-95.

Kiessling, T., *Theocriti reliquiae graece et latine*. Lipsiae 1819.

Koutzes, A., Les oeuvres médicales de Nicéphore Blémmydès selon les manuscripts existants, Πρακτικά τῆς Ακαδημίας Αθηνῶν 19 (1944/48), 56-75.

Krumbacher, K., Kasia, *SBAW* 1897:1, 305-70.

———, Die Acrostichis in der griechischen Kirchenpoesie, *SBAW* 1903, 551-691.

de Lagarde, P., - Bollig, J., Ioannis Euchaitorum metropolitae quae in Codice Vaticano Graeco 676 supersunt, *AGG* 28 (1882), 1-228.

Lehrs, F., - Dübner, F., - Ameis, C., *Poetae bucolici et didactici*. Lutetiae 1862.

Leone, P., *Johannes Tzetzes, Historiae*. Napoli 1968.

Matranga, P., *Anecdota graeca*. Romae 1850.

Mazzucchi, C., Longino in Giovanni Siculo, *Aevum* 6 (1990), 183-98.

Miller, E., *Manuelis Philae Carmina*, 2 vols. Paris 1855/1857; repr. Amsterdam 1967.

———, [ed. J. Kamateros, *Peri zôdiakou kyklou*], *Notices et extraits* 23 (1872), 53-111.

Moran, N., *Singers in Late Byzantine and Slavonic Painting*. Leiden 1986.

Munitz, J., *Theognosti Thesaurus*, CCSG 5. Turnhout - Leuven 1979.

Nissen, T., Die byzantinischen Anakreonteen, *SBAW* 1940.

Papadopoulos-Kerameus, K., Νικηφόρος Κάλλιστος Ξανθόπουλος, *ByzZ* 11 (1902), 38-49.

Sajdak, J., Spicilegium geometreum, *Eos* 33 (1930/31), 521-534.

Speck, P., *Theodoros Studites Iamben*. Berlin 1968.

Sternbach, L., Analecta byzantina, *Ceské museum Filologické* 6 (1900), 291-322.

Studemund, W., *Anecdota varia graeca: musica metrica grammatica*. Berolini 1886.

Treu, M., Manuel Holobolos, *ByzZ* 5 (1896), 53-559.

Van der Valk, M., *Eustathii ... commentarii ad Homeri Iliadem pertinentes*, 4 vols. Leiden 1976-87.

Westerink, L. *Arethas Scripta minora*, 2 vols. Lipsiae 1968-72.

———, Leo the Philosopher: *Job* and Other Poems, *ICS* 11 (1986), 193-222.

———, *Psellos poemata*. Lipsiae - Stutgardiae 1992.

INDEX LOCORUM

INDEX OF GREEK WORDS

INDEX OF SUBJECTS